KB186574

YBM
TOEFL 80+

READING

YBM TOEFL 80⁺
READING

발행인 허문호
발행처 YBM

편집 김현수, 김소리
본문 디자인 이미화, 박도순
표지 디자인 로컬앤드
마케팅 정연철, 박천산, 고영노, 김동진, 박찬경, 김윤하

초판인쇄 2024년 6월 3일
초판발행 2024년 6월 10일

신고일자 1964년 3월 28일
신고번호 제1964-000003호
주소 서울시 종로구 종로 104
전화 (02) 2000-0515 [구입문의] / (02) 2000-0463 [내용문의]
팩스 (02) 2285-1523
홈페이지 www.ybmbooks.com

ISBN 978-89-17-23953-9

YBM TOEFL 80⁺를 발행하며

어학시험 수험서 부문에서 꾸준히 베스트셀러를 출간해 온 YBM이 새롭게 변경된 TOEFL 시험에 맞추어 <YBM TOEFL 80+> 시리즈를 출간하게 되었습니다.

<YBM TOEFL 80+>는 이렇게 만들어졌습니다!

수험자의 진짜 니즈를 아는 토플 전문가들의 고득점 노하우

<YBM TOEFL 80+>는 YBM 토플연구소와 YBM 어학원 토플 대표 강사들이 공동으로 개발·집필하여 실제로 토플 시험을 준비 중인 수험자들의 니즈를 최대로 반영한 교재입니다. 토플 교육 현장에서 파악한 수험자들의 취약점 보완 및 고득점 달성을 위한 최적의 솔루션을 제공합니다.

개정 시험을 완벽 반영한 100% 최신 문항과 유형 분석

<YBM TOEFL 80+>는 2023년 7월 26일 개정 이후 시행된 시험들을 빈틈없이 분석하여 개정된 시험의 형식 외에도 문제를 구성하는 세부 요소의 개정 사항까지 완벽히 반영한 교재입니다. 달라진 토플 시험에 제대로 대비할 수 있도록 100% 신규 개발된 최신 문항과 유형 분석을 수록하였습니다.

한 권으로 빠르게 끝내는 원스탑 교재 구성

<YBM TOEFL 80+>는 문제 유형과 전략을 빠르게 이해하고 숙지할 뿐 아니라, 실제 시험에 자주 등장하는 주제를 집중적으로 학습할 수 있도록 구성하였습니다. 여기에 실제 시험과 동일한 구성의 실전 모의고사 2세트를 통해 실전감과 실력을 높이도록 하여 본 교재 한 권으로도 충분히 시험에 대비할 수 있게 해줍니다.

YBM의 모든 노하우가 집대성된 <YBM TOEFL 80+>는 수험자 여러분께 최단기 고득점의 지름길을 안내해드립니다.

YBM 토플연구소

YBM TOEFL 80⁺
READING

CONTENTS

R

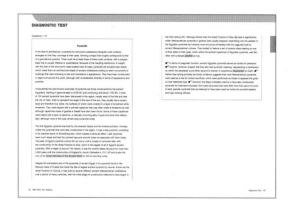

진단 테스트

최신 토플 시험 경향을 철저하게 분석하여
동일한 구성으로 제작된 진단 테스트를 통해
학습자가 자신의 실력을 정확하게 평가할 수
있도록 했다.

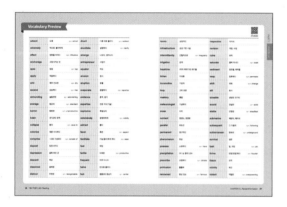

사전 어휘 학습

본격적인 토플 학습에 앞서 각 챕터의 지문에
등장하는 어휘들 중 필수 어휘들만 선별하여
동의어와 함께 제시하였다. QR코드 또는 www.
ybmbooks.com에서 다운로드 한 MP3 파일
을 들으며 어휘를 학습할 수 있도록 했다.

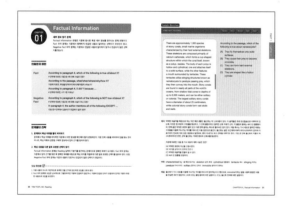

유형별 집중 훈련

파트 1에서는 각 문제 유형별로 챕터를
구성하여 토플에서 출제되는 문제 유형과 특징,
빈출 문제 패턴을 안내했다. 또한, 문제풀이
전략과 오답 포인트를 제시하여 실제 시험에
완벽하게 대비하고, 샘플 문제와 연습 문제를
풀어보면서 집중적으로 유형을 연습할 수
있도록 했다.

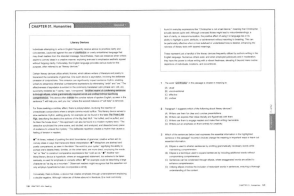

주제별 집중 훈련

파트 2에서는 주제별로 챕터를 구성하여, 역사, 예술, 인류학, 고고학, 건축학, 경제학, 심리학, 지구과학, 생물학 등 토플 최다 빈출 주제를 접할 수 있도록 했다. 긴 지문과 함께 여러 유형의 문제를 수록하여, 종합적으로 문제를 푸는 훈련을 할 수 있도록 했다.

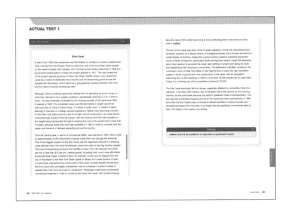

실전 모의고사

최신 출제 경향이 반영된 실전 모의고사 2세트를 실제 시험과 유사한 화면 구성과 지문 길이, 문제 난이도로 구성했다. 자신의 실력을 최종적으로 점검하여 효율적으로 실제 시험에 대비할 수 있도록 했다.

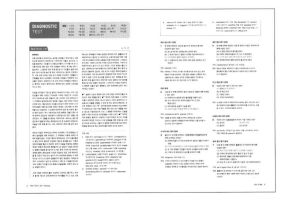

정답 및 해설

책 속의 책 형태로 제공되는 정답 및 해설에는 교재에 있는 모든 지문의 해석, 정답 및 중요 어휘와 문제 해설, 주제 관련 지식까지 수록했다. 상세한 문제 해설을 통해 학습자들이 스스로 오답의 이유를 파악하여 같은 실수를 반복하지 않도록 하는 데 도움이 되도록 했다.

 MP3 무료 다운로드 www.ybmbooks.com
(Vocabulary Preview 어휘 및 지문)

TOEFL iBT란?

TOEFL(Test of English as a Foreign Language) iBT(Internet-based test)는 미국 대학에서 수학할 비영어권 학생을 선발하기 위해 영어 구사력과 이해력을 측정하는 온라인 시험으로, 미국의 교육 기관인 ETS(Educational Testing Service)가 개발하고 운영한다. 토플은 Reading, Listening, Speaking, Writing 4개 영역으로 구성되어 있으며 모두 note-taking이 가능하다. 미국을 비롯한 영어권 국가 대학 및 대학원과 여러 기관에서 토플 점수를 인정한다.

시험영역

영역	지문 및 문항 수	시간	점수	특징
Reading	지문 총 2개 지문당 10문항	약 35분	0~30	• 다양한 주제의 긴 지문이 출제됨 • 사지선다, 지문에 들어갈 문장 삽입, 지문의 요약표를 완성하는 육지선다 문제 등이 출제됨
Listening	지문 총 5개 대화: 지문 2개 　　　지문당 5문항 강의: 지문 3개 　　　지문당 6문항	약 36분	0~30	• 캠퍼스 또는 기관 내 실제 분위기의 대화 및 강의가 출제됨 • 강의 중 전문 용어 등이 등장할 시 화면에 용어가 나오기도 함 • 사지선다, 지문 일부를 다시 듣고 풀기, 표 안에 정보 분류 또는 배열하는 형태의 문제 등이 출제됨
Speaking	지문 총 4개 독립형 1문항 통합형 3문항	약 16분 독립형: 준비 15초 　　　　답변 45초 통합형: 읽기 45초/50초 　　　　듣기 1분 30초~2분 　　　　준비 20초/30초 　　　　답변 60초	0~30	• 독립형: 주어진 주제에 대한 의견 말하기 • 통합형: 읽고 들은 내용에 기반하여 문제에 대한 답변 말하기
Writing	지문 총 2개 통합형 1문항 토론형 1문항	약 35분 통합형: 읽기 3분 　　　　듣기 2분~2분 30초 　　　　쓰기 20분 토론형: 쓰기 10분	0~30	• 통합형: 읽고 들은 내용에 기반하여 문제에 대한 답변 쓰기 　(약 150~225단어 권장) • 토론형: 토론 주제에 대한 의견 제시하기 　(100단어 이상 권장)
		약 2시간	총점 120	

시험 응시 및 성적 발표

응시 방법	• ETS 토플 웹 사이트 또는 전화상으로 접수 (조기 마감될 수 있으니, 성적이 필요한 날짜 2~3개월 전에 접수) • ETS Test Center 시험은 응시일로부터 최소 7일 전 접수, Home Edition 시험은 응시일로부터 최소 4일 전 접수
시험 장소	• ETS Test Center 또는 집에서 Home Edition 시험으로 응시 가능 (Home Edition 시험 응시를 위한 장비 및 환경 요건은 ETS 토플 웹 사이트에서 확인)
시험 비용	• 시험 접수: US$220 (한국 기준)　　• 취소한 성적 복원: US$20 • 추가 접수: US$40 추가　　　　　• 성적표 추가 발송: US$25 (기관당) 　(응시일로부터 2~7일 전에 접수할 경우)　• Speaking/Writing 재채점: US$80 (영역당) • 시험일 변경: US$60
응시 취소	• ETS 토플 웹 사이트 또는 전화상으로 취소 가능 (응시료 환불 기준 및 방법은 ETS 토플 웹 사이트에서 확인)
시험 당일	• 준비물: 　- 신분증(여권, 주민등록증, 운전면허증, 군인신분증) 　- 필기도구 및 종이는 ETS Test Center에서 제공 • Home Edition 시험 유의사항: 　- 사전에 ProctorU 프로그램을 설치하여 작동 여부 확인 　- 화이트보드 또는 투명 시트와 지워지는 마커 지참 (종이에 필기 불가) 　- 태블릿으로 시험 응시 불가하며, 시험 도중 휴대폰, 스마트워치, 듀얼 모니터 사용 및 마스크 착용 불가
성적 및 성적표	• 시험 응시일로부터 대략 4~8일 후에 온라인으로 성적 확인 가능 (이후 2일 뒤 성적표 PDF 다운로드 및 출력 가능) • 시험 접수 시 우편으로 성적표 요청한 경우, 시험 응시일로부터 약 11~15일 후에 전송 • 성적 유효 기간은 응시일로부터 2년 • MyBest Scores 제도 시행: 최근 2년간의 시험 성적 중 영역별 최고 점수를 합산하여 유효 성적으로 인정

❯ 2023년 7월 26일 기준 변경 사항
1 시험 시간 약 3시간 30분에서 2시간으로 단축
2 더미 문제 삭제
3 Listening 영역 후 휴식 없음
4 Reading: 지문 3~4개에서 2개로 축소
5 Listening: 대화 2~3개, 강의 3~4개에서 대화 2개, 강의 3개로 축소
6 Writing: 독립형 문항에서 토론형 문항으로 변경

READING 소개 및 전략

TOEFL iBT Reading은 대학 입문 수준의 학술적 주제에 대한 읽기 능력을 평가하는 데 목적이 있으므로, 여러 전공 분야와 관련된 다양한 지문들이 등장한다. 빈출 주제로는 역사, 예술, 인류학, 고고학, 건축학, 경제학, 심리학, 지구과학, 생물학 등이 있다. 문제의 답을 찾는 데 필요한 정보는 지문 안에 있기 때문에 문제를 풀기 위한 전문 지식이나 배경지식이 반드시 필요한 것은 아니다. 다만 주어진 시간 안에 답을 찾기 위해서 지문을 정확하고 빠르게 이해할 수 있어야 한다.

구성

지문 분량	문항 수	시험 시간
총 2개 지문 (지문당 700단어 내외)	총 20문항 (지문당 10문항)	35분

문제 유형

문제 유형	유형 설명	지문당 문항 수
Basic Comprehension Questions	기본적인 내용 이해하기 문제	
Factual Information	지문에서 다루는 사실적 정보를 파악하거나 세부 정보를 찾는 유형	2~5개
Vocabulary	주어진 단어 또는 구와 가장 의미가 비슷한 어휘를 찾는 유형	1~2개
Reference	지시어가 가리키는 대상을 찾는 유형	0~1개
Sentence Simplification	문장을 간략하게 요약하는 유형	0~1개
Inferencing Questions	암시된 내용 추론하기 문제	
Inference	제시된 정보를 바탕으로 추론 가능한 내용을 찾는 유형	1~2개
Rhetorical Purpose	작가의 수사적 의도를 찾는 유형	1~2개
Insert Text	제시된 문장을 알맞은 위치에 삽입하는 유형 (9번에 배치)	1개
Reading-to-Learn Questions	전체 내용 종합하기 문제	
Prose Summary	지문 전체 내용에 해당하는 요약표를 완성시키는 유형 (10번에 배치)	1개

특징

- 다른 영역과 마찬가지로 시험 중 note-taking이 허용된다.
- 지문 상단에 제목이 주어진다.
- 지문에 전문 용어나 특별한 뜻을 가진 어휘가 등장하면 그 뜻이나 개념을 설명하는 Glossary가 제공된다.

전략

<table>
<tr>
<td>

TOEFL
시험 전략

</td>
<td>

질문을 통해 문제 유형을 정확하게 파악한다.
유형별로 쓰이는 질문은 거의 규격화되어 있어, 질문을 보자마자 문제 의도를 파악할 수 있다. 한정된 시간 안에 문제가 요구하는 바를 빠르게 확인하여 필요한 정보를 지문에서 정확하게 찾아내야 한다.

글의 유형과 구조를 파악하며 읽는다.
처음부터 모든 내용을 자세하고 정확하게 이해하려고 하기보다는 빠르게 읽어 내려가면서 전체적인 주제와 핵심 어휘를 파악하는 것이 좋다. 동시에 묘사, 설명, 분류, 원인과 결과 등 글의 유형을 바탕으로 글의 구조와 단락 간의 관계를 파악하면 글의 흐름을 이해하기 훨씬 수월하다.

핵심 내용을 note-taking하는 연습을 한다.
note-taking이 허용되므로, 평소에도 글을 읽을 때 문장 간 또는 단락 간 연관성, 그리고 주제 및 주요 내용을 파악할 수 있도록 note-taking 하는 연습을 해둔다.

</td>
</tr>
<tr>
<td>

READING
실력 향상 전략

</td>
<td>

빈출 주제에 관련된 글을 꾸준히 읽는다.
TOEFL Reading 지문에 익숙해지고 기본적인 읽기 능력을 향상시키기 위해서는 빈출 주제 관련 학술 지문을 꾸준히 읽어 두는 것이 좋다. 이렇게 하면 배경지식이 쌓이게 되고 실제 시험에서 지문을 읽을 때 내용을 보다 빠르고 쉽게 파악할 수 있다.

어휘력을 높인다.
독해력은 어휘력이 바탕이 되어야 향상될 수 있다. 문제를 풀면서 잘 모르는 단어가 나오면 곧바로 단어의 의미를 확인하려고 하기보다는 문맥 안에서 의미를 추측하는 연습을 하도록 한다. 그 후 사전적 의미를 확인하여 정확하게 암기해 두도록 하자. 유의어를 함께 암기하는 것도 필수적이다.

다른 말로 바꾸어 쓰거나 요약문을 작성한다.
문제와 선택지에 등장하는 표현들은 결국 지문의 내용을 다른 말로 바꾸어 쓴 것이다. 문장에서부터 전체 지문에 이르기까지 중심 내용을 다양한 어휘와 표현으로 바꿔 쓰고 요약하는 연습을 하면 글의 주제와 주요 정보를 정확히 간파해 내는 실력을 기를 수 있다.

</td>
</tr>
</table>

READING 화면 구성

1. Reading Toolbar

TOEFL	Volume	Help	Review	Back	Next
Reading	Question 11 of 17		00:09:42	👁 Hide Time	

화면의 툴바는 시험 진행에 도움을 준다. 툴바 왼쪽에서 현재 풀고 있는 문제 번호를 확인할 수 있고, 오른쪽 상단에서 시간 확인 및 Volume 조정, 앞뒤로 문제 이동, Review 확인이 가능하다. Help 버튼으로 시험 진행 정보를 볼 수 있다

2. 시험 시작 전 Directions 화면

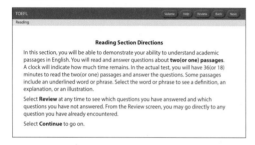

Reading 시험의 전반적 진행 방식과 툴바 버튼의 기능에 대해 간단히 설명한다.

3. 지문 화면

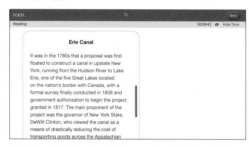

처음에는 지문만 보이고, 문제는 스크롤하며 지문 전체를 본 후 Next 버튼을 클릭하면 보인다.

4. 지문과 문제 화면

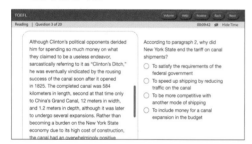

지문은 왼쪽에, 문제는 오른쪽에 위치한다. 지문의 밑줄 친 단어를 클릭하면 뜻이나 개념 설명이 Glossary 창으로 나타난다.

5. Prose Summary 문제 화면

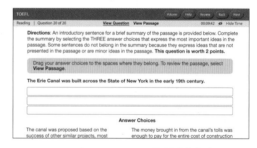

View Passage나 View Question을 클릭하면 지문 또는 문제가 보인다. 선택지를 정답 자리에 끌어오면 답이 선택되고, 선택지를 한 번 더 클릭하면 사라진다.

6. Review 화면

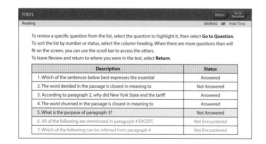

Review Questions 버튼을 클릭하면 문제 목록과 답 체크가 보이고, 문제를 선택하고 Go to Question 버튼을 클릭하면 문제로 이동한다. Return 버튼을 클릭하면 직전 화면이 보인다.

7. 시험 종료 후 Directions 화면

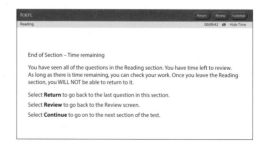

시험이 끝난 후 Directons 화면에서 Next 버튼을 클릭하면 다음 시험 영역으로 이동하며, 다시 Reading 영역으로 돌아갈 수 없다.

학습 플랜

30일 완성 학습 플랜

DAY 1	DAY 2	DAY 3	DAY 4	DAY 5
DIAGNOSTIC TEST	**PART 1** CHAPTER 01 Factual Information	**PART 1** CHAPTER 01 Factual Information	**PART 1** CHAPTER 02 Vocabulary	**PART 1** CHAPTER 02 Vocabulary

DAY 6	DAY 7	DAY 8	DAY 9	DAY 10
PART 1 CHAPTER 03 Rhetorical Purpose	**PART 1** CHAPTER 03 Rhetorical Purpose	**PART 1** CHAPTER 04 Reference	**PART 1** CHAPTER 04 Reference	**PART 1** CHAPTER 05 Sentence Simplification

DAY 11	DAY 12	DAY 13	DAY 14	DAY 15
PART 1 CHAPTER 05 Sentence Simplification	**PART 1** CHAPTER 06 Inference	**PART 1** CHAPTER 06 Inference	**PART 1** CHAPTER 07 Insert Text	**PART 1** CHAPTER 07 Insert Text

DAY 16	DAY 17	DAY 18	DAY 19	DAY 20
PART 1 CHAPTER 08 Prose Summary	**PART 1** CHAPTER 08 Prose Summary	**PART 1** 복습	**PART 2** CHAPTER 01 Humanities	**PART 2** CHAPTER 01 Humanities

DAY 21	DAY 22	DAY 23	DAY 24	DAY 25
PART 2 CHAPTER 01 Humanities	**PART 2** CHAPTER 02 Social Science	**PART 2** CHAPTER 02 Social Science	**PART 2** CHAPTER 03 Life & Natural Sciences	**PART 2** CHAPTER 03 Life & Natural Sciences

DAY 26	DAY 27	DAY 28	DAY 29	DAY 30
PART 2 CHAPTER 03 Life & Natural Sciences	**PART 2** 복습	ACTUAL TEST 1	ACTUAL TEST 2	**ACTUAL TESTS** 복습

학습 플랜 활용법

1 학습 플랜에 따라 매일의 학습 분량을 미리 계획하고, 이에 맞춰 학습 속도를 잘 조절하도록 합니다.
2 Vocabulary Preview의 어휘는 TOEFL 빈출 어휘이므로 QR코드나 www.ybmbooks.com에서 다운 받은 MP3 파일을 반복적으로 들으며 반드시 암기합니다.
3 Diagnostic Test와 Actual Tests는 실제 시험을 본다는 마음으로 note-taking을 하며 문제를 풀고, 문제를 다 푼 다음에는 지문과 문제, 문제 해설을 참고하여 오답의 이유를 분석합니다.
4 2주 만에 학습을 마무리하려면 하루에 2일치 분량을 학습하면 됩니다.

YBM TOEFL 80 +
READING

DIAGNOSTIC
TEST

DIAGNOSTIC TEST

Questions 1-10

Pyramids

In the field of architecture, a pyramid is a structure possessing triangular outer surfaces arranged so that they converge at their peak, forming a shape that roughly corresponds to that of a geometrical pyramid. There must be at least three of these outer surfaces, with a polygon base that is usually trilateral or quadrilateral. Because of the resulting distribution of weight, with the bulk of the structure's mass located near its base, pyramids are exceptionally stable, which made them an architectural staple of ancient civilizations looking to erect monuments or buildings that were imposing in size and impressive in appearance. They have been constructed in regions all around the world, although with considerable diversity in terms of appearance and purpose.

Undoubtedly the best-known examples of pyramids are those constructed by the ancient Egyptians, starting in approximately in 2700 BC and continuing until about 1700 BC. A total of 135 ancient pyramids have been discovered in the region, mostly west of the Nile and near the city of Cairo. Built to represent the angle of the rays of the sun, they usually had a square base and therefore four sides, the surfaces of which were covered in a layer of smoothed white limestone. They were topped with a pointed capstone that was often made of limestone as well, although capstones made of granite or basalt have also been found. Some of these capstones were plated with a layer of electrum, a naturally occurring alloy of gold and silver that reflects light, although none of this type remain atop pyramids today.

The first Egyptian pyramid was built by the pharaoh Djoser and his revered architect, Imhotep. Unlike the pyramids that were later constructed in the region, it was a step pyramid, consisting of six stacked layers of diminishing size, which created a terraced effect. Later pyramids were much larger and had the pointed tops and smooth sides we associate with them today. The peak of Egypt's pyramid culture did not occur until a couple of centuries later, with the construction of the Great Pyramid of Giza, which is the largest of all of Egypt's ancient pyramids. With a height of around 150 meters, it was the world's tallest structure for more than 3,000 years until the construction of England's Lincoln Cathedral in 1311 AD and is also the only of the Seven Wonders of the Ancient World to still be standing today.

Despite the impressive size of the pyramids of ancient Egypt, it is a pyramid found in the Mexican state of Puebla that holds the title of largest ancient pyramid by volume. Known as the Great Pyramid of Cholula, it was built by several different ancient Mesoamerican civilizations over a period of many centuries, with the initial stage of construction believed to have begun in the third century BC. Although shorter than the Great Pyramid of Giza, its base is significantly wider. Mesoamerican pyramids in general were usually stepped, resembling only the earliest of the Egyptian pyramids and sharing more structural similarities with the ziggurats built by ancient Mesopotamian cultures. They tended to feature a set of exterior stairs leading up one of their sides to their peak, which unlike the pointed capstones of Egyptian pyramids, was flat, often with a temple perched on top.

■(A) In terms of pragmatic function, ancient Egyptian pyramids served as tombs for pharaohs. ■(B) Experts, however, suspect that they also had symbolic meaning, representing a mechanism by which the deceased could either ascend to heaven or experience resurrection on Earth. ■(C) Rather than acting primarily as tombs, evidence suggests that most Mesoamerican pyramids were used as a site for human sacrifices, which were performed as rituals to appease the gods on their flattened tops. ■(D) However, the Maya civilization seems to have also constructed pyramids for interment purposes, from early structures that were little more than grave mounds to later, grander pyramids that are believed to have been used as tombs for powerful leaders and high-ranking officials.

1 In paragraph 1, the author mentions all of the following about pyramids EXCEPT:

(A) They are required to have at least three triangular sides.
(B) Their base must have the shape of some sort of polygon.
(C) They were constructed only with certain types of stones.
(D) Their stability made them popular with ancient civilizations.

2 Which of the following can be inferred from paragraph 2 about some Egyptian capstones?

(A) They created an imbalance in the pyramids' mass.
(B) They were a feature of only the earliest pyramids.
(C) They had several important practical functions.
(D) They made the pyramids sparkle in the sunlight.

3 The author discusses "Seven Wonders of the Ancient World" in paragraph 3 in order to

(A) suggest that pyramids are no longer impressive
(B) point out the longevity of the Great Pyramid of Giza
(C) compare the extreme size of two famous structures
(D) emphasize the height of the Great Pyramid of Giza

4 According to paragraph 3, which of the following is true of the first Egyptian pyramid?

(A) It was a collaboration of two famous architects.
(B) It was larger and smoother than later pyramids.
(C) It was made up of six layers all of different sizes.
(D) It was one of several pyramids built on a hillside.

5 The word "its" in the passage refers to

(A) the Great Pyramid of Cholula
(B) the initial stage of construction
(C) the third century BC
(D) the Great Pyramid of Giza

6 The word "perched" in the passage is closest in meaning to

(A) pitched
(B) placed
(C) merged
(D) left

7 In paragraph 4, which of the following is mentioned about the Great Pyramid of Cholula?

(A) More than a single civilization contributed to its construction.
(B) It is significantly taller and wider than the Great Pyramid of Giza.
(C) Smooth sides set it apart from other Mesoamerican pyramids.
(D) It took centuries to build and was finished in the third century BC.

8 The word "resurrection" in the passage is closest in meaning to

(A) worship
(B) leisure
(C) warfare
(D) revival

9 Look at the four squares (■) that indicate where the following sentence could be added to the passage.

Pyramids in the Americas, on the other hand, seem to have had a darker purpose.

Where would the sentence best fit? Select a square (■) to add the sentence to the passage.

10 **Directions**: An introductory sentence for a brief summary of the passage is provided below. Complete the summary by selecting the THREE answer choices that express the most important ideas in the passage. Some sentences do not belong in the summary because they express ideas that are not presented in the passage or are minor ideas in the passage. **This question is worth 2 points.**

> Drag your answer choices to the spaces where they belong. To review the passage, select **View Passage**.

The pyramid is an architectural structure that can be found across the world.

```
┌─────────────────────────────────────────────────────────┐
└─────────────────────────────────────────────────────────┘
┌─────────────────────────────────────────────────────────┐
└─────────────────────────────────────────────────────────┘
┌─────────────────────────────────────────────────────────┐
└─────────────────────────────────────────────────────────┘
```

Answer Choices

A The Egyptian pharaoh Djoser had his architect build the tallest pyramid in the world in 2700 BC.	D Mesoamerican civilizations built pyramids that had steps on their sides and a flat top.
B Most ancient Egyptian pyramids had four sides, a smooth limestone surface, and a pointed capstone on top.	E Ancient Mesoamericans and ancient Egyptians stopped building pyramids due to their unstable structure.
C Mesoamerican pyramids were known as ziggurats because of the shape of their capstones.	F Egyptian pyramids were used as tombs, while Mesoamerica pyramids were mostly used for human sacrifices.

Metabolism of Dinosaurs

There has been much controversy as to the particulars of dinosaur physiology, but none so much as that surrounding the exact nature of their thermoregulation and metabolism. The traditional view of dinosaurs has long depicted them as ungainly, sluggish creatures that were little more than overgrown, cold-blooded lizards. However, as paleontologists began to gain access to nearly complete skeletons of various dinosaur species in the late 19th century, which were being excavated from sites in the United States in large numbers, overall knowledge of their physiology began to rapidly advance.

From this new knowledge dawned the understanding that dinosaurs were likely far more active and agile than previously believed; at the same time, one prominent 19th-century biologist, Thomas Henry Huxley, a fervent proponent of Darwin's theory of evolution, proposed that dinosaurs were actually close relatives of birds rather than lizards. Despite these eye-opening ideas, perceptions of dinosaurs as cumbersome and reptilian were already firmly rooted in many people's minds, and this view remained dominant up until the mid-20th century. The 1960s, however, proved to be a period of enlightenment in paleontology, as ideas about dinosaur physiology transformed dramatically, with modern paleontologists putting forth a number of competing theories on dinosaur thermoregulation.

The idea that it is impossible to label dinosaurs as either warm-blooded or cold-blooded in the modern sense has grown in popularity, with dinosaurs viewed as having had completely different metabolisms that defy such categorization. Some scientists continue to believe that dinosaurs were cold-blooded like modern reptiles, although they now suspect that larger species had the ability to stabilize their body temperatures. These species would have regulated their body temperature through a process known as inertial homeothermy, by which a stable body temperature is maintained internally with assistance from cyclic changes in the external temperature. This outside help would be required due to the sheer mass of these dinosaurs, as it would have taken days for changes in their internal temperature to take place. There is also a school of thought that supports a model of dinosaurs that more closely resembled mammals and birds in that they were warm-blooded. Because the reign of the dinosaurs lasted for at least 130 million years, there is a high likelihood that different groups branched off and evolved metabolisms and methods of thermoregulation that differed from an earlier shared physiology.

An even more difficult undertaking for paleontologists is determining the approximate metabolic rates of various dinosaurs, a challenging task with species whose internal organs have never been observed, especially when taking into consideration the fact that these rates would have varied greatly between when these creatures were resting and when they were active. Studies of modern animals suggest that any extinct species with a resting metabolic rate that was significantly lower than its active one would not have been able to grow to the massive size that many dinosaurs achieved. Some of these larger species were likely to have been constantly engaged in an active search for sustenance, meaning that their energy expenditure would not have varied significantly whether they had resting metabolic rates that were high or low.

It has been suggested that many prehistoric species can be viewed as having possessed an "intermediate" type of metabolism at some point in the distant past. ■(A) As prehistoric mammals decreased in size, their surface area to volume ratio increased, leaving them vulnerable to heat loss, which forced them to evolve an internal temperature regulation system and become warm-blooded. ■(B) In this model, dinosaurs had low metabolic rates when at rest, a feature that would have allowed them to eat less and apply more of the nutrients they ingested toward growth. ■(C) Possessing four-chambered hearts, their aerobic capacity was high, allowing them to be quite active and not at all sluggish. ■(D) Finally, when it came to thermoregulation, it is believed they had the capacity to moderate heat loss through the expansion and contraction of blood vessels just beneath their skin.

11 Why does the author mention "the United States" in paragraph 1?

(A) To provide a reason for the existence of two types of dinosaur bones
(B) To introduce a paleontologist who proposed a revolutionary theory
(C) To indicate the source of new information about dinosaur physiology
(D) To suggest that paleontology had split into several competing groups

12 The word "agile" in the passage is closest in meaning to

(A) aggressive
(B) unintelligent
(C) cautious
(D) nimble

13 According to paragraph 2, which of the following is true of Thomas Henry Huxley?

(A) He embraced the idea of slow-moving dinosaurs.
(B) He held Darwin's theory of evolution in high regard.
(C) He confused dinosaur fossils with those of ancient birds.
(D) He participated in paleontology's age of enlightenment.

14 Which of the following can be inferred from paragraph 2 about the 1960s?

(A) An increased interest in the physiology of dinosaurs occurred.
(B) New ideas challenged Darwin's theory of evolution.
(C) Many dinosaur fossils were lost or forgotten as time passed.
(D) Paleontologists returned to traditional views after much discussion.

15 According to paragraph 3, which of the following is NOT true of modern paleontologists?

(A) Some think larger dinosaurs could keep their own body temperature stable.
(B) Some believe that the dinosaurs were warm-blooded creatures like mammals.
(C) They have found evidence that dinosaurs did not vary widely in their physiology.
(D) They have failed to come to a consensus regarding dinosaur thermoregulation.

16 Which of the sentences below best expresses the essential information in the highlighted sentence in the passage? Incorrect choices change the meaning in important ways or leave out essential information.

(A) It is difficult to estimate the metabolic rates of certain dinosaurs just by examining internal organs.

(B) Scientists suspect that metabolic rates in dinosaurs depended on whether or not they were active.

(C) Without knowing their approximate metabolic rates, it is hard to guess the behavior of dinosaurs.

(D) Learning the metabolic rates of dinosaurs is difficult due to the variation and a lack of organs to study.

17 The word "sustenance" in the passage is closest in meaning to

(A) companionship

(B) nourishment

(C) moisture

(D) shelter

18 According to paragraph 5, prehistoric animals evolved to become warm-blooded because

(A) a decrease in their size caused them to lose more heat

(B) they evolved to possess an intermediate metabolism

(C) problems with their low metabolic rates demanded it

(D) they moved to new environments to avoid dinosaurs

19 Look at the four squares (■) that indicate where the following sentence could be added to the passage.

Dinosaurs, however, did not undergo a similar reduction and were therefore able to retain this intermediate metabolism.

Where would the sentence best fit? Select a square (■) to add the sentence to the passage.

20 **Directions**: An introductory sentence for a brief summary of the passage is provided below. Complete the summary by selecting the THREE answer choices that express the most important ideas in the passage. Some sentences do not belong in the summary because they express ideas that are not presented in the passage or are minor ideas in the passage. **This question is worth 2 points.**

Drag your answer choices to the spaces where they belong. To review the passage, select **View Passage**.

The study of the physiology of dinosaurs has had a controversial history.

Answer Choices

A   It was Darwin's theory of evolution that convinced paleontologists that dinosaurs did not evolve from birds.

B   Like modern reptiles, dinosaurs had no control of their body temperature, relying instead on external factors.

C   Many scientists now believe that in terms of thermoregulation, dinosaurs were not strictly warm- or cold-blooded.

D   Because of their ratio of surface area to volume, dinosaurs did not need to evolve a warm-blooded metabolism.

E   It is believed that the low resting rates of their metabolisms prevented dinosaurs from being overly active.

F   Until the 1960s, an inaccurate view of dinosaurs as slow-moving and sluggish was prevalent in paleontology.

PART

1

QUESTION TYPES

CHAPTER 01

Factual Information

Factual information questions require the identification of specific information based on what is stated in the passage. They involve deciding which option is true or relevant to what has been presented by the author. They sometimes involve verifying which option is NOT true or NOT mentioned in the passage.

Vocabulary Preview

advent	도래	*syn.* arrival	**divert**	다른 데로 돌리다	*syn.* redirect
adversely	역으로, 불리하게		**elucidate**	설명하다	*syn.* clarify
affect	영향을 미치다	*syn.* influence	**emerge**	나오다, 생겨나다	
anchorage	고정시키는 것		**entrepreneur**	사업가	
apex	정점	*syn.* top	**equator**	적도	
apply	적용하다		**erosion**	침식	
arid	매우 건조한	*syn.* dry	**eruption**	분출	
ascend	상승하다	*syn.* rise	**evaporate**	증발하다	*syn.* vaporize
astounding	놀랄만한	*syn.* astonishing	**evidence**	흔적, 증거	
average	평균의	*syn.* standard	**expertise**	전문 지식(기술)	
barren	황량한	*syn.* unproductive	**explosive**	폭발성의	
basin	(큰 강의) 유역		**extensively**	광범위하게	*syn.* widely
collapse	붕괴	*syn.* cave-in	**extract**	뽑다	
colonize	대량 서식하다		**facet**	측면	*syn.* aspect
comprise	~으로 구성되다	*syn.* consist of	**facilitate**	가능(용이)하게 하다	*syn.* ease
deposit	침전시키다		**feat**	위업	
depression	움푹 파인 곳		**fertile**	비옥한	*syn.* productive
descent	하강		**frequent**	자주 다니다	
dissolved	용해된		**halve**	반으로 줄이다	
distinct	뚜렷한	*syn.* recognizable	**hub**	(활동의) 중심지	*syn.* center

iconic	상징적인		respective	각자의	
infrastructure	공공 기반 시설		revision	개정, 수정	
intermittently	간헐적으로	*syn.* irregularly	ruins	유적	
irrigation	관개		saturate	흠뻑 적시다	*syn.* soak
keystone	(아치 꼭대기의) 쐐기돌		sediment	침전물, 퇴적물	
lichen	지의류		seep	침투하다	*syn.* permeate
locomotive	기관차		shift	변화	*syn.* change
loop	고리 모양		silt	토사	
mastery	통달		sizeable	상당한 크기의	
meteorologist	기상학자		sound	견실한	*syn.* solid
moss	이끼		stable	안정된	*syn.* steadfast
nutrient	영양소, 영양분		submarine	해양의, 해저의	
parallel	위도선		subsequent	그 다음의	*syn.* following
permanent	영구적인		subterranean	땅속의	*syn.* underground
phenomenon	현상		survival	생존	
possess	소유하다	*syn.* have	task	일, 과업	*syn.* job
precipitation	(비·눈 등의) 강수		thrive	번영(번창)하다	*syn.* flourish
prescribe	규정하다	*syn.* dictate	tissue	조직	
protrusion	돌출부		vicinity	부근	
renowned	명성 있는	*syn.* famous	violent	격렬한	*syn.* overpowering

Factual Information

CHAPTER

01

세부 정보 찾기 문제

Factual Information 유형은 지문에 명시된 특정 세부 정보를 찾아내는 문제 유형이다. Fact 파악 문제는 지문에서 명백하게 언급된 내용과 일치하는 선택지가 무엇인지 찾고, Negative Fact 파악 문제는 지문에서 언급된 내용과 일치하지 않거나 언급되지 않은 선택지를 찾는다.

빈출문제 패턴

Fact	**According to paragraph #, which of the following is true of/about X?** ＃ 단락에 따르면, 다음 중 X에 대해 사실인 것은? **According to the passage, what/when/where/why/how X?** 지문에 따르면, 무엇을/언제/어디에서/왜/어떻게 X하는가? **According to paragraph #, X did Y because …** ＃ 단락에 따르면, X가 Y한 이유는?
Negative Fact	**According to paragraph #, which of the following is NOT true of/about X?** ＃ 단락에 따르면, 다음 중 X에 대해 사실이 아닌 것은? **In paragraph #, the author mentions all of the following EXCEPT …** 다음 중 ＃ 단락에서 글쓴이가 언급하지 않은 것은?

문제풀이 전략

1. 문제에서 핵심 어휘를 빨리 파악하기

문제에서 핵심 어휘를 파악하면 지문에서 어떤 정보를 확인해야 할지 분명해진다. 지문 전체 내용을 파악하여 답을 찾는 것이 아니라, 핵심 어휘와 관련된 구체적 정보에서 답의 근거를 찾아야 한다.

2. 핵심 내용을 다른 말로 표현한 선택지 찾기

Factual Information 문제는 Reading 실력의 기본기를 평가하는 문제이므로 정확한 독해가 요구된다. Fact 파악 문제는 지문에서 답의 근거를 찾은 후 정확한 독해를 바탕으로 핵심 의미를 적절하게 다른 말로 표현한 선택지를 골라야 한다. 또한, Negative Fact 파악 문제는 지문과 내용이 다르거나 언급되지 않은 선택지가 정답이다.

오답 포인트 ✓

1. 지문 내용이 아니라 개인적으로 유추한 것을 근거로 판단하면 오답을 고르게 된다.
2. Fact 파악 문제의 오답은 상식적으로 그럴듯하지만 지문에 언급되지 않았거나, 지문에 언급된 단어가 포함되어 있지만 지문과 무관한 내용으로 오답을 유도한다.

YBM TOEFL READING

Volume   Help   Review   Back   Next

There are approximately 1,000 species of stony corals, small marine organisms characterized by their hard external skeletons. These skeletons are composed primarily of calcium carbonate, which forms a cup-shaped structure within which the coral itself, known as a polyp, resides. The body of each polyp is hollow and cylindrical; one end attaches itself to a solid surface, while the other features a mouth surrounded by tentacles. These tentacles utilize stinging structures known as nematocysts to paralyze passing prey, which they then convey into the mouth. Stony corals are found in nearly all parts of the world's oceans, from shallow tidal zones to depths of up to 6,000 meters, and can be either solitary or colonial. The largest solitary stony corals have a diameter of about 25 centimeters, while colonial stony corals form vast atolls and reefs.

According to the passage, which of the following is true about nematocysts?

(A) They fix themselves onto solid surfaces.
(B) They cause their prey to become immobile.
(C) They can form hard external skeletons.
(D) They are shaped like a hollow cylinder.

해석 딱딱한 외골격을 특징으로 하는 작은 해양 생물인 돌산호는 약 1,000종이 있다. 이 골격들은 주로 탄산칼슘으로 이루어져 있는데, 이것은 컵 모양의 구조물을 형성하고, 그 안에 폴립이라고 알려진 산호 자체가 산다. 각 폴립의 몸체는 속이 빈 원통형이며, 한쪽 끝은 딱딱한 표면에 붙어 있고 다른 한쪽 끝에는 촉수로 둘러싸인 입이 있다. 이들 촉수는 가시 세포로 알려진 찌르는 구조물을 이용해 지나가는 먹이를 마비시킨 다음 입안으로 옮긴다. 돌산호는 얕은 조간대에서부터 최대 6,000미터 깊이에 이르기까지 전세계 거의 모든 대양에서 발견되며, 혼자 지내기도 하고 군락을 이루기도 한다. 가장 큰 단독 돌산호의 지름이 약 25센티미터인 반면, 군락 돌산호는 거대한 환초와 산호초를 형성한다.

지문에 따르면, 다음 중 가시 세포에 대해 사실은 것은?

(A) 딱딱한 표면에 자신을 고정시킨다.
(B) 먹이를 움직이지 못하게 만든다.
(C) 딱딱한 외골격을 만들어 낼 수 있다.
(D) 속이 빈 원통형 모양이다.

어휘 characterized by ~을 특징으로 하는   skeleton 골격, 뼈대   cylindrical 원통형의   tentacle 촉수   stinging 찌르는 paralyze 마비시키다   solitary 혼자의, 단독의

해설 돌산호가 가시 세포를 이용해 지나가는 먹이를 마비시켜 잡아먹는다고 했으므로, immobile이라는 말을 사용해 동일한 내용을 언급한 (B)가 정답이다. (A)와 (D)는 폴립 몸체에 대한 설명이고, (C)는 돌산호 전체에 대한 설명이다.

Root systems are organs that are primarily subterranean and play three major roles in ensuring the continued survival of plants. Their most basic function is to serve as anchorage by keeping the plant physically stable. As secondary roots grow from the plant's primary root, which is the first to emerge from the seed, they spread throughout the soil, giving the plant a firm grip on the ground and preventing it from toppling over. These same roots are further utilized to absorb water and to extract dissolved minerals from the soil, tasks that are accomplished via root hairs, threadlike protrusions extending outward from the tip of the root. Finally, nutrients, such as starches and sugars produced via the process of photosynthesis, can be stored within the tissues of the roots for later use.

According to the passage, which of the following is NOT true of root systems?

(A) They consist of a primary root and secondary roots.
(B) Their root hairs help keep plants from falling over.
(C) They can obtain dissolved minerals from the soil.
(D) Starches and sugars can be held inside them.

Ancient Roman bridges stand out as some of the empire's most iconic contributions to modern engineering. What made these impressive feats of engineering possible was the ancient Romans' mastery of the simple arch. Although evidence of arches has been found in Mesopotamian ruins from as early as the second millennium BC, it was the Romans who first used them extensively. One distinct feature of Roman arches is that they were rounded, which stands in contrast to the pointed arches later found in Gothic architecture. This semi-circular design utilized a keystone at the apex of its curve, diverting pressure more or less equally throughout the arch, which is what allowed it to bear the weight of massive structures such as bridges.

According to the passage, which of the following is true of Roman arches?

(A) They were the first arches built by humans.
(B) They were either pointed or rounded.
(C) They were copied from Gothic architecture.
(D) They were topped with a keystone.

| **Vocabulary Check** | 각 단어의 알맞은 뜻을 찾아 기호를 쓰시오.

1 subterranean _____   2 extract _____   3 ruins _____   4 divert _____

| ⓐ 유적 | ⓑ 땅속의 | ⓒ 모방 | ⓓ 뽑다 | ⓔ 다른 데로 돌리다 | ⓕ 노출된 |

EXERCISE 03

Volcanic lakes are formed after violent eruptions occur. These eruptions typically leave behind a deep depression in the surface of the Earth, created either by the eruption's explosive outward force or a subsequent inward collapse. The former geological features are known as craters, while the latter are referred to as calderas. These depressions may subsequently be filled by falling precipitation or by rising groundwater faster than the water can evaporate or seep into the ground, resulting in volcanic lakes. One of the most observable differences between volcanic lakes formed in craters versus those housed in calderas is that crater lakes tend to be more circular in shape. In addition, many crater lakes exist only intermittently, filling up and drying out repeatedly due to their unstable nature, while caldera lakes are generally larger and longer lasting.

According to the passage, volcanic lakes occur when

(A) nearby lakes begin to drain due to instability
(B) volcanic eruptions cause widespread flooding
(C) water enters a depression faster than it exits
(D) volcanic craters are transformed into calderas

EXERCISE 04

In 1948, a book by renowned educator Maria Montessori was published, elucidating the origins and key facets of her teaching method. Entitled *The Discovery of the Child*, it was a revision of one of her earlier publications, which had already been revised and republished several times. In it, she outlines guidelines on the ideal environment in which the Montessori method should be applied. These include ensuring that items such as chairs, cups, and counters are of a size suitable for the average child, rather than for adults. It also prescribes limiting the number of items in the environment to no more than a child can use, as having too many items available can adversely affect the child's ability to focus on any one task.

In the passage, which of the following is mentioned as something that should be done when creating the ideal environment for the Montessori method?

(A) minimizing available objects
(B) emphasizing age-appropriate reading activities
(C) providing detailed adult supervision
(D) offering tasks to keep children busy

| **Vocabulary Check** | 각 단어의 알맞은 동의어를 찾아 기호를 쓰시오.

1 violent _____   **2** subsequent _____   **3** renowned _____   **4** elucidate _____

| ⓐ following | ⓑ reversable | ⓒ clarify | ⓓ overpowering | ⓔ ease | ⓕ famous |

1ⓓ 2ⓐ 3ⓕ 4ⓒ

Atmospheric circulation, the large-scale movement of air across the surface of the Earth, comprises three basic types of cells, one of which is known as the Hadley cell, named in honor of the person who first described it, amateur meteorologist George Hadley. Hadley cells exist as a closed loop of circulation that forms near the equator, where moist air that has been warmed at the Earth's surface and is thus less dense begins to ascend. Meanwhile, a similar mass of air rises on the opposite side of the equator, creating a low-pressure area and causing both masses of air to move toward their respective poles. As the moist air moves away from the equator, it cools and increases in density, leading to its descent and the creation of an area of high pressure, a transformation that generally occurs in the vicinity of the 30th parallel. The air now begins to move along the surface of the Earth back toward the equator, completing the cell's cycle and producing an atmospheric phenomenon known as the trade winds.

1. **Select the TWO answer choices** that are mentioned in the passage as the reasons why moist air near the equator rises. **To receive credit, you must select TWO answer choices.**

    (A) It is circulating near the equator.
    (B) It has increased in temperature.
    (C) Its density has undergone a decrease.
    (D) It is near the trade winds.

2. According to the passage, which of the following is NOT true of Hadley cells?

    (A) They are a component of atmospheric circulation.
    (B) They occur both north and south of the equator.
    (C) They originate somewhere near the 30th parallel.
    (D) They are responsible for creating the trade winds.

| **Vocabulary Check** | 각 단어의 알맞은 뜻을 찾아 기호를 쓰시오.

1 equator _____   2 ascend _____   3 vicinity _____   4 phenomenon _____

| ⓐ 상승하다 | ⓑ 현상 | ⓒ 유지하다 | ⓓ 대류 | ⓔ 적도 | ⓕ 부근 |

1ⓔ 2ⓐ 3ⓕ 4ⓑ

EXERCISE 06

The advanced ancient civilization that thrived in Egypt for more than 3,000 years was made possible by the Nile, a northward flowing river that has an astounding total length of 6,650 kilometers and stretches from central Africa to the Mediterranean Sea. It was the Nile's annual flooding event, which deposits nutrient-rich sediment along the river's banks in late summer, that transformed an otherwise arid desert landscape into fertile farmland capable of feeding large numbers of individuals. The Nile Valley is actually covered in a thick layer of silt that allows wheat and barley to be grown in abundance, and the river itself was used to deliver life-sustaining water to these crops. Ancient Egyptian farmers created complex irrigation systems by digging channels that redirected the Nile's waters into basins, where it would saturate the soil in preparation for planting. Once the farmers' crops had been harvested, the river was utilized as a means of transportation with technologically advanced wooden boats distributing the food to the rest of the kingdom.

1. According to the passage, which of the following is true of the Nile?

(A) It floods every year near the end of summer.
(B) It created serious problems for Egyptian farmers.
(C) It unexpectedly caused the fall of ancient Egypt.
(D) It often washes away the crops of farmers.

2. In the passage, the author mentions all of the following about ancient Egyptian farmers EXCEPT

(A) how they transported their crops
(B) what they used to water their crops
(C) what kinds of crops they grew
(D) when they harvested their crops

| **Vocabulary Check** | 각 단어의 알맞은 동의어를 찾아 기호를 쓰시오.

1 thrive _____   **2** arid _____   **3** fertile _____   **4** saturate _____

| ⓐ dry | ⓑ meager | ⓒ flourish | ⓓ soak | ⓔ radiant | ⓕ productive |

ⓓ4 ⓕ3 ⓔ2 ⓒ1

In November 1963, a volcanic eruption 130 meters below sea level off the southern coast of Iceland caused the formation of a sizeable island. This submarine eruption continued for several years, ending in June 1967, at which time the newly formed island, which had been given the name Surtsey, had reached a size of 2.7 square kilometers. Although it has since been halved in area by the ongoing process of wave erosion, Surtsey has become a hub of activity for botanists, who flock to the island to study the plants that have colonized the once barren land. Surtsey's first plants were detected in the spring of 1965, followed by mosses in 1967 and lichens in 1970. In the island's first two decades, 20 separate plant species were discovered on the island, although only 10 were able to establish themselves as permanent residents, mostly due to the island's sandy soil, which was poor in nutrients. However, as birds began to frequent the island, the soil's condition improved, and in 1998, the first bush was found on Surtsey. By 2008, 69 plant species were growing on the island with two to five new species arriving each year.

1. In the passage, which of the following is mentioned about Surtsey?

    (A) how many people once lived on it
    (B) what caused its size to decrease
    (C) which plant species is the most common
    (D) who first discovered its plant life

2. According to the passage, which of the following is NOT true of Surtsey's plant life?

    (A) It has been damaged by migratory birds.
    (B) It is exhibiting increasing diversity.
    (C) It draws numerous botanists to study it.
    (D) It includes lichens as well as mosses.

| **Vocabulary Check** | 각 단어의 알맞은 뜻을 찾아 기호를 쓰시오.

1 colonize _____   2 barren _____   3 moss _____   4 frequent _____

| ⓐ 자주 다니다 | ⓑ 경치 좋은 | ⓒ 황량한 | ⓓ 이끼 | ⓔ 대량 서식하다 | ⓕ 산란 |

1 ⓔ 2 ⓒ 3 ⓓ 4 ⓐ

EXERCISE 08

There were six primary factors that facilitated the advent of the First Industrial Revolution in Great Britain in the mid-18th century. Perhaps most importantly, the nation enjoyed a high level of agricultural productivity, had a sound transportation infrastructure that included rivers, roads, canals, and ports, and was blessed with a rich supply of natural resources, most notably iron and coal. In terms of its people, Great Britain furthermore possessed a large pool of skilled workers, a stable and business-friendly government, and a large amount of financial capital available for investment. The revolution was spearheaded by the transition from the hand production of goods to the use of machines to do so, allowing for the creation of stable and efficient manufacturing processes. Steam power also played a significant role, powering many of the machines, including locomotives, that played a prominent role in this major shift in the nature of human activity. The First Industrial Revolution was later extended to other parts of the world—including continental Europe, the United States, and Japan—by the eagerness of British entrepreneurs to export their newfound expertise and the willingness of other nations to receive it.

1. According to the passage, the Industrial Revolution moved across the globe because

   (A) migrants from Britain brought new ideas from their homelands
   (B) locomotives became the main form of transportation
   (C) businesspeople from Britain wanted to spread it
   (D) invading armies forced it on defeated countries

2. In the passage, the author mentions all of the following as factors that led to the Industrial Revolution in Great Britain EXCEPT

   (A) money that could be invested
   (B) politicians who supported business
   (C) a stable transportation network
   (D) factories with dedicated workforces

| Vocabulary Check | 각 단어의 알맞은 동의어를 찾아 기호를 쓰시오.

1 facilitate _____   **2** advent _____   **3** possess _____   **4** shift _____

| ⓐ release | ⓑ have | ⓒ damage | ⓓ arrival | ⓔ expedite | ⓕ change |

1ⓔ 2ⓓ 3ⓑ 4ⓕ

YBM TOEFL 80 +
READING

Vocabulary

Vocabulary questions require the identification of the meanings of individual words or phrases as they are used in the reading passage. They involve identifying which option has a similar meaning that is relevant in the context.

Vocabulary Preview

absorb	흡수하다	*syn.* soak up	**convert**	전환시키다	*syn.* transform
accumulate	축적하다	*syn.* amass	**convey**	전하다	*syn.* communicate
alloy	합금		**countermeasure**	대응책	
ambitious	야심적인		**counterpart**	대응 관계에 있는 것	
appliance	기기, 기구		**density**	밀도	
atmosphere	(지구 및 기타 행성의) 대기		**desertification**	사막화	
boast	자랑하다		**detached**	떨어진, 분리된	*syn.* separated
bond	유대	*syn.* tie	**diameter**	지름	
boulder	(크고 둥근) 돌덩어리		**dimension**	차원	
capture	잡다, 포착하다	*syn.* seize	**disturbance**	교란, 방해	
carve	새기다	*syn.* cut	**ensue**	뒤따르다	*syn.* follow
clarity	명료함	*syn.* clearness	**equilibrium**	평형	
coalition	연합(체), 연정		**era**	시대	*syn.* age
coincide	동시에 일어나다		**evolve**	발달하다, 진화하다	*syn.* develop
commence	시작되다	*syn.* start	**expose**	노출시키다, 드러내다	
commodity	상품	*syn.* goods	**extensive**	광범위한	*syn.* far-reaching
communal	공동의		**factor**	요인	
congruence	일치, 조화, 합동		**figure**	인물, 모습	
contrast	대비		**fortuitous**	예기치 않은	*syn.* serendipitous
convention	전통, 관습	*syn.* custom	**generate**	만들어 내다	*syn.* create

installation	설치	**precursor**	선도자 _syn._ predecessor
intact	손상되지 않은 _syn._ undamaged	**principal**	주요한 _syn._ main
intellect	지성 _syn._ intelligence	**render**	(어떤 상태로) 만들다
lava	용암	**renewable**	재생 가능한
livestock	가축	**restoration**	복원
loose	느슨한 _syn._ unbound	**retreat**	후퇴하다, 물러가다
marking	(기호·형태·글자 등의) 표시	**reverse**	반전시키다
mass	질량	**revolutionary**	혁명적인, 혁명의
necessitate	필요로 하다 _syn._ require	**ritual**	(종교) 의식 _syn._ rite
notational	기호(법)의	**scent**	향기 _syn._ fragrance
ornate	화려하게 장식된 _syn._ fancy	**scorched**	불에 탄
overexploitation	과잉 개발	**smear**	문질러 바르다 _syn._ coat
pack	무리, 떼 _syn._ herd	**stir**	불러일으키다 _syn._ provoke
particle	입자	**sucrose**	자당
passionate	열정적인	**superiority**	우월성, 우세 _syn._ excellence
phase	단계 _syn._ stage	**synchronize**	동시에 발생하게 맞추다
playback	재생	**trait**	특성 _syn._ characteristic
pollen	꽃가루	**undergo**	겪다
pollination	수분(꽃가루받이)	**weathering**	풍화
practice	실행, 관행	**worship**	숭배 _syn._ reverence

Vocabulary

어휘의 의미 파악 문제

Vocabulary 유형은 지문의 음영 처리된 단어나 구와 의미가 가장 비슷한 선택지를 찾아내는 문제 유형이다. 동의어와 유의어를 찾거나, 또는 사전적 의미에서는 동의어나 유의어에 해당하지 않더라도 맥락상 대체가 가능한 단어나 구를 찾는다.

빈출문제 패턴

> **The word "X" in the passage is closest in meaning to …**
> 지문의 단어 "X"와 의미가 가장 가까운 것은?
>
> **The phrase "X" in the passage is closest in meaning to …**
> 지문의 구 "X"와 의미가 가장 가까운 것은?

문제풀이 전략

1. 사전적 동의어 먼저 찾기

먼저 평소 암기한 사전적 의미로 동일한 뜻을 가진 어휘를 찾는다. 만약 사전적 동의어가 전혀 없으면 지문의 맥락에서 쓰인 의미에 가장 가까운 어휘를 찾으면 된다.

2. 확실한 오답 선택지부터 소거하기

어휘 문제는 시간을 아낄 수 있는 문제 유형이다. 시간을 들여 고민하거나 맥락 파악을 위해 섣불리 전체 단락을 해석하려 하지 말고, 확실한 오답부터 재빨리 제외시킨 후 남은 선택지 중 가능성이 높은 것을 선택한다.

3. 동의어와 유의어, 품사별 의미를 철저히 암기하기

평소 쌓은 어휘력이 있어야 쉽고 빠르게 답을 찾을 수 있다. 동의어와 유의어를 함께 암기해 두고, 품사에 따라서 의미가 달라지는 단어는 품사별 의미도 정확하게 암기해 둔다.

오답 포인트 ✓

단어나 구를 대입했을 때 의미가 성립되는 선택지로 오답을 유도하기도 한다. 주어진 맥락과 맞지 않는데 단순히 의미가 성립된다고 해서 바로 정답으로 생각하면 안 된다.

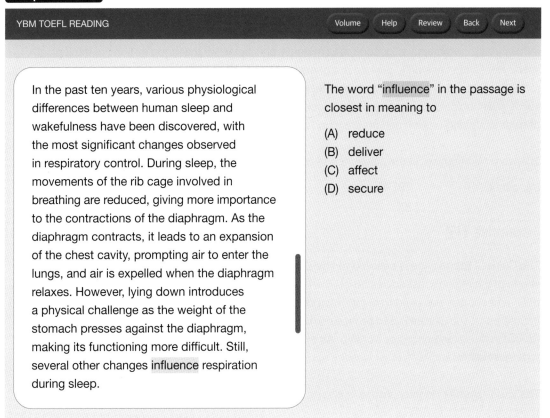

In the past ten years, various physiological differences between human sleep and wakefulness have been discovered, with the most significant changes observed in respiratory control. During sleep, the movements of the rib cage involved in breathing are reduced, giving more importance to the contractions of the diaphragm. As the diaphragm contracts, it leads to an expansion of the chest cavity, prompting air to enter the lungs, and air is expelled when the diaphragm relaxes. However, lying down introduces a physical challenge as the weight of the stomach presses against the diaphragm, making its functioning more difficult. Still, several other changes influence respiration during sleep.

The word "influence" in the passage is closest in meaning to

(A) reduce
(B) deliver
(C) affect
(D) secure

해석 지난 10년 동안 호흡 조절에서 관찰된 가장 중요한 변화와 함께 인간의 수면과 깨어 있음 사이의 다양한 생리적 차이가 발견되어왔다. 수면 중에는 호흡과 관련된 흉곽의 움직임이 줄어들어, 횡격막 수축이 더 중요해진다. 횡격막이 수축하면서 흉강이 팽창되어 공기가 폐로 들어가고, 횡격막이 이완되면서 공기가 배출된다. 그러나 누운 상태는 위의 무게가 횡격막을 압박해 제 역할을 하는 것을 더 힘들게 하면서 신체적 어려움을 초래한다. 그러나 몇 가지 다른 변화들도 수면 중 호흡에 영향을 미친다.

지문의 단어 "influence"와 의미가 가장 가까운 것은?

(A) 줄이다
(B) 전달하다
(C) 영향을 주다
(D) 확보하다

어휘 wakefulness 깨어 있음 respiratory 호흡의 rib cage 흉곽 diaphragm 횡격막 expansion 팽창
chest cavity 흉강 expel 배출하다 press against ~을 압박하다

해설 influence는 '영향을 미치다'라는 뜻이므로, 의미가 가장 가까운 것은 (C) affect이다.

EXERCISE 01

The rock cycle refers to a series of processes of the formation, transformation, and reformation of rocks through sedimentary, igneous, and metamorphic activities that span millions of geological years. Rocks are constantly pushed out of equilibrium by shifts in their environment. Sedimentary rocks, for example, consist of various-sized rock fragments, ranging from tiny clay particles to substantial boulders. These fragments become detached from their original rocks due to the effects of weathering and erosion and are transported to accumulate in basins.

The word "substantial" in the passage is closest in meaning to

(A) minor   (B) sizeable   (C) temporary   (D) distinct

EXERCISE 02

The Chinese Bronze Age is believed to have begun circa 2000 BC along the banks of the Yellow River in one of the region's first advanced civilizations. Unlike in other early cultures, where bronze, an alloy of tin and copper, was used to create weapons that were both lighter and sturdier than their stone counterparts, the Chinese used bronze primarily to craft ornate vessels, such as cauldrons and cups, for use in rituals and ancestor worship. As these utensils were a sign of prestige, possession of them was reserved for society's most wealthy and powerful.

The word "sturdier" in the passage is closest in meaning to

(A) glossier   (B) deadlier   (C) more valuable   (D) more durable

EXERCISE 03

Thomas Edison's invention of the phonograph in 1877 heralded a whole new dimension in the field of entertainment. For the first time, sounds, including spoken words and music, could be recorded and stored for playback at a later time. Nearly 20 years later, Edison once again shook up the entertainment world with a revolutionary invention; this time, it was the motion picture camera, a precursor to modern film cameras. Edison, however, was unable to sufficiently synchronize the output of his two creations, causing movies to remain silent until the mid-1920s.

The word "heralded" in the passage is closest in meaning to

(A) prevented the spread of   (B) explained the need for
(C) signaled the beginning of   (D) acted as a substitute for

| **Vocabulary Check** | 각 단어의 알맞은 뜻을 찾아 기호를 쓰시오.

1 equilibrium _____   2 detached _____   3 ornate _____   4 precursor _____

| ⓐ 화려하게 장식된 | ⓑ 변화 | ⓒ 떨어진 | ⓓ 주요한 | ⓔ 평형 | ⓕ 선도자 |

1ⓔ 2ⓒ 3ⓐ 4ⓕ

EXERCISE 04

A large-scale transition to renewable energy sources will require that we find an effective means of capturing them. When it comes to sunlight, the established solution is the installation of solar panels. These panels, which can be seen on rooftops all around the world, are made up of special cells. They absorb the light of the sun and convert it into electricity. This electricity can then be stored or used to power appliances and devices. While solar energy is the most popular form of renewable energy, there are high costs associated with it.

The word "transition" in the passage is closest in meaning to

(A) research   (B) shift   (C) completion   (D) discussion

EXERCISE 05

The oldest existing examples of proto-writing, the limited use of markings to communicate rudimentary ideas, may have been created in Europe during the Upper Paleolithic era, circa 35,000 BC. Notational signs were made next to images of animals, perhaps to convey information about their seasonal behavior that would be useful to other hunters. Later, a significant step toward the creation of an actual writing system coincided with the widespread use of pottery, when clay tokens marked with symbols were used to record numbers of livestock or other commodities.

The word "rudimentary" in the passage is closest in meaning to

(A) essential   (B) alarming   (C) ancient   (D) primitive

EXERCISE 06

The Umbrellas is an oil painting created by Pierre-Auguste Renoir over two separate periods in the 1880s. The first phase, which began early in the decade, displayed signature characteristics of the Impressionist movement, such as loose brushwork and a contrast between light and dark tones. Around 1885, having moved away from Impressionism, Renoir revisited the unfinished work and introduced muted colors and a classical linear style. Most significantly, the clothing of the principal female figure was changed to make her a member of the working class, and the titular umbrellas of the work were added to the background.

The word "muted" in the passage is closest in meaning to

(A) traditional   (B) vibrant   (C) subdued   (D) contrasting

| **Vocabulary Check** | 각 단어의 알맞은 동의어를 찾아 기호를 쓰시오.

1 capture _____   **2** convey _____   **3** loose _____   **4** principal _____

ⓐ seize   ⓑ relaxed   ⓒ regular   ⓓ main   ⓔ communicate   ⓕ involve

1ⓐ 2ⓔ 3ⓑ 4ⓓ

Scientists have already established that certain species possess extensive communication networks, and among them are elephants, which happen to be the largest land mammals. These creatures boast a well-developed social structure and employ a variety of communication methods to convey the broad spectrum of information necessary for their social interactions and daily routines. Their society is highly communal, organized around family units and social bonds. In a manner that is characteristic of a fission-fusion society, some individual elephants temporarily separate from the pack and later rejoin the larger group, which necessitates a communication system to synchronize their movements across vast areas.

1. The word "employ" in the passage is closest in meaning to

   (A) send   (B) herd   (C) utilize   (D) continue

2. The word "rejoin" in the passage is closest in meaning to

   (A) reform   (B) extend   (C) require   (D) return to

Desertification, the process through which fertile lands are rendered arid, can be caused by either natural phenomena or human activity. In both cases, the immediate effect is a catastrophic loss of vegetation in the affected area, stripping the soil of an essential protective layer that slows the twin processes of wind and water erosion. Perhaps the most common human causes of desertification are overexploitation of the soil by farmers seeking to maximize their yields in the short term and the overgrazing of livestock. There are, however, a variety of countermeasures that can be employed to slow or even reverse the effects of desertification, including reforestation and soil restoration. The former involves replanting native flora while the latter requires the provision of water and fertilizer to damaged land.

1. The word "catastrophic" in the passage is closest in meaning to

   (A) gradual   (B) inevitable   (C) disastrous   (D) continuous

2. The phrase "maximize their yields" in the passage is closest in meaning to

   (A) extend the growing season   (B) spend less money on labor
   (C) expand the sizes of their fields   (D) produce as much as possible

| **Vocabulary Check** | 각 단어의 알맞은 뜻을 찾아 기호를 쓰시오.

1 extensive _____   2 bond _____   3 overexploitation _____   4 reverse _____

| ⓐ 밀접한 | ⓑ 반전시키다 | ⓒ 유대 | ⓓ 보호하다 | ⓔ 과잉 개발 | ⓕ 광범위한 |

ⓐ4 ⓔ3 ⓒ2 ⓕ1

EXERCISE 09

Jupiter, the largest planet in the solar system, is classified as a gas giant. The reason is that it has a diameter of nearly 150,000 kilometers, is made up primarily of gas and liquid rather than solid matter, and possesses a density lower than that of the four terrestrial planets, Mercury, Venus, Earth, and Mars. The composition of its atmosphere is approximately 76 percent hydrogen and 24 percent helium with tiny amounts of methane and water vapor. While Jupiter's diameter is 11 times larger than Earth's, its mass is an astounding 318 times greater than that of our home planet. In fact, astronomers believe that Jupiter has achieved close to the maximum possible mass for a planet of its type; if it were 75 times more massive, it would likely begin fusing hydrogen atoms, create helium, and eventually transform into a star.

1. The word "approximately" in the passage is closest in meaning to

(A) about   (B) precisely   (C) properly   (D) somewhat

2. The word "fusing" in the passage is closest in meaning to

(A) rejecting   (B) joining   (C) generating   (D) attracting

EXERCISE 10

European art music underwent a significant transition at the start of the 19th century with the Classical period drawing to an end while Romantic music began to emerge. Music in the Classical period was characterized by its clarity and regular structure, a combination of features often referred to as "natural simplicity." The sonata, one of its main forms, helped lay the groundwork for the later work of Romantic composers. Romantic music differed from Classical music in that it favored emotion over intellect; it was passionate and unstructured, rejecting the conventions of Classical compositions and featuring nationalistic undertones meant to stir deep feelings. Despite these stark differences, the work of Classical composers such as Mozart had a strong influence on Romantic music and Romantic composers, including Chopin and Liszt.

1. The phrase "lay the groundwork" in the passage is closest in meaning to

(A) establish a system   (B) disprove a theory

(C) show appreciation for   (D) create a foundation

2. The word "stark" in the passage is closest in meaning to

(A) unusual   (B) discrete   (C) extreme   (D) minor

| **Vocabulary Check** | 각 단어의 알맞은 동의어를 찾아 기호를 쓰시오.

1 clarity _____   2 intellect _____   3 convention _____   4 stir _____

ⓐ intelligence   ⓑ diminish   ⓒ provoke   ⓓ clearness   ⓔ stock   ⓕ custom

ⓓ4 ⓕ3 ⓐ2 ⓓ1

The fifth century BC, specifically the period from 480 to 404 BC, was a golden age for the Greek city-state of Athens, which was experiencing a fortuitous congruence of political hegemony, economic growth, and cultural superiority. The event that marked the beginning of this period was the victory of a coalition of Greek city-states led by Athens over invading Persian armies in 478 BC. During the ensuing peace with Persia, this coalition grew imbalanced in power, with Athens emerging as the clear leader of what was essentially an Athenian empire. Pericles, an Athenian general and politician, was the most influential leader during this period. He believed in the importance of arts and literature, and he spearheaded an ambitious undertaking that brought the world many of its greatest works of architecture, including the Parthenon.

1. The word "hegemony" in the passage is closest in meaning to

(A) dominance   (B) cooperation   (C) transformation   (D) defiance

2. The word "spearheaded" in the passage is closest in meaning to

(A) mandated   (B) explored   (C) led   (D) suspended

The process by which natural communities replace one another over a period of time is known as ecological succession. There are two types of ecological succession; primary and secondary. Primary succession takes place in situations where the land is either newly formed, such as by flowing lava, or has been recently exposed, perhaps by a retreating glacier. In these cases, a pioneer species must begin the colonization process from scratch. In secondary succession, on the other hand, a disturbance destroys an existing plant community, creating a need to restart the process of ecological succession but with the soil and its nutrients still intact. This type of succession can be most clearly observed after a wildfire, when growth begins anew in the scorched soil after an entire generation of trees has been wiped out.

1. The phrase "from scratch" in the passage is closest in meaning to

(A) with great energy   (B) from the beginning
(C) with some assistance   (D) from a distance

2. The phrase "wiped out" in the passage is closest in meaning to

(A) fertilized   (B) uncovered   (C) rejuvenated   (D) removed

| **Vocabulary Check** | 각 단어의 알맞은 뜻을 찾아 기호를 쓰시오.

1 fortuitous _____   **2** coalition _____   **3** intact _____   **4** scorched _____

| ⓐ 기반 | ⓑ 연합 | ⓒ 예기치 않은 | ⓓ 손상되지 않은 | ⓔ 불에 탄 | ⓕ 심화 |

1 ⓒ 2 ⓑ 3 ⓓ 4 ⓔ

EXERCISE 13

Pollination syndromes are the collections of traits that flowers evolve through the process of natural selection. They can be formed by both nonbiological factors, such as wind and water, and biological ones, such as birds and bees. These traits include the shapes, sizes, colors, and scents of the flowers along with other features. Bee-pollinated flowers, for example, tend to be yellow or blue in color, and sucrose is often the predominant sugar in their nectar. This is in contrast to butterfly-pollinated flowers, which are usually large and pink or lavender, with strong scents and more nectar than pollen. This nectar is often secreted inside the flowers' narrow tubes, reachable only by the long tongues of butterflies. Within the scientific community, however, there is some disagreement as to how many flowers can be neatly categorized into a single classical pollination syndrome.

1. The word "predominant" in the passage is closest in meaning to

(A) fundamental　　(B) nourishing　　(C) prevalent　　(D) preceding

2. The word "secreted" in the passage is closest in meaning to

(A) extracted　　(B) concealed　　(C) transferred　　(D) digested

EXERCISE 14

The history of print can be said to have commenced with the advent of woodblock printing, a process by which symbols or images are carved into blocks of wood, which are then smeared with ink and pressed against a smooth surface, thereby transferring the image. Woodblock printing first appeared in China sometime before 220 AD with cloth being the preferred printed surface. The oldest surviving examples are fragments of silk onto which flowers had been printed in three colors. Printing on paper did not emerge as a regular practice in China until the ninth century. A copy of the *Diamond Sutra*, an ancient Buddhist text, is one of the oldest extant woodblock-printed books, with a publishing date of 868 AD. Skilled woodblock printers of this era were able to generate vast amounts of material, printing up to 2,000 sheets each day.

1. The word "fragments" in the passage is closest in meaning to

(A) sheets　　(B) garments　　(C) images　　(D) pieces

2. The word "extant" in the passage is closest in meaning to

(A) existing　　(B) anonymous　　(C) valued　　(D) recovered

| **Vocabulary Check** | 각 단어의 알맞은 동의어를 찾아 기호를 쓰시오.

1 trait _____　　　2 evolve _____　　　3 commence _____　　　4 carve _____

| ⓐ start | ⓑ transit | ⓒ imitate | ⓓ characteristic | ⓔ develop | ⓕ cut |

1ⓓ 2ⓔ 3ⓐ 4ⓕ

YBM TOEFL 80 ⁺
READING

Rhetorical Purpose

Rhetorical purpose questions require the identification of why the author has presented a particular piece of information in a particular place or manner, as rhetoric is the art of effective speaking or writing. They involve understanding the rhetorical function of a word, phrase, statement, or paragraph as it relates to the rest of the passage.

abbey	수도원	**dazzle**	압도하다, 감탄하게 하다
adjudicate	판결하다	**deficit**	부족, 결손
adorn	장식하다 *syn.* decorate	**demise**	죽음
airborne	공중에 떠 있는	**depletion**	감소
algal	조류의	**derive**	유래하다 *syn.* originate
amnesia	기억 상실	**devastating**	파괴적인
appropriate	적절한 *syn.* proper	**diminish**	줄어들다 *syn.* decrease
aquatic	수생의	**distinctive**	독특한 *syn.* distinct
assess	평가하다 *syn.* evaluate	**diverse**	다양한 *syn.* varied
attain	이르다 *syn.* reach	**divine**	신의, 신성한
basilica	(대)성당	**domain**	영역
bestow	부여하다 *syn.* impart	**domestic**	가정의
chart	지도에 기입하다	**elongated**	긴 *syn.* long
colonialism	식민주의	**encompass**	포함(망라)하다 *syn.* include
commerce	교역, 상업	**equatorial**	적도의
compensation	보상, 배상 *syn.* reparation	**erect**	세우다 *syn.* build
concentrated	집중적인	**exotic**	이국적인
consensus	의견 일치, 합의	**extinction**	멸종
cornerstone	초석, 토대	**flank**	~의 옆에 있다
culminate	정점에 이르다	**flourish**	번성하다 *syn.* thrive

forbid	금지하다	*syn.* prohibit	prompt	자극하다, 유발하다	*syn.* induce
fuel	부채질하다		prophet	예언자	
guilt	유죄		recall	기억해 내다	*syn.* recollect
hue	색조	*syn.* tint	remedy	구제책	
hypothetically	가설에 근거해서		reproduce	번식하다	
identical	동일한	*syn.* same	restrained	억제된, 절제된	
immense	엄청난	*syn.* huge	rod	막대	
impact	영향, 충격	*syn.* influence	scarce	드문, 부족한	*syn.* scant
indefinite	무기한의		shrine	신전, 성지	
innocence	무죄		staple	주요소	
insatiable	한없는, 만족할 줄 모르는		strategy	전략	
invertebrate	무척추 동물		submit	제출하다	*syn.* present
marked	현저한, 뚜렷한		tawny	황갈색의	
medieval	중세의		testimony	증언	
microbe	미생물		tilt	기울기	
microscopic	미세한		trace	극미량	
particulate	미립자		unicellular	단세포의	
penalty	처벌		variable	가변적인	*syn.* changeable
plague	괴롭히다	*syn.* trouble	verdict	판결	
portal	정문, 입구		withstand	견뎌 내다	*syn.* bear

PART 1

CHAPTER 03

Rhetorical Purpose

CHAPTER 03

수사적 의도 파악 문제

Rhetorical Purpose 유형은 글쓴이의 수사적 의도를 찾아내는 문제 유형이다. 글쓴이가 특정한 단어나 구, 문장을 특정한 위치에서 특정한 방법으로 제시하거나, 또는 특정한 단락을 강조하거나 대조하는 등의 방식으로 자신의 주장이나 견해를 효과적으로 전달하려는 것이 수사적 의도이다. 지문의 음영 처리된 단어나 구, 문장이 언급된 이유, 또는 특정 단락이 어떤 기능을 수행하는지를 통해 글쓴이의 의도를 찾아낸다.

빈출문제 패턴

Why does the author mention "X" in paragraph #?
글쓴이는 왜 # 단락에서 "X"를 언급하는가?

The author discusses "X" in paragraph # in order to …
글쓴이가 # 단락에서 "X"에 대해 논의하는 이유는?

Why does the author compare X to Y?
글쓴이는 왜 X와 Y를 비교하는가?

문제풀이 전략

1. 문장과 단락 간 논리적 맥락 파악하기

수사적 의도 파악 문제는 어떤 맥락에서 특정 단어나 구가 등장하거나, 특정 단락이 어떤 역할을 하는지를 이해하여 그 등장 배경이나 논리적 맥락을 파악해야 한다.

2. 의도나 기능을 나타내는 표현 숙지하기

수사적 의도 파악 문제에서 자주 사용되는 표현은 to illustrate(예시하다), to explain(설명하다), to compare(비교하다), to contrast(대조하다), to emphasize(강조하다), to refute(반박하다), to criticize(비판하다), to evaluate(평가하다) 등이다. 이 표현들이 맥락 안에서 구체적으로 어떤 역할을 하는지 미리 숙지해 둔다.

오답 포인트 ✓

1. 글쓴이의 의도 파악 문제는 사실적 정보를 묻는 문제와 얼핏 비슷해 보여 성급하게 오판하기 쉽다. 논리적 맥락과 관계없이 사실적 정보를 다루는 선택지가 이 유형의 빈출 오답이다.
2. 철저히 지문 맥락에 근거하여 글쓴이의 의도를 판단해야 하는데 자신의 논리로 글쓴이의 의도를 유추하는 실수도 흔하다.

What was the first city in human history? The origins of some of the earliest human civilizations can be traced back to southern Mesopotamia during the fourth millennium BC. In the latter part of that millennium, there was a significant increase in permanent settlements around the city of Uruk. This period witnessed a substantial portion of that expansion within Uruk itself, evolving into a major urban hub surrounded by several secondary settlements. Though it is difficult to accurately estimate the population, the inhabitants of Uruk were supposedly able to sustain themselves through the agricultural production from the fields surrounding the city, which they could access through their daily commutes.

Why does the author mention "agricultural production" in the passage?

(A) To give examples of agricultural products that Uruk people harvested

(B) To explain how people in one of the earliest human civilizations could survive

(C) To provide information that the expansion of Uruk was considerable

(D) To contrast how people in the city of Uruk and those in secondary cities lived differently

PART 1

CHAPTER 03

해석 인류 역사상 최초의 도시는 어디였는가? 가장 초기의 일부 인류 문명의 발단은 기원전 4000년의 남부 메소포타미아로 거슬러 올라갈 수 있다. 기원전 4000년 후반에 우루크 주변에 영구 정착지가 크게 증가했다. 이 시기에 확장의 상당 부분은 몇몇 부수 정착지에 둘러싸인 주요 도심지로 진화하던 우루크 내부에서 이루어졌다. 인구수를 정확히 추정하기는 어렵지만, 우루크 주민들은 매일 오갈 수 있는 도시 주변의 밭에서 얻은 농작물 생산을 통해 생활을 유지할 수 있었다고 추정된다.

글쓴이는 왜 지문에서 "농작물 생산"을 언급하는가?

(A) 우루크 사람들이 수확했던 농작물의 예를 들려고
(B) 초기 인류 문명들 중 한 곳의 사람들이 어떻게 생존할 수 있었는지를 설명하려고
(C) 우루크의 확장이 상당했다는 정보를 제공하려고
(D) 우루크와 주변 도시의 사람들이 어떻게 다르게 살았는지 대조하려고

어휘 be traced back to ~으로 거슬러 올라가다   settlement 정착지   witness 목격하다   hub 중심지   secondary 부수적인 inhabitant 주민   supposedly 추정상, 아마

해설 초기 인류 문명인 메소포타미아 지역의 우루크 주민들이 생존할 수 있었던 방식으로 농작물 생산이 언급되었으므로, (B)가 정답이다.

The Commercial Revolution was a period of trade-driven economic development that took place in Europe beginning in the 11th century and continuing up until the First Industrial Revolution more than 700 years later. It can be said to have culminated with the Age of Exploration, which began in the 15th century. Reawakened to the desirability of spices and other exotic goods by the Crusades, trade networks were established, and new routes were charted, leading to a boom in commerce. Geopolitically, the advent of colonialism helped fuel trade as European nations, including Portugal, Spain, and the Netherlands, began developing vast empires that stretched across the globe. Another important element was the fact that European nations were plagued by a constant deficit of silver and gold; an insatiable hunger for these precious metals, which were a cornerstone of trade with Eastern nations, led to further interest in exploring new lands.

Why does the author mention "the Crusades" in the passage?

(A) To explain why European nations gave up on colonialism
(B) To compare attitudes before and after the Age of Exploration
(C) To raise an issue on how trade had a negative impact on the world
(D) To illustrate a root cause of the European desire to explore

The inability of adults to recall events and situations that occurred before the ages of two to four is known as childhood amnesia. Although such memories are commonly referred to as having been forgotten, there is a marked difference between availability and accessibility when it comes to memory. Availability refers to whether or not the memory is actually intact and stored within the brain, while accessibility is a variable condition that is related to an individual's ability to recall the memory at any given time. This means that there may be certain memories that are available but not accessible. Early childhood memories that are personal and contain strong emotional content, such as the recollection of being given one's first pet, tend to be more accessible than public ones, such as a historical event.

The author discusses childhood pets in the passage in order to

(A) refute the concept of adults experiencing childhood amnesia
(B) contrast a typical adult memory with a childhood memory
(C) illustrate the kind of memory that is easily accessible
(D) emphasize how people are able to access unavailable memories

| **Vocabulary Check** | 각 단어의 알맞은 뜻을 찾아 기호를 쓰시오.

1 exotic _____   2 colonialism _____   3 amnesia _____   4 variable _____

| ⓐ 가변적인 | ⓑ 활발한 | ⓒ 식민주의 | ⓓ 이국적인 | ⓔ 기억 상실 | ⓕ 접근 |

1ⓓ 2ⓒ 3ⓔ 4ⓐ

EXERCISE 03

In Saint-Denis, a suburb to the north of Paris, visitors will find the Basilica of Saint-Denis, a former medieval abbey church that currently serves as a cathedral. The building is significant in terms of both its historical and architectural value, as it is adorned with many elements of early Gothic architecture. Its sculptures in particular had a powerful influence on the later development of the Gothic style, as statues of the tall, thin figures flanking the cathedral's portals and representing prophets and kings can be found in the portals of nearly every Gothic cathedral built at a later date. The statues on Saint-Denis's north portal, which were erected in 1175, are especially elongated and expressive, standing in stark contrast to the more restrained statues of Chartres Cathedral, which was built during the same period.

The author discusses "Chartres Cathedral" in the passage in order to

(A) provide an example of pre-Gothic architecture
(B) emphasize the artistic features of Saint-Denis's statues
(C) compare two construction methods from the same period
(D) give evidence that it was the inspiration for the Basilica of Saint-Denis

EXERCISE 04

The atmosphere of Mars is made up mainly of carbon dioxide with small amounts of argon and nitrogen as well as traces of oxygen and water. It also contains a high level of airborne particulates, which give the atmosphere a dusty quality and render the sky a distinctive tawny hue when viewed from the planet's surface. Due to the high concentration of atmospheric carbon dioxide and the low surface pressure of Mars, sound waves travel more slowly there than they do on Earth, resulting in the sounds themselves being diminished. In terms of climate, similarities in the tilt of the rotational axes of Mars and Earth mean that the two planets experience similar seasons although those of Mars last twice as long. There is also a wider range of temperatures on Mars with surface lows dropping to −110°C and equatorial highs reaching 35°C during the Martian summer.

Why does the author compare the tilt of Mars' axis to that of Earth's?

(A) To explain why the sky on Mars is not blue
(B) To give a reason for the lengthy seasons of Mars
(C) To show the climatic characteristics of Mars
(D) To contrast the effects of two kinds of atmospheres

| **Vocabulary Check** | 각 단어의 알맞은 동의어를 찾아 기호를 쓰시오.

1 adorn _____   **2** elongated _____   **3** hue _____   **4** diminish _____

| ⓐ release | ⓑ tint | ⓒ decorate | ⓓ phase | ⓔ long | ⓕ decrease |

1ⓒ 2ⓔ 3ⓑ 4ⓕ

Architecture flourished in ancient Mesopotamian civilizations, in part because the craft of construction was believed to be a divine gift bestowed upon humankind. Stone was scarce in the region, so clay and sunbaked bricks were the literal building blocks of early Mesopotamian architecture. Although domestic structures tended to be relatively simple and modest with a large central space surrounded by smaller rooms, public buildings were constructed to dazzle observers with both their scale and beauty. It was the ziggurat, a type of pyramid with terraced levels leading to a shrine at the apex, that was perhaps the most impressive facet of Mesopotamian architecture. Although ziggurats were religious structures, the public was forbidden to set foot inside them; they were domains reserved solely for religious officials. The other key innovation of Mesopotamian architecture was the rounded arch. It was capable of withstanding immense pressure and improved the interior airflow of the structures it supported. Ancient Roman architects were often given credit for inventing this staple of construction; however, it was already being used by Mesopotamian architects as early as the sixth century BC.

1. The author mentions "religious officials" in the passage in order to

   (A) explain why ziggurats were different from pyramids
   (B) illustrate the exclusive nature of ziggurats
   (C) emphasize the great scale and beauty of ziggurats
   (D) describe how ziggurats were used in ancient Rome

2. Why does the author mention "Ancient Roman architects" in the passage?

   (A) To demonstrate how they viewed Mesopotamia
   (B) To compare their style of construction with modern styles
   (C) To give an explanation of how they later copied ziggurats
   (D) To refute the idea that they invented arches

| **Vocabulary Check** | 각 단어의 알맞은 뜻을 찾아 기호를 쓰시오.

1 flourish _____   **2** dazzle _____   **3** shrine _____   **4** forbid _____

| ⓐ 압도하다 | ⓑ 금지하다 | ⓒ 인정하다 | ⓓ 신전 | ⓔ 번성하다 | ⓕ 유물 |

1 ⓔ 2 ⓐ 3 ⓓ 4 ⓑ

EXERCISE 06

The federal court system in the United States encompasses various types of courts that provide a means for individuals to seek legal remedies, with district courts and courts of appeals being two predominant categories within this structure. District courts, serving as general trial courts, adjudicate upon both civil and criminal cases, and the presentation of evidence and witness testimonies plays a critical role in establishing the facts and circumstances concerning the case in a district court trial. The primary responsibility of these courts is to determine the guilt or innocence of the accused and to decide on appropriate penalties and any financial compensation that may be awarded. On the other hand, courts of appeals differ in various aspects from district courts. Courts of appeals, holding what is known as appellate jurisdiction, possess the authority to review appeals, and consequently, they do not conduct trials but rather assess whether or not the district trial court adhered to proper procedures when rendering a verdict in a specific case. In the appeals process, the parties involved in the case submit their arguments in written documents, referred to as briefs, which can be quite extensive, sometimes spanning hundreds of pages.

1. Why does the author mention penalties and compensation in the passage?

   (A) To list possible means of legal redress in the United States
   (B) To explain what the main function of district courts is
   (C) To give examples of consequences faced by guilty individuals
   (D) To describe the extent of authority within the courts of appeals

2. Why does the author mention "the appeals process" in the passage?

   (A) To indicate the procedural differences between the two categories of courts
   (B) To criticize the arduous work of filing legal documents known as briefs
   (C) To point out that procedural issues may arise in the appellate jurisdiction
   (D) To emphasize how the court system is related to the justice of society

| **Vocabulary Check** | 각 단어의 알맞은 동의어를 찾아 기호를 쓰시오.

1 encompass _____　　**2** appropriate _____　　**3** compensation _____　　**4** assess _____

| ⓐ reparation | ⓑ include | ⓒ continuous | ⓓ proper | ⓔ evaluate | ⓕ praise |

Extinction pulses are sudden increases in extinction rates that take place in concentrated bursts. The Permian extinction comprised a series of such pulses, which eventually added up to the largest mass extinction event in the Earth's history. It is estimated that the Permian extinction led to the demise of around 90 percent of the Earth's species, including 95 percent of marine species. Although the general consensus within the scientific community is that the event took place over the course of 15 million years, there are some scientists who refute this, insisting that the extinctions took place over a much shorter period—a mere 200,000 years—with the majority occurring in a single 20,000-year period. Invertebrates inhabiting the warm shallows of the Earth's oceans were hit hardest by the Permian extinction, but aquatic vertebrates also experienced a devastating loss of species. Hypothetically, a rise in ocean temperatures negatively impacting nutrient cycles was the main cause of the great die-off, but other possible causes, including ozone depletion and a sudden increase in methane-producing microbes, have been proposed.

1. The author mentions "aquatic vertebrates" in the passage as an example of

(A) species that were able to survive warmer temperatures
(B) marine species that scientists were unable to classify
(C) types of fish that did not exist before the Permian extinction
(D) a category of animal that lost many species to extinction

2. The author mentions "ozone depletion" in the passage in order to

(A) refute the hypothesis that the Permian extinction lasted 15 million years
(B) introduce a possible method of avoiding extinction events in the future
(C) offer an alternative theory about the cause of the Permian extinction
(D) demonstrate how extinction pulses are linked to a rise in ocean temperatures

| **Vocabulary Check** | 각 단어의 알맞은 뜻을 찾아 기호를 쓰시오.

1 concentrated _____   **2** demise _____   **3** aquatic _____   **4** depletion _____

| ⓐ 폭발 | ⓑ 감소 | ⓒ 수생의 | ⓓ 일시적인 | ⓔ 죽음 | ⓕ 집중적인 |

1ⓕ 2ⓔ 3ⓒ 4ⓑ

EXERCISE 08

The first forms of life to inhabit the Earth are believed to have been microscopic unicellular organisms that appeared approximately four billion years ago; these were the ancestors of modern bacteria. The word bacteria derives from the Latinization of an Ancient Greek word meaning "staff," due to the fact that the first bacteria to be discovered were shaped like rods. Most modern bacteria remain unicellular and measure but a few micrometers in length. Once bacteria attain a fixed size, their growth period comes to an end. They then reproduce via a form of asexual reproduction known as binary fission, in which a single organism splits itself into two identical organisms. Under perfect conditions, such as those produced within a controlled laboratory environment, bacteria can reproduce at a fantastic rate, doubling the size of their population every 17 minutes. Outside a laboratory, however, bacteria seldom have access to a supply of nutrients sufficient enough to allow them to reproduce so rapidly for an indefinite period. The restriction in nutrients has prompted the evolution of diverse growth strategies— for instance, wild populations of bacteria tend to grow incredibly rapidly, a phenomenon that can be observed in the seasonal algal blooms that occur in certain lakes during the summer.

1. Why does the author mention "rods" in the passage?

    (A) To emphasize the size of ancient bacteria

    (B) To illustrate how bacteria were first discovered

    (C) To provide an explanation for the origins of the word "bacteria"

    (D) To describe the process by which bacteria reproduce

2. The author discusses laboratories in the passage in order to

    (A) highlight the reproduction capabilities of bacteria

    (B) provide an example of how binary fission can be harmful

    (C) suggest a potential solution to seasonal algal blooms

    (D) contrast the population size of two species of bacteria

| **Vocabulary Check** | 각 단어의 알맞은 동의어를 찾아 기호를 쓰시오.

1 prompt _____	2 attain _____	3 identical _____	4 diverse _____

ⓐ reach	ⓑ varied	ⓒ induce	ⓓ minute	ⓔ same	ⓕ defined

1ⓒ 2ⓐ 3ⓔ 4ⓑ

YBM TOEFL 80 ⁺
READING

04

Reference

Reference questions require the identification of referential relationships between words in the passage. They often involve identifying the relationship between a word or phrase and the expression or concept being referred to. Other kinds of grammatical references, such as those using *which* or *this*, are sometimes used as well.

Vocabulary Preview

accidentally	우연히		**discount**	무시하다
aid	돕다		**discriminate**	식별하다
anchor	고정시키다	*syn.* fix	**dissolve**	(관계를) 끝내다 *syn.* terminate
aperture	(작은) 구멍		**distract**	(주의를) 딴 데로 돌리다
barrier	장벽		**distress**	조난, 곤경
bind	묶다, 결속시키다		**endeavor**	노력
bleed	번지다		**endemic**	고유의, 토종의
burrow	굴을 파다		**ensure**	보장하다
camouflage	위장		**ethnicity**	인종, 민족성
ceramics	도자기류		**evaporation**	증발
circumvent	피하다	*syn.* evade	**exportation**	수출
commercial	상업적인		**extend**	길게 자라다 *syn.* stretch
compete	경쟁하다		**float**	떠다니다
consistently	지속적으로	*syn.* continuously	**frequency**	빈도
consume	먹다		**gender**	성별
continuity	연속성		**gene**	유전자
credence	믿음, 신임		**grasp**	이해하다
damp	축축한		**harsh**	혹독한 *syn.* severe
debate	논쟁, 토론		**indigenous**	원주민의
dehydration	탈수		**innovation**	혁신

intense	강렬한 *syn.* extreme	**prominently**	눈에 띄게
interbreed	이종 교배하다	**protection**	보호
interruption	방해, 중단	**realm**	영역 *syn.* domain
interspecies	이종간의	**refinement**	개선, 세련 *syn.* improvement
isolate	분리(격리)하다 *syn.* segregate	**replenish**	보충하다 *syn.* refill
maintain	유지하다 *syn.* keep	**savage**	야만인
mimic	모방하다 *syn.* imitate	**seal**	가두다, 밀봉하다
mobility	기동성	**seize**	점령하다
mucus	점액	**shape**	형성하다 *syn.* mold
multiple	다수의, 다양한	**spontaneous**	자발적인 *syn.* unplanned
notable	주목할 만한 *syn.* noteworthy	**submerged**	물속에 잠긴
numerous	수많은 *syn.* many	**tendency**	경향
objective	목적, 목표 *syn.* goal	**term**	용어, 말 *syn.* word
odds	확률, 가능성	**terrestrial**	육지에 사는
overlap	겹침	**territorial**	영토의
patronage	(예술가에 대한) 후원	**toxic**	유독성의 *syn.* poisonous
poetry	시	**tragedy**	비극
porcelain	자기	**uncharted**	지도에 표시되어 있지 않은
potential	잠재적인 *syn.* possible	**unhindered**	방해 받지 않는, 제약이 없는
pragmatic	실용적인	**vivid**	선명한

PART 1

CHAPTER 04

Reference

지시 대상 찾기 문제

Reference 유형은 지문의 음영 처리된 대명사 또는 특정 구로 된 지시어가 가리키는 대상을 찾는 문제 유형이다. 인칭대명사(she, him, it, their 등), 지시대명사(this, these, that, those 등), 부정대명사(some, one, others 등), 관계대명사(who, whose, which 등)가 주로 출제된다.

빈출문제 패턴

The word "X" in the passage refers to …

지문의 단어 "X"가 가리키는 것은?

The phrase "X" in the passage refers to …

지문의 구 "X"가 가리키는 것은?

문제풀이 전략

1. 정답은 지시어 앞쪽에서 찾기

지시어가 가리키는 대상은 항상 지시어의 앞쪽에 등장한다. 지시어가 포함된 문장과 그 앞 문장에 있을 확률이 높으므로, 문맥을 파악한 후 선택지에서 적절한 지시 대상을 선별한다.

2. 수와 의미가 일치하는 대상 선택하기

지시어와 지시 대상은 수가 일치하므로 지시어가 단수인지 복수인지가 중요한 단서가 된다. 수 일치를 바탕으로 판단하고 선택지 지문에 대입하여 의미도 통하는지 최종적으로 확인한다.

오답 포인트 ✓

1. 독해가 정확하지 않으면 지시어가 가리키는 대상을 꾸며 주는 단어를 지시 대상으로 혼동할 수 있어 주의해야 한다.
2. 지시어 주변의 명사들 중 정답과 수가 일치하는 단어로 오답을 유도하므로 반드시 대입해 보고 판단해야 한다.

YBM TOEFL READING

Around the seventeenth century, emerging European powers such as the Netherlands and England rose to prominence, resulting in declines in the economic influence of Italian cities, including Genoa, Florence, and Venice, which had once established themselves as the most significant economic hubs in Europe. These cities in northern Italy experienced an economic revival during the late thirteenth century. However, their dominance waned, and the decline was evident in the transformations observed in Venetian shipping and trade. Initially, Venice played a crucial role as an intermediary in the Adriatic Sea, where it dominated shipping services on behalf of other parties, but this intermediary function gradually diminished.

The word "themselves" in the passage refers to

(A) emerging European powers
(B) the Netherlands and England
(C) declines
(D) Italian cities

해석 17세기경 네덜란드와 영국 같은 신흥 유럽 강대국들이 두각을 나타내면서, 한때 유럽에서 가장 중요한 경제 중심지로 자리잡았던 제노바와 플로렌스, 베니스를 포함한 이탈리아 도시들의 경제적 영향력이 쇠퇴하게 되었다. 이탈리아 북부의 이 도시들은 13세기 후반에 경제 부흥을 경험했다. 그러나 그들의 지배력은 약해졌고, 베니스의 해운 및 무역에 미친 변화에서 쇠퇴가 분명히 드러났다. 처음에, 베니스는 아드리아 해에서 중개자로서 핵심적인 역할을 하며 다른 당사자들을 대신하여 해운 서비스를 지배했지만, 이 중개 역할은 서서히 감소했다.

지문에서 "themselves"가 가리키는 것은?

(A) 신흥 유럽 강대국들
(B) 네덜란드와 영국
(C) 쇠퇴
(D) 이탈리아 도시들

어휘 rise to prominence 두각을 나타내다 hub 중심지 revival 부흥 dominance 지배력 wane 약해지다
shipping 해운 intermediary 중개자; 중개의, 매개의 diminish 줄어들다

해설 이탈리아 도시들의 영향력이 쇠퇴했다고 한 다음, 지시어가 포함된 관계절에서 한때 유럽에서 가장 중요한 경제 중심지였다고 했으므로, themselves는 (D) 이탈리아 도시들임을 알 수 있다.

EXERCISE 01

While the concept of cetacean intelligence is generally accepted as scientific fact, its degree remains under debate. Dolphins, for example, seem to grasp the idea of numerical continuity but may not be capable of discriminating between numbers. One possible sign of high intelligence is interspecies cooperation; both dolphins and porpoises have been known to assist whales that have beached themselves, and there have been claims of dolphins aiding humans in distress. Dolphin tool use has also been documented as they will occasionally wrap bits of sponges around their beaks for protection while digging in the ocean floor.

The word "themselves" in the passage refers to

(A) numbers   (B) dolphins   (C) porpoises   (D) whales

EXERCISE 02

During the Hellenistic Period, an era that lasted from roughly 323 BC to 30 BC in the Greek-dominated Mediterranean region, literature thrived in multiple forms. In the realm of theater, New Comedy emerged to compete with more traditional dramatic tragedies. Poetry also flourished, with kings supporting poets with their patronage and receiving works written in their honor in return. But perhaps the most notable event of this period was the translation of Homer's *Odyssey* into Latin, an act which ensured Greek influence over Roman literature for centuries to come.

The word "their" in the passage refers to

(A) kings   (B) poets   (C) works   (D) centuries

EXERCISE 03

In allopatric speciation, a subset of a population is isolated from the rest of the species by geographic barriers that create an interruption in the gene flow, ultimately causing it to evolve into a separate species. In Australia, for instance, grey kangaroos have split into two separate species with different ranges. The western grey kangaroo is endemic to the southern portion of the country whereas the eastern grey kangaroo inhabits the eastern third. Although there is some territorial overlap, they do not interbreed in the wild.

The word "it" in the passage refers to

(A) allopatric speciation   (B) a subset of a population
(C) the rest of the species   (D) an interruption in the gene flow

---

| **Vocabulary Check** | 각 단어의 알맞은 뜻을 찾아 기호를 쓰시오.

1 grasp _____   **2** patronage _____   **3** interruption _____   **4** endemic _____

| ⓐ 방해 | ⓑ 이해하다 | ⓒ 격리된 | ⓓ 후원 | ⓔ 고유의 | ⓕ 주장하다 |

1ⓑ 2ⓓ 3ⓐ 4ⓔ

EXERCISE 04

Ceramics have long been a cornerstone of Chinese art, an unsurprising fact when considering that porcelain was a Chinese invention. It was during the Ming Dynasty that innovation in ceramics began to take off in earnest. A technical refinement in the preparation of cobalt, for example, brought an end to its tendency to bleed, introducing a heretofore impossible crispness to the edges of blue decorative images. Another significant development was the commercial exportation of porcelain on a grand scale, part of the dynasty's shift toward a market economy.

The word "its" in the passage refers to

(A) porcelain   (B) innovation   (C) the preparation   (D) cobalt

EXERCISE 05

The world's deserts are home to harsh conditions that force desert-dwelling animals to evolve specialized features and behaviors. These include high temperatures, arid soil, and vegetation that is difficult to consume. Small desert mammals survive by burrowing beneath the sand's surface during the day to circumvent the intense heat of the sun. Larger mammals, on the other hand, avoid overheating by maintaining unusually high body temperatures. As for desert birds, they take advantage of their unhindered mobility by constantly flying from one distant water source to the next.

The word "These" in the passage refers to

(A) the world's deserts   (B) harsh conditions   (C) animals   (D) behaviors

EXERCISE 06

Terrestrial snails are faced with the serious problem of dehydration, as they lose body water both through the process of evaporation and from leaving behind a trail of mucus, which is 90 percent water, as they move across surfaces. Many species can replenish lost moisture because they inhabit damp environments, but snails that live in the desert cannot do this. Instead, they seal themselves in their shells to prevent evaporation. Some accomplish this with an operculum, a hard growth on their tail that acts like a door, while others seal their shell's aperture with a thin sheet of mucus.

The word "this" in the passage refers to

(A) moving across surfaces   (B) replenishing lost moisture
(C) inhabiting damp environments   (D) living in the desert

| **Vocabulary Check** | 각 단어의 알맞은 동의어를 찾아 기호를 쓰시오.

1 refinement _____   2 harsh _____   3 circumvent _____   4 replenish _____

ⓐ severe   ⓑ refill   ⓒ improvement   ⓓ release   ⓔ evade   ⓕ dependent

1ⓒ 2ⓐ 3ⓔ 4ⓑ

The evolution of coloration within species of the animal kingdom can occur for a variety of reasons. For some, coloration provides effective camouflage that allows individuals to remain unseen by potential predators whereas others, conversely, use their coloration to attract the attention of predators by mimicking the warning colors that toxic species use to advertise the dangers they represent. Colors can also be used to dazzle attackers, such as in the case of the zebra's stripes when they move in large herds, which can distract and confuse a hungry predator. In each of these examples, coloration provides the evolutionary advantage of increasing the odds of survival. Another evolutionary advantage can be found in bright, vivid colors that aid individuals within certain species in obtaining mates, thus ensuring that their genes will be passed along to subsequent generations. Meanwhile, certain frog species have evolved the ability to lighten and darken the tone of their skin, a pragmatic ability that aids in the regulation of their body temperature.

1. The word "which" in the passage refers to

   (A) the warning colors
   (B) attackers
   (C) the zebra's stripes
   (D) large herds

2. The word "their" in the passage refers to

   (A) bright, vivid colors
   (B) individuals
   (C) certain species
   (D) mates

| **Vocabulary Check** | 각 단어의 알맞은 뜻을 찾아 기호를 쓰시오.

1 camouflage _____   2 mimic _____   3 vivid _____   4 pragmatic _____

| ⓐ 선명한 | ⓑ 모방하다 | ⓒ 실용적인 | ⓓ 단점 | ⓔ 반사하다 | ⓕ 위장 |

1 ⓕ 2 ⓑ 3 ⓐ 4 ⓒ

EXERCISE 08

The term "aquatic plant" is used to describe any species within the plant kingdom that is capable of completing its life cycle successfully submerged in water, on the water's surface, or in hydric soil, which means soil that is consistently or seasonally saturated with water, like the types present in wetlands. It is important to note that aquatic algae, which resemble aquatic plants, share numerous similarities with them, yet are not classified as such because they are not considered true plants. Aquatic plants can be categorized into smaller groups based on their growth patterns. Floating aquatic plants have their leaves and stems resting on the water's surface, with their roots trailing below but not anchored in the soil. In contrast, emergent ones are firmly rooted in the underwater soil, with their leaves and stems extending prominently above the water's surface. Another category, known as submersed aquatic plants, is also rooted in the soil, but their leaves and stems are entirely submerged, whereas suspended ones are entirely submerged without rooting in the soil.

1. The word "such" in the passage refers to

(A) wetlands
(B) aquatic algae
(C) aquatic plants
(D) numerous similarities

2. The word "their" in the passage refers to

(A) roots
(B) emergent ones
(C) leaves and stems
(D) submersed aquatic plants

| **Vocabulary Check** | 각 단어의 알맞은 동의어를 찾아 기호를 쓰시오.

1 consistently _____   **2** numerous _____   **3** anchor _____   **4** extend _____

ⓐ mostly   ⓑ continuously   ⓒ stretch   ⓓ issue   ⓔ fix   ⓕ many

It is generally accepted that during the course of fifteenth-century endeavors to discover a shorter trade route to Asia, the New World was discovered by Europeans. Christopher Columbus is famously said to have been the first European explorer to encounter land across the Atlantic Ocean, albeit accidentally, and further discoveries soon followed. With the realization of just how rich this uncharted land was in terms of gold, fertile farmland, and other resources, exploration and adventuring soon gave way to serious efforts to colonize it. Although the Americas had been settled thousands of years earlier, the European colonists gave no credence to the claims of ownership of the indigenous peoples they encountered. Discounting them as uncivilized savages, they seized their land and began to build permanent settlements on it. Spain and Portugal led the way with the earliest attempts at establishing colonies, with the Portuguese claiming what has become modern-day Brazil, while the Spanish conquered a huge swath of land stretching from South America, through Central America and Mexico, and all the way up to what is today the west coast of the United States.

1. The word "it" in the passage refers to

   (A) the Atlantic Ocean
   (B) this uncharted land
   (C) gold
   (D) exploration

2. The word "they" in the passage refers to

   (A) the European colonists
   (B) the claims of ownership
   (C) the indigenous peoples
   (D) uncivilized savages

| **Vocabulary Check** | 각 단어의 알맞은 뜻을 찾아 기호를 쓰시오.

1 endeavor _____　　　　2 credence _____　　　　3 indigenous _____　　　　4 seize _____

| ⓐ 믿음 | ⓑ 포용하는 | ⓒ 기여하다 | ⓓ 원주민의 | ⓔ 노력 | ⓕ 점령하다 |

1 ⓔ　2 ⓐ　3 ⓓ　4 ⓕ

EXERCISE 10

On the basis of group dynamics, social groups can be classified into four fundamental types: primary groups, secondary groups, collectives, and categories. Primary groups are small social groups whose members have close, personal relationships that bind them to one another, while secondary groups tend to be based on shared interests or activities and are characterized by more impersonal interactions. Comfort, support, and caring are provided within primary groups, which often can last for a lifetime and play an important role in shaping the personal identity of individuals. Secondary groups, on the other hand, are goal-oriented and temporary; group members may come and go with great frequency, with the group itself potentially dissolving once its objectives have been met. The lifespan of collectives is even briefer, as they are substantial gatherings of individuals engaging in similar activities and tend to be loosely formed as well as spontaneous. Common examples include concert audiences and people attending a conference. As for categories, they are groups that are defined by common characteristics of their members, but these types need not include any actual interactions between individuals. People's categories might include such things as their religion, gender, or ethnicity.

1. The word "them" in the passage refers to

(A) primary groups
(B) social groups
(C) members
(D) close, personal relationships

2. The phrase "these types" in the passage refers to

(A) concert audiences
(B) categories
(C) common characteristics
(D) their members

| **Vocabulary Check** | 각 단어의 알맞은 동의어를 찾아 기호를 쓰시오.

1 shape _____　　　**2** dissolve _____　　　**3** objective _____　　　**4** spontaneous _____

| ⓐ goal | ⓑ unplanned | ⓒ incite | ⓓ mold | ⓔ terminate | ⓕ morale |

1ⓓ 2ⓔ 3ⓐ 4ⓑ

Sentence Simplification

Sentence simplification questions require the identification of a sentence that has the same essential meaning as a sentence in the passage. They involve selecting a simplified version of the original sentence. The correct answer preserves the key information of the original sentence and effectively conveys its main point.

abstract	추상적인	**dominant**	우세한, 지배적인
address	(문제를) 다루다, 고심하다	**emergence**	출현 *syn.* appearance
allegory	비유, 우화	**empiricism**	경험주의
analyze	분석하다	**epoch**	시대 *syn.* era
archaeological	고고학적인	**esteemed**	존경받는 *syn.* respected
avian	조류의	**exhalation**	날숨
axis	중심축	**external**	외적인
behaviorism	행동주의	**extinct**	멸종된
bold	대담한 *syn.* daring	**femininity**	여성성
carnivore	육식 동물	**fume**	연기
cataclysmic	대재앙의 *syn.* catastrophic	**futile**	헛된 *syn.* useless
choreographer	안무가	**imitation**	모방 *syn.* copy
contraction	수축	**immerse**	~에 몰두하다 *syn.* engage
cultivate	경작하다 *syn.* grow	**inhalation**	들숨
deem	여기다 *syn.* consider	**initially**	처음에
defeat	패배	**irreversibly**	돌이킬 수 없게
define	정의하다	**lateral**	측면의, 옆으로의
delicate	섬세한 *syn.* fragile	**meteor**	운석
descend	내려가다	**migration**	이주
distinction	차이 *syn.* difference	**negate**	효력이 없게 만들다 *syn.* nullify

norm	표준 *syn.* standard	reptile	파충류
pale	흐릿한	reveal	드러내다 *syn.* disclose
physical	물리적인	rinse	씻어내다, 헹구다
poison	독살하다	scatter	흩어지다 *syn.* disperse
polish	다듬다, 광을 내다	scuff	흠을 내다
polymath	박식가, 박식한 사람	sensitive	민감한
populate	거주하다, 살다 *syn.* inhabit	spiral	나선형으로 움직이게 하다
portray	나타내다 *syn.* represent	stimulus	자극
precede	~에 앞서다 *syn.* come before	subject	(연구의) 대상
prehistoric	선사 시대의	succeed	계승하다
prey	먹이 *syn.* quarry	succumb	(병 등으로) 죽다, 쓰러지다
prolonged	장기적인	suspect	의심하다
property	속성, 특징 *syn.* characteristic	theorize	이론을 세우다 *syn.* hypothesize
propulsion	추진, 밀고 나가기	throne	왕위
psychoanalysis	정신분석	trigger	촉발하다 *syn.* cause
rage	맹위를 떨치다 *syn.* rampage	troupe	공연단
reflective	빛을 반사하는	tuber	(감자 등의) 덩이줄기
reign	통치 기간	tutor	가르치다 *syn.* teach
release	이완	unobservable	관찰 불가능한
remains	유물 *syn.* ruins	upheaval	대변동 *syn.* cataclysm

PART 1 CHAPTER 05

Sentence Simplification

CHAPTER 05

문장 재구성 문제

Sentence Simplification 유형은 지문에서 음영 처리된 문장의 핵심 내용을 다른 구조와 표현으로 재구성하여 쓴 문장을 찾는 문제이다. 중요하지 않거나 세부적인 정보는 포함하지 않는다.

빈출문제 패턴

Which of the sentences below best expresses the essential information in the highlighted sentence in the passage? Incorrect choices change the meaning in important ways or leave out essential information.

아래 문장 중 지문에서 음영 표시된 문장의 핵심 정보를 가장 잘 나타낸 것은? 오답 선택지들은 의미를 현저히 바꾸거나 핵심 정보를 생략한다.

문제풀이 전략

1. 문장을 잘라 필수 정보 파악하기

음영 처리된 문장에서 핵심 내용을 파악하는 것이 먼저이다. 접속사절, 관계절, 삽입절 등이 사용되어 길어지거나 구조가 복잡한 문장이 출제되므로, 문장을 몇 개의 의미 단위로 잘라 핵심 내용을 재빨리 찾아낸다.

2. 문장 서술 방식 파악하기

음영 처리된 문장의 서술 방식을 파악하면 선택지에서 올바르게 재구성된 문장을 찾기 쉽다. 문장을 독해하며 인과, 서사, 설명, 묘사 등 서술 방식을 파악하는 것이 필요하다.

3. 핵심 내용이 다른 말로 표현된 선택지 고르기

지문의 핵심 단어를 동의어로 바꾸어 제시하거나 핵심 문장을 다른 문장 구조로 재구성한 선택지를 고른다.

오답 포인트 ✅

1. 문장에 사용된 핵심 단어를 포함하고 있지만 교묘하게 순서 또는 원인과 결과가 바뀌어 제시되는 등의 오답을 주의해야 한다.
2. 핵심 내용이 일부 누락되고 세부적이거나 추가적인 내용이 포함된 선택지도 오답이 된다.

Plants, in their early colonization of land, confronted a variety of challenges unique to terrestrial environments. Unlike in water, there was no buoyancy to support their structures, there was no continual immersion in a nutrient-rich solution, and air caused dehydration. In response to these conditions, plants underwent evolutionary changes, developing structures that offered physical support and that preserved water as well as vessels that conveyed water and nutrients throughout the entire plant. As a result of these adaptations to dry land, certain structural characteristics emerged early in the evolution of plants, and they are now shared by almost all plants that grow on land.

Which of the sentences below best expresses the essential information in the highlighted sentence in the passage? Incorrect choices change the meaning in important ways or leave out essential information.

(A) Due to adjustments for dry conditions, evolved plants share the same niches as other plants.
(B) The emergence of structural traits resulted from plant evolution, which is exclusive to plants that found on land.
(C) By adapting to arid land, terrestrial plants could have the same structural traits as other plants.
(D) Adaptations to dry land led to the emergence of key features now widely shared by most land plants.

PART 1
CHAPTER 05

해석 식물은 육지에 정착하던 초기에, 육지 환경에서만 나타나는 다양한 어려움에 직면했다. 물속과는 달리 그들의 구조를 지지할 부력이 없었으며, 영양이 풍부한 용액에 지속적으로 담겨 있지 못했고, 공기는 수분을 빼앗아갔다. 이런 상황에 대응해, 식물은 물리적으로 지탱해 주는 구조물과 식물 전체에 물과 영양분을 실어 나르는 도관뿐 아니라 물을 보존하는 구조물을 발전시키며 진화 과정의 변화를 겪었다. 건조한 땅에 대한 이러한 적응의 결과로 식물의 진화 초기에 특정한 구조적 특징이 나타났으며, 이런 특징은 이제 육지에 사는 거의 모든 식물이 공유하고 있다.

아래 문장 중 지문에서 음영 표시된 문장의 핵심 정보를 가장 잘 나타낸 것은? 오답 선택지들은 의미를 현저히 바꾸거나 핵심 정보를 생략한다.

(A) 건조한 조건에 적응한 덕분에, 진화 식물은 다른 식물과 동일한 적합한 환경을 공유하고 있다.
(B) 식물 진화의 결과로 구조적 특성이 등장했으며, 이는 육지에서 발견되는 식물에만 해당된다.
(C) 건조한 땅에 적응함으로써 육지 식물이 다른 식물과 동일한 구조적 특성을 가질 수 있었다.
(D) 건조한 땅에 대한 적응은 이제 대부분의 육지 식물에게 널리 공유되는 주요 특성의 등장으로 이어졌다.

어휘 confront 직면하다 terrestrial 육지의 buoyancy 부력 immersion 담금, 잠금 adaptation 적응

해설 건조한 땅에 적응하는 과정의 결과로 현재 대부분의 육지 식물에게 공통되는 특성이 나타났다는 것이 핵심 정보이므로, 정답은 (D)이다.

EXERCISE 01

The daguerreotype, invented by Louis Daguerre, was the earliest widely available photographic process in the mid-19th century. It required polishing a sheet of silver-plated copper until it was as reflective as a mirror and then treating it with fumes in order to render the surface sensitive to light. Once placed in a camera, the plate was exposed for as long as deemed necessary; this depended on the intensity of the lighting. A liquid chemical treatment was then used to negate the plate's sensitivity to light, and it was rinsed, dried and sealed in a protective glass enclosure. This final step was an unavoidable necessity due to the extremely delicate nature of the plate's surface, which could be irreversibly scuffed by any contact, even the gentle wiping of a cloth.

Which of the sentences below best expresses the essential information in the highlighted sentence in the passage?

(A) The final step was sometimes skipped in order to protect the surface of the plate.
(B) The plate had to undergo the final step because its surface was easily damaged.
(C) Even the gentle wiping of a cloth could irreversibly scuff the delicate surface of the plate.
(D) It was necessary to wipe the plate with a soft cloth after the final step was finished.

EXERCISE 02

Two different schools of thought—psychoanalysis and behaviorism—are used to analyze the behavioral patterns of individuals. Behaviorists are largely focused on the external behaviors and motivations of their subjects, while psychoanalysts are more interested in what is going on in the brain. For behaviorists, attempting to understand the unobservable workings of the human mind is a futile endeavor; relying on empiricism and laboratory experimentation, they seek to prove that humans, as well as animals, are conditioned to respond to external stimuli with certain behaviors. Psychoanalysts, on the other hand, concentrate on what they believe to be the multiple layers of the human mind, and attempt to reveal how their hidden inner workings govern human behavior.

Which of the sentences below best expresses the essential information in the highlighted sentence in the passage?

(A) After observing the human mind, behaviorists seek to find how outside events influence behavior.
(B) Scientific evidence assists behaviorists in learning how humans are conditioned by stimuli.
(C) Behaviorists use experiments to study how people react to outside influences rather than trying to understand the mind.
(D) Behaviorists try to comprehend how the human brain works by performing experiments related to animal behavior.

| **Vocabulary Check** | 각 단어의 알맞은 뜻을 찾아 기호를 쓰시오.

1 sensitive _____   **2** scuff _____   **3** analyze _____   **4** futile _____

| ⓐ 분석하다 | ⓑ 보상하다 | ⓒ 헛된 | ⓓ 흠을 내다 | ⓔ 강화하다 | ⓕ 민감한 |

1ⓕ 2ⓓ 3ⓐ 4ⓒ

Ichthyosaurs, Mesozoic marine reptiles, went extinct approximately 90 million years ago, likely due to climatic upheavals. They were carnivores that ranged greatly in size and inhabited both coastal areas and the open ocean, where they fed on a variety of prey, including cephalopods. Based on their eyes, which were unusually large and surrounded by bony rings, much like the eyes of modern-day colossal squid, it has been theorized that ichthyosaurs hunted at great depths where little sunlight could reach. It is likely that they possessed the ability to descend to depths of up to 1,600 meters, by using lateral movements of their bodies as a form of propulsion so effective that it may have made them the fastest marine reptiles of their time.

Which of the sentences below best expresses the essential information in the highlighted sentence in the passage?

(A) The eyes of colossal squid may have allowed them to hunt even in places with little sunlight.
(B) The dark depths of the ocean were home to large, bony creatures such as ichthyosaurs.
(C) Living in dim places, the large eyes of ichthyosaurs likely aided them escape from predators.
(D) It is thought that ichthyosaurs hunted in deep water, since they had large eyes surrounded by bone.

In 336 BC, King Phillip II of Macedon was killed and subsequently succeeded by his son, Alexander III, who would go on to create one of the largest empires in history and become known as Alexander the Great. Before ascending to the throne at the tender age of 20, Alexander had been tutored by the esteemed philosopher Aristotle. He was renowned as a highly skilled military commander and spent the bulk of his reign immersed in a violent military campaign that raged across Western Asia, famously never suffering a single defeat on the battlefield. Alexander died at the age of 32 in the palace of the emperor of Babylon and under unclear circumstances; historians suspect that he either succumbed to malaria or was poisoned.

Which of the sentences below best expresses the essential information in the highlighted sentence in the passage?

(A) Alexander III was also known as Alexander the Great, and his father was King Phillip II of Macedon.
(B) After assassinating his father, Alexander the Great became the leader of a great empire.
(C) King Phillip II, Alexander the Great's father, died without fulfilling his aim to build the world's largest empire.
(D) Alexander the Great, who founded a vast empire, became king of Macedon after his father was killed in 336 BC.

| **Vocabulary Check** | 각 단어의 알맞은 동의어를 찾아 기호를 쓰시오.

1 prey _____   **2** theorize _____   **3** esteemed _____   **4** immerse _____

ⓐ respected   ⓑ quarry   ⓒ stock   ⓓ hypothesize   ⓔ engage   ⓕ credible

1ⓑ 2ⓓ 3ⓐ 4ⓔ

Aristotle, the ancient Greek philosopher and polymath, lived in the fourth century BC and followed in the footsteps of his teacher, Plato, by attempting to address the idea of universals, which can be roughly defined as the properties that similar objects have in common. Plato considered these universals to be abstract concepts that exist in a reality separate from the objects themselves, which are simply pale imitations of an ideal form that does not have a physical existence. This idea was most famously illustrated in his allegory of the cave, in which the material objects in the real world are portrayed as mere silhouettes cast on a cave wall by their ideal forms. Aristotle, on the other hand, believed that universals do exist in the world in which we live and can be found as qualities within the objects that represent them. In other words, while Plato believed that the ideal apple exists only in the abstract world of forms, Aristotle argued that the perfect form of an apple exists within all apples.

1. Which of the sentences below best expresses the essential information in the first highlighted sentence in the passage?

   (A) In the fourth century BC, Aristotle learned about universal truths from his teacher, Plato.
   (B) Aristotle and Plato had many ideas in common, including their views on objective properties.
   (C) Aristotle shared his teacher's interest in understanding the shared traits of like objects.
   (D) While Aristotle was a philosopher and polymath, Plato strived to understand the universe.

2. Which of the sentences below best expresses the essential information in the second highlighted sentence in the passage?

   (A) Ideal forms are like a cave in which all the objects of the world have been gathered.
   (B) In the allegory of the cave, ideas and objects are linked together by their ideal forms.
   (C) Artwork depicting ideal forms drawn on cave walls acts as an allegory for this concept.
   (D) The allegory of the cave explains the idea of how actual objects are created by their real forms.

| **Vocabulary Check** | 각 단어의 알맞은 뜻을 찾아 기호를 쓰시오.

1 define _____   2 property _____   3 imitation _____   4 allegory _____

| ⓐ 모방 | ⓑ 비유 | ⓒ 속성 | ⓓ 개척하다 | ⓔ 증거 | ⓕ 정의하다 |

1 ⓕ 2 ⓒ 3 ⓐ 4 ⓑ

The Paleogene, whose meaning in Greek is "ancient-born," is a geological period which spanned from roughly about 65 million to 23 million years ago. This period is divided into three distinct epochs by geologists, the first of which is called the Paleocene. The most significant distinction of the Paleocene from the periods that preceded it is the absence of dinosaurs, which became extinct due to a cataclysmic event at the close of the Cretaceous Era. The sudden absence of the once-dominant life form on the planet led to the emergence of new habitats and ecosystems for the Earth's remaining mammalian, avian, reptilian, and aquatic species to thrive. The extinction of dinosaurs is believed to have been triggered by a substantial meteor impact in present-day Mexico. During the early Paleocene Epoch, the Earth's climate was significantly affected by the extensive dust clouds generated by the impact, leading to a prolonged period of unnaturally cold and dark conditions. Nevertheless, by the conclusion of the epoch, conditions had returned to the warm and humid norms of the period.

1. Which of the sentences below best expresses the essential information in the first highlighted sentence in the passage?

    (A) The extinction of the dinosaurs had positive and negative effects on other species.
    (B) The sudden extinction of the previously dominant life form created opportunities for the Earth's surviving species.
    (C) Land and marine animals were threatened by new types of predators.
    (D) The dominant life form suddenly disappeared at the end of the Cretaceous Era.

2. Which of the sentences below best expresses the essential information in the second highlighted sentence in the passage?

    (A) The dust clouds derived from the collision deteriorated climatic conditions in the early Paleocene Epoch.
    (B) In the early Paleocene Epoch, dust clouds cooled and darkened the planet, which caused the collision between the Earth and a meteor.
    (C) During the early stages of the Paleocene Epoch, clouds of dust and the Earth's cold climate were combined.
    (D) The darkness and the cold of the period directly caused the extinction of the dinosaurs.

| **Vocabulary Check** | 각 단어의 알맞은 동의어를 찾아 기호를 쓰시오.

1 precede _____   **2** cataclysmic _____   **3** emergence _____   **4** trigger _____

 ⓐ put off ⓑ terrific ⓒ come before ⓓ cause ⓔ catastrophic ⓕ appearance

American dancer and choreographer Martha Graham was active for more than 70 years in both performance and education, and her unique style, known as the Graham Technique, changed the very nature of modern dance in the United States. Regarded as the first systematic modern dance technique, it relies on the opposing forces of bodily contraction and release, which are based on the inhalation and exhalation of the natural breathing cycle. Treating the spine as an axis and spiraling the torso around it is the other foundational principle of the Graham Technique. The resulting performances include, along with leaping turns, a large amount of floorwork, which is preceded by the dancers falling dramatically to the stage, with their bodies suspended momentarily in space, and ends with a rising "recovery," another example of dualism in the dancers' movements. The Graham Technique was originally designed for an all-female dance troupe although male dancers were later admitted, and it has been said that its bold style helped redefine the cultural concept of femininity.

1. Which of the sentences below best expresses the essential information in the first highlighted sentence in the passage?

(A) The first formal modern dance technique used tightening and loosening of the body instead of deep breaths.

(B) It was the first modern dance technique with a system and uses contrasting movements similar to breathing in and out.

(C) Although contracting and releasing are opposing motions, modern dance techniques use them in a natural manner.

(D) The system that created modern dance techniques is the opposite of the natural cycle people use in order to breathe.

2. Which of the sentences below best expresses the essential information in the second highlighted sentence in the passage?

(A) Despite being used only by female dancers at first, the Graham Technique was later adopted by innovative dancers.

(B) Graham admitted that male dancers helped her develop a technique that could be used by both male and female dancers.

(C) The cultural concept of gender roles is what caused the Graham Technique to have such a strong impact on dance.

(D) Graham's technique was created with female dancers in mind and influenced the way society views femininity.

| **Vocabulary Check** | 각 단어의 알맞은 뜻을 찾아 기호를 쓰시오.

1 choreographer _____   **2** inhalation _____   **3** bold _____   **4** femininity _____

| ⓐ 대담한 | ⓑ 안무가 | ⓒ 반복적인 | ⓓ 들숨 | ⓔ 여성성 | ⓕ 동의하는 |

1ⓑ 2ⓓ 3ⓐ 4ⓔ

Archaeological remains suggest that migration to the Pacific Islands may have begun more than 40,000 years ago, with every habitable island settled by the second millennium AD. Due to the fact that this region comprises approximately 10,000 islands scattered across the world's largest ocean, tracing the exact origins and the spread of Oceanian peoples is difficult, if not impossible. In the 19th century, Pacific Islanders were classified into three groups—Melanesian, Micronesian, and, Polynesian—and based on this, it was theorized that Southeast Asians populated the region in three separate waves of migration. It is believed that Melanesia was settled by Southeast Asians more than 33,000 years ago, at about the same time as Australia, with a second wave coming from the prehistoric Lapita culture about 4,000 years ago. The Lapita initially established themselves on the Bismarck Archipelago, a group of islands off the northeastern coast of New Guinea, before moving on to the Polynesian islands of Fiji, Tonga, and Samoa. By the time European contact occurred in the 16th century, Oceanian peoples had developed stone, bone, and seashell tools, were cultivating fruits and tubers, and had become skilled sailors.

1. Which of the sentences below best expresses the essential information in the first highlighted sentence in the passage?

(A) It is impossible to know how Oceanian peoples came to the Pacific Islands.
(B) Oceanian peoples most likely found it hard to spread to other islands from the one they originated from.
(C) It is not easy to determine the migration paths of Oceanian peoples due to the region's geography.
(D) It is not known exactly why Oceanian peoples scattered and failed to thrive on some Pacific Islands.

2. Which of the sentences below best expresses the essential information in the second highlighted sentence in the passage?

(A) Melanesia was likely inhabited first by Southeast Asians and much later by the Lapita culture.
(B) Melanesia was settled by Southeast Asians, who migrated to Australia about 4,000 years later.
(C) It was the second wave of migration from Melanesia and Australia that established Lapita.
(D) The people of Southeast Asia were the first to settle in Melanesia, and then followers such as Australians, who are descended from the Lapita culture, came.

| **Vocabulary Check** | 각 단어의 알맞은 동의어를 찾아 기호를 쓰시오.

1 remains _____   2 scatter _____   3 populate _____   4 cultivate _____

| ⓐ means | ⓑ grow | ⓒ disperse | ⓓ inhabit | ⓔ ruins | ⓕ goods |

1ⓔ 2ⓒ 3ⓓ 4ⓑ

YBM TOEFL 80 +
READING

Inference

Inference questions require the identification of information that is implicit in the passage, as skilled authors often leave some details to be inferred by the reader, aiming for economy of expression. They involve determining the correct answer by examining the language and information in the passage.

Vocabulary Preview

abiotic	비생물적인	**conductor**	지휘자
abundant	풍부한 *syn.* plentiful	**conflict**	(국가 간의) 충돌 *syn.* clash
adapt	적응하다 *syn.* adjust	**consolidate**	굳히다, 강화하다 *syn.* solidify
aggression	공격(성)	**contribute**	기여하다
alter	바꾸다 *syn.* modify	**decipher**	해독하다 *syn.* decode
animosity	적대감 *syn.* hostility	**determine**	알아내다, 결정하다
approach	접근 방식	**directive**	지시, 지침
arrangement	배열, 구성	**dispersal**	확산, 분산
artifact	유물	**disprove**	틀렸음을 입증하다 *syn.* refute
attract	끌어들이다 *syn.* lure	**downpour**	폭우
bare	(신체 일부를) 드러내다	**dramatic**	극적인 *syn.* striking
baton	지휘봉	**efficiency**	효율성
bear	지니다	**elevation**	고도
bonding	유대	**embrace**	(생각, 제안을) 받아들이다
brass	금관 악기	**environs**	환경, 주변
breakthrough	획기적 발견, 돌파구	**equivalent**	동등한 *syn.* equal
capacity	능력 *syn.* ability	**expanded**	확장된
cede	(영토를) 양도하다 *syn.* surrender	**expedition**	원정, 탐험
commemorate	기념하다	**expend**	(시간·노력 등을) 쓰다
compound	화합물	**forage**	먹이를 찾아 다니다

identify	확인하다		provoke	유발하다	*syn.* excite
immensely	엄청나게	*syn.* extremely	rapid	급격한	*syn.* quick
induce	유발하다	*syn.* cause	rational	이성적인	
inhabited	(사람이) 거주하는		relevant	관련 있는, 유의미한	
initial	처음의	*syn.* first	response	반응	*syn.* reaction
inscription	(새겨진) 글, 명문		scale	규모	
instinctual	본능에 따른		seemingly	겉보기에는	
internal	내부의	*syn.* inner	site	터, 장소	*syn.* location
interpret	해석하다		situated	위치하고 있는	
intriguing	흥미로운		skeptical	회의적인	*syn.* doubtful
last	지속되다	*syn.* continue	speculate	추측하다	*syn.* theorize
logic	논리		standardized	표준화된	
massive	심각한, 거대한	*syn.* huge	strings	현악기	
nomadic	유목의	*syn.* wandering	tend	가꾸다, 재배하다	
occupy	점유하다		territory	영토	
opaque	불투명한		unprecedented	전례 없는	
percussion	타악기		vary	다르다, 달라지다	*syn.* change
perpetual	영구적인, 끊임없는		vigorous	격렬한, 활발한	
pollinator	수분 매개체		woodwinds	목관 악기	
priest	사제		wrest	탈취하다	

PART 1

CHAPTER 06

Inference

CHAPTER 06

추론 문제
Inference 유형은 지문의 내용을 바탕으로 추론할 수 있는 내용을 선택지에서 고르는 문제 유형이다. 지문에 제시된 정보를 근거로 드러나지 않은 정보를 도출해내는 것이 추론이며, 그 범위는 한 문장 또는 여러 문장에 해당할 수 있다.

빈출문제 패턴

Which of the following can be inferred from paragraph # about X?
다음 중 # 단락에서 X에 대해 추론할 수 있는 것은?

The author of the passage implies that X ...
글쓴이가 X에 대해 암시하는 것은?

Paragraph # suggests which of the following about X?
다음 중 # 단락이 X에 대해 암시하는 것은?

It can be inferred from paragraph # that ...
단락에서 추론할 수 있는 것은?

문제풀이 전략

1. 지문에서 핵심 단어 찾기
문제에 제시된 핵심 단어의 위치를 지문에서 재빨리 찾아내어 정답의 근거가 되는 관련 정보들을 빠짐없이 파악해야 한다.

2. 오로지 지문에 근거하여 추론하기
정답은 결국 지문에 근거하고 있으므로 지문 내용을 정확하게 독해하는 것이 가장 중요하다. 의견 개입이나 상식적 접근 없이 오직 지문에 제시된 정보를 바탕으로 암시적 정보를 도출해 낸다.

오답 포인트 ✓

1. 지문 내용이 아닌 상식이나 지식을 근거로 판단하려다 그럴듯해 보이는 오답 선택지를 고르거나 지나치게 비약이 심한 오답 선택지를 고르게 된다.
2. Factual Information 유형과 혼동하여 지문에 언급된 것과 유사한 선택지를 찾으려고 하면 안 된다.

The southern end of Mesopotamian plain, located between the Tigris and Euphrates rivers, was where the earliest city-states in the ancient Near East appeared and the Sumer civilization emerged in the fifth millennium BC. At first glance, it may have not seemed like an ideal place to flourish because it lacked natural resources, rain was scarce, and the water present rapidly flowed across the plain during the yearly snowmelt flood. Thus, the organization of irrigation systems, particularly in directing and preserving water, was crucial. As irrigation systems were established, the amount of crops harvested increased dramatically. Such conditions enabled an elite class to emerge, likely as an organizing group, securing its position through the control of surplus crops.

Which of the following can be inferred from the passage?

(A) Civilizations flourished before the fifth millennium BC.
(B) Many civilizations found the ancient Near East the best place to live.
(C) Irrigation systems played a key role in the emergence of Sumer civilization.
(D) A few people in the highest class ruled the city-states and took all surplus crops.

해석 티그리스 강과 유프라테스 강 사이에 위치한 메소포타미아 평야의 남쪽 끝은 고대 근동의 초창기 도시 국가가 등장한 곳이자 기원전 5천년에 수메르 문명이 등장한 곳이다. 이곳은 천연 자원이 부족했고, 강우량이 매우 적었으며, 그나마 있는 물은 해마다 눈 녹은 물로 홍수가 날 때 빠르게 평원을 흘러갔기 때문에, 처음에는 문명이 번영하기에 이상적인 장소로 보이지는 않았을 것이다. 따라서 관개 시설의 조직은 특히 물을 조절하고 보존하는 데 있어 중요했다. 관개 시설이 구축되자, 작물 수확량이 극적으로 증가했다. 이러한 조건들은 엘리트층이 조직 집단으로 등장해 잉여 작물을 통제함으로써 그 지위를 견고히 할 수 있게 했다.

다음 중 지문에서 추론할 수 있는 것은?

(A) 기원전 5천년 이전에 문명이 번영했다.
(B) 많은 문명들이 고대 근동을 살기에 가장 적합한 곳으로 여겼다.
(C) 관개 시설은 수메르 문명의 등장에 중요한 역할을 했다.
(D) 소수의 최고계층 사람들이 도시 국가를 다스렸고, 모든 잉여 작물을 가져갔다.

어휘 city-state 도시 국가   civilization 문명   emerge 등장하다   flourish 번영하다   snowmelt 눈 녹은 물   irrigation 관개 preserve 보존하다   crucial 중요한   surplus 잉여의

해설 수메르 문명이 등장한 곳은 처음에는 문명이 번성할 만한 곳으로 보이지 않았지만 관개 시설 구축 후 작물 수확량이 증가하고 엘리트층이 등장했다고 했으므로, 관개 시설이 수메르 문명 등장에 중요한 역할을 했다고 유추할 수 있다. 그러므로 정답은 (C)이다.

While pollination that is accomplished by living creatures such as birds, bees, and other insects is considered biotic, there are also various forms of abiotic pollination, in which other forces, including wind and rain, serve as pollinators. The primary advantage of this is that it allows the plant to concentrate energy, which would have otherwise been expended on attracting biotic pollinators, on producing more pollen. Wind is the most common abiotic pollinator; some flowers have even evolved specific shapes that maximize the efficiency of wind-based pollen dispersal. Rain pollination, on the other hand, is utilized by only a small number of plant species. But in times of heavy downpours, plants that have adapted to this method of pollination have a significant advantage over those that rely on insect pollination.

Which of the following can be inferred from the passage about plants that rely on abiotic pollination?

(A) They produce more pollen than plants that rely on biotic pollination.
(B) They are found mainly in areas where there is little wind and a lot of rain.
(C) They have evolved to protect themselves from insects.
(D) They disperse their pollen without any assistance from external forces.

The Rosetta Stone, discovered in 1799, is an ancient Egyptian slab bearing an identical inscription in multiple languages and scripts. In 1822, a French historian, Jean Francois Champollion, used this unusual artifact as the key to deciphering Egyptian hieroglyphs. This was made possible by the fact that the stone's message, which seems to have been composed by priests commemorating a Macedonian king's ascension to the throne, was also written in Greek, a language that could be read and understood in modern times, and demotic Egyptian. The historian discovered that the direction faced by the bird and animal characters, which made up the bulk of the hieroglyphs, helped determine their meaning. This breakthrough laid the groundwork for the translation of large numbers of other ancient Egyptian hieroglyphic texts.

The author of the passage implies that Egyptian hieroglyphs

(A) were the basis of later languages such as Egyptian and Greek
(B) could be used only by ancient Egyptian priests and kings
(C) were often used to record how kings abdicated their thrones
(D) could not be understood by modern people before 1822

| Vocabulary Check | 각 단어의 알맞은 뜻을 찾아 기호를 쓰시오.

1 abiotic _____   2 dispersal _____   3 decipher _____   4 breakthrough _____

| ⓐ 해독하다 | ⓑ 생기 있는 | ⓒ 획기적 발견 | ⓓ 확산 | ⓔ 전파하다 | ⓕ 비생물적인 |

1 ⓕ 2 ⓓ 3 ⓐ 4 ⓒ

EXERCISE 03

Although some scientists remain skeptical as to the potential existence of humanlike emotions in animals, the subject has been intensely studied in a variety of species by using several different approaches. The behaviorist approach, for example, seeks to disprove the existence of animal emotions by ascribing animal behavior that resembles expressions of human emotion to nothing more than simple responses to various stimuli. Meanwhile, the comparative approach similarly embraces a simpler explanation. It follows a directive stating that animal activity should not be interpreted as being caused by higher psychological processes if it can be explained by more basic processes. Even Charles Darwin weighed in on the subject, noting that animals appear to share some of the universal emotive expressions displayed by humans, such as the baring of teeth in anger.

Which of the following can be inferred from the passage about Charles Darwin?

(A) He carefully compared different approaches to animal emotions.
(B) He doubted that animals responded to stimuli in fundamental ways.
(C) He was more open to the idea of animal emotions than behaviorists.
(D) He argued that animals can feel all the same emotions as humans.

EXERCISE 04

During the period from the 11th century to the 13th century, a series of military expeditions were organized by the Christian Church, known collectively as the Crusades. They attempted to conquer the Holy Land, comprising the city of Jerusalem and its environs, in order to free it from Muslim rule. Over the course of eight numbered major campaigns and numerous minor ones, control over the area was repeatedly wrested away in victories over Muslim forces and then ceded back in subsequent defeats. The final major crusade ended in the Europeans failing to seize any new territory. Despite the bloody nature of these conflicts and the religious animosity they stirred up, the Crusades ultimately resulted in an unprecedented cultural exchange of ideas between West and East. They brought back to Europe important theories and knowledge that it had not previously possessed.

It can be inferred from the passage that the Muslim world

(A) embraced the idea of sharing the Holy Land with Europe
(B) was in some ways more advanced than Europe
(C) had several different methods of repelling European attacks
(D) instigated the Crusades for the main purpose of spreading European culture

| **Vocabulary Check** | 각 단어의 알맞은 동의어를 찾아 기호를 쓰시오.

1 disprove _____   2 response _____   3 cede _____   4 animosity _____

| ⓐ conceal | ⓑ blame | ⓒ refute | ⓓ hostility | ⓔ reaction | ⓕ surrender |

In the 1960s, Paul D. MacLean, an American physician, proposed a theory that the human brain is essentially composed of three distinct brains working harmoniously as one. Known as the triune brain model, it encompasses the reptilian complex, the limbic system, a system of nerves and networks in the brain, and the neocortex. The neocortex, identified as the most recent evolutionary addition, occupies the frontal part of the brain and functions as the hub for logic and rational thinking. Just preceding the neocortex on the evolutionary timeline is the limbic system, situated in the central part of the brain and primarily responsible for emotional responses and social bonding. The reptilian complex, the third and oldest element in the triune brain, is often known as the reptilian brain and situated at the brain's base. It traces its origins back over 500 million years to a common ancestor of all vertebrates, encompassing mammals, reptiles, fish, and birds. This complex governs instinctual behaviors such as aggression and territoriality, ensuring the fulfillment of basic needs crucial for the species' ongoing survival. It directs us toward activities that bring pleasure and away from those that induce pain. Psychologists and behavioral scientists find the reptilian brain intriguing as it harks back to a distant era marked by scarce food and abundant predators. In contrast to the neocortex and limbic system, which remain relevant in today's civilized society, the reptilian brain can sometimes provoke seemingly irrational behavior in a modern context.

1. Which of the following can be inferred from the passage about the limbic system?

   (A) It is the most recently discovered part of the brain.
   (B) It helps the three parts of the human brain function as if they were one.
   (C) It was positioned later on the evolutionary timeline than the neocortex.
   (D) It would negatively affect social skills if it were damaged.

2. The passage suggests which of the following about the reptilian complex?

   (A) It focuses more on survival than on social cohesion.
   (B) It brings happiness and pleasure to animals.
   (C) It helps animals endure hunger and withstand exposure to environmental dangers.
   (D) It exists in the brains of all animals.

| Vocabulary Check | 각 단어의 알맞은 뜻을 찾아 기호를 쓰시오.

1 rational _____   **2** instinctual _____   **3** intriguing _____   **4** provoke _____

| ⓐ 흥미로운 | ⓑ 이성적인 | ⓒ 관찰하다 | ⓓ 본능에 따른 | ⓔ 유발하다 | ⓕ 통과하다 |

1 ⓑ 2 ⓓ 3 ⓐ 4 ⓔ

EXERCISE 06

During the Neolithic Revolution, which began around 10,000 BC and is often referred to as the Agricultural Revolution, small groups of nomadic hunter-gatherers began to form agricultural settlements. This transition can be viewed as an initial step toward the establishment of modern civilization. It was in the Middle East's Fertile Crescent that farming first began, and then other inhabited regions of the world started farming as well. While there is no consensus on what exactly triggered this world-altering change, some scientists point to a warming trend that followed the end of the last ice age as a significant contributing factor. In the Fertile Crescent, this change in climate caused wild wheat and barley to begin growing, which, in turn, encouraged nomadic peoples to settle down near these new sources of food. Other scientists, however, think there was an internal change that played a larger role in this dramatic shift in human behavior; evolutionary developments in the brain that led to rapid advances in intellectual capacity. Based on the archaeological analysis of an early site in what is now southern Türkiye, it would appear that these prehistoric farmers placed great value on art and the spiritual. Either way, humans gradually began to move away from foraging wild plants in favor of tending, at first, small gardens and later, large fields of crops.

1. Which of the following can be inferred from the passage about wheat and barley?

   (A) They thrived in southern Türkiye during the last ice age.
   (B) They require warm temperatures to grow in the wild.
   (C) They were the main target of many hunter-gatherers.
   (D) They are no longer grown in their region of origin.

2. The author of the passage implies that the earliest farmers

   (A) had to deal with extreme cold and snow
   (B) later returned to hunting and gathering
   (C) refused to take part in religious rituals
   (D) grew only modest amounts of food

| **Vocabulary Check** | 각 단어의 알맞은 동의어를 찾아 기호를 쓰시오.

1 nomadic _____   2 rapid _____   3 capacity _____   4 site _____

| ⓐ ability | ⓑ location | ⓒ quick | ⓓ cautious | ⓔ subtle | ⓕ wandering |

1 ⓕ 2 ⓒ 3 ⓐ 4 ⓑ

The atmosphere of Venus, which is often considered Earth's "sister" planet because of similarities in size and mass, is far denser and hotter than our own. Venus has an average surface temperature of about 465°C and an atmospheric pressure that is roughly equivalent to what can be found approximately 900 meters beneath the surface of Earth's oceans. Its atmosphere is composed primarily of carbon dioxide with small amounts of nitrogen. No other chemical compounds are present in anything other than trace amounts. A layer of opaque clouds made up of sulfuric acid hangs suspended above the planet, making the surface all but impossible to observe. In terms of movement, the atmosphere can be characterized as extremely active, with the upper layers engaged in a perpetual state of vigorous circulation due to winds that blow at speeds of around 360 km/h. But this number drops significantly as the elevation decreases, barely reaching about 10 km/h at the surface itself. Scientists speculate that several billion years ago, the atmosphere of Venus was much more like that of Earth and that liquid water may have existed on the planet's surface. The event that caused this to change is speculated to have been a massive greenhouse effect, created by the evaporation of this surface water, which led to an increase in the levels of various greenhouse gases.

1. The author of the passage implies that astronomers

   (A) no longer believe that Venus and Earth are similar
   (B) are closely monitoring Venus's atmospheric pressure
   (C) detected previously unknown greenhouse gases on Venus
   (D) find it difficult to study the surface of Venus from Earth

2. The passage suggests which of the following about Venus?

   (A) It will likely lose its cloud layer as its climate changes.
   (B) It may have been home to life several billion years ago.
   (C) It might have had a greater mass in the past than it does now.
   (D) It could soon experience intense wind storms on its surface.

| **Vocabulary Check** | 각 단어의 알맞은 뜻을 찾아 기호를 쓰시오.

1 equivalent _____   2 opaque _____   3 perpetual _____   4 elevation _____

| ⓐ 파장 | ⓑ 고도 | ⓒ 불투명한 | ⓓ 영구적인 | ⓔ 동등한 | ⓕ 확장 |

1 ⓔ 2 ⓒ 3 ⓓ 4 ⓑ

A typical modern orchestra is made up of four different sections of instruments—strings, woodwinds, brass, and percussion—and is led by a conductor, who directs the performance with hand gestures or a small baton. However, during the Baroque period, which lasted from about 1600 to 1750, orchestras did not have standardized sizes or compositions, both of which could vary greatly. Bach, for example, led an orchestra consisting of no more than 18 musicians, while Arcangelo Corelli employed 150 musicians in his orchestra, although only for special events. Standardization began to occur during the Classical period, which immediately followed the Baroque period, and by the first half of the 19th century it had consolidated into a set arrangement that included doubled woodwind and brass sections. This was primarily due to Beethoven requiring the change, as he utilized pairs of flutes, oboes, clarinets, bassoons, horns, and trumpets in his compositions. Later, the grand scale of Wagner's works, which were composed with an unprecedented level of complexity, led to increases in orchestral size and instrumental variety that would remain the standard for nearly a century. By the beginning of the 20th century, orchestras had grown immensely in size, with expanded string and brass sections, as well as a greater range of percussion instruments. As a result, composers now had the freedom to create even larger and more ambitious works.

1. Which of the following can be inferred from the passage about Baroque period compositions?

    (A) They required two of all the major instruments.
    (B) They were performed only on special occasions.
    (C) They were less complex than later compositions.
    (D) They focused on the woodwind and brass sections.

2. It can be inferred from the passage that Beethoven

    (A) had sufficient influence to alter the makeup of orchestras
    (B) inspired Wagner to abandon the use of orchestras altogether
    (C) was the first composer to employ an eighteen-musician orchestra
    (D) refused to include percussion instruments in his compositions

| **Vocabulary Check** | 각 단어의 알맞은 동의어를 찾아 기호를 쓰시오.

1 last _____   **2** vary _____   **3** consolidate _____   **4** immensely _____

ⓐ solidify   ⓑ continue   ⓒ randomly   ⓓ change   ⓔ extremely   ⓕ gradually

1ⓑ 2ⓓ 3ⓐ 4ⓔ

Insert Text

Insert text questions require the insertion of the provided sentence in the most appropriate location within the passage. They involve inserting the provided sentence into the passage in a way that ensures a smooth flow and maintains grammatical or logical coherence with the surrounding sentences.

Vocabulary Preview

achievement	업적	*syn.* accomplishment	**dispute**	반박하다	*syn.* challenge
acute	극심한	*syn.* severe	**drive**	추진시키다, 몰아가다	
alight	(날아가) 앉다		**elect**	선출하다	
annual	매년의, 연례의	*syn.* yearly	**encounter**	맞닥뜨리다	
arise	생기다	*syn.* emerge	**establishment**	설립	*syn.* foundation
arrange	배열하다		**exclude**	제외하다	*syn.* eliminate
article	글, 기사		**exploration**	탐사, 탐험	
categorization	분류, 범주화		**feudal**	봉건 제도의	
circulation	(신문·잡지의) 판매 부수		**focus**	초점	*syn.* emphasis
coexist	공존하다		**foolproof**	잘못될 수가 없는	*syn.* flawless
column	세로단		**fossilized**	화석화된	
combination	조합	*syn.* mixture	**fundamental**	근본적인	*syn.* basic
complement	보완하다	*syn.* supplement	**genetically**	유전적으로	
comprehension	이해		**glyph**	상형 문자	
conquest	정복		**hinder**	방해하다	*syn.* hamper
cue	단서	*syn.* hint	**independence**	독립	
currently	현재		**install**	설치하다	
date	연대를 추정하다		**institution**	제도	
detect	알아내다, 발견하다	*syn.* discover	**launch**	발사하다	
deviation	편차	*syn.* divergence	**libelous**	비방하는	

mechanism	구조, 메커니즘	**pseudonym**	필명
mold	만들다 *syn.* shape	**publish**	(신문을) 발행하다; (글을) 게재하다
native	토착의, 고유의 *syn.* indigenous	**relatively**	비교적 *syn.* comparatively
navigate	길을 찾다	**resemblance**	유사점 *syn.* likeness
officially	공식적으로	**reside**	살다 *syn.* inhabit
olfactory	후각의	**restless**	가만히 있지 못하는
oligarchic	과두 정치의	**restore**	(제도를) 부활시키다 *syn.* reinstate
order	순서; (사회적) 질서	**revival**	회복, 부활 *syn.* resurrection
organism	유기체 *syn.* creature	**shortage**	부족 *syn.* scarcity
peasant	소작농	**socioeconomic**	사회 경제적인
peril	위험 *syn.* jeopardy	**stability**	안정 *syn.* steadiness
permission	허가 *syn.* approval	**statesman**	정치가
persist	(끈질기게) 계속하다	**survive**	살아남다
physiological	생리학적인	**syllable**	음절
precisely	바로 *syn.* exactly	**transmit**	전송하다 *syn.* send
predictable	예측할 수 있는 *syn.* anticipated	**trap**	가두다, 모아두다 *syn.* confine
preference	선호 *syn.* inclination	**unfairness**	불공평
primarily	주로	**vast**	거대한 *syn.* huge
proper	적절한 *syn.* appropriate	**viewpoint**	견해 *syn.* perspective
provision	제공 *syn.* supply	**visual**	시각의 *syn.* optical

Insert Text

CHAPTER 07

문장 삽입 문제

Insert Text 문제 유형은 제시된 문장을 지문에서 가장 적절한 위치에 삽입하는 문제이다. 제시된 문장의 의미를 정확하게 파악하여, 지문 흐름상 가장 자연스럽고 앞뒤 문장들과의 문법적 또는 논리적 관계가 알맞게 연결되는 적절한 위치에 삽입하여 글을 완성한다.

빈출문제 패턴

Look at the four squares [■] that indicate where the following sentence could be added to the passage.

[A sentence in bold]

Where would the sentence best fit? Select a square [■] to add the sentence to the passage.

제시된 문장이 지문에 삽입될 수 있는 곳을 가리키는 네 개의 네모[■]를 보아라.

[삽입 문장]

이 문장이 들어갈 가장 적절한 위치는? 해당 네모[■]를 선택하여 이 문장을 지문에 삽입하여라.

문제풀이 전략

1. 제시 문장에서 단서 찾기

제시 문장에 지시어(it, this, that, such 등)가 있다면 이것이 가리키는 말을 앞 문장에서 반드시 찾아야 한다. 이를 단서로 문장 간 내용 연결을 확인할 수 있다. 연결어(however, also, therefore, for example, in fact 등) 역시 논리적 연결을 파악하는 중요한 단서가 되며, 중복되는 핵심 단어가 있는지 확인하는 것도 필수적이다.

2. 글의 흐름 파악하기

문장 간 연결뿐 아니라 단락 간 흐름을 파악하는 것도 유용하다. 대체로 설명, 논증, 예시 등의 흐름으로 이어지는 글이 많다는 점을 염두에 두고, 제시 문장이 어디에 해당할 수 있는지 논리적으로 추측하고 적용해 보아 연결이 자연스러운지 확인한다.

오답 포인트 ✅

상식이나 개인적인 판단으로 내용을 끼워 맞추려고 하면 오답을 고르기가 쉽다. 때로는 직접적인 단서 없이 문맥 속에서 정답에 대한 근거를 찾을 수 있다.

The vast quantity of Roman pottery is as noteworthy as its exceptional quality. ■(A) However, it is a challenging task to estimate the overall quantity of pottery being manufactured and utilized in a particular region because of the nature of archaeological evidence. ■(B) Archaeological findings usually represent only a part of everything that used to exist, making it challenging to determine the exact figures. ■(C) Roman settlements, particularly urban sites, are notable for the vast amount of pottery unearthed by archaeologists. ■(D) In fact, the washing and sorting of potsherds (pieces of broken pottery) constitute a significant portion of the initial excavation work due to the abundance of these artifacts. While precise quantitative estimates may remain elusive, the abundance of Roman pottery is evident in the archaeological record.

Look at the four squares [■] that indicate where the following sentence could be added to the passage.

Despite this difficulty, there is no doubt about the abundant presence of Roman pottery, especially in the Mediterranean area.

Where would the sentence best fit? Select a square [■] to add the sentence to the passage.

PART 1

CHAPTER 07

해석 로마 도자기의 양적 풍부함은 탁월한 품질만큼이나 괄목할 만하다. ■(A) 그러나 고고학적 증거의 특성 때문에 특정 지역에서 제조되고 사용되는 도자기의 전체적인 양을 추정하는 것은 어렵다. ■(B) 고고학적 유물들은 일반적으로 한 때 존재했던 모든 것 중 일부만을 나타내어, 정확한 수치를 단정하기 어렵게 만든다. ■(C) 로마의 정착지, 특히 도시 지역들은 고고학자들에 의해 발굴된 막대한 양의 도자기로 유명하다. ■(D) 사실, 도자기 파편(깨진 도자기 조각들)의 세척과 분류는 이러한 많은 양의 유물들로 인해 발굴 초기 작업의 상당한 부분을 차지한다. 정확한 양의 추정치는 여전히 파악하기 힘들 수 있지만, 로마 도자기의 막대한 양은 고고학적 기록에서 명백하게 드러난다.

제시된 문장이 지문에 삽입될 수 있는 곳을 가리키는 네 개의 네모[■]를 보아라.
이러한 어려움에도 특히 지중해 지역에서 로마 도자기의 풍부한 양에 대해서는 의심할 여지가 없다.
이 문장이 들어갈 가장 적절한 위치는? 해당 네모[■]를 선택하여 이 문장을 지문에 삽입하여라.

어휘 pottery 도자기 noteworthy 괄목할 만한 figure 수치 settlement 정착지 constitute 구성하다 excavation 발굴 estimate 추정하다; 추정치(추산) elusive 이해(파악)하기 어려운

해설 제시된 문장의 this difficulty를 단서로 앞 문장에서 어려움이 언급된다는 것을 알 수 있다. 그러므로 정확한 수치를 단정하기 어렵다는 내용의 문장 뒤와 막대한 도자기 양에 대해 설명하는 문장 앞에 위치하는 것이 자연스럽다. 따라서 정답은 (C)이다.

English geologist William Smith was studying rock strata in the early 19th century when he noticed that each stratum of rock contained mostly similar fossilized species. ■[A] Detecting a pattern in them, Smith came up with the principle of faunal succession, which states that fossilized organisms succeed one another in a predictable order. ■[B] For example, a bone of a Neanderthal will never be found in the same stratum as a bone of a dinosaur. ■[C] The reason is that they did not coexist, with dinosaurs dying out millions of years before Neanderthals first appeared. ■[D] By applying this principle, scientists can use the fossils discovered within a stratum to identify and date it.

Select a square (■) where the following sentence could be added to the passage.

There were, however, delicate distinctions, both within and between strata, that could be observed in the species.

In approximately 600 BC, the Greek city-state of Athens created an early form of democracy upon which the subsequent democracies of numerous other Greek city-states were based. Despite this, none was as stable and successful as that of Athens. ■[A] It was a direct democracy, meaning that no legislative body was elected to represent the people. ■[B] It is believed that Solon may have been the statesman who first installed a system of democracy in Athens, although this is disputed by some. ■[C] Either way, it was clearly Pericles who was the greatest, as well as the longest reigning, democratic ruler of Athens. After his death, the institution fell into peril, twice being briefly replaced by an oligarchic revolution before being restored under the rule of Eucleides. ■[D]

Select a square (■) where the following sentence could be added to the passage.

Instead, individual citizens voted on political issues themselves.

| **Vocabulary Check** | 각 단어의 알맞은 뜻을 찾아 기호를 쓰시오.

1 organism _____	2 coexist _____	3 dispute _____	4 peril _____

ⓐ 유기체	ⓑ 반박하다	ⓒ 정리하다	ⓓ 위험	ⓔ 논리	ⓕ 공존하다

1ⓐ 2ⓕ 3ⓑ 4ⓓ

EXERCISE 03

The categorization of individuals within a society into groups on the basis of socioeconomic factors, including wealth, education, and race, is known as social stratification. ■[(A)] The stratification model in modern Western cultures divides people into three social classes: upper class, middle class, and lower class. ■[(B)] This type of division between social strata can be observed clearly in feudal-type societies, where the upper noble class stands in stark contrast to the lower peasant class. ■[(C)] Generally, the more complex a society is, the more stratified it becomes. Some sociologists believe social stratification to be a positive force that arises in developed societies. ■[(D)] Others, however, have a more negative viewpoint, arguing that a lack of social mobility in stratified societies is a sign of its fundamental unfairness.

Select a square (■) where the following sentence could be added to the passage.

They view its essential purpose as the provision of continued order and stability.

EXERCISE 04

Although climate change is a natural phenomenon to some degree, it can also be caused by human activities that increase greenhouse gas levels, trapping heat within Earth's lower atmosphere. In order to determine what exactly is driving climate change today, scientists must first exclude natural variability within the climate system. Next, they must consider external yet natural drivers, such as major volcanic eruptions and deviations in Earth's solar orbit. ■[(A)] Each potential cause has its own unique fingerprint that identifies it as a driver of climate change. ■[(B)] Solar forcing, for instance, which usually causes an increase in the amount of solar energy reaching Earth, has been ruled out. ■[(C)] The reason is that its fingerprint indicates warming across the entire atmosphere, yet only the lower atmosphere is currently heating up. ■[(D)]

Select a square (■) where the following sentence could be added to the passage.

It is precisely this fact that suggests the increases in greenhouse gases are the main factor behind the current climate change.

| **Vocabulary Check** | 각 단어의 알맞은 동의어를 찾아 기호를 쓰시오.

1 viewpoint _____   **2** fundamental _____   **3** exclude _____   **4** deviation _____

ⓐ illustrate   ⓑ perspective   ⓒ divergence   ⓓ basic   ⓔ eliminate   ⓕ conclusion

1ⓑ 2ⓓ 3ⓔ 4ⓒ

PART 1 CHAPTER 07

The importance of journalism in the United States of America was made clear shortly after the country achieved independence. ■[1(A)] When the First Amendment was added to its Constitution in 1791, it guaranteed both freedom of the press and freedom of speech. ■[1(B)] Benjamin Harris published the first edition of a planned weekly newspaper, known as *Publick Occurrences*, *Both Forreign and Domestick* in 1690. ■[1(C)] It was also, unfortunately, the final edition, as Harris had failed to obtain proper permission from the British government, which at that time still ruled over the American colonies. ■[1(D)] In the 18th century, as the colonies thrived and grew, newspapers began to appear in all of the major cities. ■[2(A)] Among them was *The New-England Courant*, published by James Franklin, the older brother of Benjamin Franklin, who would go on to become one of the Founding Fathers of the United States. ■[2(B)] Benjamin Franklin's writing was published in his brother's paper, although he used a pseudonym, a common practice at the time, due to the libelous nature of many articles. ■[2(C)] During the American War of Independence, British blockades caused acute shortages of ink and paper that hindered regular publication. ■[2(D)] By the end of the war, around three dozen newspapers whose combined circulation was around 40,000 issues a week were in existence in the newly independent country.

1. Select a square (■) where the following sentence could be added to the passage.

Yet, the history of journalism in America began long before that.

2. Select a square (■) where the following sentence could be added to the passage.

In spite of this, the publishers of newspapers in the American colonies persisted.

| **Vocabulary Check** | 각 단어의 알맞은 뜻을 찾아 기호를 쓰시오.

1 libelous _____	2 acute _____	3 shortage _____	4 hinder _____

| ⓐ 부족 | ⓑ 방해하다 | ⓒ 차등 | ⓓ 학구적인 | ⓔ 극심한 | ⓕ 비방하는 |

1 ⓕ 2 ⓔ 3 ⓐ 4 ⓑ

It was on October 4, 1957, that the era of human space exploration officially began. ■[1(A)] On that day, the Soviet Union launched the first artificial satellite into space. ■[1(B)] Known as *Sputnik 1*, it orbited the Earth, transmitting radio signals for about three weeks until its batteries ran out. ■[1(C)] One month later, the Soviets launched *Sputnik 2*, which carried the first living creature, a dog named Laika, into space. ■[1(D)] Since that time, space exploration has continued to evolve and change. Perhaps the biggest achievement to date has been the landing of humans on the moon in 1969. ■[2(A)] Eight years earlier, Soviet astronaut Yuri Gagarin had become the first human in space, completing a single orbit around the Earth in a flight that lasted about an hour and a half. ■[2(B)] But on July 20, 1969, *Apollo 11*'s lunar module, the Eagle, made a successful landing on the moon, and Neil Armstrong became the first human being to walk on its surface. ■[2(C)] So far, a total of 12 astronauts have walked on the moon, but the last moonwalk took place more than 50 years ago in 1972. ■[2(D)] This is partly due to the fact that the focus of space exploration has shifted to the establishment of space stations, relatively large structures that can orbit the Earth for years and act as laboratories for the astronauts that reside within them.

1. Select a square (■) where the following sentence could be added to the passage.

    She was never expected to survive the mission, but scientists considered animal flights an essential step before human space missions.

2. Select a square (■) where the following sentence could be added to the passage.

    He and one of his fellow astronauts collected lunar rocks and dust, before they all returned to Earth safely.

| **Vocabulary Check** | 각 단어의 알맞은 동의어를 찾아 기호를 쓰시오.

1 achievement _____   2 focus _____   3 relatively _____   4 reside _____

ⓐ enthusiastically   ⓑ comparatively   ⓒ emphasis   ⓓ inhabit   ⓔ accomplishment   ⓕ domain

The ancient Maya civilization's native writing system is the only Mesoamerican writing system to have been deciphered to a substantial degree. ■[1(A)] It dates back to at least the third century BC and was in use up until the 17th century, when the Spanish conquest put an end to the once vast Maya Empire. ■[1(B)] Ancient Maya writing was referred to as "hieroglyphics" by the early European explorers who first encountered it, due to a minor resemblance to ancient Egyptian writing. ■[1(C)] It was painted onto ceramics, the walls of buildings, and paper made of bark, and it was also carved into wood or stone and molded in stucco. ■[1(D)] Unfortunately, little painted Maya writing has survived, limiting the amount of text available to archaeologists and linguists. ■[2(A)] Despite this, it is estimated that about 60 percent of extant ancient Maya writing can be understood to some degree, which allows for a basic comprehension of its structure. ■[2(B)] It was generally written in blocks and arranged into columns with a width of two blocks. ■[2(C)] Each block represents either a noun phrase or a verb phrase, and the blocks are read from left to right and from top to bottom. ■[2(D)] Surviving modern Maya languages are now written in the Latin alphabet. However, there are some who advocate for a revival of the ancient glyph system.

1. Select a square (■) where the following sentence could be added to the passage.

   In reality, however, it is more similar to modern Japanese writing with characters representing entire words complemented by glyphs that represent individual syllables.

2. Select a square (■) where the following sentence could be added to the passage.

   This process would continue until there were no columns remaining.

| **Vocabulary Check** | 각 단어의 알맞은 뜻을 찾아 기호를 쓰시오.

1 conquest _____   2 resemblance _____   3 arrange _____   4 revival _____

| ⓐ 유사점 | ⓑ 부활 | ⓒ 정복 | ⓓ 왕실 | ⓔ 배열하다 | ⓕ 청소하다 |

1 ⓒ 2 ⓐ 3 ⓔ 4 ⓑ

Bird migration is a genetically controlled phenomenon whose timing appears to be triggered primarily by changes in the length of days. ■[1(A)] These changes have an effect on the hormone levels of birds, which have been observed to become restless and more active in the days leading up to the beginning of a migration. ■[1(B)] However, there also appear to be internal mechanisms that prompt birds to begin their annual migration. ■[1(C)] Caged birds kept in conditions with no changes in day length or temperature display behavior similar to that of pre-migratory wild birds, including a preference to fly in the general direction of their species' migration. ■[1(D)] Once engaged in migration, birds navigate by utilizing their senses. Some use the sun as a compass, others detect and follow Earth's magnetic fields, and still others rely on visual landmarks and olfactory cues. In many cases, migratory navigation is accomplished by using a combination of these methods. ■[2(A)] In a phenomenon known as "spring overshoot," birds returning to their breeding grounds fly past their destinations and end up farther north than they intended. ■[2(B)] In other cases, unusually heavy winds blow birds off course. ■[2(C)] This can cause them to alight in regions thousands of kilometers outside their normal range. ■[2(D)]

1. Select a square (■) where the following sentence could be added to the passage.

   Physiological changes have been noted as well, including an increase in bodily fat deposits.

2. Select a square (■) where the following sentence could be added to the passage.

   No matter how complex these navigation techniques may be, they are far from foolproof.

| **Vocabulary Check** | 각 단어의 알맞은 동의어를 찾아 기호를 쓰시오.

1 annual _____   2 preference _____   3 visual _____   4 combination _____

| ⓐ association | ⓑ yearly | ⓒ mixture | ⓓ optical | ⓔ supportive | ⓕ inclination |

1 ⓑ 2 ⓕ 3 ⓓ 4 ⓒ

PART 1

CHAPTER 07

YBM TOEFL 80 ⁺
READING

Prose Summary

Prose summary questions require the selection of summary statements that best summarize the most important concepts discussed in the passage. A prompt is provided in the form of an introductory sentence representing the main idea of the passage, and the statements that align with the prompt should be selected to complete the summary table.

Vocabulary Preview

account	이야기, 말		**debris**	잔해 *syn.* rubble
accumulation	축적		**decline**	하락, 위축
additional	추가적인, 그 밖의 *syn.* supplementary		**defense**	방어
afford	제공하다		**demand**	필요로 하다 *syn.* need
amass	모으다, 쌓다 *syn.* collect		**destruction**	파괴
arrival	도착한 사람		**differentiate**	구분 짓다 *syn.* distinguish
artistic	예술의		**disaster**	참사 *syn.* catastrophe
assume	(권력, 책임을) 맡다 *syn.* undertake		**disruption**	혼란
broadly	폭넓게		**distant**	먼 *syn.* remote
chronological	연대순의 *syn.* sequential		**elaborate**	정교한
cite	(예로) 들다, 언급하다		**emit**	(빛·소리 등을) 내다
clash	충돌하다		**enigmatic**	불가사의한 *syn.* mysterious
composition	구성		**envision**	상상하다, 구상하다
concede	인정하다 *syn.* admit		**existence**	존재, 실재, 현존
concentric	동심원의		**extremely**	극도로 *syn.* exceedingly
concurrently	동시에, 함께		**feature**	특징 *syn.* characteristic
confirm	사실임을 확인해 주다 *syn.* verify		**fortify**	요새화하다
construct	건설하다		**generally**	일반적으로 *syn.* normally
continent	대륙		**gravel**	자갈
dangle	(들고) 달랑거리다		**heavily**	심하게

instance	경우, 사례		realistic	현실적인	
investigate	조사하다	*syn.* probe	replace	대신하다	
knowledge	지식		resident	주민	*syn.* inhabitant
literary	문학의		separation	분리	
manner	방식	*syn.* method	significant	상당한	*syn.* consequential
maritime	바다의, 해양의	*syn.* naval	source	원천, 근원	*syn.* origin
martial	호전적인	*syn.* warlike	span	(얼마의 기간에) 걸치다	
modified	변형된		spot	발견하다	
molecule	분자		strikingly	굉장히	
outskirt	변두리, 교외		subcategory	하위 범주	
perceive	감지하다, 인지하다	*syn.* recognize	suitable	적합한	*syn.* apt
potentially	잠재적으로		surround	둘러싸다	
predation	포식		tactic	전략	*syn.* strategy
present	제시하다, 나타내다	*syn.* display	theoretical	이론적인	*syn.* conceptual
prime	주된		trail	자국, 흔적	
produce	생산하다	*syn.* manufacture	typically	보통, 일반적으로	
profit	이익, 수익		universally	일반적으로	
prominent	눈에 잘 띄는	*syn.* noticeable	unpalatable	맛이 없는	
propose	의견을 제시하다		urban	도시의	
protrude	튀어나오다		variation	변이, 변화	

PART 1

CHAPTER 08

Prose Summary

CHAPTER
08

지문 요약 문제

Prose Summary 유형은 지문에서 다루는 가장 중요한 개념들을 요약한 선택지를 고르는 문제 유형이다. 요약표에 전체 지문의 주제문에 해당하는 도입 문장이 제시되는데, 선택지 6개 중 이 문장에 어울리는 요약문 3개를 선택하여 요약표를 완성하면 된다. 정답을 선택하지 못하거나 하나만 선택하면 점수를 얻지 못하고, 두 개의 정답을 선택하면 1점을, 세 개의 정답을 선택하면 2점을 얻을 수 있다.

빈출문제 패턴

Directions: An introductory sentence for a brief summary of the passage is provided below. Complete the summary by selecting the THREE answer choices that express the most important ideas in the passage. Some sentences do not belong in the summary because they express ideas that are not presented in the passage or are minor ideas in the passage. **This question is worth 2 points.**

Drag your answer choices to the spaces where they belong. To review the passage, select **View Passage.**

지시문: 지문의 간략한 요약을 위한 도입 문장이 아래에 제시되어 있다. 지문에서 가장 중요한 개념들을 나타내는 선택지 3개를 선택하여 요약을 완성하여라. 어떤 문장들은 지문에 제시되지 않거나 주요 개념이 아니므로 요약에 포함되지 않는다. **이 문제는 2점에 해당한다.**

선택지를 속하는 자리에 끌어다 놓아라. 지문을 다시 보려면 **View Passage**를 선택하여라.

문제풀이 전략

1. 요약표의 도입 문장 먼저 읽기

요약표에 제시되는 도입 문장은 전체 지문의 주제문에 해당하므로 요약을 완성하는 길잡이가 된다. 도입 문장을 먼저 읽고 요약 내용을 파악하는 것이 중요하다.

2. 단락별 주제문 찾기

전체 지문의 가장 중요한 정보는 결국 각 단락의 가장 중요한 정보에 해당한다. 다른 문제를 풀 때 미리 각 단락의 주제문 또는 중심 문장을 파악해 두면 요약 문제를 푸는 데 도움이 된다.

3. 지문과 단락의 구조 염두에 두기

학술적 성격의 지문은 중심 내용이 단락 앞부분에 제시되고 그에 대한 논증이나 예시가 뒤따르는 식의 구조가 많으므로 이를 염두에 두고 지문을 읽으면 중요한 개념을 빨리 찾을 수 있다.

오답 포인트 ✅

지문에 제시된 내용이라고 해서 무조건 답으로 선택해서는 안 된다. 너무 세부적인 정보는 내용이 맞더라도 중심 정보가 아니므로 오답이 됨을 명심해야 한다.

Renowned psychologist, philosopher, and scientist Jean Piaget was a highly influential figure in the field of developmental psychology. Piaget demonstrated his curiosity and independence from a young age, publishing a scientific paper on his observations of an albino sparrow at the age of 10. His early studies focused on mollusks, resulting in the publication of 20 papers during his late adolescence. Transitioning to psychoanalysis after obtaining his doctorate in natural science, Piaget worked at a boys' school in France, and his subsequent research on how the minds of children work and develop paved the way for the formulation of the cognitive development theory.

Assimilation, a crucial aspect of adaptation, involves children incorporating experiences into pre-existing cognitive structures. These structures, akin to reflexes present at birth, are exemplified when infants automatically use the sucking reflex for feeding, adapting it to bottles if necessary. Piaget delineated two periods for assimilation: sensorimotor and preoperational. The sensorimotor stage during infancy comprises six sub-stages: developing cognitive skills through experiences, displaying reflexes, forming habits, coordinating between vision and object interaction, understanding object permanence, and displaying insight and creativity based on experiments with external objects. These milestones signal readiness for the preoperational stage in toddlerhood, marked by the use of symbols and language, indicating intellectual growth with memory and imagination.

There are two stages to Piaget's theory of accommodation. The first is the concrete operational stage, which typically spans from approximately 7 to 11 years of age. During this stage, children develop logical thinking and an understanding of concrete events. They exhibit enhanced problem-solving abilities based on direct experiences and a comprehension of the conservation concept, which involves grasping the idea that certain properties of objects, such as quantity, volume, or numbers remain constant even when their appearance changes. Additionally, the notion of reversibility becomes apparent. Children recognize that actions can be reversed and that objects can be restored to their initial condition. Their ability to understand cause-and-effect relationships in real-world situations improves in this stage. The other is the formal operational stage, which commences from around 11 years of age and continues into adulthood. Individuals in this stage experience the development of abstract and hypothetical thinking. They can engage with concepts and ideas that are not necessarily grounded in concrete, tangible experiences. During this stage, individuals are also capable of contemplating potential outcomes and possibilities, as well as using deductive reasoning skills to solve problems.

PART 1

CHAPTER 08

Directions: An introductory sentence for a brief summary of the passage is provided below. Complete the summary by selecting the THREE answer choices that express the most important ideas in the passage. Some sentences do not belong in the summary because they express ideas that are not presented in the passage or are minor ideas in the passage. **This question is worth 2 points.**

Drag your answer choices to the spaces where they belong. To review the passage, select **View Passage**.

Piaget developed a theory of cognitive development.

Answer Choices

A   Piaget's interest in the nature of thought originated from studies and publications about albino sparrows.

B   Assimilation, the process of integrating new experiences into pre-existing frameworks, occurs in the sensorimotor and preoperational stages.

C   From the age of 11, children sometimes fail to link abstract concepts to concrete experiences.

D   In the sensorimotor stage, individuals develop the ability to engage with ideas that may not always be based on concrete experiences.

E   In the concrete operational stage, children learn to think logically and develop the concepts of conservation and reversibility.

F   Piaget's formal operational stage involves learning to think in an abstract way, use deductive reasoning, and consider possibilities.

해석 유명 심리학자이자 철학자, 그리고 과학자인 장 피아제는 발달 심리학 분야에서 대단히 영향력이 큰 인물이었다. 피아제는 어릴 때부터 호기심과 독립성을 보여, 10살에는 그의 알비노 참새 관찰 결과를 기반으로 과학 논문을 발표하기도 했다. 그의 초기 연구는 연체 동물에 초점을 맞췄으며, 청소년기 후반에 20가지 논문의 출간이라는 결과에 이르렀다. 자연 과학 분야에서 박사 학위를 취득한 후 정신 분석 분야로 넘어가면서, 피아제는 프랑스의 한 남학교에서 근무했으며, 아이들의 정신이 어떻게 작용하고 발달하는가에 관한 이후의 연구는 인지 발달 이론의 형성을 위한 길을 열어주었다.

적응의 한 가지 중요한 측면인 동화는 아이들이 이미 존재하는 인지 구조에 경험을 통합하는 과정을 수반한다. 이 구조는 태어날 때 존재하는 반사 작용과 유사한 것으로서, 유아가 우유를 먹으려 본능적으로 빨아들이는 반사 작용을 이용하는데, 필요한 경우 그것을 우유병에 적용할 때가 전형적인 예이다. 피아제는 동화를 두 기간으로 설명했는데, 감각운동기와 전조작기가 그것이다. 유아기의 감각운동기는 여섯 가지 하위 단계로 구성되며, 경험을 통한 인지 능력 발달, 반사 작용 발휘, 습관 형성, 시각과 대상 상호 작용 사이의 조정, 대상 영속성 이해, 그리고 외부 대상에 대한 실험을 바탕으로 하는 통찰력 및 창의력 발휘이다. 이 중요 단계들은 기호 및 언어의 사용이 특징인 유아기의 전조작기에 대한 준비를 암시하며, 기억력 및 상상력을 동반한 지적 성장을 나타낸다.

피아제의 조절 이론에는 두 가지 단계가 있다. 그 첫 번째는 구체적 조작기로서, 일반적으로 약 7세부터 11세에 걸쳐 나타난다. 이 단계에서 아이들은 논리적 사고와 구체적 사건에 대한 이해를 발달시킨다. 직접적인 경험을 바탕으로 한 향상된 문제 해결 능력과 보존 개념에 대한 이해를 보이는데, 보존 개념에 대한 이해란 외형이 바뀌더라도 양이나 부피, 또는 수치 같은 물체의 특정 속성들은 그대로 유지된다는 개념을 파악하는 것을 말한다. 게다가, 가역성의 개념도 분명해진다. 아이들은 행동을 거꾸로 할 수 있다는 점과 물체가 처음의 상태로 회복될 수 있다는 점을 깨닫는다. 실제 상황에서의 인과 관계를 이해하는 능력이 이 단계에서 향상된다. 나머지 하나는 형식적 조작기로서 약 11세부터 시작되어 성년기까지 지속된다. 이 단계에 있는 사람은 추상적 사고 및 가설적 사고의 발달을 경험한다. 반드시 구체적이고 실체적인 경험을 바탕으로 하지 않는 개념과 생각을 다룰 수 있다. 이 단계에서는 문제를 해결하기 위해 연역적 추리 능력을 사용할 수 있을 뿐만 아니라 잠재적인 결과와 가능성을 고려할 수도 있다.

지시문: 지문의 간략한 요약을 위한 도입 문장이 아래에 제시되어 있다. 지문에서 가장 중요한 개념들을 나타내는 선택지 3개를 선택하여 요약을 완성하여라. 어떤 문장들은 지문에 제시되지 않거나 주요 개념이 아니므로 요약에 포함되지 않는다. **이 문제는 2점에 해당한다.**

피아제는 인지 발달 이론을 발달시켰다.

(A) 사고의 특성에 대한 피아제의 관심은 알비노 참새에 관한 연구와 그 출판으로부터 비롯되었다.
(B) 새로운 경험을 이미 존재하는 체계에 통합하는 과정인 동화는 감각운동기와 전조작기에서 일어난다.
(C) 11세부터 아이들은 때때로 추상적 개념을 구체적 경험과 연결시키지 못한다.
(D) 감각운동기에서는 반드시 구체적 경험을 바탕으로 하지 않을 수도 있는 개념을 다루는 능력을 발달시킨다.
(E) 구체적 조작기에서는 아이들이 논리적으로 사고하는 법을 배우고 보존과 가역성의 개념을 발달시킨다.
(F) 피아제의 형식적 조작기는 추상적으로 사고하고, 연역적 추리를 활용하며, 가능성을 고려하는 법을 배우는 것과 관련 있다.

어휘 **1.** influential 영향력 있는 developmental psychology 발달 심리학 observation 관찰 mollusk 연체 동물
adolescence 청소년기 psychoanalysis 정신 분석 pave the way for ~을 위한 길을 터 주다
cognitive development 인지 발달

2. assimilation 동화 adaptation 적응, 적용 incorporate 통합하다 akin to ~와 유사한 reflex 반사 작용
adapt 적응하다, 적용하다 delineate 기술하다 sensorimotor stage 감각운동기 coordinate 조정하다
object permanence 대상 영속성 insight 이해, 통찰력 milestone 중요 단계 preoperational stage 전조작기

3. exhibit 보이다, 나타내다 comprehension 이해력 conservation 보존 grasp 이해하다 reversibility 가역성
reverse 되돌리다 commence 시작되다 abstract 추상적인 hypothetical 가설적인 tangible 실체적인
contemplate 고려하다 potential 잠재적인 deductive reasoning 연역적 추리

해설 지문은 피아제의 인지 발달 이론에 대해 설명하는 글이다. 동화가 일어나는 감각운동기와 전조작기, 구체적 조작기, 형식적 조작기의 특징에 대해 핵심 요지를 설명한 (B), (E), (F)가 정답이다. (A), (C), (D)는 지문 내용과 다르다.

EXERCISE 01

Although broadly defined as bodies of land surrounded on all sides by water, islands can be further broken down into several subcategories based on how they form. These include continental and barrier islands, which, despite sharing some physical similarities, are strikingly different in their manner of formation.

Continental islands, which tend to be quite large, were once attached to a continent and continue to sit upon the continental shelf. Some, such as Greenland and Madagascar, broke away when movements of the Earth's crust caused the phenomenon of continental drift to occur. On the other hand, others were formed when the Earth's rising temperatures caused glaciers to melt, leading to a significant rise in sea levels. The British Isles, for example, were once part of mainland Europe but were separated when low-lying areas were subjected to ocean flooding.

Barrier islands, in contrast, are long, narrow islands that lie parallel to a coastline, and sometimes, like continental islands, rest on the continental shelf. Their name comes from the fact that they form a barrier between the ocean and the mainland, creating a protected lagoon or sound. It is the build-up of sediment, such as sand, silt, or gravel, caused by ocean currents that are behind the formation of many barrier islands, but there are also barrier islands that were formed by melting glaciers moving slowly across the landscape and leaving behind glacial moraines, trails of piled-up debris comprising mostly rock, soil, and gravel.

Complete the summary by selecting the TWO answer choices that express the most important ideas in the passage.

Beyond their broader definition, islands can be broken down into smaller groups by the manner of their formation.

(A) Both barrier islands and continental islands have the fundamental feature of being located on a continental shelf.
(B) Continental islands share the characteristic of once having been part of a continent before some sort of separation occurred.
(C) Long, thin barrier islands are created either by the accumulation of sediment or by a glacier leaving behind a moraine.
(D) While continental islands are likely to slowly drift from place to place, barrier islands are blocked by the mainland.

| **Vocabulary Check** | 각 단어의 알맞은 뜻을 찾아 기호를 쓰시오.

1 broadly _____   2 manner _____   3 significant _____   4 debris _____

| ⓐ 방식 | ⓑ 폭넓게 | ⓒ 붙이다 | ⓓ 상당한 | ⓔ 부드럽게 | ⓕ 잔해 |

1 ⓑ 2 ⓐ 3 ⓓ 4 ⓕ

One of the earliest theoretical models used to explain urban growth was the Burgess model, named for its creator, sociologist Ernest Burgess. Proposed in the 1920s, it depicts urban land use as developing from a central business district (CBD) that sits at the city center and expands outward in concentric rings each with a different composition and purpose. The transition zone sits closest to the CBD and is a mix of residential and commercial structures, while the next zone outward, the inner suburbs, is where the homes of working class families are found. Beyond the inner suburbs lie the outer suburbs, the home of the city's middle class, and finally there is the commuter zone, where wealthy businesspeople working in the CBD reside. These zones are differentiated by the amount of money people are willing to pay to live in them, as well as the profits that businesses located within them are able to obtain.

The Burgess model has been cited as the prime influence behind the development of the multiple nuclei model in the 1940s. While this model concedes that cities may develop outward from a CBD, it proposes that additional smaller CBDs can form on the city's outskirts. This creates a more complex—and arguably more realistic—model than the one Burgess proposed, with high-rent areas being afforded a potentially shorter commute. Created at a time when the automobile was becoming the nation's preferred form of transportation, this model is based on the increased ease of mobility demanded by urban inhabitants.

Complete the summary by selecting the TWO answer choices that express the most important ideas in the passage.

Models of urban growth, such as the one created by Ernest Burgess, divide cities into different zones with different purposes.

(A) In the Burgess model, both the homes of city residents and structures used for business are found in the transition zone.
(B) The multiple nuclei model presents a more complicated version of the Burgess model containing more than one CBD.
(C) Like the Burgess model, the multiple nuclei model envisions urban areas where commuter demand for private vehicles would be high.
(D) The shape into which the Burgess model divides urban areas is a series of concentric rings with a CBD at their hub.

| **Vocabulary Check** | 각 단어의 알맞은 동의어를 찾아 기호를 쓰시오.

1 theoretical _____   2 concede _____   3 additional _____   4 demand _____

| ⓐ supplementary | ⓑ need | ⓒ conceptual | ⓓ ongoing | ⓔ admit | ⓕ decline |

1 ⓒ 2 ⓔ 3 ⓐ 4 ⓑ

The Aegean civilization, a term which originates from the Aegean Sea, typically refers to the Bronze Age societies that emerged in its vicinity. This civilization, spanning approximately 1,800 years, is categorized into three chronological periods, each characterized by a specific culture: the Cycladic culture of the Early Bronze Age, the Minoan culture of the Middle Bronze Age, and the Mycenaean culture of the Late Bronze Age.

Cycladic culture is thought to have begun in the third millennium BC, and flourished concurrently with early Egyptian and Mesopotamian civilizations. Believed to have migrated from Asia Minor, its people brought knowledge of crafting bronze weapons and tools. Around 2200 BC, a disruption occurred as new arrivals clashed with the established culture. These newcomers, giving rise to the Minoan culture, introduced horses, constructed elaborate palaces on Crete, and established a maritime network for trade with distant civilizations like Sicily and Egypt. While not universally agreed upon, some archaeologists and historians suggest that this might be considered the first advanced civilization on European soil.

Around 1450 BC, the splendid palaces of Crete suffered destruction, possibly caused by a volcanic event, and a new martial culture emerged with the Mycenaeans. The Mycenaean cities were heavily fortified, and the geometric style of art became more dominant than before, functioning as a bridge between Bronze Age and ancient Greek art. The Mycenaeans assumed control of Minoan trade routes, amassing wealth and power. They are believed to be the civilization involved in the legendary Trojan War, likely occurring around 1200 BC. However, their empire crumbled for reasons that are still debated among scholars, potentially because of a natural disaster or an invasion by the Dorians, a Greek tribe having migrated from northern mountains. Regardless, the collapse marked the demise of the Aegean civilization.

Until the 19th century, the modern world was unaware of the existence of the Aegean civilization. Ancient Greek writers termed this era the "age of heroes," yet their accounts, such as Homer's *Iliad* depicting the war between Greece and Troy, were nearly indistinguishable from myths. Besides literary hints, certain archaeological findings indicated the presence of a Bronze Age civilization in Greece.

| **Vocabulary Check** | 각 단어의 알맞은 뜻을 찾아 기호를 쓰시오.

1 chronological _____   **2** clash _____   **3** elaborate _____   **4** martial _____

| ⓐ 호전적인 | ⓑ 정교한 | ⓒ 충돌하다 | ⓓ 기념하다 | ⓔ 성실한 | ⓕ 연대기의 |

ⓐ4 ⓑ3 ⓒ2 ⓕ1

Directions: An introductory sentence for a brief summary of the passage is provided below. Complete the summary by selecting the THREE answer choices that express the most important ideas in the passage. Some sentences do not belong in the summary because they express ideas that are not presented in the passage or are minor ideas in the passage. **This question is worth 2 points.**

The Aegean culture, an ancient Greek civilization, can be categorized into three separate periods.

$$\boxed{}$$

$$\boxed{}$$

$$\boxed{}$$

(A) The term "Aegean civilization" is derived from the Aegean Sea, which is near the regions where it developed.

(B) The Aegean civilization was initially perceived as myth until archaeological findings confirmed the existence of a Bronze Age civilization in Greece.

(C) People from Asia Minor spread geometric art, often displayed on pottery and other artifacts, to the Mycenaeans.

(D) The earliest stage of the Aegean civilization is believed to have been the Cycladic culture, which was replaced by the Minoan culture.

(E) During the Bronze Age in Greece, ships were frequently used for trading through a maritime network with civilizations in Sicily and Egypt.

(F) The Mycenaean civilization, characterized by a formidable defense infrastructure and artistic accomplishments, thrived yet it underwent an enigmatic decline.

| **Vocabulary Check** | 각 단어의 알맞은 동의어를 찾아 기호를 쓰시오.

1 maritime _____   **2** distant _____   **3** amass _____   **4** disaster _____

ⓐ narrow   ⓑ remote   ⓒ naval   ⓓ collect   ⓔ catastrophe   ⓕ culture

EXERCISE 04

Numerous marine vertebrates and invertebrates as well as some terrestrial creatures, fungi, and micro-organisms possess the ability to produce and emit light, a process that is known as bioluminescence. In some cases, these species are able to produce the light themselves, while others rely on a symbiotic relationship with certain types of bacteria. Generally speaking, bioluminescence is caused by a chemical reaction involving a light-emitting molecule and an enzyme. The molecule, known as a luciferin, shows very little variation from species to species while, in contrast, the enzyme, known as a luciferase, varies widely, evidence that bioluminescence has evolved separately in more than 40 different instances across the animal kingdom.

Observations of bioluminescence date back as far as Aristotle, who noted that damp wood will sometimes emit a faint glow, but the phenomenon was not properly investigated until the late 19th century. It serves no single evolutionary purpose, with some species using it for camouflage, while others employ it to lure prey or to attract a mate. In terms of camouflage, bioluminescence is often used by marine creatures, such as some species of squid, for the purpose of counterillumination, which involves lighting up their undersides so that they match not only the brightness but also the wavelength of the light passing through the surface of the water. As a result, their silhouettes become less prominent, and predators passing below are unlikely to notice them.

Another marine creature, the anglerfish, is a prime example of a species that utilizes bioluminescence as a predation mechanism. A deep-sea fish that inhabits extremely dark environments, it dangles a modified fin protruding from between its eyes, from the inside of which symbiotic bacteria emit light in order to lure prey closer to its sizeable mouth. And on land, fireflies, a species of beetle often seen lighting up wooded areas in early summer, use their bioluminescent ability to attract a suitable mate. Scientists believe the original purpose of their bioluminescence was to serve as a warning signal in larvae, letting potential predators know that they possess an unpalatable steroid and should not be consumed, but that it later became used as part of a mating tactic employed by adults.

| **Vocabulary Check** | 각 단어의 알맞은 뜻을 찾아 기호를 쓰시오.

1 predation _____   2 protrude _____   3 suitable _____   4 tactic _____

| ⓐ 전략 | ⓑ 튀어나오다 | ⓒ 정체된 | ⓓ 적합한 | ⓔ 포식 | ⓕ 결의 |

1 ⓔ 2 ⓑ 3 ⓓ 4 ⓐ

Directions: An introductory sentence for a brief summary of the passage is provided below. Complete the summary by selecting the THREE answer choices that express the most important ideas in the passage. Some sentences do not belong in the summary because they express ideas that are not presented in the passage or are minor ideas in the passage. **This question is worth 2 points.**

Bioluminescence is a process through which living creatures produce and emit their own light.

```
┌─────────────────────────────────────────────────────────┐
│                                                         │
└─────────────────────────────────────────────────────────┘
┌─────────────────────────────────────────────────────────┐
│                                                         │
└─────────────────────────────────────────────────────────┘
┌─────────────────────────────────────────────────────────┐
│                                                         │
└─────────────────────────────────────────────────────────┘
```

(A) Bioluminescence has a variety of uses, including hiding from predators, hunting prey, and attracting a mate.

(B) Aristotle was one of the first people to observe bioluminescence, spotting it in wood that had become damp.

(C) There are two main kinds of bioluminescence—one is known as luciferin, while the other is called luciferase.

(D) It is a chemical reaction between a molecule and an enzyme that is generally the source of bioluminescence.

(E) Adult fireflies use their bioluminescence as a way of warning their larvae against eating food that is toxic.

(F) While some creatures produce bioluminescence on their own, others, like the anglerfish, rely on special bacteria.

| **Vocabulary Check** | 각 단어의 알맞은 동의어를 찾아 기호를 쓰시오.

1 produce _____   **2** generally _____   **3** investigate _____   **4** prominent _____

ⓐ unintentionally   ⓑ infinite   ⓒ probe   ⓓ manufacture   ⓔ noticeable   ⓕ normally

1 ⓓ 2 ⓕ 3 ⓒ 4 ⓔ

PART

2

THEME-BASED PRACTICE

Humanities

Humanities is an interdisciplinary field involving human culture, history, language, literature, philosophy, and art. It explores the human experience through critical analysis of cultural artifacts and texts, fostering critical thinking and a deeper understanding of societies and historical periods.

Vocabulary Preview

adopted	입양된	**dispel**	떨쳐 버리다, 없애다 *syn.* remove
aesthetic	심미적인	**dominion**	영토
alternative	대체의 *syn.* alternate	**drape**	장식하다
anticipate	예상하다 *syn.* expect	**embellished**	미화된
arguably	거의 틀림없이	**engraving**	(새긴) 문양, 조각
assert	주장하다	**eroded**	침식된
buffoonery	익살	**etch**	(뚜렷이) 새기다
carbonization	탄화	**expedient**	편리한, 편의주의의
celebratory	기념하는	**faction**	세력
coarse	조악한 *syn.* rude	**fierce**	사나운 *syn.* ferocious
conciseness	간결함	**flint**	부싯돌
conquer	정복하다 *syn.* subjugate	**forgo**	포기하다
consistency	점도	**game**	사냥감 *syn.* quarry
conspiracy	음모 *syn.* scheme	**geometric**	기하학적인
constraint	제약	**glaciated**	빙하로 덮인
consumption	소비	**impale**	찌르다 *syn.* pierce
controversy	논란 *syn.* dispute	**impassable**	통행 불가능한
cumbersome	번잡한	**implement**	기구 *syn.* tool
delicately	섬세하게	**incision**	새기기
dictator	독재자 *syn.* tyrant	**infinite**	무한한 *syn.* endless

infuse	불어 넣다	predominate	두드러지게 많다, 지배적이다
instability	불안정	prioritize	우선시하다
institutionalize	제도화하다	prosperity	번영, 번성
intrigue	모의, 음모 *syn.* plot	repertoire	목록, 레퍼토리
invasion	침략	rim	테두리
judiciously	분별력 있게	sacrifice	희생시키다
kiln	가마	satire	풍자
knead	반죽하다	scrutinize	면밀히 조사하다 *syn.* examine
limestone	석회석	sophisticated	세련된
manipulate	처리하다, 다루다	static	고정적인 *syn.* fixed
manually	수작업으로	suffice	충분하다
migrant	이주자	trance	무아지경
motif	주제	transcend	초월하다 *syn.* surpass
mundane	일상적인 *syn.* ordinary	traverse	횡단하다 *syn.* cross
mythological	신화적인	unravel	풀다
oversee	관리하다, 감독하다 *syn.* supervise	utilitarian	실용적인
peninsula	반도	valid	논리적으로 근거 있는, 타당한
pigment	안료	variant	변형 *syn.* variation
pound	두드리다 *syn.* batter	vibrant	활기찬 *syn.* lively
predate	(시간적으로) ~보다 앞서다	visualize	시각화하다

Literary Devices

Individuals attempting to write in English frequently receive advice to prioritize clarity and conciseness, cautioned against the use of unorthodox or overly embellished language that may divert readers from the intended message. Nevertheless, there are instances when writers aspire to convey ideas in a creative manner, exploring avenues to emphasize aesthetic appeal without forgoing clarity. Fortunately, the English language provides various tools for this purpose, often referred to as "literary devices."

Certain literary devices utilize artistic license, which allows writers of literature and poetry to transcend the constraints of grammar. One such device is asyndeton, involving the deliberate omission of conjunctions. This omission can significantly impact sentence rhythm, enabling writers to streamline otherwise cumbersome expressions by eliminating "ands" and "ors." The effectiveness of asyndeton is evident in the commonly translated Latin phrase *veni, vidi, vici,* succinctly rendered as "I came, I saw, I conquered." Another means of condensing sentences is through ellipsis, where grammatically required words are omitted without sacrificing comprehension. This device often mirrors the concise nature of spoken English, as seen in the sentence "I will help you, and you me," where the second instance of "will help" is removed.

For those seeking a contrary effect, there is polysyndeton, involving the insertion of unnecessary conjunctions where a simple comma would suffice. This literary device serves to slow sentence rhythm, adding gravity. An example can be found in the fable *The Three Little Pigs*, describing the destructive actions of the Big Bad Wolf: "He huffed, and he puffed, and he blew the house down." This approach can also be found in a modern mystery story: "The detective scrutinized the crime scene, and studied, and analyzed, and dissected every piece of evidence to unravel the mystery." The deliberate repetition creates a rhythm that causes a feeling of tension in readers.

■(A) At times, instead of pushing the strict boundaries of grammar, creative writers aim to convey ideas in ways that transcend literal interpretation. ■(B) Metaphors are abstract and poetic comparisons, as seen in the idiom "the world is your oyster," signifying the ability to pursue one's desires freely. Similes, on the other hand, are more direct, employing the words "as" or "like" to construct comparative expressions like "cold as ice." ■(C) Another non-literal literary device is hyperbole, where an exaggerated statement, too extreme to be taken seriously, is used for emphasis or comedic effect. ■(D) An example could be describing a large character as "as big as a mountain." Observant readers might recognize that this assertion not only employs hyperbole but also incorporates a simile.

Conversely, there is litotes, a device that creates emphasis through understatement employing a double negative. Although instances of litotes abound in literature, it is most commonly found in everyday expressions like "Christopher is not a bad dancer," meaning that Christopher actually dances quite well. Although overused litotes might lead to misunderstandings, a lack of clarity, or miscommunication, the positive effect of using it in language lies in its ability to highlight a point, attribute, or achievement without resorting to boasting. This can be particularly effective when a more subdued or understated tone is desired, enhancing the richness of literary texts with layered meanings.

These represent just a handful of the literary devices frequently utilized by authors writing in the English language. Numerous others exist, and when employed judiciously and in moderation, they have the power to infuse writing with a vibrant freshness, elevating it beyond mere routine depictions of individuals, locations, and occurrences.

1 The word "unorthodox" in the passage is closest in meaning to

    (A) usual

    (B) unconventional

    (C) effective

    (D) unclear

2 Paragraph 1 suggests which of the following about literary devices?

    (A) Writers use them for clear and concise presentations.

    (B) Writers can express their ideas literally and figuratively with them.

    (C) Writers use them to engage readers and make their writing memorable.

    (D) Writers put an emphasis on them entirely for creativity.

3 Which of the sentences below best expresses the essential information in the highlighted sentence in the passage? Incorrect choices change the meaning in important ways or leave out essential information.

    (A) Ellipsis is used to shorten sentences by omitting grammatically necessary words while maintaining comprehension.

    (B) Ellipsis is a technique used to expand sentences by including additional words without compromising comprehension.

    (C) Sentences can be condensed through ellipsis, where exaggerated words are added to enhance comprehension.

    (D) Utilizing ellipsis involves the inclusion of redundant words in sentences, ensuring a thorough understanding of the content.

4 The word "mirrors" in the passage is closest in meaning to

   (A) moderates
   (B) corresponds to
   (C) repeats
   (D) reflects

5 Why does the author mention "*The Three Little Pigs*" in paragraph 3?

   (A) To provide an example of the addition of superfluous details
   (B) To suggest that novel can be written using literary devices
   (C) To present an example of the use of polysyndeton
   (D) To explain the importance of omitting redundant conjunctions

6 The word "it" in the passage refers to

   (A) emphasis
   (B) understatement
   (C) litotes
   (D) literature

7 Look at the four squares (■) that indicate where the following sentence could be added to the passage.

   A common way of achieving this is by employing metaphors and similes—literary devices that can be used to create vivid and evocative comparisons.

   Where would the sentence best fit? Select a square (■) to add the sentence to the passage.

8 **Directions**: An introductory sentence for a brief summary of the passage is provided below. Complete the summary by selecting the THREE answer choices that express the most important ideas in the passage. Some sentences do not belong in the summary because they express ideas that are not presented in the passage or are minor ideas in the passage. **This question is worth 2 points.**

> Drag your answer choices to the spaces where they belong. To review the passage, select **View Passage**.

Numerous literary devices are used in English writing.

- [   ]
- [   ]
- [   ]

Answer Choices

A	Authors have to prioritize which literary devices are used in each sentence.	D	Asyndeton can be found in many Latin phrases.
B	The use of literary devices permits authors to write creatively without sacrificing clarity.	E	The use of literary devices can enhance writing by challenging conventional grammar rules.
C	To employ some literary devices, writers need to exclude or include specific words.	F	In the past, children's fables predominantly featured the use of literary devices.

The Rise and Fall of Rome

The ancient Roman Republic was founded in the sixth century BC and soon took control of most of the Italian peninsula. However, it was not until the third century BC that the republic began to expand its borders beyond the peninsula by advancing into and conquering neighboring territories. In some ways it was already functioning as an empire, but politically the Roman Republic was still a collective of towns and cities ruled by military commanders and overseen by a central Senate. As part of a republic, Rome's citizens elected the politicians who would represent them, unlike in a democracy, where citizens are directly involved in the nation's political decision-making. It was actually this republic system, rather than the democracy of ancient Greece, that the United States of America would be partially modeled upon nearly 2,000 years later.

By the first century BC, the ancient Roman Republic had broadened its dominion to include nearly the entire Mediterranean region, but civil wars, along with damaging political intrigue and conspiracies, had led to significant instability. In 31 BC, the victory of Octavian, later to be known as Caesar Augustus, over Mark Antony and Cleopatra led to the conquest of Egypt's Ptolemaic Kingdom and marked the beginning of Octavian's ascension to the role of the first emperor of the Roman Empire. Octavian was the adopted son of Julius Caeser, who had ruled over the Roman Republic as a virtual dictator until his famous assassination at the hands of a senator named Brutus on the Ides of March. After this shocking event, Octavian joined forces with Mark Antony, who had been one of his father's most loyal generals, to defeat the faction that organized the assassination, but the two men later became sworn enemies.

■(A) With his defeat of Mark Antony, Octavian's stunning consolidation of power became official in 27 BC. ■(B) For two centuries, the newly founded Roman Empire enjoyed unprecedented peace, prosperity, and social stability. ■(C) This period became known as Pax Romana. ■(D) Although uprisings occasionally occurred in the outer provinces, they were dealt with swiftly and mercilessly. The Roman Empire soon became one of the greatest economic and cultural powers the world had ever seen.

Under the rule of Trajan, the empire expanded to its peak in terms of territory under its control, but when power was transferred into the hands of Commodus in 180 AD, Rome began to fall into decline. This eventually led to a cataclysmic split in the Roman Empire, with the establishment of two separate imperial courts, and in 330 AD the empire's capital was moved from the city of Rome to the Greek-founded city of Byzantium, which was subsequently renamed Constantinople, after Constantine I, the first Roman emperor to convert to Christianity and the mastermind behind the eastward shift. Today, the city is known by its modern name of Istanbul and is the cultural and economic hub of the Republic of Türkiye.

This half of the empire became known as the Eastern Roman Empire or the Byzantian Empire, and it controlled the majority of the Mediterranean region, while the Western Roman Empire retained Rome, and later the nearby city of Ravenna, as its capital and ruled over a large swath of Europe. The Western Roman Empire, however, was eventually besieged by large-scale invasions, both by nearby Germanic tribes and an army of Huns led across Eurasia by the fierce warrior Attila, leading to its collapse in 476 AD. Meanwhile, the Eastern Roman Empire continued to survive, although in a somewhat diminished form, for another millennium, until the city of Constantinople fell to the invading armies of the Ottoman Empire in 1453.

1 According to paragraph 1, the Roman Republic was not a democracy because

(A) it did not have a central government ruling provinces
(B) it had no elections and was ruled by an emperor
(C) its politicians did not represent the will of the people
(D) its citizens did not directly vote on national decisions

2 The word "ascension" in the passage is closest in meaning to

(A) rise
(B) journey
(C) challenge
(D) desire

3 The word "his" in the passage refers to

(A) Julius Caesar
(B) Brutus
(C) Octavian
(D) Mark Antony

4 What is the purpose of paragraph 3 in the passage?

    (A) To describe an ideal period enjoyed by the Roman Empire

    (B) To contrast the strategies of Octavian and Mark Antony

    (C) To explain the way in which Rome chose a new leader

    (D) To illustrate the extreme changes in the Roman Senate

5 Which of the sentences below best expresses the essential information in the highlighted sentence in the passage? Incorrect choices change the meaning in important ways or leave out essential information.

    (A) The city of Constantinople got its name from the Roman emperor who first converted to Christianity in 330 AD.

    (B) Due to a schism in Rome's imperial court, many of the empire's Christian citizens began to move to the east.

    (C) The Roman Empire was separated into two parts, and the empire's capital shifted from Rome to Byzantium, which was later renamed Constantinople.

    (D) Constantine I, the first emperor of Rome, decided to unite his divided empire by seizing the city of Byzantium.

6 Which of the following can be inferred from paragraph 4 about the Roman emperor Trajan?

    (A) He was envious of Commodus.

    (B) He was a wise and efficient ruler.

    (C) He was undermined by his greed.

    (D) He was a humble and religious man.

7 Look at the four squares (■) that indicate where the following sentence could be added to the passage.

The Roman Senate granted him imperial powers over a new monarchy, with Rome designated as its seat of power and its various territories organized into provinces.

Where would the sentence best fit? Select a square (■) to add the sentence to the passage.

8 **Directions**: An introductory sentence for a brief summary of the passage is provided below. Complete the summary by selecting the THREE answer choices that express the most important ideas in the passage. Some sentences do not belong in the summary because they express ideas that are not presented in the passage or are minor ideas in the passage. **This question is worth 2 points.**

Drag your answer choices to the spaces where they belong. To review the passage, select **View Passage.**

The Roman Republic ruled the Italian peninsula but soon began to take control of neighboring territory.

Answer Choices

A The structure of the government of the United States of America is partially based on that of the Roman Republic.

B In the first century BC, Octavian, the adopted son of Julius Caesar, became the first emperor of the Roman Empire.

C Mark Antony and Octavian ruled Rome together until they were defeated by Cleopatra and the Ptolemaic Kingdom.

D Pax Romana was a period consisting of 200 years of peace and prosperity at the start of the Roman Empire.

E As Rome began to decline, it broke apart into two separate empires, one of which collapsed in the year 476 AD.

F Istanbul, a major city located in modern-day Türkiye, had two previous names, Byzantine and Constantinople.

Cave Art

Paintings and engravings found on the rock walls of caves and rock shelters have been attributed to early humans from the Upper Paleolithic period, which took place approximately 50,000 to 12,000 years ago and was the third and final phase of what is commonly known as the Stone Age. The first of these Stone Age cave paintings to be discovered in modern times was found in a Spanish cave complex known as the Cave of Altamira, with about 400 additional sites in total having been identified since then, the majority of which are located in France and Spain.

Most cave paintings were created using either red pigment made from iron oxides or black pigment made from charcoal, while the engravings seem to have been etched into soft rock walls by human fingers or through the use of flint tools in the case of harder surfaces. While some of these representations depict human beings, either in whole or as isolated body parts, the majority of cave art in all regions across all periods focuses on images of animals. In the earliest cave art, such as that found in the Chauvet-Pont-d'Arc cave in France, formidable creatures that have since become extinct predominate, including fierce cave lions and gigantic mammoths. In later cave art, more mundane animals, such as horses and bison, are more frequently depicted—interestingly, there are few images of birds or fish to be found.

Scientists believe that this art served either a symbolic or religious function, or quite possibly both. Cave art is found near cave entrances or on the exposed walls of rock shelters in many regions around the world, but art deep within caves in places where little outside light can reach is virtually exclusive to Europe. It has been theorized that Stone Age shamans would enter these caves as part of rituals in which they would experience visions after falling into a trance state and then paint them onto the walls. Another theory as to the purpose of cave art is that it was done to help bring about a successful hunt by anticipating and visualizing the various situations the hunters might face.

Some researchers have gone so far as to suggest that certain cave art images represent an early form of proto-writing. ■[A] However, it is important to note that although the animals on cave walls were often from species that could be considered expedient prey, these images do not always correspond to the animal bones found in the caves. ■[B] The Stone Age inhabitants of France's Lascaux cave complex, for example, left behind mainly reindeer bones, indicating that this was their preferred species to hunt. ■[C] However, none of the images on the walls of the cave are of reindeer, with most depicting horses. ■[D]

Another common cave art motif is the human hand, which was generally rendered via the placing of an actual hand against a rock wall. The surrounding area was then covered with pigment and the hand-shaped space in the center decorated with dots, dashes, or simplistic patterns. Based on the average size of this hand art, archaeologists believe it was primarily the work of the women of the Paleolithic communities. Although far less common than paintings and engravings, a small number of sculptures dating from this period have also been found in caves, including clay statues of bison and a life-sized model of a bear found in separate caves in the French Pyrenees mountain range. The bear statue, which is headless and believed to have once been covered in an actual bear pelt, was likely used by the community's hunters, who would repeatedly impale it with their spears.

1 The word "formidable" in the passage is closest in meaning to

(A) extinct
(B) poisonous
(C) energetic
(D) imposing

2 Why does the author mention "birds or fish" in paragraph 2?

(A) To explain how cave art benefited early humans
(B) To introduce the main religious function of cave art
(C) To give examples of animals rarely shown in cave art
(D) To suggest that these animals were often hunted

3 Which of the sentences below best expresses the essential information in the highlighted sentence in the passage? Incorrect choices change the meaning in important ways or leave out essential information.

(A) Cave art seems to be exclusive to Europe, as it has not been found in other regions of the world.
(B) While cave art is found in many regions globally, art deep within caves is unique to Europe.
(C) Cave art is limited to cave entrances or exposed rock shelter walls in many global regions.
(D) Europe is the only region where cave art is found both near cave entrances and on outside walls.

4 The word "them" in the passage refers to

(A) Stone Age shamans
(B) these caves
(C) rituals
(D) visions

5 According to paragraph 5, which of the following is NOT true about the hand images?

(A) They were made by applying pigment around a hand.
(B) They were decorated with symbols and patterns.
(C) They were part of a ritual performed by shamans.
(D) They were created mostly by female artists.

6 Which of the following can be inferred from paragraph 5 about the bear statue?

(A) It was used to practice hunting skills.
(B) It was created by female shamans.
(C) It was often moved from cave to cave.
(D) It was not as old as the wall paintings.

7 Look at the four squares (■) that indicate where the following sentence could be added to the passage.

They suspect it may have been used to share knowledge about the mating cycles of prey based on the phases of the moon.

Where would the sentence best fit? Select a square (■) to add the sentence to the passage.

8 **Directions**: An introductory sentence for a brief summary of the passage is provided below. Complete the summary by selecting the THREE answer choices that express the most important ideas in the passage. Some sentences do not belong in the summary because they express ideas that are not presented in the passage or are minor ideas in the passage. **This question is worth 2 points.**

Drag your answer choices to the spaces where they belong. To review the passage, select **View Passage**.

Art created by early humans during the Upper Paleolithic period has been found on the walls of hundreds of caves.

-
-
-

Answer Choices

A Most cave art depicts animals, such as mammoths, bison or horses, and was made using either black or red pigment.

B Bear statues have often been found in caves in France and Spain, and they may have been covered in real bear fur.

C Reindeer were the favorite prey of early human hunters, so they appear in cave art more than other animals.

D The walls of some caves containing cave art are made of soft rock, while others have much harder surfaces.

E The women of early human communities may have contributed to cave art by tracing their hands on rock walls.

F Cave art may have been created as part of a religious ritual or in preparation for a hunt.

Ancient Greek Theater

At the start of the seventh century BC, ancient Greek theater began to flourish, with the city-state of Athens serving as the hub of this cultural phenomenon. It was the Greek preference for the spoken word over the written word that ultimately led to this development. Literature was generally viewed as something dead and static that had no potential for growth or change, whereas storytelling was viewed as a living thing that possessed infinite possibilities. Around 508 BC, theater was institutionalized as the central component of the Dionysia, a festival held in honor of Dionysus, the Greek god of wine, which was divided into two separate events, the City Dionysia and the Rural Dionysia, held at different times of the year. No less than three major dramatic genres—tragedy, comedy, and the satyr play—emerged from this festival, which was later exported to other Greek cities.

The birth of Greek tragedy took place in Athens around 532 BC, during the time of Thespis, a Greek poet whose name serves as the root of "thespian," a modern English word meaning "actor." It is said Thespis was the very first person to appear on the stage as an actor, in that he was speaking the scripted words of a character. It was arguably Thespis who invented the dramatic genre that would become tragedy when he introduced a form of performance in which a single person would portray several characters, distinguishing between them through the wearing of different masks. It should be noted, however, that his importance to the development of theater is disputed by some historians, who regard him as a minor contributor rather than the "Father of Tragedy," as he is sometimes known. Up until the Hellenistic period, which began in 323 BC, all Greek tragedies were written in honor of Dionysus and performed only a single time.

Early Athenian comedy, later known as Old Comedy, was first staged at the City Dionysia in 487 BC, long after tragedy had taken hold as the most popular theatrical genre. According to Aristotle, comedies developed from the songs of celebratory festivals, but they initially failed to grab the imagination of Greek theatergoers, as few accepted them as a serious dramatic form. Despite this, comedy eventually grew into a highly structured genre in which a chorus played an important narrative role and political satire was disguised as mere acts of buffoonery. The Old Comedy of Athens told stories of laughable people who blundered in a manner that did not cause serious pain or misfortune, but the only surviving examples of comedy from this early era are eleven plays written by Aristophanes.

■(A) The third genre to be introduced to the world at the Dionysia was the satyr play, a type of short performance that bore a resemblance to both comedy and tragedy. ■(B) Satyr plays were more closely related to tragedies than comedies, as they had plotlines and language similar to those of tragedies, and one satyr play was traditionally performed alongside a series of three tragedies at the City Dionysia. ■(C) The distinction between satyr plays and other forms of theater was that they included choruses of mythological creatures with the upper body of a man and the lower body of a goat, along with coarse wordplay. ■(D) Despite this, the satyr play was seen as the only suitable performance with which to bring each City Dionysia to a conclusion.

While Greek tragedy and comedy would go on to have a huge influence on how the world views theater, with their basic structures and features still clearly observable in both modern theater and cinema, the tragicomic satyr play eventually fell out of favor with increasingly sophisticated Athenian audiences, and no more than a handful of new satyr plays were penned after the fourth century BC.

1   According to paragraph 1, which of the following is true about the Dionysia?

(A) It was exported to Athens from rural areas.
(B) It was originally a festival celebrating literature.
(C) It was financially supported by local winemakers.
(D) It was made up of two parts held separately.

2   According to paragraph 2, which of the following is NOT true about Thespis?

(A) He was the first person to perform on stage as an actor.
(B) He is considered the inventor of the dramatic genre that became tragedy.
(C) His contribution to the development of theater is undisputed by historians.
(D) He introduced a form of performance where one person portrayed several characters.

3   The word "blundered" in the passage is closest in meaning to

(A) lied
(B) erred
(C) shouted
(D) laughed

4   Which of the following can be inferred from paragraph 3 about Aristotle?

    (A) He considered theater an inferior form of art.
    (B) He helped Old Comedy become more popular.
    (C) He worried that comedy could harm children's imaginations.
    (D) He was interested in the history of theater.

5   The phrase "fell out of favor" in the passage is closest in meaning to

    (A) lost popularity
    (B) spread widely
    (C) were banned
    (D) became familiar

6   How is paragraph 5 related to paragraph 4?

    (A) Paragraph 5 questions some of the information presented in paragraph 4.
    (B) Paragraph 5 explains what later happened to the subject of paragraph 4.
    (C) Paragraph 5 summarizes the opinions given by the author in paragraph 4.
    (D) Paragraph 5 emphasizes the cultural impact of the events of paragraph 4.

7   Look at the four squares (■) that indicate where the following sentence could be added to the passage.

However, many of their themes and characters were similar to those of comedies, with both genres sharing the crowd-pleasing feature of offering audiences a happy ending.

Where would the sentence best fit? Select a square (■) to add the sentence to the passage.

8 **Directions**: An introductory sentence for a brief summary of the passage is provided below. Complete the summary by selecting the THREE answer choices that express the most important ideas in the passage. Some sentences do not belong in the summary because they express ideas that are not presented in the passage or are minor ideas in the passage. **This question is worth 2 points.**

> Drag your answer choices to the spaces where they belong. To review the passage, select **View Passage.**

Ancient Greek theater rose to prominence in the seventh century BC with the emergence of three major dramatic genres.

```
┌─────────────────────────────────────────────────────────────────────┐
│                                                                       │
└─────────────────────────────────────────────────────────────────────┘
┌─────────────────────────────────────────────────────────────────────┐
│                                                                       │
└─────────────────────────────────────────────────────────────────────┘
┌─────────────────────────────────────────────────────────────────────┐
│                                                                       │
└─────────────────────────────────────────────────────────────────────┘
```

Answer Choices

A A preference for the spoken word over the written word played a significant role in the development of Greek theater.

B Thespis, the first person to appear on stage as an actor, is universally recognized as the "Father of Tragedy."

C Early Athenian comedy, or Old Comedy, was not initially accepted as a serious dramatic form by Greek theatergoers.

D Satyr plays, the third genre introduced at the Dionysia, were more closely related to comedies than tragedies.

E Greek tragedy and comedy have had a significant influence on modern theater and cinema.

F The tragicomic satyr play remained a popular genre throughout the history of Greek theater.

The First Settlement of the Americas

Despite the traditional notion that Christopher Columbus "discovered" the New World, it has long been established that North and South America had been populated by humans who migrated there from Asia long before the first Europeans arrived. Disagreement remains, however, as to exactly when and how these ancient peoples crossed from one continent to another, and there is also considerable controversy involving the primary route through which they migrated further into the Americas.

It is believed that the first migrants arrived in North America after crossing from Beringia, a now-submerged land mass that once linked modern-day Alaska and eastern Siberia. The discovery of artifacts that seem to be linked to Pleistocene-era fauna near Clovis, a small town in the American state of New Mexico, led to a hypothesis suggesting that humans arrived in the Americas before the Ice Age had come to an end. This led to the question of how ancient people could have crossed Beringia at a time when it was completely glaciated, meaning that it would have been covered in impassable sheets of ice. The proposed answer to this question involves a land corridor that may have briefly opened up between two of these gigantic ice sheets. Ancient Asian hunters in pursuit of big game would then have traversed this corridor, becoming the first humans to settle in the Americas and gradually spreading southward and eastward throughout the two continents. This dispersal is believed to have taken place via a route that passes through the interior of North America and includes Clovis.

This is known as the Clovis-First theory, and it places the arrival of these first Americans between 13,000 and 12,600 years ago, based on advanced radiocarbon techniques used to date the artifacts found near Clovis and at other related sites. Although the fundamental facts on which this theory is based may be valid, subsequent archaeological finds strongly suggest that humans arrived in the Americas in waves of migration from Asia, some of which apparently predated the Clovis culture by thousands of years, thereby dispelling the idea of "first" in the Clovis-First theory and calling into question the concept of an inland route to Central and South America.

■(A) The coastal migration theory offers an alternative route, suggesting that the ancient peoples who first migrated to the Americas did so by traveling on foot along the coastline of northeast Asia until they reached the New World, where they continued their coastal journey southward. ■(B) A variant on this theory asserts that these migrants actually traveled on primitive boats they had managed to construct, which would have allowed them to cross between continents before the deglaciation process was complete. ■(C) Either way, this theory presents a strikingly different route than the interior passage suggested by the Clovis-First model, with a purely coastal journey bringing migrants first to Central America and later to South America. ■ (D)

This theory has drawn the endorsement of many members of the scientific community due to the fact that it explains how these new arrivals were able to spread so rapidly to coastal sites far away from Alaska, such as those discovered in southern Chile and western Venezuela. However, the theory has proven difficult to confirm definitively, mainly due to the fact that global sea levels have risen by more than 120 meters since the last glacial period ended, meaning that the coastlines these ancient people would have followed have long been submerged by the ocean, making the tracking of the exact route they traveled nearly impossible today. Despite the fact that migration routes and methods remain in question, there is a general consensus that the first humans reached the shores of the Americas approximately 15,000 to 20,000 years ago.

1   The word "fauna" in the passage is closest in meaning to

(A) gear
(B) culture
(C) wildlife
(D) soil

2   According to paragraph 2, it would have been difficult to cross Beringia during the Ice Age because

(A) its coastline had changed over the years
(B) it had been flooded before the Ice Age
(C) it was far away from North America
(D) it was covered by large slabs of ice

3   Which of the following can be inferred from paragraph 2 about the species pursued by ancient Asian hunters?

(A) They were hunted for sport rather than as a source of food.
(B) They were mostly solitary animals that did not move quickly.
(C) Their bones and skin were used to create distinctive crafts.
(D) Their remains can be found in both Asia and North America.

4 According to paragraph 3, which of the following is true about the Clovis artifacts?

    (A) They were later declared to be fake by archeologists.

    (B) Their appearance greatly differed from Asian artifacts.

    (C) Their age was determined using high-tech technology.

    (D) They included implements related to maritime activities.

5 The word "endorsement" in the passage is closest in meaning to

    (A) contempt

    (B) support

    (C) attention

    (D) funding

6 Why does the author mention "global sea levels" in paragraph 5?

    (A) To offer a reason why a migration theory cannot be verified

    (B) To give evidence that Beringia was never covered in ice sheets

    (C) To explain which route migrants likely took to South America

    (D) To suggest that early Asians did not migrate to North America

7 Look at the four squares (■) that indicate where the following sentence could be added to the passage.

Upon encountering ice barriers, they would have been able to continue onward simply by sailing around them.

Where would the sentence best fit? Select a square (■) to add the sentence to the passage.

8 **Directions**: An introductory sentence for a brief summary of the passage is provided below. Complete the summary by selecting the THREE answer choices that express the most important ideas in the passage. Some sentences do not belong in the summary because they express ideas that are not presented in the passage or are minor ideas in the passage. **This question is worth 2 points.**

> Drag your answer choices to the spaces where they belong. To review the passage, select **View Passage**.

There are several theories and controversies surrounding the migration of the first humans from Asia to the Americas.

- _____
- _____
- _____

Answer Choices

A The Clovis-First theory states the first migrants arrived in North America after crossing Beringia, but archeological evidence suggests migration from Asia predated the Clovis culture.

B The coastal migration theory suggests the first North American migrants traveled along the coastline, but this theory is difficult to confirm due to rising global sea levels.

C The origins of human migration to America are debated, with some suggesting Asians arrived before the first Europeans.

D Artifacts found near Clovis, New Mexico, suggest humans arrived in the Americas before the Ice Age ended, sparking debates about archaeological dating methods.

E Beringia, a now-submerged land mass linking Alaska and Siberia, had a minor role in human migration to the Americas, overshadowed by other land bridges that existed at the time.

F Despite uncertainties, there is a consensus that humans reached the Americas around 15,000 to 20,000 years ago.

Pottery in Ancient Egypt

The pottery of ancient Egypt served a wide variety of roles, including a number of practical household functions, specifically as vessels for the storage, preparation, transportation, and consumption of food and drinks. It was also used in rituals and has frequently been found in tombs among the various items placed there in order to accompany the deceased on their journey after death. Much has been learned about this pottery from tomb paintings and the uncovered remains of pottery workshops, including the fact that new techniques of producing pottery, rather than replacing the old ways, were simply added to the existing repertoire of the kingdom's potters. Still, by carefully examining these techniques, such as the types of incisions they made and the shapes they created, archaeologists can place each individual piece within a specific time period with some degree of confidence.

The process of creating pottery in ancient Egypt began with the selection of the appropriate materials. There is an important distinction to be made between the two most common of these, which were Nile clay and marl clay: the former was formed from eroded materials in the mountains of Ethiopia before flowing down the Nile, while the latter was formed in Egyptian limestone deposits along the banks of the Nile. Potters tended to use Nile clay for utilitarian household wares, while marl clay was preferred for decorative objects such as figural vessels, which were highly desirable items with a roughly human shape that symbolized their owner's social status and prestige.

Once gathered, the dry, hard clay needed to be softened via the addition of water. ■(A) It was then kneaded into the proper consistency, which could be accomplished either by treading on it or by splitting a large mass of clay in two and pounding the halves together. ■(B) Next, the potters would shape the clay, either manually or with the assistance of an implement designed to facilitate the process. ■(C) Finally, the firing process took place either over an open fire or inside a kiln, which is a type of primitive oven. ■(D)

The different types of decoration found on Egyptian pottery were applied at different stages of the production process, namely before, during, and after firing. In the pre-firing stage, potters often manipulated the surface of the clay in order to imprint it with a pattern designed to imitate some other type of material, such as metal, wood, or stone. Some of these patterns were incised with a sharp instrument, possibly a primitive knife or simple twig, while others were made with the potters' fingernails. A popular decorative effect that was applied during the firing process was something called a black rim, which required firing the piece within a fire pit, where carbonization would take place around the edge of the piece's opening. It is believed that it would have required a high degree of technical knowledge to produce such an effect consistently.

After the firing process had been completed, the hardened pottery was often adorned with paint, with certain styles and patterns becoming standard motifs. These included the white-cross-lined style, in which geometric patterns were painted in white or cream on a background of dark red or reddish brown; the white-background style, where colorful scenes were painted onto a white background; and the blue-painted style, featuring lotus flowers and buds painted with blue pigment as if they had been delicately draped around the neck of the pottery.

1 The word "examining" in the passage is closest in meaning to

(A) teaching
(B) demonstrating
(C) studying
(D) modernizing

2 Which of the following can be inferred from paragraph 1 about ancient Egyptian culture?

(A) There was a prevalent belief in an afterlife.
(B) There was not much respect for artisans.
(C) There were two different social classes.
(D) There were numerous kingdoms.

3 Why does the author mention "Ethiopia" in paragraph 2?

(A) To emphasize the regional importance of the Nile River
(B) To compare the pottery produced in two different areas
(C) To illustrate an external influence on Egyptian pottery
(D) To indicate the source of one material used by potters

4 The phrase "the latter" in the passage refers to

(A) ancient Egypt
(B) marl clay
(C) eroded materials
(D) the Nile

5 Which of the sentences below best expresses the essential information in the highlighted sentence in the passage? Incorrect choices change the meaning in important ways or leave out essential information.

(A) In the initial stage, potters used various materials like metal, wood, or stone to shape the clay.
(B) The primary purpose of manipulating the clay was to make it look like it was made of metal, wood, or stone.
(C) Potters often added materials such as metal, wood, or stone to the clay before firing to enhance its strength.
(D) Potters frequently changed the clay's texture to create patterns that resembled different materials.

6 According to paragraph 4, why did potters place pottery in fire pits?

(A) To create a decorative effect around the pottery's rim
(B) To make sure the surface of the clay remained soft
(C) To stop the edges of the pottery from turning black
(D) To improve the overall quality of their technical skills

7 Look at the four squares (■) that indicate where the following sentence could be added to the passage.

This often took the form of a potter's wheel, a significant technological advancement that made the creation of pottery much easier by rotating the clay on a central axis while it was being shaped.

Where would the sentence best fit? Select a square (■) to add the sentence to the passage.

8 **Directions**: An introductory sentence for a brief summary of the passage is provided below. Complete the summary by selecting the THREE answer choices that express the most important ideas in the passage. Some sentences do not belong in the summary because they express ideas that are not presented in the passage or are minor ideas in the passage. **This question is worth 2 points.**

> Drag your answer choices to the spaces where they belong. To review the passage, select **View Passage**.

Many things are known about the processes used to create pottery in ancient Egypt.

Answer Choices

A The pottery was usually made by professional craftsmen in workshops, and it had multiple incisions in it.	**D** Because potters preferred to use their fingernails to decorate pottery, there was little technological advancement.
B Two materials from different origins were used for Egyptian pottery, each chosen for specific types of wares.	**E** The pottery-making process included preparing the clay, shaping it, and firing it to create the final product.
C Pottery that had black carbonization around its rim was considered inferior, so it was often placed in tombs.	**F** After the pottery had been fired, it was often decorated in standardized patterns that were painted onto it.

02

Social Science

Social science is a branch of scientific study that looks at human behavior in a social context. Subjects such as cultural anthropology, sociology, psychology, political science, and economics could be included in this field. Its goal is to understand human social systems and relationships between individuals, eventually finding ways to improve our current society.

Vocabulary Preview

accompany	동반하다	**excessive**	과도한 *syn.* immoderate
agility	민첩성	**exclusively**	오로지
antiquity	고대	**exposure**	노출
appetite	욕구 *syn.* hunger	**familial**	가족의
biodiversity	생물 다양성	**financial**	재정의 *syn.* monetary
bolster	강화하다 *syn.* strengthen	**geographical**	지리적인
cartography	지도 제작	**grant**	주다, 부여하다
colonial	식민지의	**halt**	멈춤, 중단
commencement	시작 *syn.* beginning	**immediate**	즉각적인 *syn.* instant
coordination	조정(력)	**importation**	수입
core	핵심 *syn.* center	**impose**	강요하다, 부과하다
counteract	대응하다 *syn.* counterbalance	**inequality**	불평등
defining	본질적인 의미를 규정하는	**inevitably**	필연적으로
discord	불화 *syn.* strife	**innocent**	순수한
disposable	일회용의 *syn.* expendable	**integral**	필수불가결한
distribute	분배하다 *syn.* dispense	**intent**	목적, 의도
earmark	배정하다 *syn.* designate	**intentionally**	의도적으로 *syn.* deliberately
effectively	효과적으로	**invariably**	변함없이
enhance	향상시키다, 강화하다	**irrecoverable**	회복할 수 없는
erratically	변덕스럽게	**irreversible**	되돌릴 수 없는 *syn.* irreparable

logistical	수송의		stamina	체력	
misuse	오용, 남용	*syn.* abuse	stranglehold	숨통 조이기, 옥죄기	
mitigate	완화시키다	*syn.* alleviate	strip	박탈하다	
modification	변경	*syn.* alteration	subsequently	그 후에	
monopoly	독점		subsidy	보조금	
necessarily	반드시	*syn.* unavoidably	sufficient	충분한	
occasional	때때로 일어나는	*syn.* intermittent	surge	급증	
optimize	최적화하다		thrust	떠맡기다	
peer	또래, 동료		transaction	거래	
pioneer	개척하다		transfer	옮기다, 이동시키다	
predominantly	주로, 대부분	*syn.* mainly	ultimately	궁극적으로	*syn.* eventually
premature	너무 이른	*syn.* early	undoubtedly	의심할 여지 없이	*syn.* unquestionably
preservable	보존 가능한		unfold	전개되다	
primary	주된, 주요한	*syn.* main	uniformly	균일하게	
reliance	의존	*syn.* dependence	unsustainable	지속 불가능한	
remote	외딴	*syn.* isolated	via	~을 통해	
return	수확(물)	*syn.* yield	virtual	사실상의	
rift	균열		vital	필수적인	
rural	시골의		wane	시들해지다	*syn.* dwindle
severe	극심한	*syn.* drastic	whet	자극하다, 돋우다	*syn.* stimulate

Spice Trade

The spice trade dates back to antiquity, when the ancient civilizations of Asia, Africa, and Europe first began to engage in commerce involving a wide variety of cultivated spices, including ginger, nutmeg, and cinnamon. ■(A) Some of the earliest maritime trade routes were plied by Indonesian sailors, who were transporting the spices grown in Southeast Asia to India and the island of Sri Lanka as early as 1500 BC. ■(B) In time, these trade lanes expanded both in volume and scope, growing to include the Middle East and parts of eastern Africa by the first millennium AD. ■(C) It was during this time that spice traders actually colonized Madagascar, arriving there from modern-day Indonesia after crossing the Indian Ocean on outrigger canoes and finding this large land mass off the coast of Africa to be uninhabited. ■(D)

Around this same time, the Kingdom of Axum, located in what is now Ethiopia, managed to conquer the Red Sea and, taking advantage of its geographical placement between the Indian Ocean and the Mediterranean Sea, seized a significant measure of control over the maritime trade routes bringing spices from the East to the then-thriving Roman Empire. These routes culminated at the edges of the Red Sea, where the spices were unloaded and transported overland to the shores of the Mediterranean. However, by the seventh century, with the rise of Islam in the Arab world, the dominance of Axum gradually waned, and Arab traders took the helm of the spice trade, transporting spices from Southeast Asia to the merchants of the eastern and central Mediterranean regions, who then conveyed them to the markets of Europe, where demand for them was growing.

Although it was the overland routes across Asia that had originally whet the European appetite for exotic spices, as cartography and shipbuilding technology continued to advance, maritime routes soon became absolutely vital to the spice trade, allowing it to grow by leaps and bounds. By the start of the 12th century, the Turks had become the masters of the trade routes passing from the Indian Ocean, through the Red Sea, and overland into the Mediterranean. Everything changed, however, with the commencement of the Crusades, a series of holy wars between Christians and Muslims, at the end of the 11th century, as increased exposure to Eastern cultures led to a rise in demand for spices—black pepper in particular—in the West.

Because of this, the Italian maritime republics of Venice and Genoa became increasingly active in the importation and distribution of spices, until the point where they had established a virtual monopoly on trade between Europe and Asia, a situation that brought them great wealth and power, and continued until the 15th century. In 1498, however, the Portuguese explorer and navigator Vasco da Gama pioneered a new trade route connecting Europe to the Indian Ocean. Known as the Cape Route, it involved sailing around the Cape of Good Hope, located on the very southern tip of the African continent. Although fraught with dangers, this route allowed merchants to avoid passing through the Red Sea and Mediterranean Sea, thereby breaking the stranglehold of Venice and Genoa, and thrusting Portugal into a major role in the spice trade that eventually allowed this small European nation to establish a vast colonial empire.

Ultimately, the spice trade had an impact on all of the regions involved in it that went far beyond simple commercial transactions. It facilitated several major exchanges of not only technology but also religion and culture, changing the face of civilization and representing perhaps the world's first steps towards globalization.

1 Which of the following can be inferred from paragraph 1 about ancient Indonesian civilization?

(A) It did not put an emphasis on agriculture.
(B) It learned about trade from its neighbors.
(C) It was not interested in global commerce.
(D) It had advanced maritime technology.

2 The word "culminated" in the passage is closest in meaning to

(A) outlasted
(B) extended
(C) initiated
(D) concluded

3 Which of the sentences below best expresses the essential information in the highlighted sentence in the passage? Incorrect answer choices change the meaning in important ways or leave out essential information.

(A) Axum maintained its dominance over the Arab world until the rising European demand for spices changed the balance of power.
(B) As Islam became more powerful, Southeast Asian spice traders lost interest in exchanges of commerce with Europe.
(C) In the seventh century, control over the spice trade between Asia and Europe had been transferred from Axum to the Arab world.
(D) The seventh century marked the beginning of a brand new spice trade when European nations began growing their own spices.

4 The phrase "by leaps and bounds" in the passage is closest in meaning to

(A) rapidly
(B) erratically
(C) naturally
(D) gradually

5 Why does the author mention "the Crusades" in paragraph 3?

(A) To indicate the cause of a rise in the demand for spices in Europe
(B) To suggest that the spice trade caused a rift between East and West
(C) To contrast the different approaches to trade between East and West in the 11th century
(D) To show how Eastern merchants had a positive effect on Europe

6 According to paragraph 4, what allowed Portugal to become a major participant in the spice trade?

(A) a victory over Muslim armies in the Middle East
(B) a change in the shipbuilding technology of Europe
(C) the establishment of a new maritime trade route
(D) the creation of an overland route from the Red Sea

7 Look at the four squares (■) that indicate where the following sentence could be added to the passage.

These same spices then made their way to the Greek and Roman empires via overland routes.

Where would the sentence best fit? Select a square (■) to add the sentence to the passage.

8 **Directions**: An introductory sentence for a brief summary of the passage is provided below. Complete the summary by selecting the THREE answer choices that express the most important ideas in the passage. Some sentences do not belong in the summary because they express ideas that are not presented in the passage or are minor ideas in the passage. **This question is worth 2 points.**

> Drag your answer choices to the spaces where they belong. To review the passage, select **View Passage**.

The global spice trade has had a long and interesting history.

> ☐

> ☐

> ☐

Answer Choices

A The spice trade switched from maritime routes to predominantly overland routes after the 15th century.	D A major shift in dominance over the spice trade occurred when a Portuguese explorer created a new maritime trade route.
B Control of the route between the Indian Ocean and the Mediterranean Sea repeatedly changed hands over the centuries.	E The spice trade began around 1500 BC, with Southeast Asian sailors bringing spices to India and Sri Lanka.
C The Cape of Good Hope, located on the southern tip of Africa, presented many dangers for spice merchants.	F Venice and Genoa fought alongside several Muslim countries during the Crusades in order to defend the spice trade.

The Environmental Problem of Overlogging

The practice of logging involves felling trees, dividing their trunks into sections of various lengths, and then transporting the resulting logs to a sawmill for further processing. In the past, this was accomplished exclusively by hand, and in certain colder parts of the world logging continues to be done in a manual fashion, as loggers fell each tree with an axe in winter, subsequently transporting the logs via sleds drawn by draft animals, such as horses or oxen, to the banks of a frozen river. When the spring thaw comes and the ice melts, they are floated down the river to an awaiting sawmill.

However, in most modernized countries around the world, logging has become a highly mechanized process, with felling achieved through the use of chainsaws or even, on plantations where trees are harvested en masse, with a machine that is capable of cutting down multiple trees in a single motion. The logs are transported through the use of motorized vehicles, including trucks, tractors and, in some cases in particularly remote areas, helicopters. While this use of modern technology is not at all surprising and undoubtedly offers countless benefits to logging companies, it has contributed to the serious environmental problem of overlogging.

Overlogging can be defined as the overexploitation of forests as a natural resource that is unsustainable and has the potential to lead to both irrecoverable deforestation and the permanent destruction of wildlife habitats. However, while the ease of cutting down, cutting up, and transporting trees created by the use of heavy machinery and modern methods has encouraged overlogging in some areas, it is by no means the sole cause of the problem. Overlogging, along with a number of other forms of environmental degradation, is often a partial consequence of subsidies, which are financial incentives offered by governments in order to encourage or discourage certain commercial activities. In the United States, for example, the National Forest Service uses taxpayer dollars to support logging companies in the engineering and construction of logging roads located in national forests. Although the ultimate intent of granting such subsidies is to contribute to the strengthening of the national economy, in this case and numerous others, environmental groups consider it to be a misuse of government funds.

Consumer demand for certain unsustainable products is another significant factor in overlogging. Disposable tissues, for example, including toilet paper, paper towels, and facial tissues, may be convenient and affordable items that many consumers consider essential to their daily routines, yet their production has become a driving force behind the overlogging that is destroying forests around the world. Although many consumers are now turning to products that do not require wood pulp as part of their manufacturing process, such as facial tissues made from 100 percent bamboo fibers, such alternative products currently represent only a very small percentage of the overall market. And in some parts of the world, overlogging is not strictly a byproduct of capitalism and consumerism. In rural China, for example, it is the demand for wood to be used as fuel in households that is causing excessive logging to occur.

The effects of overlogging on the world's forests is severe and widespread, as once-forested areas are reduced to brushlands that offer little shelter to indigenous wildlife and are susceptible to flooding. ■(A) The consequences of overlogging can sometimes be mitigated by requiring logging companies to earmark a portion of their earnings for reforestation. ■(B) This may include activities such as the planting of biologically diverse and regionally appropriate saplings in deforested areas. ■(C) Although not a solution to the problem of overlogging, reforestation can have a positive impact on both regional biodiversity and the quality of life enjoyed by the local population. ■(D)

1 The word "they" in the passage refers to

(A) loggers
(B) the logs
(C) sleds
(D) the banks

2 According to paragraph 3, why does the US government give money to logging companies to build roads?

(A) To promote tourism in national parks
(B) To speed up technological development
(C) To bolster their reforestation efforts
(D) To make the nation financially stronger

3 Which of the following best expresses the essential information in the highlighted sentence in the passage? Incorrect answer choices change the meaning in important ways or leave out essential information.

(A) Along with destroying the Earth's forest, overlogging drives up the demand of household items.
(B) Despite their convenience, disposable tissues contribute significantly to global deforestation.
(C) Although people enjoy the convenience of paper products, buying them contributes to overlogging.
(D) By using disposable tissues instead of other paper products, consumers can help prevent overlogging.

4 The word "byproduct" in the passage is closest in meaning to

(A) indicator
(B) opposite
(C) consequence
(D) competitor

5 Which of the following can be inferred from paragraph 4 about rural China?

(A) There is much local opposition to logging activity.
(B) Biodiversity has been improved by reforestation.
(C) Overlogging has been worsened by modernization.
(D) People burn firewood to keep their homes warm.

6 All of the following are mentioned in paragraph 5 about reforestation EXCEPT:

(A) It can be funded by logging company profits.
(B) It has been enhanced by mechanization.
(C) It involves planting young trees outdoors.
(D) It improves the lives of the local residents.

7 Look at the four squares (■) that indicate where the following sentence could be added to the passage.

Fortunately, this is not always an irreversible situation.

Where would the sentence best fit? Select a square (■) to add the sentence to the passage.

8 **Directions**: An introductory sentence for a brief summary of the passage is provided below. Complete the summary by selecting the THREE answer choices that express the most important ideas in the passage. Some sentences do not belong in the summary because they express ideas that are not presented in the passage or are minor ideas in the passage. **This question is worth 2 points.**

> Drag your answer choices to the spaces where they belong. To review the passage, select **View Passage**.

Logging is the practice of cutting down trees and bringing them to a sawmill.

```
┌──────────────────────────────────────────────────────────────┐
│                                                                │
└──────────────────────────────────────────────────────────────┘
┌──────────────────────────────────────────────────────────────┐
│                                                                │
└──────────────────────────────────────────────────────────────┘
┌──────────────────────────────────────────────────────────────┐
│                                                                │
└──────────────────────────────────────────────────────────────┘
```

Answer Choices

A Government subsidies to logging companies and the use of unsustainable products are two factors that encourage overlogging.

B Facial tissues that are made from bamboo rather than wood pulp are an environmentally friendly alternative.

C Building logging roads in national parks can lessen the damage caused by the heavy machinery of logging companies.

D The modernization of logging techniques, including the use of mechanical devices, has contributed to overlogging.

E The negative effects of overlogging can be partially offset by reforestation activities such as planting trees.

F Overlogging is more likely to take place in colder regions where loggers usually transport logs after the spring thaw.

The Role of Play in Child Development

Modern parents and educators now view play as an essential component of children's development, providing them with a way to stay active and healthy while simultaneously learning social skills and enjoying time spent alone or with their peers. However, when it comes to developmental benefits, not all forms of play are created equal. It is important to ensure that a significant portion of children's leisure time is dedicated to freely chosen play.

Freely chosen play comprises a wide variety of activities that share the quality of allowing children to make their own decisions about the play and to control the direction in which it goes. This requires that they rely on their own instincts, interests, and imagination without being steered or encouraged by a parent or other adult, either directly or indirectly. Perhaps the defining feature of freely chosen play is the fact that there is no right or wrong way to engage in it. Children require this type of unstructured play from the moment they are born all the way up until their teenage years in order to optimize their physical and mental health, as well as to ensure that they acquire sufficient life skills to thrive as successful adults.

Play in general equips children with the tools they will need for future success in three fundamental ways: mentally, physically, and socially. ■(A) In terms of mental development, play provides children with opportunities to strengthen their confidence, independence, and curiosity. ■(B) Perhaps most importantly, it forces them to cope with challenging situations. ■(C) Physically, the benefits of certain types of play are obvious—when taking part in enjoyable activities that involve running, jumping, throwing, or catching, kids are taking important steps toward developing their agility, stamina, and coordination. ■(D)

Finally, play that involves interaction with other children helps kids develop the types of social skills that will allow them to build healthy, rewarding relationships as they grow older. Although group play invariably involves conflicts, disagreement, and perhaps even tears, parents must learn not to discount these types of incidents as purely negative, no matter how unpleasant they may be when they occur. These moments of discord go hand in hand with times of harmony such as sharing and taking turns during play, and they teach kids to explore their feelings, deal with powerful emotions, and express themselves effectively.

Play can also be a means through which parents interact with their children in a fun and relaxing manner that helps strengthen familial bonds. However, it is important that when taking part in or simply supporting the play activities of their children, parents pay careful attention not to control the direction the play takes or to impose rules or limitations on it, except for those required to maintain a certain standard of safety. The reason is that play is, at its fundamental core, about freedom and choice; having an adult make all of the decisions will strip the experience of much of its innocent joy and leave the child bereft of developmental benefits.

As part of their play, it is not uncommon for children to create challenges for themselves and to intentionally introduce an element of uncertainty. Although in certain situations and under some circumstances this may create a level of risk that parents wish to avoid, this too is an integral part of play. Through it, children are able to test themselves and determine exactly what their own limits are, while learning how to deal with risky situations, a skill that will inevitably prove useful later in life.

1 The word "simultaneously" in the passage is closest in meaning to

(A) at the same time
(B) in a strange way
(C) with some doubt
(D) for a good reason

2 According to paragraph 2, which of the following is NOT true about freely chosen play?

(A) The children themselves determine how it unfolds.
(B) There is no correct or incorrect way of engaging in it.
(C) Parents are needed to guide children in the right direction.
(D) It should be enjoyed by children from birth until their teens.

3 Which of the following can be inferred about children who do NOT experience unstructured play?

(A) They can create their own structured play.
(B) They will be more focused on schoolwork.
(C) They have less of a chance of being injured.
(D) They are more likely to struggle as adults.

4 The author discusses conflicts during play in paragraph 4 in order to

(A) warn parents about a possible consequence of unstructured play
(B) suggest that freely choosing the direction of play can be risky
(C) explain how both good and bad moments in play have benefits
(D) compare two different types of play commonly enjoyed by children

5 The word "bereft" in the passage is closest in meaning to

(A) deprived
(B) assured
(C) replaced
(D) enhanced

6 According to paragraph 6, which of the following can children learn through play?

(A) what to do in a frustrating environment
(B) what they can and cannot do
(C) how to follow the rules of the game
(D) how to impress their peers with their abilities

7 Look at the four squares (■) that indicate where the following sentence could be added to the passage.

All of these physical skills will later be essential in a myriad of daily situations above and beyond the playing field.

Where would the sentence best fit? Select a square (■) to add the sentence to the passage.

8 **Directions**: An introductory sentence for a brief summary of the passage is provided below. Complete the summary by selecting the THREE answer choices that express the most important ideas in the passage. Some sentences do not belong in the summary because they express ideas that are not presented in the passage or are minor ideas in the passage. **This question is worth 2 points.**

> Drag your answer choices to the spaces where they belong. To review the passage, select **View Passage**.

Today, play is considered to be a vital part of a child's development.

```
┌─────────────────────────────────────────────────────┐
│                                                       │
└─────────────────────────────────────────────────────┘
┌─────────────────────────────────────────────────────┐
│                                                       │
└─────────────────────────────────────────────────────┘
┌─────────────────────────────────────────────────────┐
│                                                       │
└─────────────────────────────────────────────────────┘
```

Answer Choices

A A strictly regulated balance of structured and unstructured play will provide the most advantages to children.

B Some of the play children engage in should be freely chosen to ensure that they learn the skills needed to succeed in life.

C Freely chosen play can help children develop useful skills, but only if their parents provide clear boundaries.

D Brief periods of play can be enjoyable for parents who choose to participate in it with their children.

E Parents should allow children to make their own decisions during play and should not worry about occasional conflicts.

F Play provides children with important benefits that can be mental, physical, or social in nature.

Agriculture and Population Growth

The rapid growth of the human population during the Holocene epoch was primarily fueled by a shift from the nomadic lifestyle of hunter-gatherer tribes to settled agricultural communities. These communities focused on producing and storing easily preservable food, contributing significantly to the population surge. Accompanying this population increase was the global emergence of new socioeconomic systems that had two beneficial effects on farming communities: first, they ensured a higher caloric return from each unit of land that was being farmed; and second, they created an enhanced capacity for the distribution of great quantities of food to large numbers of people.

The development of agriculture, however, did not necessarily have an immediate and powerful impact on every culture, nor did it uniformly affect all regions of the globe in its earliest stages, as some communities moved much more slowly toward a reliance on farming than others, with some even continuing to focus on foraging as their primary means of acquiring food. Based on available archeological evidence, it would seem that a common feature of many ancient communities was the employment of food-acquisition strategies that combined certain elements of both foraging and farming.

Along with an increase in populations, perhaps the most notable effect of the transition to an agricultural society could be seen in the impact it had on the natural environment surrounding early settlements, which underwent significant modification in order to better meet human needs. ■(A) It has been suggested that the advent of such landscape transformation efforts can serve to delineate the border between the end of the Holocene epoch, which is said to have begun approximately 12,000 years ago, and the beginning of what has been proposed as the current epoch, known as the Anthropocene. ■(B) Many experts have actually rejected the very concept of the Anthropocene, instead continuing to view the Holocene as the current epoch. ■(C) Either way, this negative human impact on the physical environment resulted in a variety of problems, including deforestation and soil erosion, both of which plagued early agricultural communities and caused them great harm. ■(D)

Despite this, agricultural systems continued to be improved and implemented, and, as a direct result, populations continued to grow. Societies became more and more complex, as politically distinct states began to form, and large urban centers sprouted up all across the world. Yet another negative consequence of the development of agriculture was a worsening of the social inequality that existed within these ancient civilizations, which were nevertheless able to greatly expand their production of essential crops and continue to distribute food to their growing populations.

Even with this overall increased availability of food, the rapid increase in the number of people was accompanied by an increase in sickness, which in turn caused a decrease in the average human lifespan. Although the misery brought about by all of this disease and premature death did not bring human population growth to a halt, it likely had the effect of slowing it down somewhat, as did a range of logistical difficulties related to dealing with a suddenly expanded population, such as food shortages and a lack of other basic resources. All of these potential obstacles to continued population growth, however, were eventually circumvented through technological advancements and cultural innovations.

Today, with advances in technology and medicine taking place at a faster rate than ever before, many of agriculture's less desirable effects have been more or less counteracted, allowing our planet's population to continue growing in leaps and bounds. As of the beginning of 2024, the global population was estimated to stand at more than eight billion individuals.

1 Which of the following best expresses the essential information in the highlighted sentence in the passage? Incorrect answer choices change the meaning in important ways or leave out essential information.

(A) The population increase caused a change in the focus of socioeconomic systems from food production to food distribution.
(B) As people began to move away from farming communities, two new socioeconomic systems were needed to protect the agricultural industry.
(C) Despite an increase in the caloric value of farmed crops, the new socioeconomic systems could not deliver food to enough people.
(D) New socioeconomic systems increased the overall amount of calories in the food produced through farming and helped deliver it to large populations.

2 According to paragraph 2, which of the following is true about foraging?

(A) It replaced farming as a means of food acquisition.
(B) It had a powerful impact on ancient economies.
(C) It took place in only a handful of the world's regions.
(D) It was used alongside farming by ancient people.

3 The word "delineate" in the passage is closest in meaning to

(A) weaken
(B) discuss
(C) define
(D) cross

4 Which of the following can be inferred from paragraph 4 about social inequality?

(A) It existed before the population growth caused by agriculture.
(B) It was reduced by the introduction of political organizations.
(C) It caused many people to transition from foraging to farming.
(D) It prevented average people from obtaining enough nutrition.

5 Why does the author mention "the average human lifespan" in paragraph 5?

(A) To show how an increased access to food benefited people
(B) To emphasize a negative consequence of population growth
(C) To suggest that a sharp reduction in disease had taken place
(D) To explain why farming was needed to prevent food shortages

6 The word "it" in the passage refers to

(A) the misery
(B) premature death
(C) human population growth
(D) a halt

7 Look at the four squares (■) that indicate where the following sentence could be added to the passage.

It must be noted, however, that this idea has not been widely accepted.

Where would the sentence best fit? Select a square (■) to add the sentence to the passage.

8 **Directions**: An introductory sentence for a brief summary of the passage is provided below. Complete the summary by selecting the THREE answer choices that express the most important ideas in the passage. Some sentences do not belong in the summary because they express ideas that are not presented in the passage or are minor ideas in the passage. **This question is worth 2 points.**

> Drag your answer choices to the spaces where they belong. To review the passage, select **View Passage**.

The transition to an agricultural society played a large role in expanding the rate of human population growth.

- [   ]
- [   ]
- [   ]

Answer Choices

A After a sudden increase in the human population, many ancient civilizations were forced to stop foraging and start farming.	D Communities that embraced agriculture made changes to their natural surroundings, which had negative consequences.
B Some experts believe the Holocene epoch is ongoing, but others assert that it has ended and the Anthropocene has begun.	E Innovations and advances in technology were not enough to neutralize the negative effects of agriculture and population growth.
C Agriculture did not instantly have a strong effect everywhere, as foraging continued to play a large role in some areas.	F Increased populations caused more sickness and shorter lifespans, which slowed population growth but did not stop it.

CHAPTER 03

Life & Natural Sciences

Life and natural sciences is a broad field of study that encompasses disciplines related to the understanding of living organisms, their interactions with the environment, and underlying natural phenomena. It fosters a comprehensive understanding of the interconnectedness of various scientific domains.

Vocabulary Preview

abrasion	마모	*syn.* erosion	**crumble**	부스러지다	*syn.* fall apart
accelerate	가속화하다	*syn.* hasten	**deactivate**	정지시키다	
accuracy	정확성		**decayed**	부패한	*syn.* rotten
acquire	얻다	*syn.* obtain	**deploy**	(효율적으로) 활용하다	
altitude	고도		**elude**	~에게 이해되지 않다	
amensalistic	편해 공생의		**embryo**	배아	
anther	꽃밥		**equation**	방정식	
attrition	소모		**eternal**	영원한	*syn.* everlasting
avert	방지하다	*syn.* prevent	**exceed**	초과하다	*syn.* surpass
baffle	당황하게 만들다	*syn.* bewilder	**excrete**	배설하다	
biome	생물군계		**fasten**	고정시키다	*syn.* affix
boost	높이다, 촉진하다		**feasibility**	실현 가능성	
cessation	중단	*syn.* termination	**fern**	양치류	
chromosome	염색체		**ferocity**	맹렬함, 흉포함	
clonal	복제의		**fertilization**	수정	
collide	충돌하다	*syn.* crash	**fragmentation**	분절증식	
compelling	강력한, 설득력 있는		**fungus**	균류	
concordance	일치		**futility**	헛됨, 무가치	
contradict	부정하다, 반박하다		**flyby**	저공 비행	
crack	균열	*syn.* fissure	**gamete**	생식 세포	

glitch	결함 *syn.* defect	**mutation**	돌연변이
haustorium	기생근	**mutualistic**	상리 공생의
horizon	층위	**niche**	범위
humus	부엽토	**offspring**	자손 *syn.* descendant
imminent	임박한 *syn.* impending	**orbit**	궤도를 돌다
immobile	움직이지 못하는, 부동의	**organelle**	세포 기관
immortal	불멸의 *syn.* undying	**overlook**	간과하다 *syn.* miss
inadvertent	의도하지 않은 *syn.* unintended	**parasitic**	기생의
inexorable	거침 없는 *syn.* unrelenting	**peat**	토탄
inflict	(영향 등을) 가하다	**perpetuate**	영속화하다
integrity	완전한 상태	**perspective**	관점 *syn.* viewpoint
intricate	복잡한 *syn.* complicated	**pistil**	암술
juxtaposition	병렬	**proportion**	비율 *syn.* portion
lipid	지방질	**replication**	복제
longevity	장수, 수명	**roam**	배회하다 *syn.* wander
lure	유혹하다 *syn.* entice	**sapling**	어린 나무
manifest	나타나다	**senescence**	노쇠
meticulous	세심한 *syn.* careful	**stamen**	수술
micro-organism	미생물	**unbridled**	걷잡을 수 없는
mitosis	체세포 분열	**vortex**	소용돌이

PART 2

CHAPTER 03

Soil Formation

The surface of the Earth is covered with a relatively thin layer of soil made up mostly of organic materials and mineral particles derived from the weathering of rocks, along with air, water, and living organisms, all of which are engaged in a slow yet constant interaction. Although often overlooked, soil is an essential component of the planet's ecosystem—it is from the soil that plants obtain the nutrients they need to grow and reproduce, and these plants are the main food source of many of the Earth's animals, including human beings.

The formation of soil occurs over time, resulting in two main types: the topsoil, which is the layer of soil closest to the surface, and the subsoil, which is located directly beneath it. ■ (A) These can be further divided into smaller layers known as horizons. ■ (B) Most of the Earth's soils contain three horizons. The A horizon is located within the topsoil, and it is rich in humus, nutrients, and organic matter; this is the layer where the highest level of biological activity takes place, as it is home to the slowly spreading roots of trees and plants, along with burrowing insects, earthworms, and micro-organisms. ■ (C) Beneath the A horizon lies the B horizon, a layer of subsoil rich in clay. It is not as fertile as the A horizon, it is lighter in color, and it is home to far less biological activity, but it is here that the greatest amount of moisture can be found. ■ (D) The C horizon is the next level down, and it is made up primarily of a layer of rock that, as it is gradually weathered by natural forces, serves as a source of much of the soil found in the A and B horizons.

Some of this weathering is physical in nature, such as the abrasion that occurs when chunks of rock collide with one another. Other forms of physical weathering include changes in temperature and the formation of frost. There are also chemical weathering processes that accelerate the breakdown of rock into soil, which occur when the minerals found within rock react with water, air, or chemicals. Finally, there is biological weathering—this is the breakdown of rocks by living creatures. The activity of burrowing animals, for example, can allow water or air to penetrate rock, gradually causing it to crumble; the roots of plants also contribute to weathering, as they work their way into cracks in the surface of rock, expanding over time and leading to splits in the rock's structure.

As the minerals from this weathered rock form the basis of soil, the type of rock that has been broken down will have a strong influence on the characteristics of the soil it creates. Soils that have been formed from granite, for example, tend to be sandy and are not particularly fertile, while soils created by weathered basalt are often quite fertile and full of clay, provided the conditions under which they form are sufficiently moist.

Along with these minerals, soil contains high levels of decayed organic matter. When plants die, their stems, leaves, and roots return to the soil from which they grew; this process also occurs when they are consumed by animals and then excreted in the form of waste. And when these same animals die, their bodies too will be broken down and transformed into a component of the soil. As these animal and plant remains, along with animal waste, are consumed by the bacteria, worms, and fungi living in the soil, they are eventually transformed into organic matter such as humus, peat or charcoal, causing the composition and characteristics of the soil to undergo significant changes.

1 Which of the sentences below best expresses the essential information in the highlighted sentence? Incorrect answer choices change the meaning in important ways or leave out essential information.

(A) Despite requiring plants to thrive, soil can be created by the bodies and waste of certain animals.

(B) Soil is important because plants cannot survive without it, and people and animals need to eat plants.

(C) Unlike most plants and animals, human beings rely on soil to provide them with the food they need.

(D) The least essential component of soil is the nutrients it contains, but few people are aware of this.

2 The word "it" in the passage refers to

(A) time
(B) the topsoil
(C) the surface
(D) the subsoil

3 Paragraph 2 suggests which of the following about topsoil?

(A) It is more fertile than subsoil.
(B) It is less common than subsoil.
(C) It forms less quickly than subsoil.
(D) It contains more clay than subsoil.

4   **Select the TWO answer choices** that are mentioned in paragraph 2 as being features of the A horizon that make it distinct from other horizons. **To receive credit, you must select TWO answer choices.**

(A) plenty of organic matter
(B) the presence of greatest amount of moisture
(C) the highest level of biological activity
(D) a source of much of the soil

5   The word "penetrate" in the passage is closest in meaning to

(A) escape from
(B) pass into
(C) fall under
(D) go around

6   According to paragraph 4, some soils made from basalt are fertile and full of clay because

(A) they are near a layer of granite
(B) they contain little organic matter
(C) they can be found deep underground
(D) they form in a wet environment

7   Look at the four squares (■) that indicate where the following sentence could be added to the passage.

Because of its composition, which includes a great deal of organic materials, it is darker in color than the other horizons.

Where would the sentence best fit? Select a square (■) to add the sentence to the passage.

8 **Directions**: An introductory sentence for a brief summary of the passage is provided below. Complete the summary by selecting the THREE answer choices that express the most important ideas in the passage. Some sentences do not belong in the summary because they express ideas that are not presented in the passage or are minor ideas in the passage. **This question is worth 2 points.**

Drag your answer choices to the spaces where they belong. To review the passage, select **View Passage**.

A layer of soil covers the surface of the Earth.

-
-
-

Answer Choices

A The weathering of rocks, which is caused by natural forces, forms the mineral component of soil.	D After plants and animals die, their bodies decay and become the organic matter that makes up part of the soil.
B Topsoil contains a large number of rocks, which slowly break down when they collide with one another.	E Burrowing insects, earthworms, and micro-organisms can be found in A horizon.
C The Earth's soil can be divided into two main parts, topsoil and subsoil, which usually contain three horizons.	F The soil found in areas that are moist are more likely to possess a thick layer of rock between their topsoil and subsoil.

Interactions Among Species

Across both the plant and animal kingdoms, biologists have identified numerous cases in which a pair of species existing in close physical proximity have evolved to interact in very specific ways. Generally speaking, these interspecies relationships can be categorized as being either mutualistic, parasitic, or amensalistic.

Simply put, mutualism refers to a relationship between two species in which both species receive significant benefits. When it comes to plants, mutualism plays a key role in ensuring that terrestrial ecosystems remain healthy and functioning, mostly due to the fact that approximately 80 percent of all land plants rely on a mutualistic relationship with various species of fungi living in their root systems beneath the surface of the soil. This particular mutualistic relationship involves the exchange of inorganic materials for organic ones. More specifically, the fungi provide the plants with a variety of minerals they have extracted from the soil, while the plants share the sugars or lipids they have generated through the process of photosynthesis with the fungi. It is also possible for plant species to establish mutualistic relationships with animal species, a type of situation that can be most easily observed in plants that bear fruit that is eaten by certain animals. The animals receive the nutrients provided by the fruit they consume and in turn furnish the plants with an effective method of dispersing their seeds, which are excreted in the animals' waste.

Parasitism, on the other hand, is a markedly more one-sided relationship between two species, one of which receives benefits at the expense of the other. Parasitic plants are found in nearly every biome on the planet, represented by approximately 4,500 species that make up about one percent of all flowering plants. These parasitic plants all share the unique characteristic of possessing a specialized organ, called a haustorium, that is capable of penetrating the soft tissues of another plant, thereby fastening the two plants together and allowing the parasite to extract a variety of resources from the host, which can include water, nitrogen, carbon, and sugars. The negative effects that can be inflicted on the host plants by their parasites are wide-ranging, but the most common consequences are severely stunted growth and a higher than usual mortality rate. Some parasitic plants have even evolved the ability to locate a suitable host by detecting certain chemicals emitted into the air by the host's shoots or into the soil by its roots.

Much like parasitism, amensalism is an asymmetric relationship between a pair of species in which one of the two is ultimately harmed or killed. The difference between the two is that in amensalism, the unharmed species receives no direct benefit from the relationship. ■(A) There are two basic types of amensalism in the world of plants, the first being rooted in competition, as a larger or more powerful organism uses its size or strength to prevent a smaller, weaker rival from acquiring an essential resource. ■(B) In some cases, the root system of the mature tree may also be capable of absorbing all of the nutrients and water in the surrounding soil, leaving none for the sapling. While the mature tree is not affected by this interaction, the sapling is likely to die. ■(C) In the other type of amensalism, known as antagonism, one organism actively deploys specialized chemicals to kill or damage the other. ■(D) This can be observed in the interactions between a species of tree known as the black walnut and the herbaceous plants that grow within its root zone, in which the tree secretes a substance into the soil that is fatal to the plants.

1   Why does the author mention "photosynthesis" in paragraph 2?

(A) To show how organisms in mutualism receive benefits
(B) To explain the process that allows certain plants to bear fruit
(C) To suggest that plant species have an advantage over animals
(D) To illustrate a vital role played by the root systems of fungi

2   According to paragraph 2, which of the following is true of mutualism?

(A) A small proportion of plants rely on it.
(B) It often involves plants providing minerals and taking sugar.
(C) Plants can have mutualistic relationships with animals.
(D) Only one participant is impacted by the interaction.

3   The word "stunted" in the passage is closest in meaning to

(A) exposed
(B) hindered
(C) accelerated
(D) mimicked

4 According to paragraph 3, which of the following is true of parasitic plants?

(A) They kill off a small percentage of flowering plants each year.
(B) They do not grow as quickly as most non-parasitic plants.
(C) They produce large amounts of resources to attract hosts.
(D) They can be observed in virtually every biome across the globe.

5 The word "asymmetric" in the passage is closest in meaning to

(A) hostile
(B) abnormal
(C) enduring
(D) uneven

6 Which of the following can be inferred from paragraph 4 about the black walnut tree?

(A) There is usually little vegetation growing at its base.
(B) It is often taller and wider than other nearby trees.
(C) It carefully protects the saplings of its own species.
(D) There may be many different kinds of herbaceous plants near its roots.

7 Look at the four squares (■) that indicate where the following sentence could be added to the passage.

For example, when a sapling begins to grow next to a mature tree of another species, the mature tree may cast a shadow that will deprive the sapling of the sunlight it needs in order to survive.

Where would the sentence best fit? Select a square (■) to add the sentence to the passage.

8 **Directions**: An introductory sentence for a brief summary of the passage is provided below. Complete the summary by selecting the THREE answer choices that express the most important ideas in the passage. Some sentences do not belong in the summary because they express ideas that are not presented in the passage or are minor ideas in the passage. **This question is worth 2 points.**

Drag your answer choices to the spaces where they belong. To review the passage, select **View Passage.**

There are three basic types of interspecies relationships: mutualism, parasitism, and amensalism.

-

-

-

Answer Choices

A In mutualism, two species engage in a relationship from which both receive benefits.

B Amensalistic relationships are interactions in which both species are either harmed or killed.

C Parasitic plants draw benefits from another type of plant in a way that causes harm to the second species.

D Mutualistic species compete for the same resources, but only one is ultimately successful.

E Amensalism is a relationship where one species is harmed without directly benefiting the other.

F In parasitism, an animal species provides benefits to a plant species, such as when bees pollinate flowers.

Telomeres and Telomerase

The human body is composed of numerous components, comprising trillions of specialized cells, and each of these cells contains a crucial organelle called the nucleus. Within these nuclei, there are chromosomes—sophisticated assemblies of thread-like structures housing genetic blueprints transmitted across generations. Commonly referred to as our "genes," this genetic code encompasses four distinct biological compounds, identified as nucleobases or simply "bases," intricately pairing and linking to form the elongated, spiraled chain-like structures constituting our DNA. In the course of mitosis, the cellular replication mechanism, this genetic material undergoes duplication, with one-half remaining within the original cell and the other half being transferred to the newly formed cell. To safeguard the precision and integrity of this crucial process, our chromosomes are endowed with protective telomeres, which help prevent glitches and errors.

Protective telomeres, situated at the terminal ends of our chromosomes, are intricate structures that constitute a DNA sequence consisting of up to 15,000 repeated base pairs. They play a pivotal role in the meticulous regulation of mitosis, preventing the inadvertent loss of chromosomal DNA and averting the accidental fusion of chromosomes. The consequences of such occurrences could be catastrophic, introducing fatal flaws in the replicated DNA. Thus, telomeres emerge as indispensable guardians, ensuring the precision of cellular replication. But during regulation, the telomeres are prone to suffering damage. With each division of their host cells, telomeres experience a gradual attrition of up to 200 base pairs. Over time, this cumulative loss progressively diminishes the telomere's length until it reaches a threshold known as "critical length," signaling the cessation of replication and inevitably leading to cell death. This erosion, however, encounters a counteracting force in the form of telomerase—a remarkable enzyme comprising RNA and proteins. Possessing the unique capability to append base pair sequences to our telomeres, telomerase acts as a protective shield, elongating these structures and thereby staving off the imminent onset of cell death.

Diverging from the widespread presence of telomeres, the operational domain of telomerase is notably confined within specific niches of the human body. Its activity is predominantly observed in fetal tissue and cancerous tumors, as well as in germ cells, which possess the unique potential to evolve into either sperm or eggs. Outside these specialized realms, it infrequently manifests in the body's other cells, and when it is present, its activity is minimal. This scenario allows the unbridled erosion of telomeres to transpire, consequently facilitating the aging and ultimate demise of cells—a phenomenon termed senescence. In stark contrast, cells with more active telomerase experience what is more or less a balance between the opposing forces of addition and erosion. This balance effectively halts the relentless attrition of telomeres, thereby preserving their length. Theoretically, such cells possess the capability to perpetuate growth and division indefinitely, earning them the colloquial designation of "immortal cells." This contrasting behavior underscores the pivotal role of telomerase in cellular longevity, presenting a fascinating juxtaposition between the inexorable march of senescence in its absence and the potential perpetuity encapsulated in its presence.

In light of this, the notion of immortal cells captivates scientists studying the causes and consequences of human aging, as well as those investigating cancer cell behavior in the interest of potentially eliminating this deadly disease. ■(A) Telomerase in human cancer cells exhibits activity up to 20 times higher than it does in normal body cells. ■(B) Discovering a way to deactivate telomerase activity could significantly enhance the feasibility of treating and potentially curing cancer. ■(C) Moreover, there is optimistic anticipation that identifying an on-off switch for telomerase might, in the distant future, extend the human lifespan indefinitely. ■(D) This prospect is likened to a scientific equivalent of the mythological fountain of youth, offering hope for groundbreaking advancements in the field.

1   Which of the sentences below best expresses the essential information in the highlighted sentence? Incorrect answer choices change the meaning in important ways or leave out essential information.

(A) Our genetic code, called genes, is known to include nucleobases that form the entire DNA of human beings.
(B) Genes can be divided into four parts of the biological blueprint, which are called nucleobases, and eventually build DNA structures.
(C) Our genes are composed of four distinct nucleobases that pair and link to create the spiraled structures of our DNA.
(D) The genetic code of human beings appears to be made up of four compounds that convert themselves into long and spiral shapes.

2   According to paragraph 1, what is the role of telomeres during mitosis?

(A) It prevents flaws and errors.
(B) It helps create multiple versions of cells.
(C) It protects the DNA that remains in a gene.
(D) It makes chromosomes grow as fast as possible.

3   The word "constitute" in the passage is closest in meaning to

(A) depend on
(B) make up
(C) separate from
(D) differ from

4 Paragraph 2 suggests which of the following about cell death?

    (A) After they die, cells can be revived.

    (B) It never occurs in host cells in important positions.

    (C) Telomerase accelerates the end of cells.

    (D) It can be caused by a gradual decrease in telomeres.

5 The word "it" in the passage refers to

    (A) the human body

    (B) telomerase

    (C) fetal tissue

    (D) sperm

6 Why does the author mention "immortal cells" in paragraph 3?

    (A) To explain how difficult it is to balance attrition and erosion

    (B) To compare cellular growth and cellular demise

    (C) To illustrate the function of telomerase

    (D) To introduce a way people can survive cancer

7 Look at the four squares (■) that indicate where the following sentence could be added to the passage.

This heightened telomerase activity significantly contributes to the resilience of cancer, challenging all known medical treatments and potential cures, none of which have proven reliably effective so far.

Where would the sentence best fit? Select a square (■) to add the sentence to the passage.

8   **Directions**: An introductory sentence for a brief summary of the passage is provided below. Complete the summary by selecting the THREE answer choices that express the most important ideas in the passage. Some sentences do not belong in the summary because they express ideas that are not presented in the passage or are minor ideas in the passage. **This question is worth 2 points.**

> Drag your answer choices to the spaces where they belong. To review the passage, select **View Passage.**

Telomeres and telomerase play important roles in cellular replication.

```
┌─────────────────────────────────────────────────┐
│                                                   │
└─────────────────────────────────────────────────┘
┌─────────────────────────────────────────────────┐
│                                                   │
└─────────────────────────────────────────────────┘
┌─────────────────────────────────────────────────┐
│                                                   │
└─────────────────────────────────────────────────┘
```

Answer Choices

A Telomeres protect our chromosomes, but they get shorter each time a cell divides, which eventually leads to cell death.

B Cells without any active telomerase will keep growing and dividing indefinitely, which makes them "immortal" in a way.

C Cells depend on telomeres to prevent mitosis from occurring too rapidly, which can lead to the formation of cancerous tumors.

D Telomerase, an enzyme that prevents telomeres from getting too short, is found mostly in fetal tissue, cancerous tumors, and germ cells.

E Telomeres start out with about 200 base pairs, but telomerase continuously adds base pairs until the cell dies.

F Telomerase is more active in cancer cells than in normal cells, so finding a way to turn it off could help in the treatment of cancer.

Age of the Universe

In the past, scientists did not have a concrete grasp on the age of the universe, as they had neither the means to make the necessary measurements nor the knowledge to formulate accurate theories. In fact, all the way up until the beginning of the 20th century, the majority of the world's most respected scientists believed that the universe was eternal and existed in something they referred to as a "steady state," meaning that it had never experienced any large-scale changes and never would. Therefore, in their eyes, any attempt to put an age on the universe was an exercise in futility.

Acceptance of the idea that the universe was actually millions, or even billions, of years old first began to take hold in the 18th century, but it was not until the mid-19th century that the first formal scientific theories suggesting that the universe was indeed finite were formulated. These were based on studies of thermodynamics and the concept of entropy, which contradicted the notion of an infinite universe by indicating that within one everything would be the same temperature, which would therefore preclude even the possibility of the existence of stars or life. In 1915, when Albert Einstein published his groundbreaking theory of general relativity, he did so under the prevailing assumption that the universe was infinite and existed in a steady state, later using the theory to construct a static cosmological model of the universe. Because of this fundamental error, he found it necessary to add a repulsive force to his equations that would counterbalance the effects of gravity and account for the presumed steady state of the universe.

This view of a static universe, however, was soon challenged by the work of Edwin Hubble, an American astronomer who, while observing what were thought to be clouds of dust and gas within the Milky Way, realized he was actually gazing at galaxies outside of our own. ■(A) These galaxies were determined to be immense in size and extremely far away; further analysis suggested that they were steadily moving away from the Milky Way, and that the farther away these galaxies were, the faster they were moving, all of which was compelling evidence that the universe is not static at all and is actually expanding. ■(B) The very first scientific estimate of the age of the universe emerged from a calculation that sought to determine when all of the matter in the universe first began moving outward and away from a single point. ■(C) However, due to the fact that Hubble's rough calculation of the distance of the galaxies he observed was far too conservative, the number that he came up with as the age of the universe was much too low. ■(D)

The most accurate method currently employed by today's astronomers when they endeavor to establish a measurement of the universe's age involves direct observations of the universe in an early state, an approach that has yielded an approximate age of 13.8 billion years. Based on the concordance of numerous studies, some of which have included the monitoring of microwave background radiation, the range of uncertainty for this measurement has been reduced to a mere 20 million years in either direction, meaning that it can be considered impressively precise. It is by measuring background radiation in space that the post-Big Bang cooling time of the universe can be estimated, which, when combined with measurements of the rate at which the universe is expanding, can provide an approximate age of the universe. The narrow range of this estimated age corresponds with that of the oldest observable star (from the perspective of Earth) in the universe, further boosting confidence in its accuracy.

1   According to paragraph 2, Einstein needed to add a repulsive force to his equation because

(A) galaxies outside the Milky Way had been found
(B) it was based on a fundamental misconception
(C) he no longer believed the universe was infinite
(D) the concept of gravity was not yet understood

2   Which of the following can be inferred from paragraph 3 about Edwin Hubble?

(A) He was primarily focused on studying the Milky Way.
(B) He discovered that the universe is static and unchanging.
(C) He made groundbreaking observations of galaxies outside the Milky Way.
(D) He disproved Albert Einstein's theory of general relativity.

3   The word "monitoring" in the passage is closest in meaning to

(A) rejection
(B) sequencing
(C) precision
(D) tracking

4 Which of the sentences below best expresses the essential information in the highlighted sentence? Incorrect answer choices change the meaning in important ways or leave out essential information.

(A) It is only by learning the approximate age of the universe that scientists can understand the reason it cooled off and began to expand so quickly after the Big Bang took place.

(B) The age of the universe can be estimated by measuring radiation in space, and then determining how long it took to cool off after the Big Bang and how fast it is expanding.

(C) Despite measuring the radiation caused by the Big Bang when the universe first began to expand, scientists were unable to accurately estimate the universe's age.

(D) Many things can be learned by studying the Big Bang, including how hot the universe will eventually become, how fast it is expanding, and how old it is.

5 The word "its" in the passage refers to

(A) this estimated age
(B) the oldest observable star
(C) Earth
(D) the universe

6 How is paragraph 4 related to paragraph 3?

(A) It explains the origins of the incorrect information paragraph 3.
(B) It shows the scientific impossibility of the theory in paragraph 3.
(C) It provides the essential details of the calculation in paragraph 3.
(D) It describes the modern application of the discovery in paragraph 3.

7 Look at the four squares (■) that indicate where the following sentence could be added to the passage.

Despite this, the groundwork for today's more precise estimates was laid by the formula derived from his observations, now known as Hubble's Law.

Where would the sentence best fit? Select a square (■) to add the sentence to the passage.

8 **Directions**: An introductory sentence for a brief summary of the passage is provided below. Complete the summary by selecting the THREE answer choices that express the most important ideas in the passage. Some sentences do not belong in the summary because they express ideas that are not presented in the passage or are minor ideas in the passage. **This question is worth 2 points.**

Drag your answer choices to the spaces where they belong. To review the passage, select **View Passage**.

It was not until recently that scientists were able to estimate the age of the universe.

Answer Choices

A Albert Einstein made two great breakthroughs—the theory of relativity and a cosmological model of the universe.	D The discovery of distant universes beyond the Milky Way caused scientists to question the Big Bang theory.
B The observations of Edwin Hubble led to the understanding that the universe is dynamic and expanding.	E Studies showed that the further away objects in space are from one another, the faster they move in opposite directions.
C In the past, scientists believed the universe was infinite and existed in a steady state without change.	F By measuring radiation, scientists estimated the universe to be 13.8 billion years old.

Plant Reproduction

It is through the act of reproduction that plants and animals produce offspring, thereby passing their genes on to a new generation and ensuring the continuation of their respective species. When it comes to reproduction, however, there is a notable difference between flora and fauna. Whereas a fox can freely roam a forest in search of a suitable mate, plants are for the most part immobile and therefore must overcome greater challenges in order to proliferate. Although plant reproduction can take on numerous forms, each of these can be classified as either sexual reproduction or asexual reproduction.

■(A) Sexual reproduction entails the fusion of gametes from two different sources. ■(B) In plants that produce flowers, it is within these that the reproductive organs are contained. ■(C) The anther, a small cap atop a stalk called the stamen, produces grains of pollen, each of which contains a set of male chromosomes. ■(D) In order to initiate reproduction, these grains must attach themselves to the stigma, the sticky top of the pistil, which is where the male and female reproductive cells are brought together. This process is known as pollination. Plants can either self-pollinate—which occurs when the anther and stigma are located in the same flower or in different flowers of the same plant—or cross-pollinate by transferring the pollen from an anther of one plant to a stigma of another.

Cross-pollination can be accomplished in a number of different ways. Some flowering plants rely on other organisms, usually insects such as bees or butterflies, to cross-pollinate, luring them to an awaiting store of sugary nectar via the colors, shapes, and scents of their flowers. As the insects feed, their bodies are coated in a dusting of the stamen's pollen, and they carry it with them to the next flower they visit. Others are pollinated by the wind— these plants can often be identified by their petalless flowers and the large amounts of pollen they produce, both of which serve to expedite the process of reproduction. However it is accomplished, successful pollination culminates in the fertilization of egg cells, which triggers the development of seeds that will eventually grow into a new generation of plants.

Asexual reproduction, on the other hand, is a very different process requiring no assistance from any external forces. New life is created without the fusion of gametes, and for this reason, it results in clonal offspring that are genetic duplicates of the single parent plant, assuming that no mutations occur during the process. Asexual reproduction comprises two main forms, the first being vegetative reproduction, and the second being apomixis. In vegetative reproduction, a portion of the parent plant produces the offspring, such as in the case of budding, wherein repeated cell division concentrated in a single site on the body of the plant forms a bud, which eventually detaches and grows into a clone of the parent. Another form of asexual vegetative reproduction, found most commonly in molds and lichen, is fragmentation. This involves a parent plant splitting apart upon achieving maturation, thereby producing a genetic clone.

The other primary form of asexual reproduction in the plant kingdom, apomixis, can be observed in such common species as Kentucky blue grass and the dandelion. Like sexual reproduction, it involves the development and eventual dispersal of seeds; however, the seeds do not originate from fertilized embryos, and as in all other forms of asexual reproduction, they mature into clones of the parent plant. This type of reproduction is common in some flowering plants and ferns but is rarely found in other types of seed-producing plants.

1   Why does the author mention "a fox" in paragraph 1?

(A) To give an example of a serious danger faced by plants
(B) To emphasize the rarity of asexual reproduction in animals
(C) To explain why some plants need two types of reproduction
(D) To contrast plant reproduction with animal reproduction

2   The word "proliferate" in the passage is closest in meaning to

(A) dominate
(B) migrate
(C) harden
(D) multiply

3   Which of the following can be inferred from paragraph 3 about the stamen?

(A) It is located near the plant's supply of nectar.
(B) It is the same color as the petals of the flower.
(C) It is not required in plants that cross-pollinate.
(D) It cannot produce pollen if it has an anther.

4 The word "expedite" in the passage is closest in meaning to

(A) scatter
(B) transform
(C) accelerate
(D) coordinate

5 According to paragraph 4, which of the following is true about budding?

(A) Large numbers of cells in close proximity split in two.
(B) The parent plant breaks into two parts when it matures.
(C) The participation of certain outside elements is necessary.
(D) A single seed develops from a small amount of pollen grains.

6 According to paragraph 5, which of the following is NOT true of apomixis?

(A) It requires the production of seeds.
(B) It can be either sexual or asexual.
(C) It creates offspring that are clonal.
(D) It is frequently utilized by ferns.

7 Look at the four squares (■) that indicate where the following sentence could be added to the passage.

This ensures that the offspring will differ genetically from both of the parents.

Where would the sentence best fit? Select a square (■) to add the sentence to the passage.

8 **Directions**: An introductory sentence for a brief summary of the passage is provided below. Complete the summary by selecting the THREE answer choices that express the most important ideas in the passage. Some sentences do not belong in the summary because they express ideas that are not presented in the passage or are minor ideas in the passage. **This question is worth 2 points.**

> Drag your answer choices to the spaces where they belong. To review the passage, select **View Passage**.

There are two main forms of plant reproduction: sexual and asexual.

```
┌─────────────────────────────────────────────────────────────┐
│                                                               │
└─────────────────────────────────────────────────────────────┘
┌─────────────────────────────────────────────────────────────┐
│                                                               │
└─────────────────────────────────────────────────────────────┘
┌─────────────────────────────────────────────────────────────┐
│                                                               │
└─────────────────────────────────────────────────────────────┘
```

Answer Choices

A Apomixis is a form of sexual reproduction that involves the dispersal of seeds that mature into genetically diverse offspring.

B In sexual reproduction, a portion of the parent plant breaks away and develops into a genetically identical clone.

C In asexual reproduction, new life is created without the fusion of gametes, resulting in clonal offspring.

D Cross-pollination takes place between two separate plants, while self-pollination involves a single plant.

E Unlike plants, animals wishing to reproduce can move from place to place, searching for a suitable individual to mate with.

F Sexual reproduction in plants involves the fusion of gametes from two different sources and is often facilitated by pollination.

Jupiter's Atmosphere

Jupiter, the largest planet in the solar system and the fifth farthest planet from the Sun, is a gas giant with a mass so large that it exceeds the combined mass of all the other planets in the solar system by a factor of more than two and a half. The planet, which is named for the king of the gods in ancient Roman mythology, is covered in a perpetual layer of clouds made up of ammonia crystals, with an atmosphere that extends downward for approximately 3,000 kilometers beneath this layer.

The ammonia cloud layer itself is believed to have a depth of about 50 kilometers and to be composed of a band of thinner clouds resting atop a band of thicker ones. ■(A) Having detected flashes of lightning in Jupiter's atmosphere, scientists suspect that there may also be a layer of water clouds, somewhat similar to those found in the atmosphere of Earth, hidden directly beneath the ammonia clouds. ■(B) The *Juno* spacecraft, which was launched by NASA in 2011 and has been orbiting Jupiter on a research mission since 2016, has also detected shallow lightning high in the planet's atmosphere. ■(C) Unlike the more powerful lightning below, it seems to be generated by the ammonia clouds. ■(D)

Perhaps the best-known atmospheric feature of Jupiter is the Great Red Spot, a storm that may have been observed by astronomers on Earth as early as 1665 and continues to baffle scientists with its size, longevity, and ferocity. The storm is an enormous vortex rotating in a counterclockwise direction, just south of the planet's equator at a maximum altitude of about eight kilometers above the clouds below. Once deemed larger than Earth and considered a permanent feature of the planet, the Great Red Spot is now believed to be gradually decreasing in size, based on observations made by the Hubble Space Telescope and various space probes that have conducted missions in the vicinity of Jupiter. The exact source of its distinct red color continues to elude science, but the most likely explanation is that it is the result of an ongoing reaction between ammonia and acetylene.

In 2017, another unusual atmospheric feature was discovered on Jupiter, this one located near the planet's north pole and dubbed the "Great Cold Spot" by astronomers. Along with its impressive size of approximately 24,000 kilometers in length and 12,000 kilometers in width, its most noteworthy feature is its temperature, which is estimated to be about 200°C lower than that of its surroundings. While little has been learned about it to date, it is believed to be a giant vortex similar to the Great Red Spot, and despite the fact that its shape and strength change with some regularity, with the entire storm virtually disappearing from time to time, it has remained in the same general area since it was first observed.

As for the atmosphere itself, it has proven to be predominantly made up of molecular hydrogen, accounting for approximately 90 percent of the atmosphere, and helium, which comprises slightly less than 10 percent, a proportion that roughly corresponds with that of the Sun and shows little variation from the composition of the planet as a whole. Nitrogen, sulfur, and noble gas can also be found in Jupiter's atmosphere, but these exist in a relative proportion that exceeds the Sun's by a factor of approximately three. Other chemical compounds that have been found in much smaller amounts include methane, ammonia, and water, with this last element being of great interest to the scientific community. During one of its flybys near the planet's equator, *Juno* took a sample of the atmosphere, the subsequent analysis of which revealed that water molecules make up 0.25 percent of Jupiter's atmosphere.

1 According to paragraph 2, which of the following is true about Jupiter's lightning?

(A) The *Juno* mission had some difficulties detecting it.
(B) It is created by a reaction between two layers of clouds.
(C) There is a very high concentration of ammonia inside it.
(D) There appear to be two types with two different sources.

2 The author discusses "the Hubble Space Telescope" in paragraph 3 in order to

(A) provide the source of some essential information
(B) explain how an atmospheric feature was discovered
(C) suggest that human activity is affecting Jupiter
(D) compare the relative size of two different storms

3 The word "it" in the passage refers to

(A) Jupiter
(B) its distinct red color
(C) science
(D) the most likely explanation

4 The word "dubbed" in the passage is closest in meaning to

    (A) installed

    (B) estimated

    (C) named

    (D) detected

5 Which of the sentences below best expresses the essential information in the highlighted sentence? Incorrect answer choices change the meaning in important ways or leave out essential information.

    (A) The extreme variation between molecular hydrogen and helium is what makes the atmosphere of Jupiter as unstable as the Sun's surface.

    (B) The amounts of hydrogen and helium in Jupiter's atmosphere are very different, whereas on the Sun the two amounts are roughly the same.

    (C) Jupiter's atmosphere is made up mostly of hydrogen and helium, in percentages that are similar to those of both the entire planet and the Sun.

    (D) Jupiter has an atmosphere that contains a lot of hydrogen and little helium, which makes it the planet that most closely resembles the Sun.

6 Which of the following can be inferred from paragraph 5 about the water in Jupiter's atmosphere?

    (A) It was found in the atmosphere in the past but no longer exists.

    (B) It will be the subject of further investigation by space probes.

    (C) It has a different chemical makeup than water found on Earth.

    (D) It increases in amount the closer one gets to Jupiter's equator.

7 Look at the four squares (■) that indicate where the following sentence could be added to the passage.

The electrical discharge generated by this lightning is significantly more powerful than that created by Earth's lightning.

Where would the sentence best fit? Select a square (■) to add the sentence to the passage.

8 **Directions**: An introductory sentence for a brief summary of the passage is provided below. Complete the summary by selecting the THREE answer choices that express the most important ideas in the passage. Some sentences do not belong in the summary because they express ideas that are not presented in the passage or are minor ideas in the passage. **This question is worth 2 points.**

> Drag your answer choices to the spaces where they belong. To review the passage, select **View Passage**.

Jupiter, the largest planet in the solar system, has an interesting atmosphere.

- _____
- _____
- _____

Answer Choices

A	The main component of Jupiter's atmosphere is molecular hydrogen, followed by a much smaller amount of helium.
B	The temperature of Jupiter's atmosphere is much lower than expected and has been decreasing in recent years.
C	*Juno* is a spacecraft that was launched by NASA and is now orbiting Jupiter to study the planet's atmosphere.
D	Scientists have observed a storm known as the Great Red Spot, which has gradually changed in size, in Jupiter's atmosphere.
E	A layer of clouds made of ammonia crystals covers the entire planet, creating lightning.
F	Due to its great distance from the Sun, Jupiter has more water in its atmosphere than any other planet except Earth.

YBM TOEFL 80 ⁺
READING

ACTUAL
TESTS

Erie Canal

It was in the 1780s that a proposal was first floated to construct a canal in upstate New York, running from the Hudson River to Lake Erie, one of the five Great Lakes located on the nation's border with Canada, with a formal survey finally conducted in 1808 and government authorization to begin the project granted in 1817. The main proponent of the project was the governor of New York State, DeWitt Clinton, who viewed the canal as a means of drastically reducing the cost of transporting goods across the Appalachian Mountains, which stood as a geographical obstacle between New York and the nation's quickly developing west.

Although Clinton's political opponents derided him for spending so much money on what they claimed to be a useless endeavor, sarcastically referring to it as "Clinton's Ditch," he was eventually vindicated by the rousing success of the canal soon after it opened in 1825. The completed canal was 584 kilometers in length, second at that time only to China's Grand Canal, 12 meters in width, and 1.2 meters in depth, although it was later to undergo several expansions. Rather than becoming a burden on the New York State economy due to its high cost of construction, the canal had an overwhelmingly positive financial impact, with the revenue from the tolls imposed on the freight being transported through it covering the cost of its construction in less than 10 years, although these tolls were later abolished in 1882 in order to compete with the newly built network of railways spreading across the country.

The Erie Canal's peak, in terms of commercial traffic, was reached in 1855, when a total of approximately 33,000 shipments of goods made their way through the waterway. One of the biggest impacts of the Erie Canal was the significant reduction in shipping costs between New York and the Midwest, where the nation's farming industry resided. The cost of transporting products from Buffalo to New York City reduced from $100 per ton to less than $10 per ton, making goods, including food, much more affordable across the East Coast. A barrel of flour, for example, could now be shipped from the city of Rochester to the New York State capital of Albany for a mere fraction of what it would have cost before the construction of the canal. Another benefit derived from the Erie Canal, this one largely unexpected, was an increase in tourism in areas of upstate New York once shunned by vacationers. Passenger boats lined up alongside commercial freighters in order to cruise up and down the canal, with tourists enjoying leisurely views of the wilderness lining it and contributing even more revenue to the state's **coffers**.

The era of Erie Canal was also a time of great migration, of both the international and domestic varieties, as a steady stream of immigrants flowed out of Europe and into the United States of America, fueling the young country's massive westward expansion. Some of these immigrants, particularly those arriving from Ireland, joined the extensive labor force needed to excavate the canal, later settling in small towns along its route and establishing Irish American communities. The settlement of Buffalo, located in the northwest corner of New York State on the frigid shores of Lake Erie, also benefited greatly in terms of growth from the construction of the canal, with its population ballooning from 2,000 residents in 1820 to more than 18,000 people just 20 years later. Today, it is a thriving city with a population of around 275,000.

The Erie Canal eventually fell into disuse, negatively affected by competition first from railroads, in the early 20th century, and in the latter half of the century by the trucking industry, as the automobile became the nation's preferred mode of transportation. The last regularly scheduled shipping service on the canal shut down permanently in 1994, and while the Erie Canal today continues to attract handfuls of curious tourists and recreational boaters from the area, it no longer has any significant commercial value to New York State or the country as a whole.

Glossary	⊠
coffers: funds that are available for an organization or government to spend	

It was in the 1780s that a proposal was first floated to construct a canal in upstate New York, running from the Hudson River to Lake Erie, one of the five Great Lakes located on the nation's border with Canada, with a formal survey finally conducted in 1808 and government authorization to begin the project granted in 1817. The main proponent of the project was the governor of New York State, DeWitt Clinton, who viewed the canal as a means of drastically reducing the cost of transporting goods across the Appalachian Mountains, which stood as a geographical obstacle between New York and the nation's quickly developing west.

Which of the sentences below best expresses the essential information in the highlighted sentence in the passage? Incorrect choices change the meaning in important ways or leave out essential information.

(A) It was the governor of New York State that envisioned the canal as a more cost-effective means of transporting goods across the mountains.

(B) After DeWitt Clinton became the governor of New York, he had to overcome many obstacles to build the canal.

(C) The canal had to be built across the Appalachian Mountains, which separate New York from the American west.

(D) The canal made it easier to ship items to people in the west because DeWitt Clinton was an elected governor.

Although Clinton's political opponents derided him for spending so much money on what they claimed to be a useless endeavor, sarcastically referring to it as "Clinton's Ditch," he was eventually vindicated by the rousing success of the canal soon after it opened in 1825. The completed canal was 584 kilometers in length, second at that time only to China's Grand Canal, 12 meters in width, and 1.2 meters in depth, although it was later to undergo several expansions. Rather than becoming a burden on the New York State economy due to its high cost of construction, the canal had an overwhelmingly positive financial impact, with the revenue from the tolls imposed on the freight being transported through it covering the cost of its construction in less than 10 years, although these tolls were later abolished in 1882 in order to compete with the newly built network of railways spreading across the country.

The word "derided" in the passage is closest in meaning to

(A) ridiculed
(B) analyzed
(C) abandoned
(D) supported

Although Clinton's political opponents derided him for spending so much money on what they claimed to be a useless endeavor, sarcastically referring to it as "Clinton's Ditch," he was eventually vindicated by the rousing success of the canal soon after it opened in 1825. The completed canal was 584 kilometers in length, second at that time only to China's Grand Canal, 12 meters in width, and 1.2 meters in depth, although it was later to undergo several expansions. Rather than becoming a burden on the New York State economy due to its high cost of construction, the canal had an overwhelmingly positive financial impact, with the revenue from the tolls imposed on the freight being transported through it covering the cost of its construction in less than 10 years, although these tolls were later abolished in 1882 in order to compete with the newly built network of railways spreading across the country.

According to paragraph 2, why did New York State end the tariff on canal shipments?

(A) To satisfy the requirements of the federal government

(B) To speed up shipping by reducing traffic on the canal

(C) To be more competitive with another mode of shipping

(D) To include money for a canal expansion in the budget

The Erie Canal's peak, in terms of commercial traffic, was reached in 1855, when a total of approximately 33,000 shipments of goods made their way through the waterway. One of the biggest impacts of the Erie Canal was the significant reduction in shipping costs between New York and the Midwest, where the nation's farming industry resided. The cost of transporting products from Buffalo to New York City reduced from $100 per ton to less than $10 per ton, making goods, including food, much more affordable across the East Coast. A barrel of flour, for example, could now be shipped from the city of Rochester to the New York State capital of Albany for a mere fraction of what it would have cost before the construction of the canal. Another benefit derived from the Erie Canal, this one largely unexpected, was an increase in tourism in areas of upstate New York once shunned by vacationers. Passenger boats lined up alongside commercial freighters in order to cruise up and down the canal, with tourists enjoying leisurely views of the wilderness lining it and contributing even more revenue to the state's coffers.

The word "shunned" in the passage is closest in meaning to

(A) developed
(B) inspected
(C) avoided
(D) defined

The Erie Canal's peak, in terms of commercial traffic, was reached in 1855, when a total of approximately 33,000 shipments of goods made their way through the waterway. One of the biggest impacts of the Erie Canal was the significant reduction in shipping costs between New York and the Midwest, where the nation's farming industry resided. The cost of transporting products from Buffalo to New York City reduced from $100 per ton to less than $10 per ton, making goods, including food, much more affordable across the East Coast. A barrel of flour, for example, could now be shipped from the city of Rochester to the New York State capital of Albany for a mere fraction of what it would have cost before the construction of the canal. Another benefit derived from the Erie Canal, this one largely unexpected, was an increase in tourism in areas of upstate New York once shunned by vacationers. Passenger boats lined up alongside commercial freighters in order to cruise up and down the canal, with tourists enjoying leisurely views of the wilderness lining it and contributing even more revenue to the state's coffers.

What is the purpose of paragraph 3?

(A) To contrast two different causes given in paragraph 2
(B) To give details about an idea introduced in paragraph 2
(C) To show the cause of a negative effect in paragraph 2
(D) To offer the author's opinion of an idea in paragraph 2

The era of Erie Canal was also a time of great migration, of both the international and domestic varieties, as a steady stream of immigrants flowed out of Europe and into the United States of America, fueling the young country's massive westward expansion. Some of these immigrants, particularly those arriving from Ireland, joined the extensive labor force needed to excavate the canal, later settling in small towns along its route and establishing Irish American communities. The settlement of Buffalo, located in the northwest corner of New York State on the frigid shores of Lake Erie, also benefited greatly in terms of growth from the construction of the canal, with its population ballooning from 2,000 residents in 1820 to more than 18,000 people just 20 years later. Today, it is a thriving city with a population of around 275,000.

All of the following are mentioned in paragraph 4 EXCEPT:

(A) Europeans were immigrating to the United States in large numbers.

(B) Americans were migrating in a westward direction as the nation expanded.

(C) Cities on the East Coast decreased in size while those in the Midwest grew.

(D) Irish immigrants who came to work on the canal settled down in New York.

The era of Erie Canal was also a time of great migration, of both the international and domestic varieties, as a steady stream of immigrants flowed out of Europe and into the United States of America, fueling the young country's massive westward expansion. Some of these immigrants, particularly those arriving from Ireland, joined the extensive labor force needed to excavate the canal, later settling in small towns along its route and establishing Irish American communities. The settlement of Buffalo, located in the northwest corner of New York State on the frigid shores of Lake Erie, also benefited greatly in terms of growth from the construction of the canal, with its population ballooning from 2,000 residents in 1820 to more than 18,000 people just 20 years later. Today, it is a thriving city with a population of around 275,000.

Which of the following can be inferred from paragraph 4 about the city of Buffalo?

(A) It initially opposed the proposal to build the Erie Canal.

(B) It experienced only a temporary increase in total residents.

(C) It has one of the most diverse populations in New York State.

(D) It is located near the place where the Erie Canal meets Lake Erie.

The Erie Canal eventually fell into disuse, negatively affected by competition first from railroads, in the early 20th century, and in the latter half of the century by the trucking industry, as the automobile became the nation's preferred mode of transportation. The last regularly scheduled shipping service on the canal shut down permanently in 1994, and while the Erie Canal today continues to attract handfuls of curious tourists and recreational boaters from the area, it no longer has any significant commercial value to New York State or the country as a whole.

According to paragraph 5, which of the following is true of the Erie Canal today?

(A) It is smaller and its commercial traffic flows in only one direction.

(B) It has been paved over and now is used as a highway for truckers.

(C) It continues to be important to both the national and state economies.

(D) It is visited by small numbers of tourists and rarely used for shipping.

The Erie Canal's peak, in terms of commercial traffic, was reached in 1855, when a total of approximately 33,000 shipments of goods made their way through the waterway. ■(A) One of the biggest impacts of the Erie Canal was the significant reduction in shipping costs between New York and the Midwest, where the nation's farming industry resided. The cost of transporting products from Buffalo to New York City reduced from $100 per ton to less than $10 per ton, making goods, including food, much more affordable across the East Coast. ■(B) A barrel of flour, for example, could now be shipped from the city of Rochester to the New York State capital of Albany for a mere fraction of what it would have cost before the construction of the canal. ■(C) Another benefit derived from the Erie Canal, this one largely unexpected, was an increase in tourism in areas of upstate New York once shunned by vacationers. ■(D) Passenger boats lined up alongside commercial freighters in order to cruise up and down the canal, with tourists enjoying leisurely views of the wilderness lining it and contributing even more revenue to the state's coffers.

Look at the four squares [■] that indicate where the following sentence could be added to the passage.

East Coast businesses shipping machinery and manufactured products from their factories to customers in the Midwest experienced a similar financial boon.

Where would the sentence best fit? Select a square [■] to add the sentence to the passage.

Directions: An introductory sentence for a brief summary of the passage is provided below. Complete the summary by selecting the THREE answer choices that express the most important ideas in the passage. Some sentences do not belong in the summary because they express ideas that are not presented in the passage or are minor ideas in the passage. **This question is worth 2 points.**

Drag your answer choices to the spaces where they belong. To review the passage, select **View Passage**.

The Erie Canal was built across the State of New York in the early 19th century.

-
-
-

Answer Choices

A   The canal was proposed based on the success of other similar projects, most notably the Grand Canal in China.

B   As other types of transportation, including trains and trucks, became more popular, shippers stopped using the canal.

C   Buffalo was a small settlement on the shores of Lake Erie that grew rapidly in size due to the canal's construction.

D   The money brought in from the canal's tolls was enough to pay for the entire cost of construction in less than 10 years.

E   The canal quickly lowered the cost of shipping between New York and the Midwest, causing a drop in prices.

F   As Americans began to migrate west, New York State struggled to find enough laborers to work on the canal.

Water on Mars

Beginning with the first use of rudimentary telescopes to study the heavens, early astronomers engaged in earnest discussion over whether water could be found on the planet Mars. Although the "canals" and "oceans" that they initially observed have long since been explained away as unrelated natural features, thanks to modern technology and space exploration we now know two important facts: first, that there is water on Mars, although it is found almost exclusively in the form of ice, with small amounts of water vapor existing in the atmosphere; and second, that water in liquid form may have existed in great quantities in the past.

Most of the ice currently found on Mars is of the subterranean variety, although it is visible on the planet's north polar ice cap and is believed to be hidden beneath the permanent layer of carbon dioxide ice of the south polar ice cap. A total of more than five million cubic kilometers of ice is known to exist on or near the surface of Mars, which if melted would cover the entire planet in 35 meters of water. The pressing questions that remain are to what extent water existed in its liquid state some time in the distant past, and whether or not it flowed freely and in copious amounts across the planet's surface.

Nearly four billion years ago, the atmosphere of Mars is believed to have been denser and its surface temperatures higher, meaning that extensive amounts of liquid water could have existed, perhaps in the form of a massive ocean that covered one-third of the planet. There is also the possibility that smaller bodies of liquid water existed in more recent years, possibly including freshwater lakes that would have been hospitable to microbial life. When NASA's Mariner 9 spacecraft began orbiting Mars in 1971, it captured more than 7,000 images of the planet's surface, many of which gifted astronomers with their first hard evidence, in the form of geomorphic features, that liquid water had once existed in significant quantities.

Since that time, approximately 40,000 Martian river valleys have been mapped out by researchers, tracing the routes that flowing water had once traveled, some of them covering thousands of kilometers, eroding the surface bedrock along the way and carving out deep valleys much like those found in some regions of our planet. Also included in these images were evidence of streams that had broken off into multiple branches, an indicator that they had most likely been formed by falling rain.

Along with these streams and river valleys, a considerable number of lake basins have been identified on Mars. Some of these are roughly equal in size to Earth's largest lakes and were evidently fed by the rivers that once ran through the planet's valleys. Like the streams, some of these lakes may have been formed by precipitation, while others seem to have been created by rising groundwater. It was once assumed that these lakes dated back to the distant past when the overall environment of Mars was relatively warm and wet. It has been hypothesized that some sort of cataclysmic event—possibly volcanic activity, meteorite impacts, or a change in the planet's orbit—caused the atmosphere to warm up to the point where subterranean ice began to melt and form lakes.

Another strong indicator that water once flowed freely on Mars is the deltas that have been spotted in some of the planet's lake beds, fan-shaped patterns formed from sediments deposited into the lakes long ago by rivers. These deltas are considered significant due to the fact that they would have required both deep water and a long period of time in order to form. Also, had this water not remained stable in terms of level over a considerable time, the sediment would have been washed away. All of this geomorphic evidence points strongly toward there having been a time when Mars possessed abundant liquid water, an especially notable piece of information when considering that this is one of the fundamental features required to support life.

Beginning with the first use of rudimentary telescopes to study the heavens, early astronomers engaged in earnest discussion over whether water could be found on the planet Mars. Although the "canals" and "oceans" that they initially observed have long since been explained away as unrelated natural features, thanks to modern technology and space exploration we now know two important facts: first, that there is water on Mars, although it is found almost exclusively in the form of ice, with small amounts of water vapor existing in the atmosphere; and second, that water in liquid form may have existed in great quantities in the past.

Why does the author mention "early astronomers" in paragraph 1?

(A) To emphasize the importance of the invention of the telescope
(B) To compare different theories about the origins of Mars' water
(C) To illustrate the immense size of Mars' ancient canals and oceans
(D) To introduce a misconception about water on Mars from the past

Most of the ice currently found on Mars is of the subterranean variety, although it is visible on the planet's north polar ice cap and is believed to be hidden beneath the permanent layer of carbon dioxide ice of the south polar ice cap. A total of more than five million cubic kilometers of ice is known to exist on or near the surface of Mars, which if melted would cover the entire planet in 35 meters of water. The pressing questions that remain are to what extent water existed in its liquid state some time in the distant past, and whether or not it flowed freely and in copious amounts across the planet's surface.

The word "copious" in the passage is closest in meaning to

(A) abundant
(B) fluctuating
(C) decreasing
(D) unknowable

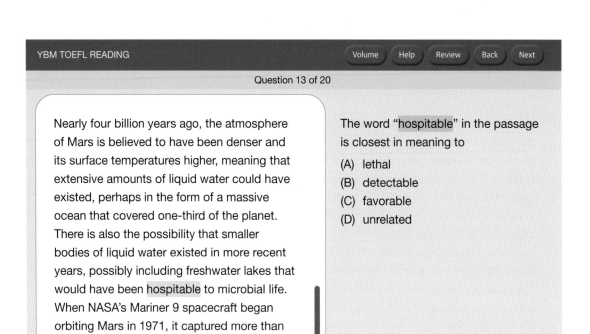

Nearly four billion years ago, the atmosphere of Mars is believed to have been denser and its surface temperatures higher, meaning that extensive amounts of liquid water could have existed, perhaps in the form of a massive ocean that covered one-third of the planet. There is also the possibility that smaller bodies of liquid water existed in more recent years, possibly including freshwater lakes that would have been hospitable to microbial life. When NASA's Mariner 9 spacecraft began orbiting Mars in 1971, it captured more than 7,000 images of the planet's surface, many of which gifted astronomers with their first hard evidence, in the form of geomorphic features, that liquid water had once existed in significant quantities.

The word "hospitable" in the passage is closest in meaning to

(A) lethal
(B) detectable
(C) favorable
(D) unrelated

Nearly four billion years ago, the atmosphere of Mars is believed to have been denser and its surface temperatures higher, meaning that extensive amounts of liquid water could have existed, perhaps in the form of a massive ocean that covered one-third of the planet. There is also the possibility that smaller bodies of liquid water existed in more recent years, possibly including freshwater lakes that would have been hospitable to microbial life. When NASA's Mariner 9 spacecraft began orbiting Mars in 1971, it captured more than 7,000 images of the planet's surface, many of which gifted astronomers with their first hard evidence, in the form of geomorphic features, that liquid water had once existed in significant quantities.

According to paragraph 3, which of the following is true of Mariner 9?

(A) It landed in a Martian river valley to search for water.

(B) It collected Martian soil samples and analyzed them.

(C) It took the first photographs of the large ocean on Mars.

(D) It provided proof that liquid water once existed on Mars.

Since that time, approximately 40,000 Martian river valleys have been mapped out by researchers, tracing the routes that flowing water had once traveled, some of them covering thousands of kilometers, eroding the surface bedrock along the way and carving out deep valleys much like those found in some regions of our planet. Also included in these images were evidence of streams that had broken off into multiple branches, an indicator that they had most likely been formed by falling rain.

Which of the sentences below best expresses the essential information in the highlighted sentence in the passage? Incorrect choices change the meaning in important ways or leave out essential information.

(A) The surface of Mars is made of bedrock, which causes the water flowing across it to pass through many deep valleys.

(B) Researchers have used river valleys to identify the paths of thousands of rivers eroded into the surface of Mars by flowing water.

(C) After much research, scientists concluded that about 40,000 of the valleys found on Mars no longer contain any flowing rivers.

(D) Studies of thousands of river valleys on Mars have shown that they are much longer and deeper than those found on Earth.

Along with these streams and river valleys, a considerable number of lake basins have been identified on Mars. Some of these are roughly equal in size to Earth's largest lakes and were evidently fed by the rivers that once ran through the planet's valleys. Like the streams, some of these lakes may have been formed by precipitation, while others seem to have been created by rising groundwater. It was once assumed that these lakes dated back to the distant past when the overall environment of Mars was relatively warm and wet. It has been hypothesized that some sort of cataclysmic event—possibly volcanic activity, meteorite impacts, or a change in the planet's orbit—caused the atmosphere to warm up to the point where subterranean ice began to melt and form lakes.

Select the TWO answer choices from paragraph 5 that describe the ways Martian lakes may have formed. **To receive credit, you must select TWO answers.**

(A) Rain fell when the atmosphere of Mars was warmer.

(B) A large ocean began to dry up, leaving behind lakes.

(C) An eruption on the planet changed ice to liquid water.

(D) Chunks of ice from space crashed into the planet.

Another strong indicator that water once flowed freely on Mars is the deltas that have been spotted in some of the planet's lake beds, fan-shaped patterns formed from sediments deposited into the lakes long ago by rivers. These deltas are considered significant due to the fact that they would have required both deep water and a long period of time in order to form. Also, had this water not remained stable in terms of level over a considerable time, the sediment would have been washed away. All of this geomorphic evidence points strongly toward there having been a time when Mars possessed abundant liquid water, an especially notable piece of information when considering that this is one of the fundamental features required to support life.

According to paragraph 6, deltas formed in Martian lake beds because

(A) groundwater began to heat up and rise to the surface of the planet

(B) large rivers flowing fast and strong cut deep grooves into the bedrock

(C) rocks and soil were swept into them by rivers over long periods of time

(D) a shift in the planet's orbit resulted in its surface becoming unstable

Another strong indicator that water once flowed freely on Mars is the deltas that have been spotted in some of the planet's lake beds, fan-shaped patterns formed from sediments deposited into the lakes long ago by rivers. These deltas are considered significant due to the fact that they would have required both deep water and a long period of time in order to form. Also, had this water not remained stable in terms of level over a considerable time, the sediment would have been washed away. All of this geomorphic evidence points strongly toward there having been a time when Mars possessed abundant liquid water, an especially notable piece of information when considering that this is one of the fundamental features required to support life.

In paragraph 6, the author implies that water on Mars

(A) most likely existed for a very brief time long ago
(B) may indicate that there was once life on the planet
(C) could have been the source of the water on Earth
(D) might come and go in a cycle that takes centuries

Along with these streams and river valleys, a considerable number of lake basins have been identified on Mars. ■(A) Some of these are roughly equal in size to Earth's largest lakes and were evidently fed by the rivers that once ran through the planet's valleys. ■(B) Like the streams, some of these lakes may have been formed by precipitation, while others seem to have been created by rising groundwater. ■(C) It was once assumed that these lakes dated back to the distant past when the overall environment of Mars was relatively warm and wet. ■(D) It has been hypothesized that some sort of cataclysmic event—possibly volcanic activity, meteorite impacts, or a change in the planet's orbit—caused the atmosphere to warm up to the point where subterranean ice began to melt and form lakes.

Look at the four squares [■] that indicate where the following sentence could be added to the passage.

Research conducted in 2010, however, uncovered evidence of lakes near the equator of the planet that date from a considerably more recent period.

Where would the sentence best fit? Select a square [■] to add the sentence to the passage.

Directions: An introductory sentence for a brief summary of the passage is provided below. Complete the summary by selecting the THREE answer choices that express the most important ideas in the passage. Some sentences do not belong in the summary because they express ideas that are not presented in the passage or are minor ideas in the passage. **This question is worth 2 points.**

Drag your answer choices to the spaces where they belong. To review the passage, select **View Passage**.

Astronomers have long been interested in whether there is water on Mars.

-
-
-

Answer Choices

A It is now known that there is water on Mars, mostly in the form of ice, and that liquid water may have existed in large amounts.

B There are large ice caps covering the poles of Mars, but they are made up of only frozen carbon dioxide rather than water.

C Researchers thought they had discovered lakes near the equator of Mars, but they were just deposits of frozen groundwater.

D There are large lake beds on the surface of Mars, some of which include deltas created by rivers flowing into them.

E Images taken by a NASA spacecraft have revealed geomorphic evidence of flowing water, including thousands of river valleys.

F Early astronomers looked at Mars through crude telescopes and mistakenly believed they were seeing canals and oceans.

ACTUAL TEST 2

Herbivores' Impact on Plant Diversity

Plant diversity is a crucial element needed to maintain the health and functionality of the Earth's ecosystems. Herbivores play an essential role in ensuring that this diversity is not lost. The traditional view of the relationship between herbivores and plant diversity was fairly simplistic—it was believed that the vegetative consumption of herbivores protected diversity by precluding any one species from attaining dominance over its rival species. This is important because once a species becomes dominant, it gradually eliminates the subordinate species that share its habitat through a process known as competitive exclusion, by which the weaker species are denied access to the resources of the ecosystem. However, while the fundamental ideas behind this line of thinking remain valid, scientists now understand that the reality of the situation is more convoluted.

Generally, the feeding habits of herbivores do lead to an increase in plant diversity. In a healthy, productive ecosystem, where the environment provides plants with all of the resources they require to grow and reproduce, a moderate level of herbivore feeding can actually increase the productivity of the ecosystem and lead to an increase in total biomass. As the herbivores feed on the dominant plant species, they reduce its population and free up additional resources for subordinate species, thereby maintaining diversity. In less productive ecosystems, however, the opposite may occur. Because there is not an abundance of resources, the feeding behavior of herbivores can create a situation where only the strongest, most tolerant species are able to survive, while the more fragile ones succumb to extinction, which obviously leads to a reduction in plant diversity.

The size of the herbivores involved is another factor that helps determine their impact on the biodiversity of the ecosystem. For example, one of the most important resources required by plant species is sunlight, which they compete for by growing taller and casting shadows across their shorter rivals. The presence of large herbivores, however, can reduce the advantage of taller plant species, as they are more likely to be targeted for consumption. In terms of mass, the smaller the herbivores, the less of an impact they are likely to have, as creatures with little mass require fewer nutrients and cause only minor disturbances in the physical environment. Large herbivores, however, have a much greater impact, as they consume large amounts of the dominant plant species and also dig up the ground, which actually improves the quality of the soil by preventing it from compacting and introducing additional oxygen into it. They also leave behind a great deal of fecal matter, which, along with dispersing the seeds of the species they have consumed, increases the nutrients of the soil, all of which allows for an overall increase in the growth of the ecosystem's plants.

Although herbivores tend to consume an ecosystem's dominant plant species, in some cases they will target subordinate species simply due to their higher palatability. Because of this, in areas where herbivores feed in large numbers, the palatability of plants can affect which species become dominant, with less palatable plants more likely to attain dominance. Plants will often offset their susceptibility to herbivores due to palatability by resorting to something called a "growth-defense trade-off." Simply put, in order to activate any of a variety of defense mechanisms against hungry herbivores, plants must reallocate their internal resources to the detriment of their own growth. These defenses can be physical, such as sharp thorns or a layer of wax across their outer surface, or chemical, as in the case of toxins that adversely affect the health of herbivores or even **volatile organic compounds**, known as VOCs, that are released into the air and attract predators of the herbivores. As a result, although the plants experience a reduction in their individual size and overall mass, they ensure their continued survival.

Glossary	⊠

volatile organic compounds (VOCs): gaseous chemical substances produced by organisms such as plants in order to communicate with one another and protect themselves from external threats

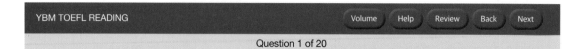

Plant diversity is a crucial element needed to maintain the health and functionality of the Earth's ecosystems. Herbivores play an essential role in ensuring that this diversity is not lost. The traditional view of the relationship between herbivores and plant diversity was fairly simplistic—it was believed that the vegetative consumption of herbivores protected diversity by precluding any one species from attaining dominance over its rival species. This is important because once a species becomes dominant, it gradually eliminates the subordinate species that share its habitat through a process known as competitive exclusion, by which the weaker species are denied access to the resources of the ecosystem. However, while the fundamental ideas behind this line of thinking remain valid, scientists now understand that the reality of the situation is more convoluted.

The word "convoluted" in the passage is closest in meaning to

(A) artificial
(B) beneficial
(C) complicated
(D) unappreciated

Plant diversity is a crucial element needed to maintain the health and functionality of the Earth's ecosystems. Herbivores play an essential role in ensuring that this diversity is not lost. The traditional view of the relationship between herbivores and plant diversity was fairly simplistic—it was believed that the vegetative consumption of herbivores protected diversity by precluding any one species from attaining dominance over its rival species. This is important because once a species becomes dominant, it gradually eliminates the subordinate species that share its habitat through a process known as competitive exclusion, by which the weaker species are denied access to the resources of the ecosystem. However, while the fundamental ideas behind this line of thinking remain valid, scientists now understand that the reality of the situation is more convoluted.

Which of the following best expresses the essential information in the highlighted sentence? Incorrect answer choices change the meaning in important ways or leave out essential information.

(A) The importance of being dominant is what drives some species to destroy their rivals through competition.

(B) It is necessary to eliminate the subordinate species in order to allow the more dominant ones to survive.

(C) The reason this happens is because dominant species do not have to compete for the ecosystem's resources.

(D) This matters because dominant species kill off weaker ones by blocking them from the resources they need.

Generally, the feeding habits of herbivores do lead to an increase in plant diversity. In a healthy, productive ecosystem, where the environment provides plants with all of the resources they require to grow and reproduce, a moderate level of herbivore feeding can actually increase the productivity of the ecosystem and lead to an increase in total biomass. As the herbivores feed on the dominant plant species, they reduce its population and free up additional resources for subordinate species, thereby maintaining diversity. In less productive ecosystems, however, the opposite may occur. Because there is not an abundance of resources, the feeding behavior of herbivores can create a situation where only the strongest, most tolerant species are able to survive, while the more fragile ones succumb to extinction, which obviously leads to a reduction in plant diversity.

According to paragraph 2, which of the following is true about the relationship between herbivores and ecosystems?

(A) Highly productive ecosystems face the greatest threat to diversity from feeding herbivores.

(B) Herbivores reduce diversity in less productive ecosystems by causing weaker species to die.

(C) The greater an ecosystem's plant diversity is, the fewer resources it has available to offer.

(D) Subordinate plant species suffer the most when herbivores consume the dominant species.

The size of the herbivores involved is another factor that helps determine their impact on the biodiversity of the ecosystem. For example, one of the most important resources required by plant species is sunlight, which they compete for by growing taller and casting shadows across their shorter rivals. The presence of large herbivores, however, can reduce the advantage of taller plant species, as they are more likely to be targeted for consumption. In terms of mass, the smaller the herbivores, the less of an impact they are likely to have, as creatures with little mass require fewer nutrients and cause only minor disturbances in the physical environment. Large herbivores, however, have a much greater impact, as they consume large amounts of the dominant plant species and also dig up the ground, which actually improves the quality of the soil by preventing it from compacting and introducing additional oxygen into it. They also leave behind a great deal of fecal matter, which, along with dispersing the seeds of the species they have consumed, increases the nutrients of the soil, all of which allows for an overall increase in the growth of the ecosystem's plants.

Why does the author mention "dig up the ground" in paragraph 3?

(A) To explain how herbivores benefit the soil
(B) To introduce a way that plants reproduce
(C) To suggest that strong plants have deep roots
(D) To describe a feeding method of herbivores

The size of the herbivores involved is another factor that helps determine their impact on the biodiversity of the ecosystem. For example, one of the most important resources required by plant species is sunlight, which they compete for by growing taller and casting shadows across their shorter rivals. The presence of large herbivores, however, can reduce the advantage of taller plant species, as they are more likely to be targeted for consumption. In terms of mass, the smaller the herbivores, the less of an impact they are likely to have, as creatures with little mass require fewer nutrients and cause only minor disturbances in the physical environment. Large herbivores, however, have a much greater impact, as they consume large amounts of the dominant plant species and also dig up the ground, which actually improves the quality of the soil by preventing it from compacting and introducing additional oxygen into it. They also leave behind a great deal of fecal matter, which, along with dispersing the seeds of the species they have consumed, increases the nutrients of the soil, all of which allows for an overall increase in the growth of the ecosystem's plants.

In paragraph 3, the author mentions all of the following about large herbivores EXCEPT:

(A) They can protect an ecosystem's plant diversity by feeding on taller plants.

(B) Their diet requires few nutrients, ensuring that they cause little disruption.

(C) They often disturb the soil, which keeps it loose and increases its oxygen levels.

(D) Their dung helps spread the seeds of some plants and adds nutrients to the soil.

The size of the herbivores involved is another factor that helps determine their impact on the biodiversity of the ecosystem. For example, one of the most important resources required by plant species is sunlight, which they compete for by growing taller and casting shadows across their shorter rivals. The presence of large herbivores, however, can reduce the advantage of taller plant species, as they are more likely to be targeted for consumption. In terms of mass, the smaller the herbivores, the less of an impact they are likely to have, as creatures with little mass require fewer nutrients and cause only minor disturbances in the physical environment. Large herbivores, however, have a much greater impact, as they consume large amounts of the dominant plant species and also dig up the ground, which actually improves the quality of the soil by preventing it from compacting and introducing additional oxygen into it. They also leave behind a great deal of fecal matter, which, along with dispersing the seeds of the species they have consumed, increases the nutrients of the soil, all of which allows for an overall increase in the growth of the ecosystem's plants.

Which of the following can be inferred from paragraph 3 about tall plants?

(A) They exist only in ecosystems that are not especially productive.

(B) They require fewer means of defending themselves than short ones.

(C) They are in a more convenient position for large herbivores to eat.

(D) They are more likely to be subordinate species than dominant ones.

Although herbivores tend to consume an ecosystem's dominant plant species, in some cases they will target subordinate species simply due to their higher palatability. Because of this, in areas where herbivores feed in large numbers, the palatability of plants can affect which species become dominant, with less palatable plants more likely to attain dominance. Plants will often offset their susceptibility to herbivores due to palatability by resorting to something called a "growth-defense trade-off." Simply put, in order to activate any of a variety of defense mechanisms against hungry herbivores, plants must reallocate their internal resources to the detriment of their own growth. These defenses can be physical, such as sharp thorns or a layer of wax across their outer surface, or chemical, as in the case of toxins that adversely affect the health of herbivores or even volatile organic compounds, known as VOCs, that are released into the air and attract predators of the herbivores. As a result, although the plants experience a reduction in their individual size and overall mass, they ensure their continued survival.

The word "susceptibility" in the passage is closest in meaning to

(A) vulnerability
(B) invisibility
(C) capability
(D) hostility

Although herbivores tend to consume an ecosystem's dominant plant species, in some cases they will target subordinate species simply due to their higher palatability. Because of this, in areas where herbivores feed in large numbers, the palatability of plants can affect which species become dominant, with less palatable plants more likely to attain dominance. Plants will often offset their susceptibility to herbivores due to palatability by resorting to something called a "growth-defense trade-off." Simply put, in order to activate any of a variety of defense mechanisms against hungry herbivores, plants must reallocate their internal resources to the detriment of their own growth. These defenses can be physical, such as sharp thorns or a layer of wax across their outer surface, or chemical, as in the case of toxins that adversely affect the health of herbivores or even volatile organic compounds, known as VOCs, that are released into the air and attract predators of the herbivores. As a result, although the plants experience a reduction in their individual size and overall mass, they ensure their continued survival.

According to paragraph 4, why do plants sacrifice their growth?

(A) They want to go unnoticed by herbivores.
(B) They are unable to access enough nutrients.
(C) They share resources with subordinate species.
(D) They focus more of their energy on self-defense.

The size of the herbivores involved is another factor that helps determine their impact on the biodiversity of the ecosystem. ■[(A)] For example, one of the most important resources required by plant species is sunlight, which they compete for by growing taller and casting shadows across their shorter rivals. ■[(B)] The presence of large herbivores, however, can reduce the advantage of taller plant species, as they are more likely to be targeted for consumption. ■[(C)] In terms of mass, the smaller the herbivores, the less of an impact they are likely to have, as creatures with little mass require fewer nutrients and cause only minor disturbances in the physical environment. ■[(D)] Large herbivores, however, have a much greater impact, as they consume large amounts of the dominant plant species and also dig up the ground, which actually improves the quality of the soil by preventing it from compacting and introducing additional oxygen into it. They also leave behind a great deal of fecal matter, which, along with dispersing the seeds of the species they have consumed, increases the nutrients of the soil, all of which allows for an overall increase in the growth of the ecosystem's plants.

Look at the four squares [■] that indicate where the following sentence could be added to the passage.

The thinning of their population increases light availability at lower levels, and therefore leads to greater plant diversity.

Where would the sentence best fit? Select a square [■] to add the sentence to the passage.

Directions: An introductory sentence for a brief summary of the passage is provided below. Complete the summary by selecting the THREE answer choices that express the most important ideas in the passage. Some sentences do not belong in the summary because they express ideas that are not presented in the passage or are minor ideas in the passage. **This question is worth 2 points.**

Drag your answer choices to the spaces where they belong. To review the passage, select **View Passage**.

Herbivores play an important role in maintaining the diversity of plants.

-
-
-

Answer Choices

A	Large herbivores can cause serious physical damage to ecosystems by digging holes that disturb the soil.	D	VOCs are physical defenses that plants use against herbivores, such as sharp thorns and dangerous toxins.
B	Herbivore feeding can strengthen productive ecosystems, but it may reduce the plant diversity of less productive ones.	E	Herbivores tend to target plant species with higher palatability, which are more likely to attain dominance in areas where herbivores feed in large numbers.
C	Plant biodiversity is affected by the size of herbivores, with smaller ones causing minor disturbances while larger ones significantly alter ecosystems.	F	In order to develop ways to protect themselves from herbivores, some species will restrict their own growth.

Salt Production and Trade in China

Salt has played an outsize role in the history of China, asserting a powerful influence over the nation's social and economic development. One reason for this is the fact that salt is not only a component behind one of the "five flavors" considered essential to Chinese cuisine but also one of the proverbial "seven necessities of life." Historically, there were five types of salt across the region, with sea salt existing in the greatest abundance. In Sichuan, workers utilized drilling technology to access well salt, draining subterranean salt pools deep beneath the surface of the Earth. In Western China, lake and earth salt were extracted from water and soil respectively, while rock salt was collected from caves located in Shaanxi and Gansu. The competency of each successive Chinese government was judged largely on how well it managed the production and distribution of salt, with related policies sparking passionate social debate over private wealth and the nature of governance itself.

Early governments took it upon themselves to directly control the production and sale of salt. In 1368 AD, when the Ming dynasty was founded, the new government continued to directly control the production and sale of salt like its predecessors. However, officials later devised a system that allowed merchants to purchase certificates granting them the right to buy government salt, which could then be sold only within limited markets. This unconventional melding of state monopoly and free market eventually proved to be disastrous, as merchants began reselling their certificates, salt was hoarded, and speculation drove up prices. Expensive government salt could not compete with black-market salt, but rather than making it cheaper, officials raised its price even further in order to meet tax revenue quotas. This made contraband salt even more attractive, and soon two-thirds of the salt on the market was coming from outside the government monopoly, leading to a series of national crises.

During the Ming dynasty, the ocean was the primary source of salt, with seawater being either boiled down or allowed to sit in the sun until evaporation took place in order to extract its salt. Prison labor was sometimes employed to carry out this time-intensive process, but it was more commonly conducted by the members of households that had been designated official salt producers by the government. Throughout the Ming dynasty, the number of these salt producers plummeted, as families fled from the burdensome requirements heaped upon them by the government. Meanwhile, critics of salt policies continued to employ poetry and fiction to argue against the wisdom and morality of using salt to exploit the poor while enriching government officials.

In the mid-17th century, the Qing dynasty was founded, replacing the Ming dynasty and eventually bringing with it much-needed salt policy reform. The salt industry was now centered in the city of Yangzhou, due to the fact that it is located on the banks of the Yangzi River, which was used to transport salt to the north. The Yangzhou merchants controlled the region's salt rights, making them exceedingly rich and powerful, although they needed to constantly ply the emperor with gifts and praise to prevent him from rescinding these rights. Government salt superintendents also enriched themselves, either by underreporting tax revenues and pocketing the difference or by accepting gifts from salt merchants who were beholden to them. Once again, corruption flourished, and salt revenues fell.

In 1820, the Daoguang Emperor ascended to the throne and, facing a financial crisis caused by the troublesome opium trade, made fiscal reform his top priority. He handed the responsibility of reforming the salt industry to an official named Tao Zhu. Tao responded by eradicating the old system left over from the Ming dynasty and replacing it with what was more or less an open market. Merchants who remained in good standing with the government could now purchase as much salt as they wished and sell it wherever they pleased. Although these changes did not immediately bring about the benefits Tao had promised, forcing him to retire, it created a more adaptable system that gradually improved the overall management of the salt trade.

Salt has played an outsize role in the history of China, asserting a powerful influence over the nation's social and economic development. One reason for this is the fact that salt is not only a component behind one of the "five flavors" considered essential to Chinese cuisine but also one of the proverbial "seven necessities of life." Historically, there were five types of salt across the region, with sea salt existing in the greatest abundance. In Sichuan, workers utilized drilling technology to access well salt, draining subterranean salt pools deep beneath the surface of the Earth. In Western China, lake and earth salt were extracted from water and soil respectively, while rock salt was collected from caves located in Shaanxi and Gansu. The competency of each successive Chinese government was judged largely on how well it managed the production and distribution of salt, with related policies sparking passionate social debate over private wealth and the nature of governance itself.

The word "sparking" in the passage is closest in meaning to

(A) analyzing
(B) initiating
(C) resolving
(D) banning

Salt has played an outsize role in the history of China, asserting a powerful influence over the nation's social and economic development. One reason for this is the fact that salt is not only a component behind one of the "five flavors" considered essential to Chinese cuisine but also one of the proverbial "seven necessities of life." Historically, there were five types of salt across the region, with sea salt existing in the greatest abundance. In Sichuan, workers utilized drilling technology to access well salt, draining subterranean salt pools deep beneath the surface of the Earth. In Western China, lake and earth salt were extracted from water and soil respectively, while rock salt was collected from caves located in Shaanxi and Gansu. The competency of each successive Chinese government was judged largely on how well it managed the production and distribution of salt, with related policies sparking passionate social debate over private wealth and the nature of governance itself.

According to paragraph 1, which of the following is NOT true of salt?

(A) Salt extracted from seawater was the most common type.

(B) Salt was stored in deep wells that were created with drills.

(C) In some places, rock salt was gathered from within caves.

(D) Salt management was a major criteria for judging regimes.

Early governments took it upon themselves to directly control the production and sale of salt. In 1368 AD, when the Ming dynasty was founded, the new government continued to directly control the production and sale of salt like its predecessors. However, officials later devised a system that allowed merchants to purchase certificates granting them the right to buy government salt, which could then be sold only within limited markets. This unconventional melding of state monopoly and free market eventually proved to be disastrous, as merchants began reselling their certificates, salt was hoarded, and speculation drove up prices. Expensive government salt could not compete with black-market salt, but rather than making it cheaper, officials raised its price even further in order to meet tax revenue quotas. This made contraband salt even more attractive, and soon two-thirds of the salt on the market was coming from outside the government monopoly, leading to a series of national crises.

The word "them" in the passage refers to

(A) governments
(B) officials
(C) merchants
(D) certificates

Early governments took it upon themselves to directly control the production and sale of salt. In 1368 AD, when the Ming dynasty was founded, the new government continued to directly control the production and sale of salt like its predecessors. However, officials later devised a system that allowed merchants to purchase certificates granting them the right to buy government salt, which could then be sold only within limited markets. This unconventional melding of state monopoly and free market eventually proved to be disastrous, as merchants began reselling their certificates, salt was hoarded, and speculation drove up prices. Expensive government salt could not compete with black-market salt, but rather than making it cheaper, officials raised its price even further in order to meet tax revenue quotas. This made contraband salt even more attractive, and soon two-thirds of the salt on the market was coming from outside the government monopoly, leading to a series of national crises.

The word "contraband" in the passage is closest in meaning to

(A) unauthorized
(B) discontinued
(C) inexpensive
(D) replicated

During the Ming dynasty, the ocean was the primary source of salt, with seawater being either boiled down or allowed to sit in the sun until evaporation took place in order to extract its salt. Prison labor was sometimes employed to carry out this time-intensive process, but it was more commonly conducted by the members of households that had been designated official salt producers by the government. Throughout the Ming dynasty, the number of these salt producers plummeted, as families fled from the burdensome requirements heaped upon them by the government. Meanwhile, critics of salt policies continued to employ poetry and fiction to argue against the wisdom and morality of using salt to exploit the poor while enriching government officials.

In paragraph 3, the author mentions all of the following about extracting sea salt EXCEPT:

(A) Natural evaporation was sometimes utilized.

(B) The process took a lengthy period to complete.

(C) Prisoners were sometimes forced to do the work.

(D) It was managed by members of the royal household.

In the mid-17th century, the Qing dynasty was founded, replacing the Ming dynasty and eventually bringing with it much-needed salt policy reform. The salt industry was now centered in the city of Yangzhou, due to the fact that it is located on the banks of the Yangzi River, which was used to transport salt to the north. The Yangzhou merchants controlled the region's salt rights, making them exceedingly rich and powerful, although they needed to constantly ply the emperor with gifts and praise to prevent him from rescinding these rights. Government salt superintendents also enriched themselves, either by underreporting tax revenues and pocketing the difference or by accepting gifts from salt merchants who were beholden to them. Once again, corruption flourished, and salt revenues fell.

According to paragraph 4, salt superintendents underreported taxes because

(A) they lacked the resources they needed
(B) they were asked to do so by the emperor
(C) they took pity on the local salt merchants
(D) they wanted to keep some for themselves

In the mid-17th century, the Qing dynasty was founded, replacing the Ming dynasty and eventually bringing with it much-needed salt policy reform. The salt industry was now centered in the city of Yangzhou, due to the fact that it is located on the banks of the Yangzi River, which was used to transport salt to the north. The Yangzhou merchants controlled the region's salt rights, making them exceedingly rich and powerful, although they needed to constantly ply the emperor with gifts and praise to prevent him from rescinding these rights. Government salt superintendents also enriched themselves, either by underreporting tax revenues and pocketing the difference or by accepting gifts from salt merchants who were beholden to them. Once again, corruption flourished, and salt revenues fell.

Why does the author mention "the Yangzi River" in paragraph 4?

(A) To explain the reason behind Yangzhou's great influence

(B) To describe a positive change made by the Qing dynasty

(C) To contrast the salt production methods of two dynasties

(D) To give a detail about how salt tax revenues were spent

In 1820, the Daoguang Emperor ascended to the throne and, facing a financial crisis caused by the troublesome opium trade, made fiscal reform his top priority. He handed the responsibility of reforming the salt industry to an official named Tao Zhu. Tao responded by eradicating the old system left over from the Ming dynasty and replacing it with what was more or less an open market. Merchants who remained in good standing with the government could now purchase as much salt as they wished and sell it wherever they pleased. Although these changes did not immediately bring about the benefits Tao had promised, forcing him to retire, it created a more adaptable system that gradually improved the overall management of the salt trade.

Which of the following can be inferred from paragraph 5 about Tao Zhu?

(A) He was focused on opium rather than salt.

(B) He faced heavy criticism for his new system.

(C) He had family connections to the Ming dynasty.

(D) He failed to consider long-term implications.

In the mid-17th century, the Qing dynasty was founded, replacing the Ming dynasty and eventually bringing with it much-needed salt policy reform. ■(A) The salt industry was now centered in the city of Yangzhou, due to the fact that it is located on the banks of the Yangzi River, which was used to transport salt to the north. ■(B) The Yangzhou merchants controlled the region's salt rights, making them exceedingly rich and powerful, although they needed to constantly ply the emperor with gifts and praise to prevent him from rescinding these rights. ■(C) Government salt superintendents also enriched themselves, either by underreporting tax revenues and pocketing the difference or by accepting gifts from salt merchants who were beholden to them. ■(D) Once again, corruption flourished, and salt revenues fell.

Look at the four squares [■] that indicate where the following sentence could be added to the passage.

Things, however, did not start out well.

Where would the sentence best fit? Select a square [■] to add the sentence to the passage.

Directions: An introductory sentence for a brief summary of the passage is provided below. Complete the summary by selecting the THREE answer choices that express the most important ideas in the passage. Some sentences do not belong in the summary because they express ideas that are not presented in the passage or are minor ideas in the passage. **This question is worth 2 points.**

Drag your answer choices to the spaces where they belong. To review the passage, select **View Passage**.

Historically, salt was considered an important economic and social factor in China.

-
-
-

Answer Choices

A The Ming and Qing dynasties adopted different policies to control the production and distribution of salt.

B During the Qing dynasty, an official appointed by the emperor undertook the reformation of the salt industry, which failed anyway.

C During the Ming dynasty, the combination of a state monopoly on salt and free market ideas resulted in multiple crises.

D Salt producers sold their goods on the black market, causing a dangerous drop in government salt prices.

E Despite the challenges the Qing dynasty faced in reforming the corrupt salt industry, their fiscal reforms paid off later.

F In certain parts of China, salt was obtained through a method that involved collecting it from caves.

YBM TOEFL 80+
READING

세부 정보 찾기 문제

1 첫 번째 단락에서 다음 중 글쓴이가 피라미드에 대해
언급하지 않은 것은?
(A) 최소한 세 개의 삼각형 면이 있어야 한다.
(B) 그 토대가 반드시 일종의 다각형 모양이어야 한다.
(C) 오직 특정한 종류의 돌로만 지어졌다.
(D) 그 안정성으로 인해 고대의 여러 문명 사회에서 인기
있었다.

어휘 stability 안정성

해설 피라미드가 적어도 세 개의 삼각형 면으로 되어 있고, 토대
부분이 다각형 모양이며, 고대 문명 사회들의 건축학적 주요
산물이었다는 내용은 있지만, 특정한 돌로 지어졌다는
내용은 제시되어 있지 않으므로, (C)가 정답이다.

추론 문제

2 다음 중 두 번째 단락에서 일부 이집트의 갓돌에 대해 추론할
수 있는 것은?
(A) 피라미드의 질량에 있어 불균형을 만들어 냈다.
(B) 오직 가장 초기의 피라미드들만 지니고 있던
특징이었다.
(C) 여러 중요한 실용적 기능을 했다.
(D) 피라미드들이 햇빛에 반짝이도록 만들었다.

어휘 imbalance 불균형 sparkle 반짝이다

해설 갓돌들 중 일부는 빛을 반사하는 호박금으로 도금되어
있었다는 설명에서 햇빛을 반사해 반짝였던 것을 유추할 수
있으므로, (D)가 정답이다.

수사적 의도 파악 문제

3 글쓴이가 세 번째 단락에서 "고대 세계의 7대 불가사의"에
대해 논의하는 이유는?
(A) 피라미드들이 더 이상 인상적이지 않다는 점을 시사하기
위해
(B) 기자의 대 피라미드가 오래 지속되었음을 지적하기 위해
(C) 두 가지 유명한 구조물의 극단적 규모를 비교하기 위해
(D) 기자의 대 피라미드의 높이를 강조하기 위해

어휘 longevity 오래 지속됨, 장수

해설 기자의 대 피라미드가 고대 세계의 7대 불가사의 중에서
오늘날에도 여전히 서 있는 유일한 것이라고 하면서 아주
오랫동안 존재해 온 구조물임을 나타냈으므로, 정답은 (B)이다.

세부 정보 찾기 문제

4 세 번째 단락에 따르면, 다음 중 최초의 이집트 피라미드에
대해 사실인 것은?
(A) 두 유명 건축가의 합작품이었다.
(B) 이후의 피라미드들보다 더 크고 더 매끈했다.
(C) 크기가 모두 다른 6개의 층으로 되어 있었다.
(D) 언덕에 지어진 몇몇 피라미드들 중 하나였다.

어휘 collaboration 합작(품), 공동 작업(물)

해설 최초의 이집트 피라미드가 계단식 피라미드로서 크기가
줄어들면서 쌓인 6개의 층으로 구성되어 있다고 했으므로,
(C)가 정답이다.

지시 대상 찾기 문제

5 지문의 단어 "its"가 가리키는 것은?
(A) 촐룰라의 대 피라미드
(B) 첫 축조 단계
(C) 기원전 3세기
(D) 기자의 대 피라미드

해설 its 앞에 기자의 대 피라미드와 비교하는 말이 쓰여 있어 its가
앞선 문장에 언급된 촐룰라의 대 피라미드를 가리킨다는 것을
알 수 있다. 그러므로 정답은 (A)이다.

어휘의 의미 파악 문제

6 지문의 단어 "perched"와 의미가 가장 가까운 것은?
(A) 경사진   (B) 놓여 있는
(C) 합쳐진   (D) 남겨진

해설 perched는 '자리잡고 있는'이라는 뜻을 나타내므로, 의미가
가장 가까운 (B) placed가 정답이다.

세부 정보 찾기 문제

7 다음 중 네 번째 단락에서 촐룰라의 대 피라미드에 대해
언급된 것은?
(A) 하나 이상의 문명 사회가 그 건축에 기여했다.
(B) 기자의 대 피라미드보다 훨씬 더 높고 더 넓다.
(C) 매끄러운 면들로 인해 메소아메리카의 다른
피라미드들과 구분된다.
(D) 짓는 데 수세기가 걸렸으며 기원전 3세기에 완성되었다.

어휘 set A apart from B A를 B와 구분 짓다

해설 촐룰라의 대 피라미드가 수세기에 걸쳐 여러 다른 고대
메소아메리카 문명 사회에 의해 지어졌다고 했으므로, 정답은
(A)이다.

어휘의 의미 파악 문제

8 지문의 단어 "resurrection"과 의미가 가장 가까운 것은?
(A) 숭배
(B) 여가
(C) 전쟁
(D) 부활

해설 resurrection은 '부활'을 의미하므로 동일한 뜻을 가진 (D) revival이 정답이다.

문장 삽입 문제

9 제시된 문장이 지문에 삽입될 수 있는 곳을 가리키는 네 개의 네모[■]를 보아라.

반면에 아메리카의 피라미드들은 더 암울한 목적을 지니고 있었던 것으로 보인다.

이 문장이 들어갈 가장 적절한 위치는? 해당 네모[■]를 선택하여 이 문장을 지문에 삽입하여라.
(A)　　　(B)　　　(C)　　　(D)

해설 주어진 문장은 대조를 나타내는 on the other hand와 함께 아메리카 피라미드들이 지니고 있던 부정적인 측면을 언급했다. 따라서 고대 이집트 피라미드들이 지니고 있던 긍정적인 의미를 설명하는 문장 뒤에 위치해 그와 대조적인 내용이 이어져야 흐름이 자연스럽다. 그러므로 정답은 (C)이다.

지문 요약 문제

10 지시문: 지문의 간략한 요약을 위한 도입 문장이 아래에 제시되어 있다. 지문에서 가장 중요한 개념들을 나타내는 선택지 3개를 선택하여 요약을 완성하여라. 어떤 문장들은 지문에 제시되지 않거나 주요 개념이 아니므로 요약에 포함되지 않는다. **이 문제는 2점에 해당한다.**

피라미드는 전 세계에 걸쳐 찾아볼 수 있는 건축 구조물이다.

(A) 이집트의 파라오 조세르는 기원전 2700년에 그의 건축가에게 세계에서 가장 높은 피라미드를 짓게 했다.
(B) 대부분의 고대 이집트 피라미드들에는 네 개의 면과 매끈한 석회석 표면, 그리고 꼭대기에 뾰족한 갓돌이 있었다.
(C) 메소아메리카 피라미드들은 갓돌의 모양 때문에 지구라트라고 알려져 있었다.
(D) 메소아메리카 문명 사회들은 측면에 계단이 있고 꼭대기는 평평한 피라미드를 지었다.
(E) 고대 메소아메리카인들과 고대 이집트인들은 불안정한 구조 때문에 피라미드 건축을 중단했다.
(F) 이집트 피라미드들은 무덤으로 쓰인 반면, 메소아메리카 피라미드들은 주로 인신 제물을 바치는 데 쓰였다.

해설 피라미드에 대한 지문에서 고대 이집트 피라미드의 모양과 표면용 재료, 그리고 갓돌의 형태에 대한 설명, 메소아메리카 피라미드의 특징에 대한 설명, 이집트 피라미드와 메소아메리카 피라미드 사이의 용도 차이에 대한 설명이 차례로 나오므로, 정답은 (B), (D), (F)이다. (A)는 지문에 언급되지 않았고, (C)와 (E)는 지문 내용과 다르다.

---

pp. 21-25

Questions 11-20

공룡의 신진대사

공룡 생리 기능의 자세한 사실에 대한 논란이 많이 있어 왔지만, 그들의 체온 조절과 신진대사의 정확한 특징을 둘러싼 논란은 그렇게 많지 않다. 공룡에 대한 전통적인 관점은 그들을 덩치 큰 냉혈 도마뱀에 지나지 않는 보기 흉하고 둔한 생물체로 오랫동안 묘사해 왔다. 하지만 고생물학자들이 19세기 후반에 미국 곳곳에서 대량으로 발굴되던 다양한 공룡 종의 거의 완전한 뼈대들을 접하기 시작하면서, 공룡의 생리 기능에 대한 전반적인 지식이 빠르게 발전하기 시작했다.

이 새로운 지식으로부터 공룡들이 이전에 생각했던 것보다 아마 훨씬 더 활동적이고 민첩했을 것이라는 점이 이해되기 시작했고, 동시에 19세기에 유명했던 생물학자이자 다윈의 진화론에 대한 열렬한 지지자였던 토머스 헨리 헉슬리가 공룡들이 실제로는 도마뱀이 아니라 조류와 가까운 동족이라고 제안했다. 이 괄목할 만한 아이디어들에도 불구하고, 크고 무거운 파충류 같은 동물이라는 공룡에 대한 인식은 이미 많은 사람들의 마음 속에 단단히 뿌리 박혀 있었으며, 이러한 관점은 20세기 중반까지 계속 지배적이었다. 하지만 1960년대는 고생물학 분야에 있어 계몽의 시기였던 것으로 드러났는데, 현대의 고생물학자들이 공룡의 체온 조절에 관해 경쟁하듯 다수의 이론들을 제시하면서 공룡 생리 기능에 대한 아이디어들이 극적으로 변했기 때문이다.

공룡에게 현대적인 의미의 온혈 동물 또는 냉혈 동물이라는 꼬리표를 붙이는 것이 불가능하다는 견해가 인기를 끌게 되면서, 공룡은 그런 분류가 불가능한 완전히 다른 신진대사를 지닌 것으로 여겨졌다. 일부 과학자들은 공룡이 현대의 파충류 같은 냉혈 동물이었다고 계속 믿고 있지만, 이제 몸집이 더 큰 종은 체온을 안정시킬 능력을 지니고 있었을 것으로 추측하고 있다. 이 종은 관성 항온성이라고 알려진 과정을 통해 체온을 조절했을 텐데, 그로 인해 외부 온도의 주기적 변화에 도움을 받아 내부적으로 안정적인 체온이 유지된다. 이 외부적 도움은 순전히 이 공룡들의 몸집으로 인해 필요했을 텐데, 내부의 체온 변화가 일어나는 데 며칠이 걸렸을 것이기 때문이다. 온혈 동물이라는 점에서 포유류 및 조류와 더 가까이 닮은 공룡 모델을 지지하는 학설도 있다. 공룡의 지배가 적어도 1억 3천만 년 동안 지속되었기 때문에, 여러 다른 집단이 갈라져 나오면서 이전에 공유되었던 생리 기능과 다른 신진대사 및 체온 조절 방식을 발달시켰을 가능성이 높다.

고생물학자들에게 훨씬 더 어려운 일은 다양한 공룡들의 대략적인 신진대사율을 밝혀내는 것인데, 이는 내장이 한 번도 관찰된 적이 없는 종을 대상으로 하는 까다로운 일로서, 특히 이 비율은 이 생물체들이 쉬고 있을 때와 활동적이었을 때 크게 달랐을 것이라는 사실을 고려해 볼 때 그렇다. 현대 동물 연구에 따르면 휴식 중의 신진대사율이 활동 상태의 대사율보다 훨씬 더 낮았던 모든 멸종된 종은 많은 공룡들이 도달했던 거대한 크기로 자랄 수 없었을 것임을 시사한다. 이 더 큰 종들 중 일부는 지속적으로 적극적인 자양물 탐색 활동을 펼쳤을 가능성이 있는데, 이는 그 종들이 갖고 있던 휴식 중 신진대사율의 높고 낮음에 상관없이 그 에너지 소비가 크게 다르지 않았을 것임을 의미한다.

많은 선사 시대 종들이 아주 먼 과거의 어느 시점엔가 '중간' 유형의 신진대사를 갖고 있었던 것으로 볼 수 있다는 점이 제기된 바 있다. ■(A) 선사 시대의 포유류는 크기가 줄어들면서 부피 대비 표면적 비율이 늘어나 열 손실에 취약해졌고, 이로 인해 어쩔 수 없이 내부 체온 조절 체계를 발전시켜 온혈 동물이 되었다. ■(B) 이 모델에서, 공룡들은 쉴 때 낮은 신진대사율을 갖고 있었는데, 이러한 특징으로 인해 더 적게 먹으면서 섭취한 영양분을 성장하는 데 더 많이 돌릴 수 있었을 것이다. ■(C) 심실이 4개인 심장이 있어 유산소능력이 뛰어났기 때문에, 상당히 활동적이고 전혀 둔하지 않을 수 있었다. ■(D) 마지막으로 체온 조절이라는 측면에서 봤을 때, 이들은 피부 바로 아래에 있는 혈관의 확장 및 수축을 통해 열 손실을 완화할 수 있는 능력을 지니고 있었던 것으로 여겨지고 있다.

지문 어휘

1. controversy 논란 particulars 자세한 사실 physiology 생리 기능 nature 특징, 본질 thermoregulation 체온 조절 metabolism 신진대사 ungainly 보기 흉한 sluggish 둔한, 느릿느릿한 paleontologist 고생물학자 access 접근, 접촉 skeleton 골격 excavate 발굴하다
2. dawn 이해되기 시작하다 fervent 열렬한 proponent 지지자 eye-opening 괄목할 만한 perception 인식 cumbersome 크고 무거운 reptilian 파충류의 dominant 지배적인 enlightenment 계몽 paleontology 고생물학 put forth ~을 제시하다
3. defy (설명 등이) 불가능하다 stabilize 안정시키다 inertial homeothermy 관성 항온성(부피 대비 표면적의 비율이 작아져 체온이 잘 내려가지 않음) cyclic 주기적인 sheer 순전한 school of thought 학설, 학파 reign 지배, 통치 branch off 갈라지다, 나뉘다
4. undertaking 일 internal organ 내장 extinct 멸종한 expenditure 소비
5. intermediate 중간의 surface area to volume ratio 부피 대비 표면적 비율 vulnerable to ~에 취약한 ingest 섭취하다 four-chambered 심실이 4개인 aerobic capacity 유산소능력(몸이 에너지 전환을 하는 과정 중 유산소적으로 이루어지는 과정의 에너지 전환능력) contraction 수축

수사적 의도 파악 문제

11 글쓴이는 왜 첫 번째 단락에서 "미국"을 언급하는가?
(A) 두 종류의 공룡 뼈가 존재하는 이유를 제공하기 위해
(B) 혁신적인 이론을 제안한 한 고생물학자를 소개하기 위해
(C) 공룡의 생리 기능에 대한 새로운 정보의 출처를 나타내기 위해
(D) 고생물학이 몇몇 경쟁 그룹으로 세분화되었음을 시사하기 위해

어휘 revolutionary 혁신적인

해설 19세기 후반 미국에서 다양한 공룡 종의 거의 완전한 골격이 발굴되면서 공룡의 생리 기능에 대한 전반적인 지식이 빠르게 발전했다고 했으므로, (C)가 정답이다.

어휘의 의미 파악 문제

12 지문의 단어 "agile"과 의미가 가장 가까운 것은?
(A) 공격적인
(B) 우둔한
(C) 조심스러운
(D) 민첩한

해설 agile은 '민첩한'이라는 뜻으로 사용되었으므로, 같은 의미를 가진 (D) nimble이 정답이다.

세부 정보 찾기 문제

13 두 번째 단락에 따르면, 다음 중 토머스 헨리 헉슬리에 대해 사실인 것은?
(A) 느리게 움직이는 공룡이라는 개념을 수용했다.
(B) 다윈의 진화론을 높이 평가했다.
(C) 공룡 화석을 고대 조류의 것과 혼동했다.
(D) 고생물학의 계몽 시대에 참여했다.

해설 토머스 헨리 헉슬리가 다윈의 진화론에 대한 열렬한 지지자였다고 했으므로, 정답은 (B)이다.

추론 문제

14 다음 중 두 번째 단락에서 1960년대에 대해 추론할 수 있는 것은?
(A) 공룡의 생리 기능에 대한 관심이 증가했다.
(B) 새로운 개념들이 다윈의 진화론에 도전장을 냈다.
(C) 시간이 흐름에 따라 많은 공룡 화석이 분실되거나 잊혀졌다.
(D) 고생물학자들이 많은 논의 끝에 전통적인 관점으로 돌아갔다.

해설 1960년대가 고생물학 분야에서 계몽의 시기였다는 말과 함께 공룡의 생리 기능과 관련된 생각이 크게 바뀌어 많은 이론이 제시되었다는 설명에서 공룡의 생리 기능에 대한 관심이 증가했음을 유추할 수 있다. 그러므로 (A)가 정답이다.

세부 정보 찾기 문제

15 세 번째 단락에 따르면, 다음 중 현대의 고생물학자들에 대해 사실이 아닌 것은?
(A) 일부 학자들은 더 큰 공룡들이 체온을 안정적으로 유지할 수 있었다고 생각한다.
(B) 일부 학자들은 공룡들이 포유류와 같은 온혈 동물이었다고 생각한다.
(C) 공룡들이 생리 기능에 있어 크게 다르지 않았다는 증거를 발견했다.
(D) 공룡의 체온 조절과 관련해 합의에 이르지 못했다.

어휘 come to a consensus 합의에 이르다

해설 일부 학자들이 몸집이 더 큰 공룡 종이 체온을 안정시킬 능력을 지니고 있었던 것으로 생각하고 있으며, 포유류와 더 닮은 공룡 모델을 지지하는 학설도 존재하고, 일부 학자들이 여전히 파충류로 믿거나 포유류나 조류와 더 가깝게 생각하며 합의에 이르지 못했다는 점이 제시되어 (A), (B), (D)는 사실이다. 그러나 (C)는 언급되어 있지 않다.

문장 재구성 문제

16 아래 문장 중 지문에서 음영 표시된 문장의 핵심 정보를 가장 잘 나타낸 것은? 오답 선택지들은 의미를 현저히 바꾸거나 핵심 정보를 생략한다.
(A) 단순히 내장을 살펴보는 것만으로는 특정 공룡들의 신진대사율을 추정하기 어렵다.
(B) 과학자들은 공룡들의 신진대사율이 그들이 활동적이었는지의 여부에 달려 있었다고 추측한다.
(C) 대략적인 신진대사율을 알지 못하면 공룡들의 행동을 추측하기 어렵다.
(D) 차이 및 연구할 장기가 없기 때문에 공룡들의 신진대사율을 알기가 어렵다.

어휘 estimate 추정하다

해설 공룡의 내장이 전혀 관찰된 적이 없고 공룡이 쉴 때와 활동적일 때의 차이 때문에 공룡들의 신진대사율을 밝히기 어렵다는 요지를 모두 포함하고 있는 (D)가 정답이다.

어휘의 의미 파악 문제

17 지문의 단어 "sustenance"와 의미가 가장 가까운 것은?
(A) 동료애 (B) 자양분
(C) 수분 (D) 피신처

해설 sustenance는 '자양물'이라는 뜻으로 사용되었으므로, 유사한 뜻을 가진 (B) nourishment가 정답이다.

세부 정보 찾기 문제

18 다섯 번째 단락에 따르면, 선사 시대 동물들이 진화해 온혈 동물이 된 이유는?
(A) 크기 감소로 인해 열을 더 많이 잃게 되었기 때문에
(B) 중간 정도의 신진대사율을 지니도록 진화했기 때문에
(C) 낮은 신진대사율 문제로 인해 그럴 필요가 있었기 때문에
(D) 공룡을 피하기 위해 새로운 환경으로 이주했기 때문에

해설 선사 시대 포유류가 크기가 줄어들고 부피 대비 표면적 비율이 늘어나 열 손실에 취약해지면서, 내부 체온 조절 체계를 발전시켜 온혈 동물이 되었다고 했으므로, 정답은 (A)이다.

문장 삽입 문제

19 제시된 문장이 지문에 삽입될 수 있는 곳을 가리키는 네 개의 네모[■]를 보아라.

하지만 공룡들은 유사한 감소를 겪지 않았고, 그에 따라 이 중간 정도의 신진대사를 유지할 수 있었다.

이 문장이 들어갈 가장 적절한 위치는? 해당 네모[■]를 선택하여 이 문장을 지문에 삽입하여라.
(A) (B) (C) (D)

어휘 reduction 감소 retain 유지하다

해설 주어진 문장은 대조를 나타내는 however와 함께 공룡이 유사한 감소를 겪지 않았다고 했다. 따라서 포유류가 크기 감소로 인해 온혈 동물로 변화한 과정을 설명하는 문장 뒤에 놓여 그와 반대되는 공룡의 경우를 언급하는 흐름이 되어야 문맥이 자연스럽다. 그러므로 (B)가 정답이다.

지문 요약 문제

20 **지시문:** 지문의 간략한 요약을 위한 도입 문장이 아래에 제시되어 있다. 지문에서 가장 중요한 개념들을 나타내는 선택지 3개를 선택하여 요약을 완성하여라. 어떤 문장들은 지문에 제시되지 않거나 주요 개념이 아니므로 요약에 포함되지 않는다. **이 문제는 2점에 해당한다.**

공룡의 생리 기능에 대한 연구는 논란이 많은 역사를 지니고 있다.

(A) 공룡이 조류에서 진화하지 않았다는 점을 고생물학자들에게 납득시킨 것은 다윈의 진화론이었다.
(B) 현대의 파충류와 마찬가지로 공룡들도 체온 조절 능력이 없어서, 대신 외부 요소에 의존했다.
(C) 현재 많은 과학자들이 체온 조절 측면에 있어 공룡들이 엄밀히 온혈 또는 냉혈 동물이 아니었다고 생각한다.
(D) 부피 대비 표면적 비율 때문에 공룡들은 온혈 신진대사를 발전시킬 필요가 없었다.
(E) 휴식 중의 낮은 신진대사율이 공룡들을 지나치게 활동적이지 못하게 막은 것으로 여겨지고 있다.
(F) 1960년대까지는 공룡을 느리게 움직이고 둔한 것으로 보는 부정확한 관점이 고생물학 분야에서 일반적이었다.

어휘 strictly 엄밀히 inaccurate 부정확한

해설 공룡의 신진대사를 주제로 한 지문에서 공룡을 명확하게 온혈 동물 또는 냉혈 동물로 분류하는 것이 불가능하다는 과학계의 생각, 부피 대비 표면적 비율과 관련된 공룡의 진화에 대한 내용, 고생물학 분야에서 1960년대까지 이어지던 공룡에 대한 부정확한 관점을 설명한 (C), (D), (F)가 정답이다. (A)와 (E)는 지문에서 다루지 않은 내용이고, (B)는 지문 내용과 다르다.

PART 1

CHAPTER 01 Factual Information

EXERCISE   pp. 32-37

정답 | **01** (B) **02** (D) **03** (C) **04** (A) **05** 1.(B), (C)
2.(C)   **06** 1.(A) 2.(D) **07** 1.(B) 2.(A)
08 1.(C) 2.(D)

01

뿌리계는 주로 땅속에 있는 기관으로 식물의 지속적인 생존을 보장하는 세 가지 중요한 역할을 한다. 가장 기본적인 기능은 식물을 물리적으로 안정되게 유지시킴으로써 고정해 주는 역할을 하는 것이다. 씨앗에서 처음으로 나오는 식물의 원뿌리에서 곁뿌리들이 나오면서 이 곁뿌리들이 땅 전체로 퍼져, 식물을 땅에 단단히 고정시켜 주고 쓰러지지 않게 해 준다. 이 같은 뿌리들은 더 나아가 물을 흡수하고 흙에서 용해된 광물질을 뽑아내는 데 이용되는데, 이는 뿌리 끝에서 바깥으로 뻗은 실 같은 돌출부인 뿌리털을 통해서 이루어지는 일이다. 마지막으로, 광합성 과정을 통해 생산된 녹말과 당분 등의 영양소들은 나중에 사용될 수 있도록 뿌리 조직 내에 저장될 수 있다.

지문 어휘

subterranean 땅속의 anchorage 고정시키는 것
emerge 나오다, 생겨나다 grip 잡음 topple over 쓰러지다
extract 뽑다 dissolved 용해된 threadlike 실 같은
protrusion 돌출부 starch 녹말, 탄수화물 photosynthesis
광합성 tissue 조직

지문에 따르면, 다음 중 뿌리계에 대해 사실이 아닌 것은?
(A) 원뿌리와 곁뿌리로 이루어져 있다.
(B) 뿌리털은 식물이 쓰러지지 않게 해 준다.
(C) 흙에서 용해된 광물질을 얻을 수 있다.
(D) 녹말과 당분이 그 안에 저장되어 있을 수 있다.

어휘 fall over 넘어지다, 쓰러지다

해설 식물이 쓰러지지 않게 해주는 것은 뿌리털이 아닌 곁뿌리이기 때문에 (B)가 정답이다. 원뿌리에서 곁뿌리가 자라나 뿌리계를 이루고, 뿌리계는 광물질을 뽑아내며 녹말과 당분 등의 영양소를 저장할 수 있다고 했으므로 (A), (C), (D)는 사실이다.

02

고대 로마의 다리는 로마 제국이 현대 공학 기술에 기여한 가장 상징적인 것의 일부로 부각된다. 이 같은 공학 기술상의 인상적인 위업을 이룰 수 있었던 것은 고대 로마인들이 단순

한 아치에 통달했기 때문이었다. 기원전 2천년 정도로 이른 시기의 메소포타미아 유적에서도 아치의 흔적이 발견되고는 있지만, 그것을 처음으로 광범위하게 사용한 것은 로마인들이었다. 로마 아치의 한 가지 두드러진 특징은 형태가 둥글었다는 것인데, 이는 후에 고딕 건축물에서 발견되는 뾰족한 아치와 대조를 이룬다. 이 반원형의 디자인은 곡선의 정점에 쐐기돌을 사용해 압력을 아치 전체로 거의 균등하게 분산시켜 주었는데, 이것이 바로 다리 같은 거대한 구조물의 무게를 그 아치가 지탱할 수 있게 해 주었다.

지문 어휘

iconic 상징적인 feat 위업 mastery 통달 ruins 유적
extensively 광범위하게 keystone (아치 꼭대기의) 쐐기돌
apex 정점 divert 다른 데로 돌리다

지문에 따르면, 다음 중 로마의 아치에 대해 사실인 것은?
(A) 인간이 건설한 최초의 아치였다.
(B) 끝이 뾰족하거나 둥글었다.
(C) 고딕 건축물을 모방했다.
(D) 꼭대기에 쐐기돌이 있었다.

어휘 topped with 꼭대기에 ~이 있는

해설 로마 아치는 정점에 쐐기돌을 사용했다고 했으므로 (D)가 정답이다. 메소포타미아 아치가 이미 존재했고 로마 아치는 둥글었으며, 고딕 건축물은 후세에 나왔다고 했으므로 (A), (B), (C)는 지문 내용과 다르다.

03

화산 호수는 격렬한 분출이 일어난 후에 생성된다. 이 같은 분출은 보통 지구 표면에 깊게 파인 부분을 남기는데, (이것은) 분출로 인한 외적인 폭발력이나 뒤이은 안으로의 붕괴에 의해 생성되는 것이다. 전자의 지질학적 특징은 분화구로 알려져 있고, 반면에 후자는 칼데라라고 불린다. 이처럼 움푹 파인 부분은 나중에 물이 증발하거나 땅속으로 스며드는 속도보다 더 빠르게 내리는 빗물이나 불어나는 지하수로 가득 찰 수 있으며, 이로 인해 화산 호수가 만들어진다. 분화구에 형성되는 화산 호수와 칼데라에 자리잡은 화산 호수 사이의 가장 주목할 만한 차이점 중 하나는 분화구 호수가 모양이 더 둥근 편이라는 것이다. 게다가, 다수의 분화구 호수는 불안정한 속성 때문에 반복적으로 물이 찼다가 말랐다가 하면서 간헐적으로만 존재하고, 반면에 칼데라 호수는 전반적으로 크기가 더 크고 더 오래 남아 있다.

지문에 따르면, 화산 호수가 생성되는 때는?
(A) 불안정성 때문에 인근 호수가 마르기 시작할 때
(B) 화산 폭발로 광범위한 범람이 일어날 때
(C) 물이 빠져나가는 속도보다 더 빠르게 움푹 파인 곳으로
유입될 때
(D) 화산 분화구가 칼데라로 변형될 때

어휘 drain 물이 빠지다, 말라버리다 instability 불안정성

해설 증발하거나 땅속으로 스며드는 물의 속도보다 더 빠르게
빗물이나 지하수가 분화구로 유입될 때 화산 호수가 생긴다고
했으므로, (C)가 정답이다.

04

1948년에 유명한 교육학자 마리아 몬테소리의 책이 출판되
어, 몬테소리 교육 방식의 기원과 주요 측면들을 설명했다.
<아이의 발견>이라는 제목의 이 책은, 그녀의 이전 출판물
중 하나를 개정한 것으로, 이미 여러 차례 개정되어 재판된
적이 있었다. 그 책에서 그녀는 몬테소리 방식이 적용되어야
하는 이상적 환경에 관한 지침을 간단하게 설명한다. 이 지침
에는 의자, 컵, 카운터 같은 물품이 반드시 성인이 아니라 평
균 아동에게 적합한 크기여야 한다는 것이 포함된다. 이 책은
또한 주위 물품의 개수를 아이가 이용할 수 있는 수준 이내로
제한할 것을 규정하고 있는데, 너무 많은 물품을 가지게 되면
어떤 한 가지 과제에 집중하는 아이의 능력에 역효과를 미칠
수 있기 때문이다.

다음 중 지문에서 몬테소리 방식에 이상적인 환경을 만들 때
해야하는 것으로 언급한 것은?
(A) 사용 가능한 물품의 수 최소화
(B) 나이에 맞는 읽기 활동 강조
(C) 상세한 성인의 감독 제공
(D) 아이들을 바쁘게 하기 위한 과제 제공

어휘 age-appropriate 나이에 맞는 supervision 감독

해설 주위 물품의 수를 아이가 이용할 수 있는 수준 이내로 제한하는
규정이 있다고 했으므로, (A)가 정답이다. (B), (C), (D)는
언급되지 않았다.

05

대기 순환, 즉 지표면 전역에 걸친 대규모 공기 이동은 세 가
지 기본 유형의 순환으로 이루어져 있는데, 그 중 하나가 해
들리순환이라고 알려져 있으며, 이 순환에 대해 최초로 설명
한 아마추어 기상학자 조지 해들리를 기려 붙여진 이름이다.
해들리순환은 적도 부근에 형성되는 폐쇄형 순환고리 형태
로 존재하며, 이곳에서 지표면에서 가열되어 밀도가 더 낮은
습한 공기가 상승하기 시작한다. 한편, 적도 반대편에서도 유
사한 공기 덩어리가 상승해 저기압 지대가 만들어지고, 이 두
공기 덩어리가 각자의 극을 향해 이동하게 된다. 습한 공기는
적도에서 멀어지면서 냉각되고 밀도가 높아져, 하강하게 되
면서 고기압 지대를 만드는데, 일반적으로 위도 30도선 부
근에서 이런 변화가 발생한다. 이제 공기는 다시 적도를 향해
지표면을 따라 이동하기 시작하고, 순환의 주기가 완료되면
무역풍으로 알려진 대기 현상이 나타난다.

1 지문에서 적도 부근의 습한 공기가 상승하는 이유로 언급된
것 두 개를 고르시오. 두 개를 골라야 점수가 인정된다.
(A) 적도 부근에서 순환하고 있다.
(B) 온도가 높아졌다.
(C) 밀도가 낮아졌다.
(D) 무역풍 가까이에 있다.

어휘 undergo 겪다

해설 적도 부근에서 가열되어 밀도가 낮아진 습한 공기가 상승하기
시작한다고 했으므로, (B)와 (C)가 정답이다.

2 지문에 따르면, 다음 중 해들리순환에 대해 사실이 아닌
것은?
(A) 대기 순환의 한 구성 요소이다.
(B) 적도의 북쪽과 남쪽에서 발생한다.
(C) 위도 30도선 부근에서 시작된다.
(D) 무역풍이 발생하는 원인이다.

어휘 component 구성 요소

해설 해들리순환이 적도 부근에서 처음 형성되어 각자의 극
방향으로 이동한 후 위도 30도선 부근에 이르면 변화한다고
했으므로, (C)가 정답이다.

이집트에서 선진 고대 문명이 3천년 이상 번영할 수 있었던 것은 나일강 때문이었는데, 나일강은 놀랄만한 길이인 6,650킬로미터에 이르며 중앙 아프리카에서 지중해까지 북쪽으로 흐르는 강이다. 메마른 사막 지형이었을 곳을 수많은 사람들을 먹여 살릴 만한 비옥한 농지로 변화시킨 것은 매년 발생하는 나일강의 범람이었는데, 이로 인해 늦여름 강둑을 따라 영양분이 풍부한 침전물(토사)이 쌓였다. 나일 계곡은 실제로 밀과 보리가 풍부하게 자랄 수 있는 두꺼운 토사 층으로 뒤덮여 있고, 강 자체도 이들 농작물에 생명 유지에 필요한 물을 대주는 데 이용되었다. 고대 이집트 농부들은 나일강의 물 방향을 강 유역으로 바꾸는 수로를 파서 복합 관개 시설을 만들었는데, 나일강은 그곳에서 작물을 심으려고 준비 중인 땅을 흠뻑 적셔 주곤 했다. 일단 농부들의 작물이 수확되면 기술적으로 발달한 나무 배들이 식량을 왕국 내 여타 지역으로 분배하면서 나일강이 교통 수단으로 이용되었다.

지문 어휘

thrive 번영(번창)하다 Mediterranean Sea 지중해 deposit 침전시키다 sediment 침전물, 퇴적물 arid 매우 건조한 fertile 비옥한 silt 토사 irrigation 관개 channel 수로 redirect ~의 방향을 바꾸다 basin (큰 강의) 유역 saturate 흠뻑 적시다

1 지문에 따르면, 다음 중 나일강에 대해 사실인 것은?
(A) 매년 늦여름 무렵에 범람한다.
(B) 이집트 농부들에게 심각한 문제들을 일으켰다.
(C) 뜻하지 않게 고대 이집트의 멸망을 야기했다.
(D) 종종 농부들의 농작물을 쓸어 간다.

어휘 fall 멸망, 몰락 wash away ~을 쓸어 가다

해설 매년 발생하는 나일강의 범람으로 늦여름에 침전물이 쌓였다고 했으므로, (A)가 정답이다. (B), (C), (D)는 언급되지 않았다.

2 다음 중 지문에서 글쓴이가 고대 이집트 농부들에 대해 언급하지 않은 것은?
(A) 농작물을 수송한 방법
(B) 농작물에 물을 대기 위해 사용한 것
(C) 재배한 농작물의 종류
(D) 농작물을 수확한 시기

어휘 transport 수송하다

해설 농작물 수확 시기에 관한 언급은 없으므로 (D)가 정답이다. 수확한 농작물은 나무 배들을 이용해 분배했고, 관개 시설을 이용해 물을 댔으며, 나일 계곡에서 밀과 보리가 자랐다고 했으므로, (A), (B), (C)는 지문 내용과 일치한다.

1963년 11월, 아이슬란드 남부 해안 부근 해저 130미터 지점의 화산 분출로 상당히 큰 섬이 생겨났다. 이 해저 폭발은 몇 년간 계속되다 1967년 6월에 끝이 났는데, 슈르체이라고 명명된 새로 형성된 이 섬은 그 시점에 크기가 2.7평방 킬로미터에 이르렀다. 슈르체이 섬은 계속되는 파랑침식 과정 때문에 지금은 크기가 절반으로 줄었음에도 식물학자들의 활동 중심지가 되었으며, 이들은 한때 불모지였던 곳에서 대량으로 서식하는 식물들을 연구하기 위해 이 섬으로 모여든다. 슈르체이 섬의 첫 번째 식물이 1965년 봄에 발견되었고, 뒤이어 1967년에 이끼가, 1970년에 지의류가 발견되었다. 영양분이 부족한 섬의 모래흙 때문에 비록 10종만이 영구 거주자로서 자리잡을 수 있었지만, 섬이 생기고 첫 20년 동안 서로 다른 20종의 식물이 이 섬에서 발견되었다. 하지만, 새들이 이 섬을 자주 드나들기 시작하면서 토질이 개선되었고, 1998년에는 슈르체이 섬에서 최초의 덤불이 발견되었다. 2008년 무렵에는 식물 69종이 섬에 서식하고 있었고, 매년 2~5종의 새로운 종이 유입되었다.

지문 어휘

sizeable 상당한 크기의 halve 반으로 줄이다 wave erosion 파랑침식 hub (활동의) 중심지 colonize 대량 서식하다 barren 황량한 moss 이끼 lichen 지의류 establish oneself 자리잡다, 정착하다 frequent 자주 다니다

1 다음 중 지문에서 슈르체이 섬에 대해 언급된 것은?
(A) 한때 그곳에 살았던 사람 수
(B) 섬의 크기가 줄어든 원인
(C) 가장 흔한 식물 종
(D) 섬에서 식물을 처음 발견한 사람

어휘 common 흔한

해설 계속되는 파랑침식으로 섬의 크기가 절반으로 줄었다고 했으므로, (B)가 정답이다. (A), (C), (D)는 언급되지 않았다.

2 지문에 따르면, 다음 중 슈르체이 섬의 식물에 대해 사실이 아닌 것은?
(A) 철새들에 의해 손상되었다.
(B) 다양성이 늘어나고 있다.
(C) 그것을 연구하려는 많은 식물학자들을 끌어들인다.
(D) 이끼는 물론 지의류도 포함한다.

어휘 migratory bird 철새

해설 자주 드나드는 새들로 인해 섬의 토질이 개선되고 덤불까지 발견됐다고 했으므로, 지문의 내용과 일치하지 않는 것은 (A)이다.

18세기 중엽 영국에서 1차 산업혁명의 도래를 가능하게 했던 여섯 가지 주요 요소가 있었다. 아마도 가장 중요한 것은 영국이 높은 수준의 농업 생산성을 누리고 있었고, 강, 도로, 운하, 항구 등을 포함한 견실한 공공 수송 기반 시설을 확보하고 있었으며, 천연자원, 특히 철과 석탄을 풍부하게 공급받는 축복을 누리고 있었다는 것이다. 더욱이 인력 측면에서 영국은 대규모의 숙련된 노동 인력과 안정적이면서 기업 친화적인 정부, 그리고 투자에 투입할 대량의 금융 자본을 확보하고 있었다. 손으로 하는 제품 생산에서 기계를 이용한 생산으로 전환되는 과정이 산업혁명을 앞장서서 이끌었고, 이를 통해 안정적이면서 효율적인 제조 과정이 창출되었다. 증기력 또한 기관차를 비롯해 인간 활동 본질의 주요한 변화를 주도하는 많은 기계들에 동력을 공급하며 중요한 역할을 담당했다. 1차 산업혁명은 새롭게 발견한 자신들의 전문 지식을 수출하려는 영국 사업가들의 열의와 이를 받아들이려는 다른 나라들의 적극성으로 이후 유럽 대륙, 미국, 일본을 비롯한 세계의 여타 지역으로 확산되었다.

지문 어휘

facilitate 가능(용이)하게 하다 advent 도래 sound 견실한
infrastructure 공공 기반 시설 possess 소유하다 pool
이용 가능 인력 spearhead 앞장서서 이끌다 power 동력을
공급하다 locomotive 기관차 shift 변화 entrepreneur
사업가 expertise 전문 지식(기술)

1 지문에 따르면, 산업혁명이 전 세계로 퍼져 나간 이유는?
(A) 영국 이민자들이 고국에서 새로운 사상을 가지고 나갔기 때문에
(B) 기관차가 주요 수송 방식이 되었기 때문에
(C) 영국 사업가들이 산업혁명을 확산시키고 싶어 했기 때문에
(D) 침략군이 패배한 나라에 산업혁명을 강요했기 때문에

어휘 migrant 이주자, 이민자 force 강요하다
해설 새롭게 발견한 전문 지식을 수출하려는 영국 사업가들의 열의가 확산의 원인이라고 했으므로, (C)가 정답이다.

2 다음 중 지문에서 글쓴이가 영국의 산업혁명을 이끈 요인들로 언급하지 않은 것은?
(A) 투자할 수 있었던 돈
(B) 사업을 지지했던 정치인들
(C) 안정적인 수송망
(D) 헌신적인 노동자들이 있는 공장

어휘 dedicated 헌신적인 workforce 노동자, 노동 인구
해설 투자에 투입할 대량의 금융 자본이 있었으며, 정부가 기업 친화적이었고, 견실한 수송 기반 시설이 있었다고 했지만, 공장 관련 내용은 없으므로 (D)가 정답이다.

CHAPTER 02 Vocabulary

EXERCISE pp. 44-49

정답 | 01 (B) **02** (D) **03** (C) **04** (B) **05** (D) **06** (C)
07 1.(C) 2.(D) **08** 1.(C) 2.(D) **09** 1.(A) 2.(B)
10 1.(D) 2.(C) **11** 1.(A) 2.(C) **12** 1.(B) 2.(D)
13 1.(C) 2.(B) **14** 1.(D) 2.(A)

암석 순환은 바위가 수백만 년의 지질 연대에 걸쳐 퇴적, 화성(火成), 변성 활동을 통해 암석이 형성되고, 변형되며, 또 재형성되는 일련의 과정을 가리킨다. 암석은 환경 변화로 인해 평형 상태에서 밀려나도록 끊임없이 압력을 받는다. 예를 들어, 퇴적암은 미세한 점토 입자에서 상당히 큰 돌덩어리에 이르기까지 다양한 크기의 암석 조각들로 이루어져 있다. 이 조각들은 풍화와 침식의 영향으로 원래 암석에서 떨어져 나간 다음 실려 나가 강 유역에 축적된다.

지문 어휘

sedimentary 퇴적의 igneous 화성의 metamorphic
변성의 equilibrium 평형 fragment 조각, 파편 particle 입자
boulder (크고 둥근) 돌덩어리 detached 떨어진, 분리된
weathering 풍화

지문의 단어 "substantial"과 의미가 가장 가까운 것은?
(A) 중요하지 않은
(B) 상당한
(C) 일시적인
(D) 뚜렷한

해설 substantial은 '(크기가) 상당한'이라는 뜻으로 사용되었으므로, 유사한 뜻을 나타내는 (B) sizeable이 정답이다.

중국 청동기 시대는 기원전 약 2000년에 황허강 유역을 따라 이 지역 최초의 선진 문명 중 한 곳에서 시작된 것으로 보인다. 돌 무기보다 더 가볍고 견고한 무기를 만들기 위해 주석과 구리의 합금인 청동이 사용되었던 다른 초기 문명들과는 달리, 중국인들은 주로 종교 의식이나 조상 숭배에 쓰이는 가마솥이나 컵 같은 화려하게 장식된 그릇들을 만드는 데 청동을 사용했다. 이런 그릇들은 명망의 상징이었기 때문에, 그것을 소유하는 것은 사회에서 가장 돈 많고 힘있는 사람들에게만 가능했다.

지문 어휘

circa 약, ~경 alloy 합금 counterpart 대응 관계에 있는 것 craft (공예품 등을) 만들다 ornate 화려하게 장식된 vessel 그릇 cauldron 가마솥 ritual (종교) 의식 worship 숭배 prestige 명망, 위신

지문의 단어 "sturdier"와 의미가 가장 가까운 것은?
(A) 더 광택 있는　　　　(B) 더 치밀적인
(C) 더 가치 있는　　　　(D) 더 내구성 있는

해설 sturdier는 '견고한'이라는 뜻의 형용사 sturdy의 비교급 형태이므로, (D) more durable이 정답이다.

토마스 에디슨의 1877년 축음기 발명은 엔터테인먼트 분야에 있어 완전히 새로운 차원을 예고했다. 최초로, 음성과 음악을 비롯한 소리들이 차후 재생을 위해 녹음되고 저장될 수 있게 되었다. 20년 가까이 지나 에디슨은 또 다시 혁명적인 발명품으로 엔터테인먼트 세계를 뒤흔들었는데, 이번에는 현대 필름 카메라의 선도자격인 활동사진 카메라였다. 하지만 에디슨은 자신의 두 창작물의 출력을 충분히 일치시키지 못했고, 이로 인해 1920년대 중반까지도 영화는 무성 상태였다.

지문 어휘

phonograph 축음기 dimension 차원 playback 재생 shake up 뒤흔들다 motion picture 활동사진, 영화 precursor 선도자 synchronize 동시에 발생하게 맞추다, (영상과 음향 따위를) 일치시키다

지문의 단어 "heralded"와 의미가 가장 가까운 것은?
(A) 확산을 막았다
(B) 필요성을 설명했다
(C) 시작임을 암시했다
(D) 대체제 역할을 했다

해설 heralded는 '(시작될 것임을) 예고했다'라는 뜻이므로, 의미가 가장 비슷한 것은 (C) signaled the beginning of이다.

재생 에너지원으로의 대규모 전환은 그 에너지원을 포착하는 효율적인 수단을 찾아야 할 필요성을 야기할 것이다. 햇빛에 관해서라면, 지금까지의 해결책은 태양광 패널을 설치하는 것이다. 전 세계 옥상에서 볼 수 있는 이 패널은 특별한 전지들로 이루어져 있다. 이 전지들은 태양광을 흡수해 전기로 변환시킨다. 그 다음에 이 전기는 저장되거나 기구 또는 장치들에 동력을 공급하는 데 사용될 수 있다. 태양 에너지는 가장 많이 통용되는 재생 에너지 형태이지만 관련 비용이 높다.

지문 어휘

capture 잡다, 포착하다 when it comes to ~에 관해서라면 installation 설치 cell 전지 convert 전환시키다 appliance 기기, 기구 associated with ~와 관련된

지문의 단어 "transition"과 의미가 가장 가까운 것은?
(A) 연구　　　　　　　　(B) 변화
(C) 완료　　　　　　　　(D) 토의

해설 transition은 '전환'을 의미하므로, 의미가 가장 비슷한 (B) shift가 정답이다.

가장 기본적인 생각을 전달하기 위해 제한적으로 사용하는 표시인 원시 문자 중 현존하는 가장 오래된 예는 기원전 약 35,000년에 후기 구석기 시대에 유럽에서 발명되었을 수 있다. 동물 이미지 옆에 기호 표시를 붙였는데, 아마도 동물들의 계절적 행동과 관련해 다른 사냥꾼들에게 유용할 수 있는 정보를 전하기 위해서였을 것이다. 이후, 실제 문자 체계 창출을 향한 중대한 발걸음이 도기의 광범위한 사용과 때를 맞추어 시작되었는데, 바로 이 시기에 상징 부호가 표시된 점토 토큰이 가축이나 여타 상품들의 숫자를 기록하는 데 사용되었다.

지문 어휘

proto-writing 원시 문자 marking (기호·형태·글자 등의) 표시 Upper Paleolithic 후기 구석기 시대 notational 기호(법)의 convey 전하다 coincide 동시에 일어나다 clay token 점토 토큰(모양에 따라 다른 수량을 나타냄) livestock 가축 commodity 상품

지문의 단어 "rudimentary"와 의미가 가장 가까운 것은?
(A) 본질적인
(B) 놀라운
(C) 고대의
(D) 원시 단계의

해설 rudimentary는 '가장 기본적인, 발달되지 않은'이란 뜻으로, 의미가 가장 비슷한 것은 (D) primitive이다.

<우산>은 피에르 오귀스트 르누아르가 1880년대 각기 다른 두 시기에 그린 유화이다. 1880년대 초기에 시작된 첫 번째 단계에서는 느슨한 붓놀림, 밝은 색조와 어두운 색조의 대비 같은 인상주의 운동의 전형적인 특징을 보여주었다. 1885년 무렵에 이미 인상주의에서 멀어진 르누아르는 완성하지 않았던 그 그림을 다시 꺼내 부드러운 색채와 선을 살린 고전주의 양식을 도입했다. 가장 중요한 것은 중심이 되는 여성 인물의 옷차림이 노동자 계층처럼 보이게 바뀌었고, 그림 제목의 유래가 된 우산들이 작품 배경에 추가되었다는 것이다.

지문 어휘

phase 단계 characteristic 특징 loose 느슨한 brushwork 붓놀림 contrast 대비 linear 선의 principal 주요한 figure 인물, 모습 titular 표제(이름)의 유래가 된

지문의 단어 "muted"와 의미가 가장 가까운 것은?
(A) 전통적인
(B) 선명한
(C) 부드러운
(D) 대조적인

해설 muted는 '(색이) 부드러운'이란 뜻으로 사용되었으므로, 동일한 뜻의 (C) subdued가 정답이다.

과학자들은 특정 종들이 광범위한 의사소통 체계를 갖추고 있음을 이미 규명했으며, 그 종들 중 하나가 가장 큰 육상 포유류인 코끼리이다. 이 생명체들은 잘 발달된 사회 구조를 자랑하며, 다양한 소통 방식을 이용해 사회적 상호 작용이나 일상적인 일들을 수행하는 데 필요한 폭넓은 정보를 전달한다. 그들의 사회는 가족 단위와 사회적 유대를 중심으로 조직된 매우 공동체적인 사회이다. 분열-융합 사회의 특징대로, 일부 코끼리들은 개별적으로 무리에서 잠시 벗어나 있다가 나중에 더 큰 무리에 다시 합류하며, 이로 인해 광대한 영역에 걸친 코끼리들의 이동이 동시에 이루어지게 하기 위한 의사 전달 체계가 필요하다.

지문 어휘

establish 규명하다 extensive 광범위한 boast 자랑하다 communal 공동의 bond 유대 fission-fusion society (동물 행동학) 분열-융합 사회 pack 무리, 떼 necessitate 필요로 하다 vast 광대한

1 지문의 단어 "employ"와 의미가 가장 가까운 것은?
   (A) 보내다
   (B) 이동하다
   (C) 이용하다
   (D) 지속하다

해설 employ는 '이용하다'라는 뜻으로 쓰였으므로, 정답은 (C) utilize이다.

2 지문의 단어 "rejoin"과 의미가 가장 가까운 것은?
   (A) 개혁하다
   (B) 연장하다
   (C) 필요로 하다
   (D) ~으로 돌아가다

해설 rejoin은 '다시 합류하다'라는 뜻이므로, 유사한 뜻을 나타내는 (D) return to가 정답이다.

비옥한 땅이 건조해지는 과정인 사막화는 자연 현상이나 인간의 행동에 의해 야기될 수 있다. 어떤 경우이든, 그 즉각적인 결과는 영향을 받은 지역 내에서 파멸적인 초목 손실이 발생한다는 것이고, 이로 인해 바람과 물로 인한 이중 침식 과정을 지연시켜 줄 필수적 보호층이 땅에서 사라지게 된다. 아마도 인간이 사막화를 초래하게 된 가장 흔한 원인은 단기간에 산출량을 극대화하려는 농부들에 의한 과도한 토지 사용, 그리고 과도한 가축 방목일 것이다. 하지만 숲의 재조성과 토질 복원 등 사막화의 영향을 늦추거나 심지어 반전시키는 데 이용될 만한 다양한 대응책이 있다. 전자는 토종 식물들을 옮겨 심는 것이 수반되고, 후자는 손상된 땅에 물이나 비료를 공급하는 것이 필요하다.

지문 어휘

desertification 사막화 render (어떤 상태로) 만들다 vegetation 초목 strip A of B A에서 B를 앗아가다 overexploitation 과잉 개발 overgrazing 과도 방목 countermeasure 대응책 reverse 반전시키다 restoration 복원 flora 식물상 fertilizer 비료

1 지문의 단어 "catastrophic"과 의미가 가장 가까운 것은?
   (A) 점차적인
   (B) 불가피한
   (C) 처참한
   (D) 지속적인

해설 catastrophic은 '파멸적인'이라는 뜻이므로, 의미가 가장 비슷한 것은 (C) disastrous이다.

2 지문의 구 "maximize their yields"와 의미가 가장 가까운 것은?
   (A) 성장 시기를 연장하다
   (B) 임금 지출을 줄이다
   (C) 밭의 크기를 확장하다
   (D) 최대량을 산출하다

해설 maximize their yields는 '산출량을 극대화하다'라는 뜻이므로, 정답은 (D) produce as much as possible이다.

태양계에서 가장 큰 행성인 목성은 거대 기체 행성으로 분류
된다. 목성 지름이 대략 150,000킬로미터에 달하고, 주로
고체가 아닌 가스와 액체로 이루어져 있으며, 4개의 지구형
행성, 즉 수성, 금성, 지구, 화성보다 밀도가 낮기 때문이다.
목성 대기권의 구성 성분은 대략 수소가 76퍼센트, 헬륨이
24퍼센트이고 아주 적은 양의 메탄과 수증기가 있다. 목성은
지름이 지구 지름의 11배지만, 질량은 우리 고향 행성 지구
보다 놀랍게도 318배나 더 크다. 사실상 천문학자들은 목성
이 비슷한 유형의 행성으로서 가능한 최고 질량에 근접했다
고 믿고 있다. 만약 목성이 75배 더 크다면, 수소 원자 융합
을 시작해 헬륨을 생성하고 결국 항성으로 바뀔 것이다.

지문 어휘

classify 분류하다 gas giant 거대 기체 행성 diameter 지름
density 밀도 terrestrial planet 지구형 행성(가스가 아닌
고체로 된 행성) composition 구성, 구성 요소 atmosphere
(지구 및 기타 행성의) 대기 water vapor 수증기 mass 질량
hydrogen atom 수소 원자

1 지문의 단어 "approximately"와 의미가 가장 가까운 것은?
(A) 대략
(B) 정확히
(C) 적절히
(D) 약간

해설 approximately는 '대략'을 뜻하므로, 유사한 뜻의 (A) about
이 정답이다.

2 지문의 단어 "fusing"과 의미가 가장 가까운 것은?
(A) 거절하기
(B) 합치기
(C) 발생시키기
(D) 끌어들이기

해설 fusing은 '융합하기'라는 뜻을 나타내므로, 의미가 가장 비슷한
(B) joining이 정답이다.

10

유럽의 예술 음악은 19세기 들어서 고전주의 시대가 끝나고
낭만주의 음악이 출현하기 시작하면서 중대한 변화를 겪었
다. 고전주의 시대 음악은 명료함과 규칙적인 구조가 특징으
로, 종종 '자연스러운 단순함'이라고 일컬어지는 특징들이 결
합된 것이다. 그 주요 형식 중 하나인 소나타는 이후 낭만주
의 작곡가들의 작품을 위한 기반을 다지는 데 도움이 되었다.
낭만주의 음악은 지성보다 감성을 선호했다는 점에서 고전주
의 음악과 달랐다. 낭만주의 음악은 열정적이고 체계가 없었
으며, 고전주의 작곡법의 전통을 거부했고, 깊은 감정을 불러
일으키기 위한 민족주의적 함의를 특징으로 담고 있었다. 이
같은 극명한 차이에도 불구하고, 모차르트 같은 고전주의 작

곡가들의 작품은 낭만주의 음악과 쇼팽이나 리스트 같은 낭
만주의 작곡가들에게 강한 영향을 미쳤다.

지문 어휘

undergo 겪다 clarity 명료함 in that ~라는 점에서
intellect 지성 passionate 열정적인 unstructured 체계가
없는 convention 전통, 관습 nationalistic 민족주의적인
undertone 숨은 뜻, 함의 stir 불러일으키다

1 지문의 구 "lay the groundwork"와 의미가 가장 가까운
것은?
(A) 체계를 구축하다
(B) 이론이 틀렸음을 입증하다
(C) ~에 고마움을 표하다
(D) 기반을 세우다

해설 lay the groundwork는 '기반을 다지다'라는 뜻이므로,
의미가 가장 비슷한 것은 (D) create a foundation이다.

2 지문의 단어 "stark"와 의미가 가장 가까운 것은?
(A) 색다른
(B) 별개의
(C) 극심한
(D) 중요하지 않은

해설 stark는 '극명한'이라는 뜻을 나타내므로, 의미가 가장 비슷한
(C) extreme이 정답이다.

기원전 5세기, 구체적으로 말해 기원전 480년에서 404년
까지의 기간은 그리스 도시 국가 아테네의 황금기로, 정치적
패권과 경제 성장, 그리고 문화적 우수성이 예상치 않게 한데
어우러지는 상황을 누리고 있었다. 이 시기의 도래를 알린 사
건은 아테네가 이끄는 그리스 도시 국가 연합이 기원전 478
년 페르시아 침략군에 맞서 승리한 것이었다. 뒤이어 페르시
아와 평화가 이루어지는 시기에, 이 연합체는 아테네가 본질
적으로 아테네 제국이었던 곳의 명백한 지도자로 부상하면서
점차 권력 관계의 균형을 잃게 되었다. 아테네의 장군이자 정
치가였던 페리클레스가 이 시기에 가장 영향력 있는 지도자
였다. 그는 예술과 문학의 중요성을 믿었으며, 파르테논 신전
을 포함하여 세상에 가장 위대한 건축물들을 많이 가져다 준
야심 찬 사업에 앞장섰다.

지문 어휘

specifically 구체적으로 말하면 fortuitous 예기치 않은
congruence 일치, 조화, 합동 superiority 우월성, 우세
coalition 연합(체), 연정 ensue 뒤따르다 undertaking
(중요한) 일, 사업

1 지문의 단어 "hegemony"와 의미가 가장 가까운 것은?
(A) 권세
(B) 협조
(C) 변형
(D) 저항

해설 hegemony는 '패권'이라는 뜻이므로, 가장 비슷한 뜻을 가진 (A) dominance가 정답이다.

2 지문의 단어 "spearheaded"와 의미가 가장 가까운 것은?
(A) 명령했다
(B) 탐구했다
(C) 이끌었다
(D) 중단했다

해설 spearheaded는 '앞장섰다'를 뜻하므로, 의미가 가장 비슷한 것은 (C) led이다.

12

자연 군락이 일정 기간에 걸쳐 다른 군락으로 대체되는 과정은 생태 천이로 알려져 있다. 생태 천이에는 1차와 2차, 이렇게 두 가지 유형이 있다. 1차 천이는 유동 용암 등으로 땅이 새롭게 형성되거나, 아마도 물러나는(작아지는) 빙하 때문에 땅이 최근에 노출되는 등의 상황에서 일어난다. 이런 경우, 선도 종이 군집화 과정을 처음부터 새롭게 시작해야 한다. 반면에 2차 천이에서는 교란 요소가 기존의 식물 군락을 파괴시켜 생태 천이 과정을 다시 시작해야 할 필요가 생기지만, 흙과 영양분은 손상되지 않고 남아 있다. 이런 유형의 천이는 산불이 난 후에 가장 분명하게 관찰할 수 있는데, 이 때는 한 세대의 나무들 전체가 완전히 파괴된 후 불에 탄 흙 속에서 식물이 새로 자라기 시작한다.

지문 어휘

ecological succession 생태 천이 lava 용암 retreat 후퇴하다, 물러나다 colonization (식물의) 군집화, 대량 서식 disturbance 교란, 방해 intact 손상되지 않은 wildfire 산불 scorched 불에 탄 generation 세대, (동식물) 한 단계 생명 주기

1 지문의 구 "from scratch"와 의미가 가장 가까운 것은?
(A) 힘차게
(B) 처음부터
(C) 약간의 도움을 받아
(D) 멀리서

해설 from scratch는 '처음부터'라는 뜻이므로, 정답은 (B) from the beginning이다.

2 지문의 구 "wiped out"과 의미가 가장 가까운 것은?
(A) 비료를 준
(B) 노출된
(C) 활기를 되찾은
(D) 제거된

해설 wiped out은 '완전히 파괴된'을 뜻하므로, 의미가 가장 비슷한 것은 (D) removed이다.

13

수분 증후군이란 꽃들이 자연 도태 과정을 거치며 발달하는 특성들의 집합체이다. 그것은 바람이나 물 같은 비생물학적 요인에 의해 생길 수도 있고, 새나 벌 같은 생물학적 요인으로 생길 수도 있다. 이 같은 특성들 중에는 꽃의 모양, 크기, 색깔, 향기, 그 밖의 특징들이 포함된다. 예를 들어, 벌이 꽃가루를 옮긴 꽃들은 노란색이나 파란색을 띠는 경향이 있고, 꿀 속의 가장 지배적인 당분이 자당인 경우가 많다. 이것은 나비가 꽃가루를 옮긴 꽃들과 대조되는데, 이런 꽃들은 대개 크기가 크면서 분홍이나 연보라색을 띠고, 향이 강하며 꽃가루보다 꿀이 더 많이 들어 있다. 이 꿀은 종종 꽃의 좁은 관 안에 숨겨져 있어서, 나비들의 긴 혀를 통해서만 닿을 수 있다. 하지만, 과학계 내에서는 얼마나 많은 종류의 꽃을 단 하나의 전형적인 수분 증후군으로 정확하게 분류할 수 있는지에 대해 다소 견해가 엇갈린다.

지문 어휘

pollination 수분(꽃가루받이) trait 특성 evolve 발달하다, 진화하다 natural selection 자연 선택, 자연 도태 nonbiological 비생물학적인 factor 요인 scent 향기 sucrose 자당 nectar 꿀, 과즙 in contrast to ~와 대조되어 pollen 꽃가루

1 지문의 단어 "predominant"와 의미가 가장 가까운 것은?
(A) 근본적인
(B) 영양가 있는
(C) 우세한
(D) 선행하는

해설 predominant는 '지배적인'이라는 뜻이므로, 유사한 뜻을 나타내는 (C) prevalent가 정답이다.

2 지문의 단어 "secreted"와 의미가 가장 가까운 것은?
(A) 추출한
(B) 감춰진
(C) 이전된
(D) 소화된

해설 secreted는 '숨겨진'이라는 뜻으로 사용되었으므로, 정답은 의미가 가장 비슷한 (B) concealed이다.

인쇄의 역사는 목재 덩어리에 부호나 그림을 새긴 다음 잉크를 문질러 발라 매끄한 표면에 대고 눌러 이미지를 그대로 옮기는 과정인 목판 인쇄의 도래와 함께 시작되었다고 할 수 있다. 목판 인쇄는 서기 220년 이전 어느 때인가 중국에서 처음 등장했으며 천 표면에 인쇄하는 것이 선호되었다. 현재까지 남아 있는 가장 오래된 예는 세 가지 색으로 꽃들이 인쇄되어 있는 비단 조각들이다. 종이 인쇄는 9세기가 되어서야 중국에서 일반적인 관행으로 등장했다. 고대 불교 경전인 <금강반야바라밀경>은 현존하는 가장 오래된 목판본 중 하나로, 출판일자가 서기 868년으로 되어 있다. 이 시기에 숙련된 목판 인쇄공들은 하루 최대 2,000장까지 인쇄해 방대한 양의 인쇄물을 만들어 낼 수 있었다.

지문 어휘

commence 시작되다 advent 도래, 출현 woodblock printing 목판 인쇄 carve 새기다 smear 문질러 바르다 practice 실행, 관행 generate 만들어 내다

1 지문의 단어 "fragments"와 의미가 가장 가까운 것은?
(A) 종이들
(B) 의복들
(C) 그림들
(D) 조각들

해설 fragments는 '조각들'이라는 뜻이므로, 의미가 가장 비슷한 (D) pieces가 정답이다.

2 지문의 단어 "extant"와 의미가 가장 가까운 것은?
(A) 존재하는
(B) 익명의
(C) 소중한
(D) 되찾은

해설 extant는 '현존하는'이라는 뜻이므로, 유사한 뜻을 나타내는 (A) existing이 정답이다.

CHAPTER 03 Rhetorical Purpose

EXERCISE
pp. 56-61

정답 | 01 (D) **02** (C) **03** (B) **04** (C) **05** 1.(B) 2.(D)
06 1.(B) 2.(A) **07** 1.(D) 2.(C) **08** 1.(C) 2.(A)

상업 혁명은 유럽에서 일어난 무역 중심의 경제 발전 시기로, 11세기에 시작해 700년 이상이 지난 1차 산업 혁명기까지 계속되었다. 상업 혁명은 대항해 시대와 더불어 절정에 이르렀다고 할 수 있는데, 이 시대는 15세기에 시작되었다. 십자군 전쟁으로 향료 및 기타 이국적 물품에 대한 열망이 되살아나자, 무역 망이 확립되고 새로운 무역로가 지도에 기입되고, 이로 인해 교역 붐이 일어났다. 지정학적으로는, 포르투갈, 스페인, 네덜란드를 포함한 유럽 국가들이 전 세계를 아우르는 거대한 제국들을 개발하기 시작하면서, 식민주의의 출현이 무역을 부채질하는 역할을 했다. 또 다른 주요 요인은 유럽 국가들이 은과 금의 지속적인 부족으로 고통을 겪었다는 사실인데, 동양 국가들과의 교역에서 토대가 되었던 이들 귀금속에 대한 한없는 갈망이 새로운 땅을 탐험하는 데 더 큰 관심을 갖게 만들었다.

지문 어휘

culminate 정점에 이르다 Age of Exploration 대항해 시대 exotic 이국적인 the Crusades 십자군 전쟁 chart 지도에 기입하다 commerce 교역, 상업 geopolitically 지정학적으로 colonialism 식민주의 fuel 부채질하다 plague 괴롭히다 deficit 부족, 결손 insatiable 한없는, 만족할 줄 모르는 cornerstone 초석, 토대

글쓴이는 왜 지문에서 "십자군 전쟁"을 언급하는가?
(A) 유럽 국가들이 식민주의를 포기한 이유를 설명하려고
(B) 대항해 시대를 전후해서 태도의 변화를 비교하려고
(C) 무역이 전 세계에 미친 부정적인 영향에 대해 문제를 제기하려고
(D) 유럽인들의 탐험 욕구의 근본 원인을 설명하려고

어휘 raise an issue 문제를 제기하다

해설 상업혁명을 가속화시킨 원인들을 설명하면서, 그 원인들 중 하나인 탐험 욕구가 십자군 전쟁을 계기로 생겼다고 했으므로, (D)가 정답이다.

성인이 2~4세 이전에 일어났던 사건이나 상황을 기억해 내지 못하는 것은 아동기 기억 상실로 알려져 있다. 그런 기억들은 대개 망각되었다고 일컬어지지만, 기억에 있어서 입수 가능성과 접근 가능성 사이에는 현저한 차이가 있다. 입수 가능성은 기억이 실제로 손상되지 않은 채 뇌 속에 저장되어 있는지 여부를 가리키고, 접근 가능성은 특정 시점의 기억을 불러낼 수 있는 개개인의 능력과 관련된 가변적 조건이다. 이는 입수할 수는 있지만 접근할 수는 없는 어떤 기억들이 존재할 수 있다는 뜻이다. 처음으로 반려동물을 선물 받은 기억처럼 개인적이면서 강한 감정적 내용을 담고 있는 아주 어린 적 기억들은 역사적 사건 같은 공적인 기억들보다 더 접근 가능한 경향이 있다.

지문 어휘

recall 기억해 내다 amnesia 기억 상실 marked 현저한, 뚜렷한 availability 입수 가능성 accessibility 접근 가능성 intact 손상되지 않은 variable 가변적인 recollection 기억

글쓴이가 지문에서 어린 시절의 반려동물에 대해 논의하는 이유는?
(A) 성인이 아동기 기억 상실을 경험한다는 개념을 반박하기 위해
(B) 전형적인 성인 기억과 어린 시절 기억을 대조하기 위해
(C) 쉽게 접근할 수 있는 유형의 기억을 예를 들어 설명하기 위해
(D) 사람들이 입수할 수 없는 기억에 어떻게 접근할 수 있는지 강조하기 위해

어휘 refute 반박하다 concept 개념

해설 개인적이고 감정적이어서 접근이 잘 되는 기억의 예로 어린 시절 처음 가지게 된 반려동물이 언급되었으므로, (C)가 정답이다.

파리 북쪽의 교외 지역인 생드니에 가면 방문자들은 예전 중세 시대 때에는 수도원 교회였지만 지금은 대성당으로 쓰이는 생드니 대성당을 볼 수 있다. 이 건물은 역사적으로는 물론, 초기 고딕 건축의 여러 요소로 장식되었기 때문에, 건축적 가치의 측면에서도 중요하다. 특히 이곳의 조각들은 이후 고딕 양식의 발전에 강한 영향을 미쳤는데, 그 사실은 생드니 성당 입구들 옆에 있는 예언자와 왕의 모습을 한 크고 얇은 인물 조각상들이 나중에 지어진 거의 모든 고딕 성당의 입구에서 발견되는 것으로 알 수 있다. 1175년에 세워진 생드니 성당 북쪽 입구의 조각상들은 특히 형태가 길고 표정이 풍부해서, 같은 시기에 지어진 샤르트르 대성당의 더 절제된 조각상들과 극명한 대조를 이룬다.

지문 어휘

basilica (대)성당 medieval 중세의 abbey 수도원 cathedral 대성당 in terms of ~의 측면에서 adorn 장식하다 flank ~의 옆에 있다 portal 정문, 입구 prophet 예언자 erect 세우다 elongated 긴 stand in contrast to ~와 대조를 이루다 stark 극명한 restrained 억제된, 절제된

글쓴이가 지문에서 "샤르트르 대성당"을 논의하는 이유는?
(A) 고딕 시대 이전 건축물의 예를 들기 위해
(B) 생드니 조각상들의 예술적 특성을 강조하기 위해
(C) 같은 시기의 두 가지 건축 기법을 비교하기 위해
(D) 생드니 대성당에 영감을 주었다는 증거를 제시하기 위해

어휘 feature 특징 inspiration 영감

해설 샤르트르 대성당에 있는 조각상들의 절제된 특성과 비교해 생드니의 조각상들이 특히 길고 표정이 풍부하다고 강조하고 있다. 그러므로 (B)가 정답이다.

화성의 대기는 이산화탄소가 대부분이고 극미량의 산소와 물, 그리고 적은 양의 아르곤 및 질소로 이루어져 있다. 또한 공중에 떠다니는 미립자도 높은 수준으로 포함하고 있는데, 이 때문에 대기권에 먼지가 많고, 화성 표면에서 바라볼 때 하늘이 독특한 황갈색 색조를 띠게 만든다. 고농도의 대기권 이산화탄소와 화성 표면의 낮은 압력 때문에 화성에서는 음파가 지구상에서보다 더 느리게 이동하며, 이로 인해 소리 자체가 줄어든다. 기후 측면에서 보면, 화성과 지구의 자전축 기울기가 비슷하기 때문에, 비록 화성의 계절이 두 배 더 길기는 하지만 두 행성이 유사한 계절을 경험한다. 또한 화성의 기온은 범위가 더 넓어, 표면 최저 온도가 섭씨 영하 110도까지 떨어지고 적도 부근의 최고 기온은 화성의 여름에 섭씨 35도에 이른다.

지문 어휘

carbon dioxide 이산화탄소 trace 극미량 airborne 공중에 떠 있는 particulate 미립자 tawny 황갈색의 hue 색조 concentration 농도 diminish 줄어들다 tilt 기울기 rotational axis 자전축 equatorial 적도의 Martian 화성의

글쓴이는 왜 화성 자전축의 기울기와 지구 자전축의 기울기를 비교하는가?
(A) 화성의 하늘이 푸른색이 아닌 이유를 설명하려고
(B) 화성의 계절이 긴 이유를 설명하려고
(C) 화성의 기후 특성을 밝히려고
(D) 두 종류 대기권의 영향을 대조하려고

어휘 lengthy 긴, 늘어진

해설 화성과 지구의 자전축 기울기가 비슷해 기후적 측면에서 두 행성의 계절도 유사하다고 했으므로, (C)가 정답이다.

고대 메소포타미아 문명에서는 건축이 번성했는데, 부분적으로는 건설 기술이 인간에게 부여된 신의 선물이라는 믿음이 있었기 때문이었다. 이 지역에서는 돌이 드물었기 때문에, 진흙과 햇볕에 말린 벽돌이 말 그대로 초기 메소포타미아 건축의 기본 구성 요소였다. 가정용 구조물은 커다란 중앙 공간을 작은 방들이 둘러싸고 있는 형태로 비교적 단순하고 수수한 편이었지만, 공공 건물들은 그 규모나 아름다움에서 보는 사람들을 압도하게 건설되었다. 메소포타미아 건축물에서 아마도 가장 인상적인 측면은, 계단식 경사면을 따라가면 정상에 신전이 나오는 일종의 피라미드, 즉 지구라트였다. 지구라트는 종교적인 구조물이지만 일반 평민들은 그 안에 들어가는 게 금지되어 있었고, 종교 지도자들만을 위한 영역이었다. 메소포타미아 건축물의 또 다른 주요 혁신은 둥근 아치였다. 이 아치는 엄청난 압력을 견딜 수 있었으며, 지탱하고 있는 구조물의 내부 공기가 더 잘 흐르게 했다. 고대 로마의 건축가들이 건축의 이러한 주요소를 발명했다고 공로를 인정받기도 했지만, 아치는 일찍이 기원전 6세기에 메소포타미아 건축가들에 의해 이미 사용되고 있었다.

지문 어휘

flourish 번성하다 divine 신의, 신성한 bestow 부여하다
scarce 드문, 부족한 literal 문자 그대로의 building block
구성 요소 domestic 가정의 modest 수수한 dazzle
압도하다, 감탄하게 하다 terraced 계단식의 shrine 신전, 성지
facet 측면 forbid 금지하다 domain 영역 withstand 견뎌
내다 give credit for ~의 공로를 인정하다 staple 주요소

1 글쓴이는 무엇을 위해 지문에서 "종교 지도자들"을
언급하는가?
(A) 지구라트가 피라미드와 다른 이유를 설명하기 위해
(B) 지구라트의 배타적인 면을 보여주기 위해
(C) 지구라트의 엄청난 크기와 아름다움을 강조하기 위해
(D) 지구라트가 고대 로마에서 어떻게 이용되었는지
설명하기 위해

어휘 exclusive 배타적인, 독점적인

해설 지구라트가 종교적 구조물이었지만 평민이 들어오는 것이
금지된 배타적인 곳이었음을 설명하려고 언급한 것이므로,
(B)가 정답이다.

2 글쓴이는 왜 지문에서 "고대 로마의 건축가들"을 언급하는가?
(A) 그들이 메소포타미아를 어떻게 여겼는지 보여주기 위해
(B) 그들의 건축 양식을 현대적 양식과 비교하기 위해
(C) 그들이 후에 어떻게 지구라트를 모방했는지 설명하기
위해
(D) 그들이 아치를 발명했다는 생각을 반박하기 위해

어휘 view 여기다, 보다 copy 모방하다

해설 고대 로마 건축가들이 아치를 만들었다고 믿는 경우도
있었지만, 사실은 그보다 훨씬 전에 메소포타미아 건축가들이
아치를 사용했다고 했다. 그러므로 정답은 (D)이다.

미국의 연방 법원 체제는 법적 구제책을 찾는 개개인에게 필요한 수단을 제공하는 다양한 유형의 법원들을 포함하며, 지방 법원과 상소 법원이 이 구조 내에서 주요한 두 개 범주에 속한다. 일반 사실심 법정 역할을 하는 지방 법원은 민사와 형사 소송을 판결하며, 증거나 목격자 증언을 제시함으로써 지방 법원에서 재판하는 소송 사건과 관련해 사실과 정황을 입증하는 데 결정적인 역할을 한다. 이들 지방 법원의 주요 임무는 피고의 유무죄 여부를 밝히고 적절한 처벌과 인정될 수 있는 금전적 배상을 결정하는 일이다. 반면에, 상소 법원은 여러 측면에서 지방 법원과 다르다. 항소심 재판권이라는 것을 보유한 상소 법원은 상소를 심리할 수 있는 권한을 지니며, 따라서 재판은 하지 않고 지방 법원이 특정 사건에 판결을 내림에 있어서 타당한 절차를 충실히 지켰는지 여부를 평가한다. 이 상소 과정에서 소송 사건에 연루된 당사자들은 자신들의 주장을 소송 사건 적요서라는 서류 형태로 제출하는데, 이것은 상당히 광범위해 때로는 수백 페이지에 달하기도 한다.

지문 어휘

federal court 연방 법원 encompass 포함(망라)하다
remedy 구제책 district court 지방 법원 court of appeal
상소 법원 predominant 주요한, 우세한 trial court
사실심(1심) 법정 adjudicate 판결하다 civil 민사상의
criminal 형사상의 testimony 증언 trial 재판 guilt 유죄
innocence 무죄 the accused 피고 appropriate 적절한
penalty 처벌 compensation 보상, 배상 award (배상금
등을) 인정하다, 주다 appellate jurisdiction 항소심 재판권
assess 평가하다 adhere to ~을 충실히 지키다 verdict 판결
submit 제출하다 brief 소송 사건 적요서

1 글쓴이는 왜 지문에서 처벌과 배상을 언급하는가?
(A) 미국에서 법적 배상을 받을 수 있는 수단을 나열하기
위해
(B) 지방 법원의 주요 기능이 무엇인지 설명하기 위해
(C) 죄 지은 사람이 직면하는 결과의 예를 들기 위해
(D) 상소 법원이 갖는 권한의 범위를 설명하기 위해

어휘 redress 보상, 배상 consequence 결과

해설 지방 법원의 주요 임무가 피고의 유무죄를 밝히고, 처벌과
금전적 배상을 결정하는 것이라고 했다. 그러므로 (B)가
정답이다.

2 글쓴이는 왜 지문에서 "상소 과정"을 언급하는가?
(A) 두 가지 범주의 법원 간 절차상의 차이점을 나타내기
위해
(B) 사건 적요서라는 법률 서류를 제출하는 고된 일을
비판하려고
(C) 항소심 재판권에 절차상의 문제가 발생할 수 있음을
지적하기 위해
(D) 법원 체계가 사회 정의와 어떻게 연관되는지 강조하기
위해

어휘 arduous 고된 file (증서·서류를) 정식으로 제출하다

해설 유무죄를 가리는 지방 법원과 절차에 대한 심의만 하는 상소 법원을 비교하고 있으므로, (A)가 정답이다.

어휘 hypothesis 가설 alternative 대안의

해설 대양 온도 상승뿐 아니라 오존 파괴도 종 페름기 멸종을 야기시켰을 수 있는 다른 원인들 중 하나라고 했다. 그러므로 (C)가 정답이다.

07

멸종 맥박은 집중적으로 몰아서 발생하는 형태로 멸종 속도가 급격하게 증가하는 것이다. 페름기 멸종은 그와 같은 일련의 맥박들로 이루어졌는데, 이것이 합쳐져 결국 지구 역사상 최대 규모의 멸종 사건이 발생하게 된 것이다. 페름기 멸종으로, 95퍼센트의 해양 생물 종을 포함해, 지구에 사는 종의 약 90퍼센트가 죽은 것으로 추정된다. 과학계의 일반적인 합의는 이 사건이 1500만 년에 걸쳐 일어났다는 것이지만, 멸종이 훨씬 더 짧은 기간 내에, 즉 단지 20만 년에 걸쳐 일어났고 그 중에서도 다수는 2만 년이라는 단일 기간에 발생했다며, 이를 반박하는 과학자도 일부 있다. 지구 대양의 따뜻하고 얕은 곳에 사는 무척추 동물들이 페름기 멸종에 가장 큰 타격을 받았지만, 수생 척추 동물들도 엄청난 종 손실을 겪었다. 가설에 근거해 볼 때, 영양소 순환에 부정적인 영향을 미치는 대양 온도 상승이 이 엄청난 멸종의 주요 원인이었지만, 오존 파괴와 메탄가스를 발생시키는 미생물의 급격한 증가를 포함한 다른 가능한 원인들도 제기되고 있다.

지문 어휘

extinction pulse 멸종 맥박 concentrated 집중적인
demise 죽음 consensus 의견 일치, 합의 refute 반박하다
invertebrate 무척추 동물 shallows (강·바다의) 얕은 곳
aquatic 수생의 vertebrate 척추 동물 devastating 파괴적인
hypothetically 가설에 근거해서 die-off (동식물 개체의) 멸종,
집단사 depletion 감소 microbe 미생물

1 글쓴이는 지문에서 "수생 척추 동물"을 무엇의 예로 언급하는가?
(A) 더 따뜻한 기온에서 살아남을 수 있었던 종들
(B) 과학자들이 분류할 수 없었던 수생 종들
(C) 페름기 멸종 이전에는 존재하지 않았던 어종들
(D) 다수 종이 사라져 멸종에 이른 동물의 범주

어휘 classify 분류하다

해설 해저의 따뜻하고 얕은 곳에 서식하는 무척추 동물 이외에 페름기 멸종으로 타격을 받은 예로 수생 척추 동물을 들었으므로, (D)가 정답이다.

2 글쓴이가 지문에서 "오존 파괴"를 언급하는 이유는?
(A) 페름기 멸종이 1,500만 년 지속되었다는 가설을 반박하기 위해
(B) 미래에 멸종 사건을 피하게 해 주는 가능한 방법을 소개하기 위해
(C) 페름기 멸종의 원인에 대해 대안 이론을 제시하기 위해
(D) 멸종 맥박이 대양 온도 상승과 어떻게 연관되는지 보여주기 위해

08

지구상에 서식했던 최초의 생명 형태는 약 40억 년 전에 등장한 미세한 단세포 생물이었을 것으로 여겨지는데, 이들은 현대 박테리아의 조상이었다. 박테리아라는 말은 '지팡이'를 의미하는 고대 그리스어가 라틴화 한 것에서 유래하며, 이는 최초로 발견된 박테리아가 막대 같은 모양이었다는 사실 때문이었다. 대부분의 현대 박테리아는 단세포 상태로 남아 있으며 길이가 기껏해야 몇 마이크로미터밖에 되지 않는다. 박테리아는 일정한 크기에 도달하면 성장기가 멈춘다. 그러면 박테리아는 한 개의 생명체가 두 개의 동일한 생명체로 쪼개지는 이분법이라는 무성생식을 통해 번식한다. 통제된 실험실 환경에서 생산되는 것 같이 완벽한 조건 하에서라면, 박테리아는 굉장한 속도로 번식해 17분마다 개체 수가 두 배로 늘어날 수 있다. 하지만, 실험실 밖에서 박테리아는 무기한으로 그토록 빠르게 번식하게 해줄 만큼 충분한 영양분을 공급받기 어렵다. 영양분 제한은 다양한 성장 전략을 발전시켰는데, 예를 들어, 야생 박테리아 개체군은 엄청나게 빠르게 성장하는 경향이 있는데, 이는 여름철 특정 호수들에서 발생하는 계절적 조류 대증식에서 관찰할 수 있는 현상이다.

지문 어휘

inhabit 서식하다 microscopic 미세한 unicellular 단세포의
derive 유래하다 Latinization 라틴화 staff 지팡이 rod 막대
attain 이르다 reproduce 번식하다 asexual reproduction
무성생식 binary fission 이분법 identical 동일한 indefinite
무기한의 diverse 다양한 strategy 전략 algal 조류의

1 글쓴이는 왜 지문에서 "막대"를 언급하는가?
(A) 고대 박테리아의 크기를 강조하기 위해
(B) 박테리아가 어떻게 처음 발견되었는지 설명하기 위해
(C) '박테리아'라는 말의 유래를 설명하기 위해
(D) 박테리아가 번식하는 과정을 설명하기 위해

해설 최초로 발견된 박테리아의 모양이 막대와 비슷했기 때문에, '지팡이'를 뜻하는 고대 그리스어가 라틴화 한 말에서 박테리아라는 말이 유래했다고 했으므로, (C)가 정답이다.

2 글쓴이가 지문에서 연구실을 언급하는 이유는?
(A) 박테리아의 번식 능력을 강조하기 위해
(B) 이분법이 어떻게 해로울 수 있는지에 대한 예를 들기 위해
(C) 계절적 조류 대증식에 대한 가능한 해결책을 제안하기 위해
(D) 두 종의 박테리아의 개체군 크기를 대조하기 위해

해설 박테리아가 급격하게 번식하는 데 완벽한 조건의 예로 환경이 통제된 실험실을 들었으므로, (A)가 정답이다.

CHAPTER 04 Reference

EXERCISE pp. 68-73

정답 | 01 (D) 02 (A) 03 (B) 04 (D) 05 (B) 06 (B)
07 1.(C) 2.(B) 08 1.(C) 2.(D) 09 1.(B) 2.(A)
10 1.(C) 2.(B)

01

고래의 지능이라는 개념이 과학적 사실로 널리 받아들여지고 있지만, 어느 정도인지는 아직 논쟁 중이다. 예를 들어, 돌고래들은 숫자의 연속성이라는 개념은 이해하는 것 같지만, 숫자들을 구별하지는 못하는 것 같다. 높은 지능을 보여 줄 수 있는 한 징후는 서로 다른 종들 간의 협력인데, 돌고래들과 쇠돌고래들 모두 해변으로 밀려온 고래들을 돕는 것으로 알려져 있고, 돌고래들이 조난 당한 인간들을 돕는다는 주장도 있어 왔다. 돌고래의 기구 사용 또한 기록되고 있는데, 돌고래들은 해저 바닥을 팔 때 부리를 보호하려고 때로는 부리에 스폰지 조각을 감싸기도 한다.

지문 어휘

cetacean 고래(목)의 debate 논쟁, 토론 grasp 이해하다
numerical 수의 continuity 연속성 discriminate 식별하다
interspecies 이종간의 porpoise 쇠돌고래 aid 돕다
distress 조난, 곤경 document (상세한 내용을) 기록하다

지문의 단어 "themselves"가 가리키는 것은?
(A) 숫자들 (B) 돌고래들
(C) 쇠돌고래들 (D) 고래들

해설 서로 다른 종들이 협력하는 예로 돌고래와 쇠돌고래들이 해변으로 밀려온 고래들을 돕는 상황을 언급하고 있다. 해변에 밀려온 대상이 고래들이므로, (D)가 정답이다. 또한, 재귀대명사 themselves의 주체가 whales인 것도 답을 찾을 수 있는 단서이다.

02

그리스의 지배를 받던 지중해 지역에서 기원전 약 323년부터 기원전 30년까지 지속됐던 헬레니즘 시대에는 문학이 다양한 형태로 융성했다. 연극 영역에서는, 신희극이 출현해 보다 극적인 전통 비극과 경쟁했다. 시 또한 번창했는데, 왕들이 후원을 통해 시인들을 지원하고 그 보답으로 그들을 기려 쓰여진 작품들을 헌정 받았다. 하지만 아마도 이 시기에 가장 주목할 만한 사건은 호머의 <오딧세이>를 라틴어로 번역한 것으로, 이는 차후 몇 세기 동안 로마 문학에 미치는 그리스의 영향력을 보장해 주는 작업이었다.

지문 어휘

Hellenistic 헬레니즘의 Mediterranean 지중해의 realm 영역 tragedy 비극 poetry 시 patronage (예술가에 대한) 후원 in one's honor ~에게 경의를 표하여, ~을 기려 in return 보답으로 notable 주목할 만한 translation 번역 ensure 보장하다

지문의 단어 "their"가 가리키는 것은?
(A) 왕들 (B) 시인들
(C) 작품들 (D) 세기들

해설 왕들이 시인들을 후원하고 그 보답으로 그들을 기리는 작품을 헌정 받았다고 했으므로, their는 (A)를 가리킨다.

03

이소적 종분화에서는 한 개체군 중 일부가 유전자 이동의 방해 요소가 되는 지리적 장벽에 의해 그 종의 나머지와 분리되어 결국 별개 종으로 진화하게 된다. 예를 들어, 호주에서는 회색캥거루가 분리되어 서로 다른 분포 구역에 서식하는 두 종이 되었다. 서부회색캥거루는 호주 남쪽 지역의 고유 종이고, 동부회색캥거루는 동부 지역의 3분의 1에 해당하는 지역에 서식한다. 지리적으로 겹치는 부분이 있지만, 이들은 야생 상태에서는 이종 교배를 하지 않는다.

지문 어휘

allopatric speciation 이소적 종분화 subset 부분 집합
population 개체군 isolate 분리[격리]하다 barrier
장벽 interruption 방해, 중단 gene 유전자 ultimately
결국 range (동식물의) 분포 구역 endemic 고유의, 토종의
territorial 영토의 overlap 겹침 interbreed 이종 교배하다

지문의 단어 "it"이 가리키는 것은?
(A) 이소적 종분화
(B) 한 개체군 중 일부
(C) 그 종의 나머지
(D) 유전자 이동의 방해 요소

해설 한 개체군 중 일부가 지리적 장벽에 의해 분리되어 결국은 그것(it)이 별개 종으로 진화한다고 했다. 그러므로 it은 분리되는 주체인 (B)이다.

04

도자기는 오랫동안 중국 예술의 근본이었고, 이는 자기가 중국에서 발명된 것이라는 점을 생각해 보면 놀랍지 않은 사실이다. 도자기의 혁신이 본격적으로 시작된 것은 명 왕조 때였다. 예를 들어, 암청색 안료 준비 면에서의 기술 개선이 그것의 번지는 속성을 없애 주었고, 푸른색 장식 이미지들의 가장자리에 이전에는 불가능했던 깔끔함을 가져다 주었다. 또 다른 중요한 발전은 자기의 대규모 상업적 수출이었는데, 이는 명 왕조가 시장 경제로 나아가는 변화의 한 부분이었다.

지문 어휘

ceramics 도자기류 porcelain 자기 Ming Dynasty 명 왕조 take off 시작하다 in earnest 진지하게, 본격적으로 refinement 개선, 세련 bring an end to ~을 끝내다 tendency 경향 bleed 번지다 heretofore 지금까지는 crispness (티, 구김 없는) 깔끔함 commercial 상업적인 exportation 수출

지문의 단어 "its"가 가리키는 것은?
(A) 자기   (B) 혁신
(C) 준비   (D) 암청색 안료

해설 암청색 안료를 다루는 기술이 발전해서 its, 즉 암청색 안료의 번지는 속성이 없어졌다고 했으므로, 정답은 (D)이다.

05

전 세계의 사막들은 사막에 서식하는 동물들이 특별한 특성과 행동들을 발달시킬 수밖에 없게 만드는 혹독한 조건들의 본거지이다. 이들 중에는 고온, 건조한 토양, 먹기 힘든 식물 등이 포함된다. 작은 사막 포유류들은 강렬한 태양열을 피하기 위해 낮 동안에는 모래 표면 아래로 파고 들어감으로써 생존한다. 반면, 큰 포유류들은 아주 높은 체온을 유지함으로써 과열 상태를 피한다. 사막에 사는 새들의 경우, 멀리 떨어진 한 수원에서 다음 수원으로 끊임없이 날아다님으로써 제약 없는 기동성을 이용한다.

지문 어휘

harsh 혹독한 force 강요하다 specialized (특별한 기능이나 환경에) 특화된 consume 먹다 burrow 굴을 파다 circumvent 피하다 intense 강렬한 maintain 유지하다 as for ~의 경우 take advantage of ~을 이용하다 unhindered 방해 받지 않는, 제약이 없는 mobility 기동성

지문의 단어 "These"가 가리키는 것은?
(A) 전 세계의 사막들
(B) 혹독한 조건들
(C) 동물들
(D) 행동들

해설 사막은 동물들이 서식하기 힘든 혹독한 조건들을 가지고 있다고 한 다음, 지시어가 포함된 문장에서 그 예들(고온, 건조한 토양, 먹기 힘든 식물)을 들고 있다. 따라서 These가 가리키는 것은 (B)이다.

06

육생 달팽이는 심각한 탈수 문제에 직면해 있는데, 이는 증발 과정을 통해서 그리고 표면을 돌아다니면서 수분이 90퍼센트인 점액 자국을 남김으로써 체내 수분을 잃기 때문이다. 많은 종들이 축축한 환경에서 서식하기 때문에 잃어버린 수분을 보충할 수 있지만, 사막에 사는 달팽이들은 이것을 할 수 없다. 대신 그 달팽이들은 증발을 막기 위해 껍데기 속에 몸을 숨긴다. 어떤 달팽이들은 꼬리 부분에 딱딱하게 자라 문 같은 역할을 하는 숨문 뚜껑을 이용해 이를 수행하며, 어떤 달팽이들은 껍데기의 구멍을 얇은 점막으로 막는다.

지문 어휘

terrestrial 육지에 사는 dehydration 탈수 evaporation 증발 trail 자국, 흔적 mucus 점액 replenish 보충하다 damp 축축한 seal 가두다, 밀봉하다 operculum 숨문 뚜껑 aperture (작은) 구멍

지문의 단어 "this"가 가리키는 것은?
(A) 표면을 돌아다니기
(B) 잃어버린 수분 보충하기
(C) 축축한 환경에 서식하기
(D) 사막에 살기

해설 but을 중심으로 앞 뒤 문장이 대조되는 내용을 제시한다. 축축한 환경에서는 수분을 보충할 수 있지만, 사막에서는 '이것'을 할 수 없다고 했으므로, (B)가 정답이다.

07

동물계의 종에서는 다양한 이유로 체색의 진화가 일어날 수 있다. 어떤 종들의 경우, 체색은 효과적인 위장 수단이 되어 잠재적 포식자의 눈에 띄지 않도록 해 주고, 또 다른 종들의 경우 정반대로 독성 종들이 자신들이 가진 위험성을 알리려고 사용하는 경계색을 모방함으로써 포식자의 주의를 끌기 위해 체색을 이용한다. 색깔은 또한 큰 무리를 지어 이동하는 얼룩말의 줄무늬 경우처럼, 공격자들을 현혹하는 데 쓰이기도 하는데, 이것은 굶주린 포식자의 주의를 딴 데로 돌리고 혼동시킬 수 있다. 이 각각의 예들에서 체색은 생존 확률을 높여주는 진화상의 이점을 제공한다. 또 다른 진화상의 이점은 특정 종 내에서 각 개체들이 짝을 얻도록 돕고 그리하여 그들의 유전자가 다음 세대로 전달되는 것을 보장해 줄 수 있는 밝고 선명한 색깔에서 찾아 볼 수 있다. 한편, 어떤 개구리 종은 피부 색조를 밝거나 어둡게 할 수 있는 능력을 발달시켰는데, 이는 체온 조절에 도움이 되는 실용적인 능력이다.

지문 어휘

camouflage 위장 potential 잠재적인 predator 포식자
mimic 모방하다 toxic 유독성의 advertise 널리 알리다
distract (주의를) 딴 데로 돌리다 advantage 이점 odds
확률, 가능성 vivid 선명한 obtain 획득하다 mate 짝
pragmatic 실용적인 regulation 조절

1 지문의 단어 "which"가 가리키는 것은?
(A) 경계색
(B) 공격자들
(C) 얼룩말의 줄무늬
(D) 큰 무리

해설 얼룩말의 줄무늬가 공격자들을 현혹할 수 있다고 언급한 후,
which 관계절에서 이것이 포식자의 주의를 딴 데로 돌리고
혼동시킬 수 있다고 했다. 그러므로 which가 가리키는 것은
(C)이다.

2 지문의 단어 "their"가 가리키는 것은?
(A) 밝고 선명한 색깔
(B) 각 개체들
(C) 특정 종
(D) 짝

해설 밝고 선명한 색깔이 각 개체들을 도와 짝을 얻게 하고 그들의
유전자도 전달하게 해 준다고 했으므로, (B)가 정답이다.

'수생 식물'이라는 용어는 식물계에서 물에 잠기거나, 수면
위, 또는 습지에 있는 유형처럼 지속적 또는 계절적으로 물에
젖어 있는 토양을 뜻하는 습윤 토양에서 성공적으로 생애 주
기를 완료할 수 있는 종을 설명하는 데 쓰인다. 수생 식물과
비슷한 수생 조류는 수생 식물과 유사점이 많기는 하지만 진
짜 식물로 간주되지 않기 때문에, 그렇게 분류되지는 않는다
는 점에 유의하는 게 중요하다. 수생 식물은 생육 방식에 따
라 더 작은 분류군으로 분류될 수 있다. 부유 식물은 뿌리가
아래쪽으로 늘어져 있지만 흙 속에 고정되어 있지는 않은 채,
잎과 줄기를 수면 위에 띄우고 있다. 이와 달리 정수 식물은
잎과 줄기는 눈에 띄게 수면 위로 뻗어 있으면서, 물속 토양
에 굳게 뿌리를 내리고 있다. 침수 식물로 알려진 또 다른 범
주 역시 흙 속에 뿌리를 내리고 있지만 잎과 줄기는 완전히
물에 잠겨 있고, 반면에 떠 있는 수생 식물은 흙 속에 뿌리를
내리지 않은 채 물에 완전히 잠겨 있다.

지문 어휘

term 용어, 말 submerged 물속에 잠긴 hydric 습윤한
consistently 지속적으로 wetland 습지 numerous 수많은
float 떠다니다 trail (가지 따위가) 늘어지다 anchor 고정시키다
extend 길게 자라다 prominently 눈에 띄게 suspended
(물속 또는 공중에) 떠 있는

1 지문의 단어 "such"가 가리키는 것은?
(A) 습지
(B) 수생 조류
(C) 수생 식물
(D) 수많은 유사점

해설 수생 조류는 수생 식물과 유사점도 많지만 그렇게(such)
분류되지는 않는다고 했으므로, such가 가리키는 것은
(C)이다.

2 지문의 단어 "their"가 가리키는 것은?
(A) 뿌리
(B) 정수 식물
(C) 잎과 줄기
(D) 침수 식물

해설 침수 식물을 설명하면서, 뿌리도 땅에 박혀 있고 그것의 잎과
줄기도 물속에 잠겨 있다고 말하고 있으므로, their는 (D)를
가리킨다.

15세기에 유럽인들이 아시아로 가는 더 짧은 무역로를 발견
하려고 노력하던 와중에 신세계가 발견되었다는 것은 널리
인정되는 사실이다. 크리스토퍼 콜럼버스가 우연이기는 하지
만, 대서양을 가로질러 육지와 맞닥뜨린 최초의 유럽 탐험가
였다고 많은 사람들이 말해 왔고, 곧이어 더 많은 발견이 뒤
따랐다. 지도에 표시되지 않은 이 땅이 금과 비옥한 농지, 기
타 자원의 측면에서 얼마나 풍요로운지 깨닫게 되면서, 탐험
과 모험은 곧 그것을 식민지화하려는 진지한 노력으로 바뀌
었다. 아메리카 대륙이 이미 수천 년 전에 정착지가 되어 있
었지만, 유럽인 식민지 개척자들은 그들이 마주친 원주민들
의 소유권 주장에 신빙성을 부여하지 않았다. 원주민들을 미
개한 야만인이라고 무시하면서 그들은 원주민들의 땅을 점령
하고 그 위에 영구 정착지를 건설하기 시작했다. 스페인과 포
르투갈이 최초로 식민지 건설을 시도하며 앞장서, 포르투갈
인들은 오늘날의 브라질 땅을 차지했고, 스페인 사람들은 남
아메리카에서 중앙아시아와 멕시코를 거쳐 오늘날의 미국 서
해안에 이르는 광대한 땅을 정복했다.

지문 어휘

endeavor 노력 encounter 마주치다 albeit ~이기는 하지만
accidentally 우연히 realization 깨달음 uncharted 지도에
표시되어 있지 않은 give way to ~으로 바뀌다 colonize
식민지로 만들다 credence 믿음, 신임 indigenous 원주민의
discount 무시하다 uncivilized 미개한 savage 야만인
seize 점령하다 swath (길고 넓은) 땅

1 지문의 단어 "it"이 가리키는 것은?
(A) 대서양
(B) 지도에 표시되지 않은 이 땅
(C) 금
(D) 탐험

해설 지도에 나오지도 않는 땅의 가치를 발견하고 그것(it)을
식민지로 만들기 위해 노력하게 되었다고 했으므로, it은 (B)를
가리킨다.

2 지문의 단어 "they"가 가리키는 것은?
(A) 유럽인 식민지 개척자들
(B) 소유권 주장
(C) 원주민들
(D) 미개한 야만인들

해설 they는 원주민들이 땅 주인임을 인정하지 않고 그 땅을 점령한
사람들이므로, 바로 앞에 언급한 (A)를 가리킨다.

10

집단 역학에 근거해 사회 집단은 1차 집단, 2차 집단, 단체,
부류, 이렇게 네 개의 기본 유형으로 분류될 수 있다. 1차 집
단은 구성원들이 서로를 결속시켜 주는 친밀하고 개인적인
관계를 맺는 작은 사회 집단인데, 2차 집단은 공동의 이해 관
계나 활동에 근거하는 경향이 있고 보다 개인적인 것이 개입
되지 않은 상호 작용을 특징으로 한다. 위안, 지지, 배려는 1
차 집단에서 제공되는데, 이것은 평생 지속되는 경우가 많고
개인의 정체성을 형성하는 데 중요한 역할을 한다. 반면에 2
차 집단은 목표 지향적이면서 일시적인데, 구성원들이 아주
빈번히 들어왔다 나갔다 할 수 있고, 목표를 이루고 나면 집
단 자체가 해체될 수도 있다. 단체는 수명이 더욱 더 짧은데,
그들은 동일한 활동에 참여하는 개개인이 상당한 규모로 모
인 것으로 자발적이면서도 느슨하게 형성되는 경향이 있기
때문이다. 흔한 예로 음악회 청중과 학회에 참석한 사람들을
들 수 있다. 부류의 경우, 구성원들의 공통적인 특성에 따라
정의되는 집단이기는 하지만, 이 유형은 개개인 간의 어떤 실
제적인 상호 작용도 포함할 필요가 없다. 사람들의 부류에는
종교, 성별, 인종 등이 포함될 수 있다.

지문 어휘

group dynamics 집단 역학 bind 묶다, 결속시키다
interests 이익, 이해 관계 impersonal 개인적인 것이 개입되지
않은 shape 형성하다 identity 정체성 goal-oriented
목표 지향적인 frequency 빈도 dissolve (관계를) 끝내다
objective 목적, 목표 lifespan 수명 spontaneous 자발적인
gender 성별 ethnicity 인종, 민족성

1 지문의 단어 "them"이 가리키는 것은?
(A) 1차 집단
(B) 사회 집단
(C) 구성원들
(D) 친밀하고 개인적인 관계

해설 1차 집단의 구성원들이 친밀한 관계를 맺고 있으며 그 관계가
그들(them)을 묶어준다고 했으므로, them은 (C)를 가리킨다.

2 지문의 구 "these types"가 가리키는 것은?
(A) 음악회 청중
(B) 부류
(C) 공통적인 특성
(D) 그 구성원들

해설 지시어가 포함된 문장 바로 앞에 부류라는 사회 집단 유형에
관한 설명이 시작되었고, but에 이어 이들 유형에 대한 설명이
이어지므로, (B)가 정답이다.

CHAPTER 05 Sentence Simplification

EXERCISE   pp. 80-85

정답 | **01** (B) **02** (C) **03** (D) **04** (D) **05** 1.(C) 2.(D)
06 1.(B) 2.(A) **07** 1.(B) 2.(D) **08** 1.(C) 2.(A)

01

루이 다게르가 발명한 다게레오타입은 19세기 중반에 최초
로 널리 이용된 사진술이었다. 이 기술은 은도금한 구리 판을
거울처럼 빛을 반사할 때까지 광을 낸 다음, 표면을 빛에 민
감하게 만들기 위해 판에 연기 처리를 한다. 판을 카메라에
넣은 다음, 필요하다고 생각되는 만큼 노출시켰는데, 이것은
빛의 강도에 따라 달랐다. 그런 다음, 액체 화학 약품 처리로

빛에 대한 판의 민감성을 없애고, 헹군 다음 말려서 보호용
유리 케이스 안에 봉했다. 이 마지막 단계는 판 표면의 극도
로 섬세한 성질 때문에 꼭 필요한 과정이었는데, 어떠한 접
촉, 심지어 천으로 부드럽게 닦기만 해도 돌이킬 수 없는 흠
집이 생길 수 있기 때문이었다.

지문 어휘

polish 다듬다, 광을 내다 plate 도금하다; (금속) 판 reflective
빛을 반사하는 fume 연기 render (어떤 상태로) 만들다
sensitive 민감한 deem 여기다 intensity 강도 negate
효력이 없게 만들다 rinse 씻어내다, 헹구다 delicate 섬세한
irreversibly 돌이킬 수 없게 scuff 흠을 내다

아래 문장 중 지문에서 음영 표시된 문장의 핵심 정보를 가장 잘 나타낸 것은?
(A) 판의 표면을 보호하기 위해 마지막 단계는 때때로 생략되었다.
(B) 표면이 쉽게 손상되기 때문에 판은 마지막 단계를 거쳐야만 했다.
(C) 천으로 부드럽게 닦는 것만으로도 판의 섬세한 표면에 돌이킬 수 없는 흠집이 생길 수 있었다.
(D) 마지막 단계가 끝나면 부드러운 천으로 판을 닦아야 했다.

어휘 skip 생략하다 undergo 겪다

해설 핵심 내용은 쉽게 흠집이 날 정도로 판 표면이 섬세하다는 조건 때문에 마지막 단계가 필수적이라는 것이므로, (B)가 정답이다.

02

개인의 행동 패턴을 분석하는 데에는 정신분석과 행동주의라는 두 가지 다른 학설이 이용된다. 행동주의 심리학자들은 주로 대상의 외적 행동과 동기에 집중하고, 반면에 정신분석 학자들은 뇌 속에서 일어나는 일에 더 관심을 갖는다. 행동주의 심리학자들에게는 관찰 불가능한 인간의 심리 작용을 이해하려고 시도하는 것 자체가 헛된 노력이며, 경험주의와 연구실 실험에 의존해 인간은 동물과 마찬가지로 특정 행동을 통해 외적 자극에 반응하게 되어 있다는 것을 증명하고자 한다. 반면에, 정신분석 학자들은 인간 심리의 다층성이라고 믿는 것에 집중하며, 숨겨진 내면의 작용이 인간 행동을 어떻게 지배하는지 보여주려고 한다.

지문 어휘

school of thought 학설 psychoanalysis 정신분석
behaviorism 행동주의 analyze 분석하다 external 외적인
subject (연구의) 대상 unobservable 관찰 불가능한
futile 헛된 empiricism 경험주의 stimulus 자극 (pl. stimuli)
reveal 드러내다 govern 지배하다

아래 문장 중 지문에서 음영 표시된 문장의 핵심 정보를 가장 잘 나타낸 것은?
(A) 행동주의 심리학자들은 인간의 마음을 관찰한 후, 외부 사건이 행동에 어떻게 영향을 미치는지 찾아내려고 한다.
(B) 과학적 증거의 도움으로 행동주의 심리학자들은 인간이 어떻게 자극에 좌우되는지 알아낸다.
(C) 행동주의 심리학자들은 마음을 이해하려고 애쓰기보다 실험을 통해 인간이 어떻게 외부 영향에 반응하는지 연구한다.
(D) 행동주의 심리학자들은 인간의 뇌가 어떻게 작용하는지 이해하기 위해 동물의 행동에 관련된 실험을 한다.

어휘 comprehend 이해하다 perform 행하다

해설 행동주의 심리학자들은 인간의 심리 작용을 이해하려 하지 않고, 실험을 통해 외적 자극에 반응하는 인간의 행동을 연구한다는 것이 핵심 내용이다. 그러므로 (C)가 정답이다.

03

중생대 해양 파충류인 어룡은 아마도 기후 대변동으로 인해 대략 9천만 년 전에 멸종했다. 어룡은 육식 동물로 크기가 굉장히 다양했고 해안 지역과 먼바다 모두에서 두족류 동물을 비롯해 다양한 먹이를 잡아먹으며 서식했다. 마치 요즘의 콜로살오징어처럼 유난히 큰 데다가 둥근 뼈로 둘러싸인 그들의 눈에 근거해서, 어룡들이 햇빛이 거의 닿지 않는 아주 깊은 곳에서 먹이를 찾았다는 이론이 주장되어 왔다. 어룡들은 최대 1,600미터 깊이까지 내려갈 수 있는 능력이 있었던 것 같고, 이는 몸의 측면 움직임을 추진 수단의 하나로 사용해서였을 텐데, 아주 효과적이어서 그 당시 어룡은 가장 빠른 해양 파충류로 자리매김했을 것으로 보인다.

지문 어휘

ichthyosaur 어룡 Mesozoic 중생대의 reptile 파충류
extinct 멸종된 upheaval 대변동 carnivore 육식 동물
range (양·크기 등의 범위가) 다양하다 feed on ~을 먹고 살다
prey 먹이 cephalopod 두족류 동물 theorize 이론을 세우다
lateral 측면의, 옆으로의 propulsion 추진, 밀고 나가기

아래 문장 중 지문에서 음영 표시된 문장의 핵심 정보를 가장 잘 나타낸 것은?
(A) 콜로살오징어는 눈 덕분에 햇빛이 거의 비치지 않는 곳에서도 먹이를 찾는 게 가능했을 것이다.
(B) 어두운 심해에는 어룡처럼 크고 뼈가 굵은 생명체들이 살고 있었다.
(C) 어두운 곳에 서식했기 때문에, 어룡들의 큰 눈이 포식자로부터 도망가는 데 도움이 되었을 것이다.
(D) 어룡들은 뼈로 둘러싸인 큰 눈을 가지고 있었기 때문에, 깊은 물속에서 먹이를 잡았을 것으로 여겨진다.

어휘 escape 달아나다, 탈출하다 predator 포식자

해설 둥근 뼈로 둘러싸인 유난히 큰 눈을 가지고 있었다는 사실에 근거해 어룡이 깊은 물속에서 먹이를 찾았다는 이론이 있어왔다는 요지를 잘 나타낸 것은 (D)이다.

04

기원전 336년 마케도니아의 필립 2세가 살해되고 이어 그의 아들인 알렉산더 3세가 왕위를 계승했는데, 그는 역사상 가장 큰 제국 중 하나를 건설하고 알렉산더 대왕이라고 알려질 인물이었다. 20세라는 어린 나이에 왕위에 오르기 전, 알렉산더는 존경받는 철학자 아리스토텔레스에게 가르침을 받았다. 그는 노련한 군 사령관으로 명성이 높았고 통치 시기 대부분을 서아시아를 아우르며 맹위를 떨친 격렬한 전투에 몰두한 채 보냈는데, 전장에서 단 한 번도 패배하지 않은 것으로 유명하다. 알렉산더는 바빌론 황제의 성에서 석연치 않은 상황 하에 32세의 나이에 사망했다. 역사가들은 그가 말라리아로 죽었거나 독살당한 것으로 의심하고 있다.

지문 어휘

succeed 계승하다 ascend 오르다 throne 왕위 tutor 가르치다 esteemed 존경받는 reign 통치 기간 immerse ~에 몰두하다 rage 맹위를 떨치다 defeat 패배 battlefield 전장 suspect 의심하다 succumb (병 등으로) 죽다, 쓰러지다 poison 독살하다

아래 문장 중 지문에서 음영 표시된 문장의 핵심 정보를 가장 잘 나타낸 것은?
(A) 알렉산더 3세는 알렉산더 대왕이라고도 알려져 있었고, 그의 아버지는 마케도니아의 필립 2세였다.
(B) 알렉산더 대왕은 아버지 필립 2세를 암살한 후 대제국의 지도자가 되었다.
(C) 알렉산더 대왕의 아버지 필립 2세는 세계 최대의 제국을 건설하겠다는 목표를 달성하지 못하고 사망했다.
(D) 거대한 제국을 건설한 알렉산더 대왕은 아버지가 기원전 336년 살해된 후 마케도니아의 왕이 되었다.

어휘 assassinate 암살하다 fulfill 달성하다

해설 핵심 내용은 알렉산더 대왕이 아버지가 암살된 후 왕위에 올랐고 후에 큰 제국을 건설하게 된다는 것이다. 그러므로 답은 (D)이다.

05

고대 그리스의 철학자이자 박식가인 아리스토텔레스는 기원전 4세기에 살면서, 스승인 플라톤의 발자취를 좇아 보편성이라는 개념을 다루고자 했는데, 보편성이란 유사한 사물들이 공통으로 가지고 있는 속성이라고 대략 정의될 수 있다. 플라톤은 이 보편성을 사물 자체와는 별개로 현실 세계에 존재하는 추상적인 개념이라고 생각했는데, 사물이란 물리적으로 존재하지 않는 이상적인 형태를 단순히 엉성하게 모방한 것이기 때문이다. 이 개념은 그의 유명한 동굴의 비유에 잘 설명되어 있는데, 실제 세계에 존재하는 물체로서의 사물은 그 사물의 이상적인 형태가 동굴 벽에 그림자로 드리워져 나타난 것에 불과하다. 반면, 아리스토텔레스는 보편성이란 우리가 살고 있는 이 세상에 실제 존재하며 사물 안에서 그 사물이 보여주는 특성으로서 모습을 드러낸다고 믿었다. 다시 말해, 플라톤이 이상적인 사과가 추상적인 형태의 세계 안에서만 존재한다고 믿은 반면, 아리스토텔레스는 사과의 완벽한 형태가 모든 사과 안에 존재한다고 주장했다.

지문 어휘

polymath 박식가, 박식한 사람 address (문제를) 다루다, 고심하다 define 정의하다 property 속성, 특성 abstract 추상적인 pale 흐릿한 imitation 모방 physical 물리적인 allegory 비유, 우화 portray 나타내다 silhouette 그림자, 실루엣 cast (그림자를) 드리우다

1 아래 문장 중 지문에서 음영 표시된 첫 번째 문장의 핵심 정보를 가장 잘 나타낸 것은?
(A) 기원전 4세기에 아리스토텔레스는 스승인 플라톤에게서 보편적인 진리를 배웠다.
(B) 아리스토텔레스와 플라톤은 객관적 속성에 관한 견해를 비롯해 많은 생각을 공유했다.
(C) 아리스토텔레스는 스승과 마찬가지로 유사한 사물의 공통된 특성을 이해하는 데 관심이 있었다.
(D) 아리스토텔레스가 철학자이자 박식가인 반면에 플라톤은 세계를 이해하기 위해 노력했다.

어휘 objective 객관적인 strive 노력하다, 분투하다

해설 아리스토텔레스는 스승의 뒤를 이어 유사한 물체의 공통된 특성인 보편성을 다루었다는 것이 주요 내용이므로, (C)가 정답이다.

2 아래 문장 중 지문에서 음영 표시된 두 번째 문장의 핵심 정보를 가장 잘 나타낸 것은?
(A) 이상적인 형태는 이 세상의 모든 사물이 모여 있는 동굴과 같다.
(B) 동굴의 비유에서 개념과 사물은 이상적인 형태에 의해 같이 연결되어 있다.
(C) 동굴 벽에 그려진 이상적인 형태를 나타내는 그림은 이 개념을 위한 비유 역할을 한다.
(D) 동굴의 비유는 현실의 사물이 그것의 실재 형태에 의해 어떻게 만들어지는지에 대한 개념을 설명한다.

어휘 depict 묘사하다

해설 물리적인 사물은 이상적인 형태에 의해 동굴 벽면에 비춰진 그림자에 불과하다는 것을 동굴의 비유가 설명한다는 것이 요지이다. 그러므로 답은 (D)이다.

06

그리스어로 '고대에서 태어난'을 뜻하는 고제3기는 대략 6,500만 년 전에서부터 2,300만 년 전까지에 걸친 지질 시대이다. 이 시기는 지질학자들에 의해 세 개의 별개 시대로 나뉘며, 그 중 첫 번째가 팔레오세이다. 앞서 존재했던 시기들과 팔레오세의 가장 두드러진 차이점은 공룡이 없었다는 것인데, 공룡은 백악기 시대 끝 무렵 대재앙적인 사건으로 인해 멸종했다. 한때 지배종이었던 생명체가 지구상에서 갑작스럽게 사라지자, 지구에 남아있던 포유류, 조류, 파충류, 수생 종들이 번성할 수 있는 새로운 서식지와 생태계가 출현했다. 공룡의 멸종은 오늘날의 멕시코 지역에 발생한 엄청난 운석 충돌로 촉발되었다고 여겨진다. 팔레오세 초기에는 지구의 기후가 그 충돌 때문에 발생한 대규모 먼지 구름의 영향을 크게 받아, 비정상적으로 춥고 어두운 상태가 장기간 지속되었다. 그럼에도 불구하고, 이 시기가 끝날 무렵에는 따뜻하고 습한 원래의 표준 환경으로 돌아갔다.

Paleogene 고(古)제3기 epoch 시대 Paleocene (Epoch) 팔레오세 distinction 차이 precede ~에 앞서다 cataclysmic 대재앙의 Cretaceous Era 백악기 시대 dominant 우세한, 지배적인 emergence 출현 ecosystem 생태계 mammalian 포유류의 avian 조류의 reptilian 파충류의 trigger 촉발하다 meteor 운석 prolonged 장기적인 norm 표준

1 아래 문장 중 지문에서 음영 표시된 첫 번째 문장의 핵심 정보를 가장 잘 나타낸 것은?

    (A) 공룡의 멸종은 다른 종들에게 긍정적인 영향과 부정적인 영향을 미쳤다.

    (B) 앞서 지배적이었던 생명체의 갑작스러운 멸종은 지구상에 살아남은 종들에게 기회가 되었다.

    (C) 육지와 해양 동물들이 새로운 형태의 포식자들에게 위협을 받았다.

    (D) 지배종이던 생명체가 백악기 말에 갑자기 사라졌다.

어휘 opportunity 기회 threaten 위협하다

해설 지배종이 갑자기 사라진 지구 환경이 원인이 되어, 다른 여러 종들이 살기 좋게 변했다는 결과를 가져온 것이 핵심 내용이므로, 정답은 (B)이다.

2 아래 문장 중 지문에서 두 번째 음영 표시된 문장의 핵심 정보를 가장 잘 나타낸 것은?

    (A) 그 충돌로 생긴 먼지 구름은 팔레오세 초기의 기후 상태를 악화시켰다.

    (B) 팔레오세 초기에 먼지 구름이 지구를 차갑고 어둡게 만들었으며, 이로 인해 지구와 운석 사이에 충돌이 발생했다.

    (C) 팔레오세 초기 단계에 먼지 구름과 지구의 찬 기후가 결합되어 있었다.

    (D) 그 시기의 어둠과 추위는 직접적으로 공룡의 멸종을 야기했다.

어휘 collision 충돌 deteriorate 악화시키다

해설 팔레오세 초기에 운석 충돌 때문에 먼지 구름이 발생했고 이로 인해 기후 환경이 장기간 나빠졌다는 것이 요지이다. 그러므로 정답은 (A)이다.

07

미국의 무용수이자 안무가인 마사 그레이엄은 공연과 교육 양 분야에서 70년 이상 활동했으며, 그레이엄 기술이라고 알려진 그녀만의 독특한 스타일은 미국 현대 무용의 본질 자체를 변화시켰다. 최초의 체계적인 현대 무용 기술로 여겨지는 그 스타일은 신체의 수축과 이완이라는 서로 반대되는 힘에 의존하는데, 이는 자연스러운 호흡 주기의 들숨과 날숨을 기반으로 한다. 척추를 기본 축으로 삼아 그 주변으로 몸통을 나선형으로 움직이는 것이 그레이엄 기술의 또 다른 기본 원

리이다. 그렇게 해서 나오는 그녀의 춤에는 도약 회전과 더불어 많은 마루 동작이 포함되는데, 무용수들이 몸을 공중에 순간적으로 띄웠다가 무대로 극적으로 떨어지는 동작이 먼저 앞서고, 몸을 일으키는 '회복' 동작으로 끝을 맺어, 무용수 동작의 이원성을 보여주는 또 다른 예가 된다. 그레이엄 기술은 남성 무용수가 후에 들어오기는 했지만 원래 전원 여성인 무용단을 위해 고안된 것이었으며, 그 대담한 스타일이 여성성에 대한 문화적 개념을 재정립하는 데 도움이 되었다고 평가된다.

choreographer 안무가 rely on ~에 의존하다 contraction 수축 release 이완 inhalation 들숨 exhalation 날숨 axis 중심축 spiral 나선형으로 움직이게 하다 torso 몸통 momentarily 순간적으로 dualism 이원성 troupe 공연단 bold 대담한 femininity 여성성

1 아래 문장 중 지문에서 첫 번째 음영 표시된 문장의 핵심 정보를 가장 잘 나타낸 것은?

    (A) 최초의 공식적인 현대 무용 기술은 깊은 호흡 대신 신체의 수축과 이완을 이용했다.

    (B) 그것은 체계를 갖춘 최초의 현대 무용 기술이었으며, 들숨 및 날숨과 유사한 대비 동작을 사용한다.

    (C) 수축과 이완이 서로 반대되는 동작이지만, 현대 무용 기술에서는 이들을 자연스러운 방식으로 사용한다.

    (D) 현대 무용 기술을 창조해 낸 체계는 사람들이 호흡하기 위해 사용하는 자연스러운 주기와 반대가 된다.

어휘 breathe 호흡하다

해설 그레이엄 기술은 최초의 체계적인 현대 무용 기술로, 들숨과 날숨에 근거한 신체의 수축과 이완에 의존한다는 것이 핵심 내용이므로, 정답은 (B)이다.

2 아래 문장 중 지문에서 두 번째 음영 표시된 문장의 핵심 정보를 가장 잘 나타낸 것은?

    (A) 그레이엄 기술은 처음에는 여성 무용수들만 사용했지만, 이후 혁신적인 무용수들에 의해 채택되었다.

    (B) 그레이엄은 남성 무용수들의 도움으로 남성과 여성 무용수들이 함께 사용할 수 있는 기술을 개발했다고 인정했다.

    (C) 그레이엄 기술이 춤에 그토록 강한 영향을 미쳤던 것은 성 역할에 대한 문화적 개념 때문이었다.

    (D) 그레이엄 기술은 여성 무용수들을 염두에 두고 만들어졌으며, 사회가 여성성을 바라보는 방식에 영향을 미쳤다.

어휘 innovative 혁신적인 admit 인정하다, 시인하다

해설 그레이엄 기술은 원래 여성 무용단을 위해 개발되었고, 여성성에 대한 개념을 바꾸는 역할을 했다는 것이 핵심 내용이다. 그러므로 답은 (D)이다.

고고학 유물에 따르면 태평양 섬들로 이주가 시작된 것은 4만 년 이전이었을 것으로 보이며, 서기 2000년 무렵에는 거주 가능한 모든 섬에 사람들이 정착했다. 이 지역이 세계 최대의 대양에 흩어져 있는 대략 1만 개의 섬으로 이루어져 있다는 사실 때문에, 오세아니아 종족들의 정확한 기원과 분포를 추적한다는 것은 불가능하지는 않지만 어렵다. 19세기에 태평양 제도의 주민들은 멜라네시안, 미크로네시안, 폴리네시안, 이렇게 세 그룹으로 분류되었고, 이에 근거해 동남아시아인들이 세 차례의 서로 다른 이주 물결을 타고 와 이 지역에 거주하게 됐다는 이론이 정립되었다. 멜라네시아에는 대략 오스트레일리아와 같은 시기인 3만 3천 년 이전에 동남아시아인들이 정착했는데, 제2차 물결은 약 4천 년 전 선사시대 라피타 문화권에서부터 온 것으로 보인다. 라피타인들은 처음에 뉴기니 북동 해안 인근에 모여 있는 섬들인 비스마르크 제도에 정착했다가, 계속해서 피지, 통가, 사모아 같은 폴리네시아 섬들로 이동했다. 16세기 들어 유럽과의 접촉이 일어날 무렵에 오세아니아 종족들은 돌과 뼈, 조개껍데기로 만든 도구를 개발했고, 과일과 덩이줄기들을 재배하고 있었으며, 상당히 숙련된 뱃사람이 되어 있었다.

지문 어휘

archaeological 고고학적인 remains 유물 migration 이주 scatter 흩어지다 populate 거주하다, 살다 prehistoric 선사시대의 initially 처음에 Bismarck Archipelago 비스마르크 제도 cultivate 경작하다 tuber (감자 등의) 덩이줄기

1 아래 문장 중 지문에서 첫 번째 음영 표시된 문장의 핵심 정보를 가장 잘 나타낸 것은?
(A) 오세아니아 종족들이 어떻게 태평양의 섬들에 오게 되었는지는 알 수 없다.
(B) 오세아니아 종족들은 그들이 원래 살던 섬에서 다른 섬들로 퍼져 나가는 것을 분명 어렵게 여겼을 것이다.
(C) 그 지역의 지형 때문에 오세아니아 종족들의 이주 경로를 알아내는 것은 쉽지 않다.
(D) 오세아니아 종족들이 흩어져 나가 태평양 섬들에서 번성하지 못한 이유는 정확히 알려져 있지 않다.

어휘 determine 알아내다, 밝히다 path 길

해설 태평양 지역의 지형 때문에 오세아니아 종족들이 어디서 와서 어떻게 퍼졌는지 알기 어렵다는 것이 핵심 내용이므로, (C)가 정답이다.

2 아래 문장 중 지문에서 두 번째 음영 표시된 문장의 핵심 정보를 가장 잘 나타낸 것은?
(A) 멜라네시아는 처음에는 동남아시아인들이, 한참 후에는 라피타 문화권 사람들이 거주했을 것이다.
(B) 동남아시아인들은 멜라네시아에 정착했다가, 약 4천 년 후에 오스트레일리아로 이주했다.
(C) 라피타를 세운 것은 멜라네시아와 오스트레일리아에서 온 제2차 이주 물결이었다.
(D) 동남아시아 사람들이 멜라네시아에 최초로 정착했고, 이어 라피타 문화권의 후손인 오스트레일리아 사람들 등이 뒤따라 왔다.

어휘 be descended from ~의 후손이다

해설 멜라네시아에는 처음에 동남아시아인들이, 이후 라피타 문화권 사람들이 이주해 왔다는 것이 핵심 내용이므로, 정답은 (A)이다.

CHAPTER 06 Inference

EXERCISE
pp. 92-97

정답 | 01 (A) 02 (D) 03 (C) 04 (B) 05 1.(D) 2.(A)
06 1.(B) 2.(D) 07 1.(D) 2.(B) 08 1.(C) 2.(A)

새와 벌, 그리고 다른 곤충들 같이 살아 있는 생물에 의해 이루어지는 수분을 생물적이라고 한다면 바람과 비 같은 다른 힘이 수분의 매개체 역할을 하는 여러 형태의 비생물적 수분도 존재한다. 이것의 주요 장점은 식물이 에너지를 더 많은 꽃가루를 생산하는 데 집중할 수 있게 해 준다는 것인데, 그렇지 않았다면 생물적 수분 매개체를 유인하는 데 다 써버렸을 것이다. 바람은 가장 흔한 비생물적 수분 매개체로, 어떤 꽃들은 바람에 기반한 꽃가루 확산의 효율성을 극대화하는 특정 형태를 발달시키기도 한다. 한편, 비 수분은 소수의 식물 종에 의해서만 이용된다. 하지만 폭우가 내릴 때는 이런 수분 방식에 적응한 식물들이 곤충 수분에 의존하는 식물보다는 상당한 이점이 있다.

지문 어휘

pollination 수분(꽃가루받이) biotic 생물의 abiotic 비생물적인 pollinator 수분 매개체 primary 주요한 expend (시간·노력 등을) 쓰다 attract 끌어들이다 pollen 꽃가루 evolve 발달시키다 maximize 극대화하다 efficiency 효율성 dispersal 확산, 분산 downpour 폭우 adapt 적응하다

다음 중 지문에서 비생물적 수분에 의존하는 식물들에 대해 추론할 수 있는 것은?
(A) 생물적 수분에 의존하는 식물보다 더 많은 꽃가루를 생산한다.
(B) 바람이 거의 불지 않고 비가 많이 오는 지역에서 주로 발견된다.
(C) 곤충들로부터 자신을 보호할 수 있도록 진화해 왔다.
(D) 외적인 힘의 도움 없이 꽃가루를 확산시킨다.

어휘 protect 보호하다 assistance 도움

해설 비생물적 수분을 하는 식물들은 수분 매개체인 생물을 유인할 필요가 없어 꽃가루 생산에 더 집중할 수 있다고 했으므로, 더 많은 꽃가루를 생산할 수 있음을 유추할 수 있다. 그러므로 (A)가 정답이다.

02

1799년에 발견된 로제타석(石)은 여러 언어와 문자로 동일한 내용의 글을 새겨 놓은 고대 이집트의 석비이다. 1822년에 프랑스의 역사가 장 프랑수아 샹폴리옹은 이 독특한 유물을 이집트 신성문자를 해독하는 실마리로 이용했다. 이것이 가능했던 것은 한 마케도니아 왕의 즉위를 기념하는 사제들에 의해 작성된 것으로 보이는 그 석비의 내용이 현대에도 읽고 이해될 수 있는 언어인 그리스어로 그리고 고대 이집트 민중문자로도 쓰여졌다는 사실 때문이었다. 이 역사가는 이들 신성문자의 대부분을 차지하는 새와 동물 모양의 글자들이 향해 있는 방향이 글의 의미를 파악하는 데 도움이 된다는 것을 발견했다. 이 획기적 발견은 다른 수많은 고대 이집트 신성문자 글들을 번역하는 토대가 되었다.

지문 어휘

slab (돌, 목재로 된) 판, 비 bear 지니다 inscription (새겨진) 글, 명문 script 문자 artifact 유물 decipher 해독하다 Egyptian hieroglyphs 이집트 신성문자 priest 사제 commemorate 기념하다 ascension (높은 지위에) 오름 demotic Egyptian 이집트 민중문자 character 글자, 부호 breakthrough 획기적 발견, 돌파구 lay the groundwork for ~의 토대가 되다

글쓴이가 이집트 신성문자에 대해 암시하는 것은?
(A) 이집트어나 그리스어 같은 후대 언어들의 토대였다.
(B) 고대 이집트의 사제들과 왕들만 사용할 수 있었다.
(C) 왕들이 퇴위하는 방식을 기록하는 데 자주 이용되었다.
(D) 1822년 전에는 현대인들이 이해할 수 없었다.

어휘 abdicate 왕위에서 물러나다

해설 1822년에 로제타석을 이용해 이집트 신성문자를 해독했다는 설명에서 이전에는 신성문자를 해독할 수 없었음을 추론할 수 있다. 그러므로 정답은 (D)이다.

03

동물들에게 인간과 같은 감정이 존재할 가능성에 대해 일부 과학자들이 여전히 회의적이기는 하지만, 이 주제는 다양한 종을 대상으로 몇몇 다른 접근 방식을 사용해 강도 높게 연구되어 왔다. 예를 들어, 행동주의 접근법은 인간의 감정 표현과 유사한 동물의 행동을 다양한 자극에 대한 단순 반응에 불과하다고 여김으로써 동물의 감정이 존재한다는 것 자체가 틀렸음을 입증하려고 애쓴다. 한편, 비교 접근법도 마찬가지로 더 간단한 설명 방식을 택한다. 그것은 동물의 행동이 더 기본적 과정으로 설명될 수 있다면, 높은 수준의 심리적 과정에 의해 야기된 것으로 해석해서는 안 된다고 하는 지침을 따른다. 심지어 찰스 다윈도 이 주제에 끼어들며, 화가 나서 이빨을 드러내는 것처럼 인간에게서 보여지는 보편적인 감정 표현을 동물들이 일부 공유하는 것으로 보인다고 언급했다.

지문 어휘

skeptical 회의적인 approach 접근 방식 disprove 틀렸음을 입증하다 ascribe A to B A를 B에 속하는 것으로 여기다 response 반응 comparative 비교의 embrace (생각, 제안을) 받아들이다 directive 지시, 지침 interpret 해석하다 weigh in (논쟁 등에) 끼어들다 bare (신체 일부를) 드러내다

다음 중 지문에서 찰스 다윈에 대해 추론할 수 있는 것은?
(A) 동물의 감정에 대한 여러 다른 접근법을 신중하게 비교했다.
(B) 동물들이 근본적인 방식으로 자극에 반응한다는 것을 의심했다.
(C) 동물의 감정이라는 개념에 행동주의자들보다 마음이 더 열려 있었다.
(D) 동물은 인간과 똑같은 감정을 느낄 수 있다고 주장했다.

어휘 respond 반응하다 fundamental 근본적인

해설 앞선 접근법들이 동물의 감정을 단순한 반응이나 수준 낮은 차원에서 발생한 것으로 여긴 반면, 다윈은 동물과 인간의 감정 표현에 공통점이 일부 있다고 했으므로, 동물의 감정에 대해 더 수용적이었음을 유추할 수 있다. 그러므로 정답은 (C)이다.

04

11세기에서 13세기에 이르는 시기에 일련의 군사 원정이 기독교 교회에 의해 조직되었는데, 일괄하여 십자군 전쟁이라고 한다. 그들은 예루살렘과 그 주변으로 이루어진 성지를 이슬람의 지배로부터 해방시키기 위해 정복하려고 했다. 총 여덟 차례의 주요 전투와 수많은 소규모 전투들을 치르는 과정에서 이슬람 세력에 승리하면 그 지역에 대한 통치권을 빼앗아 오고, 뒤이어 패배하면 통치권을 다시 빼앗기는 일이 반복되었다. 마지막 주요 전투는 유럽인들이 새로운 영토를 전혀 점령하지 못한 채 끝이 났다. 이런 충돌의 피비린내 나는 특성과 그 충돌이 불러온 종교적 적대감에도 불구하고, 십자군 전쟁은 결과적으로 동서양 간의 전례 없는 문화적 사상 교류를 가져왔다. 십자군 전쟁은 유럽에 이전에는 없던 중요한 이론과 지식을 전해 주었다.

expedition 원정, 탐험 the Crusades 십자군 전쟁 environs 환경, 주변 Muslim 이슬람 교도 number 합한 수가 총 ~이 되다 campaign 전투 wrest 탈취하다 cede (영토를) 양도하다 seize 점령하다 territory 영토 conflict (국가 간의) 충돌 animosity 적대감 unprecedented 전례 없는

이슬람 세계에 대해 지문에서 추론할 수 있는 것은?
(A) 성지를 유럽과 나눠가진다는 생각을 받아들였다.
(B) 어떤 면에서 유럽보다 선진적이었다.
(C) 유럽의 공격을 격퇴시킬 몇 가지 다른 방법들을 가지고 있었다.
(D) 유럽 문화를 확산시키는 것을 주요 목적으로 십자군 전쟁을 부추겼다.

어휘 repel 격퇴하다 instigate 부추기다

해설 십자군 전쟁으로 동서양 간의 교류가 이루어져 유럽인들이 이전에 갖고 있지 못했던 중요한 이론과 지식을 얻게 되었다고 했으므로, 이슬람 문화가 어떤 면에서는 더 선진적이었음을 유추할 수 있다. 그러므로 (B)가 정답이다.

05

1960년대에 미국의 의사 폴 D. 맥클린은 인간의 뇌가 기본적으로 하나처럼 조화롭게 작동하는 세 개의 별개 뇌로 이루어져 있다는 이론을 제기했다. 삼위일체 뇌 모델이라고 알려진 이것은 파충류 복합체, 뇌의 신경 및 네트워크 조직인 변연계, 그리고 신피질을 포함한다. 진화상으로 가장 최근에 추가된 것으로 밝혀진 신피질은 뇌의 앞부분을 차지하며 논리와 이성적 사고의 중추 기능을 한다. 진화 연대표상에서 신피질 바로 앞서 있는 것이 변연계로, 뇌 중앙에 위치하며 주로 정서적 반응과 사회적 유대를 담당한다. 삼위일체 뇌 모델에서 세 번째이면서 가장 오래된 부분은 파충류 복합체로, 종종 파충류의 뇌라고도 하며 뇌 기저부에 자리잡고 있다. 그 기원은 포유동물, 파충류, 어류, 조류를 포함하는 모든 척추동물의 공통 조상이 있는 5억여 년 전으로 거슬러 올라간다. 이 복합체는 공격과 세력권 유지 습성 같은 본능적 행위를 관장해, 종의 지속적 생존을 위해 꼭 필요한 기본 욕구를 충족하도록 보장해 준다. 이 복합체는 기쁨을 가져다 주는 행동을 하도록 이끌고, 고통을 유발하는 활동을 하지 않게 유도한다. 심리학자와 행동주의 과학자들은 파충류의 뇌를 흥미롭게 여기는데, 그것이 부족한 식량과 수많은 포식자를 특징으로 하는 오래 전 시대를 상기시키기 때문이다. 오늘날의 문명 사회에서도 유의미한 신피질과 변연계와는 대조적으로, 파충류의 뇌는 때때로 현대의 맥락에서는 비이성적으로 보일 행동을 유발할 수 있다.

지문 어휘

physician 의사 triune 삼위일체의 reptilian 파충류의 limbic system 변연계 neocortex 신피질 occupy 점유하다 logic 논리 rational 이성적인 timeline 연대표 situated 위치하고 있는 responsible for ~을 담당하는 bonding 유대

instinctual 본능에 따른 aggression 공격(성) territoriality 세력권 유지 습성 induce 유발하다 intriguing 흥미로운 hark back to ~을 상기시키다 abundant 풍부한 relevant 관련 있는, 유의미한 provoke 유발하다 seemingly 겉보기에는 irrational 비이성적인

1 다음 중 지문에서 변연계에 대해 추론할 수 있는 것은?
(A) 뇌에서 가장 최근에 발견된 부분이다.
(B) 인간 뇌의 세 부분이 마차 하나처럼 기능하도록 돕는다.
(C) 진화 연대표상에서 신피질보다 뒤쪽에 놓여 있다.
(D) 손상될 경우 사회적 기능에 부정적인 영향을 미칠 수 있다.

해설 변연계가 사회적 유대를 담당한다고 했으므로, 손상되면 사회적 기능에 나쁜 영향을 미칠 것임을 추론할 수 있다. 그러므로 정답은 (D)이다.

2 다음 중 지문이 파충류 복합체에 대해 암시하는 것은?
(A) 사회적 화합보다 생존에 더 집중한다.
(B) 동물에게 행복과 기쁨을 가져다 준다.
(C) 동물이 배고픔을 견디고 환경적 위험에 노출되어도 버틸 수 있게 돕는다.
(D) 모든 동물의 뇌 속에 존재한다.

어휘 cohesion 화합, 응집 exposure to ~에 노출됨

해설 파충류 복합체는 공격 및 세력권 유지 습성 등을 담당해 종이 지속적으로 생존하게 한다는 설명에서 사회적 화합보다 생존을 중시한다는 것을 알 수 있다. 그러므로 (A)가 정답이다.

06

기원전 10,000년 무렵에 시작되어 흔히 농업 혁명이라고도 불리는 신석기 혁명 시기에, 적은 무리의 유목민 수렵채집인들이 농업 정착지를 만들기 시작했다. 이 같은 변화는 현대 문명 건설을 향한 첫발로 볼 수 있다. 농업이 처음 시작된 것은 중동의 비옥한 초승달 지대에서였고, 세계의 다른 거주 지역에서도 농사를 짓기 시작했다. 정확히 무엇이 세상을 변화시킨 이런 변화를 불러왔는지에 대해 의견이 일치하지 않지만, 일부 과학자들은 마지막 빙하기가 끝난 후 뒤이어 나타난 온난화 경향을 중요한 기여 요인으로 지적한다. 비옥한 초승달 지대에서는 이 같은 기후 변화로 야생 밀과 보리가 자라기 시작했고, 이것이 결국 유목민들에게 이 새로운 식량원 가까이에 정착하도록 장려했다. 하지만 또 다른 과학자들은 인간 행동이 이처럼 극적으로 전환하는 데 더 큰 역할을 한 내적인 변화가 있었다고 생각하는데, 그것은 바로 지적 능력의 급격한 향상을 불러온 뇌의 진화적 발전이었다. 오늘날의 튀르키예 남부에 해당하는 옛 터에 대한 고고학적 분석에 따르면, 이곳의 선사시대 농부들은 예술과 영적인 것에 큰 가치를 두었던 것으로 보인다. 어느 쪽으로든 인간들은 점차 야생 식물을 찾아 다니던 것에서 멀어지고 가꾸는 쪽으로 기울었는데, 처음에는 작은 뜰을 그리고 나중에는 큰 농작물 밭을 가꾸게 되었다.

지문 어휘

Neolithic Revolution 신석기 혁명 nomadic 유목의 initial 처음의 Fertile Crescent 비옥한 초승달 지대 inhabited (사람이) 거주하는 consensus 의견 일치 alter 바꾸다 contribute 기여하다 dramatic 극적인 rapid 급격한 capacity 능력 site 터, 장소 forage 먹이를 찾아 다니다 tend 가꾸다, 재배하다

1 다음 중 지문에서 밀과 보리에 대해 추론할 수 있는 것은?
(A) 마지막 빙하기 때 튀르키예 남부 지역에서 번성했다.
(B) 야생에서 자라려면 따뜻한 기온이 요구된다.
(C) 많은 수렵채집인들의 주요 표적이었다.
(D) 더 이상 원산지에서 재배되지 않는다.

어휘 thrive 번성하다 target 표적

해설 마지막 빙하기가 끝나고 기후가 따뜻해지면서 야생 밀과 보리가 자라기 시작했다고 했으므로, 밀과 보리가 야생에서 자라려면 따뜻한 기온을 필요로 한다는 것을 추론할 수 있다. 그러므로 정답은 (B)이다.

2 글쓴이가 최초의 농부들에 대해 암시하는 것은?
(A) 극한의 추위와 눈을 상대해야 했다.
(B) 후에 수렵과 채집으로 돌아갔다.
(C) 종교 의식에 참여하기를 거부했다.
(D) 별로 많지 않은 식량만 재배했다.

어휘 refuse 거부하다 ritual 의식 modest 그다지 많지 않은

해설 농부들이 식물 채집에서 가꾸기로 전환할 때 처음에는 작은 뜰부터 시작했다는 설명에서 양이 많지 않았음을 암시하고 있다. 그러므로 (D)가 정답이다.

07

크기와 질량의 유사성 때문에 종종 지구의 '자매'라고 여겨지는 금성의 대기는 우리의 대기보다 밀도가 훨씬 더 높고 더 뜨겁다. 금성의 평균 표면 온도는 섭씨 약 465도이며, 대기압은 지구의 해양 표면 아래 900미터 정도 되는 지점에서의 압력과 거의 같다. 금성의 대기는 주로 이산화탄소로 구성되어 있고 질소가 소량 있다. 극소량을 제외하고는 그 밖의 화학적 화합물은 어디에도 존재하지 않는다. 황산으로 이루어진 불투명한 구름층이 금성 상공에 떠 있어서, 표면을 관찰하는 것이 거의 불가능하다. 움직임 측면에서 볼 때, 금성의 대기권은 극도로 활동적인 것이 특징이라고 할 수 있는데, 그 상층부는 시속 약 360킬로미터로 부는 바람 때문에 끊임 없이 활발한 순환 상태를 유지한다. 하지만 이 수치는 고도가 떨어질수록 상당히 낮아져, 표면에서는 시속 약 10킬로미터밖에 되지 않는다. 과학자들은 수십억 년 전에는 금성의 대기가 지구와 훨씬 더 비슷했으며 표면에 액체 상태의 물이 존재했을지도 모른다고 추측한다. 이런 상태를 변화하게 만든 사건은 지표수가 증발하면서 발생한 심각한 온실 효과였을 것으로 추측되는데, 이것은 또한 여러 온실가스 수치의 증가로 이어졌다.

지문 어휘

Venus 금성 equivalent 동등한 nitrogen 질소 compound 화합물 opaque 불투명한 sulfuric acid 황산 suspend (공중에) 뜨다 all but 거의 engaged in ~에 관여하는 perpetual 영구적인, 끊임없는 vigorous 격렬한, 활발한 elevation 고도 speculate 추측하다 massive 심각한, 거대한

1 글쓴이가 천문학자에 대해 암시하는 것은?
(A) 금성과 지구가 더 이상 비슷하지 않다고 믿는다.
(B) 금성의 대기압을 면밀히 추적하고 있다.
(C) 전에는 알려지지 않았던 금성의 온실가스를 찾아냈다.
(D) 지구에서 금성 표면을 연구하는 게 어렵다고 여긴다.

해설 불투명한 구름층 때문에 금성 표면을 관찰하는 게 거의 불가능하다는 말에서 지구에서 금성 표면을 연구하는 게 어려울 것임을 추론할 수 있다. 그러므로 정답은 (D)이다.

2 다음 중 지문이 금성에 대해 암시하는 것은?
(A) 기후 변화로 구름층을 잃게 될 것이다.
(B) 수십억 년 전에 생명체의 본거지였을 수도 있다.
(C) 과거에는 지금보다 더 큰 질량을 가졌을지도 모른다.
(D) 표면에서 곧 심한 폭풍이 일어날 수도 있다.

해설 수십억 년 전에는 금성의 대기가 지구와 많이 비슷했고 물도 존재했을지 모른다는 설명은 생명체의 존재 가능성을 암시한 것이다. 그러므로 (B)가 정답이다.

08

전형적인 현대 오케스트라는 현악기, 목관 악기, 금관 악기, 타악기, 이렇게 네 개의 서로 다른 악기 섹션으로 이루어지며, 손 동작이나 작은 지휘봉으로 연주를 지휘하는 지휘자가 이끈다. 하지만 약 1600년부터 1750년까지 지속되었던 바로크 시대에는 오케스트라가 표준화된 규모와 구성을 갖추지 않아 둘 다 많이 달라질 수 있었다. 예를 들어, 바흐는 단지 18명의 음악가로 구성된 오케스트라를 이끌었고, 반면에 아르칸젤로 코렐리는 오로지 특별한 행사만을 위해서였지만, 자신의 오케스트라에 150명의 음악가를 고용했다. 바로크 시대를 바로 뒤따른 고전주의 시대에는 표준화가 나타나기 시작했고, 19세기 전반 즈음에는 두 배로 늘어난 목관 악기와 금관 악기 섹션을 포함하는 고정된 구성으로 굳어졌다. 이것은 주로 베토벤이 자신의 작품에서 플루트, 오보에, 클라리넷, 바순, 호른, 트럼펫을 두 개씩 사용하면서 변화를 요구했기 때문이었다. 이후, 전례 없는 수준으로 복잡하게 작곡된 바그너 작품의 엄청난 규모 때문에 거의 한 세기 동안 표준으로 남을 정도로 오케스트라의 규모와 악기 다양성이 확장되었다. 20세기 초에는 오케스트라가 규모 면에서 엄청나게 커져서 타악기 범위가 훨씬 넓어졌을 뿐만 아니라 현악기와 금관 악기 섹션도 확대되었다. 그 결과, 이제 작곡가들은 훨씬 더 방대하고 더 야심 찬 작품들을 자유롭게 창작할 수 있게 되었다.

지문 어휘

strings 현악기 woodwinds 목관 악기 brass 금관 악기
percussion 타악기 conductor 지휘자 baton 지휘봉
last 지속되다 standardized 표준화된 composition 구성
vary 다르다, 달라지다 consolidate 굳히다, 강화하다
set 정해진, 고정된 arrangement 배열, 구성 immensely
엄청나게 expanded 확장된

1 다음 중 지문에서 바로크 시대 작품에 대해 추론할 수 있는
것은?
(A) 모든 주요 악기들을 두 개씩 필요로 했다.
(B) 특정한 경우에만 연주되었다.
(C) 이후의 작품에 비해 덜 복잡했다.
(D) 목관 악기와 금관 악기 섹션에 치중했다.

어휘 occasion (특정한) 경우

해설 바로크 시대 이후 고전주의 시대에 베토벤과 바그너를
거치면서 오케스트라 구성이 확장되었고 작품이 더
복잡해졌다고 했으므로, 바로크 시대 작품은 이후 작품에 비해
덜 복잡했다고 추론할 수 있다. 그러므로 정답은 (C)이다.

2 지문에서 베토벤에 대해 추론할 수 있는 것은?
(A) 오케스트라의 구성을 변화시킬 만큼 충분한 영향을
미쳤다.
(B) 바그너가 오케스트라 사용을 완전히 단념하도록 영감을
주었다.
(C) 음악가 18명으로 구성된 오케스트라를 이용한 최초의
작곡가였다.
(D) 자신의 작품에 타악기를 포함시키는 것을 거부했다.

어휘 makeup 구성 inspire 영감을 주다 abandon 단념하다

해설 19세기 전반에 오케스트라가 커진 이유가 베토벤이 자신의
작품에서 여러 악기를 각각 두 개씩 쓰고자 했기 때문이라는
설명에서 그가 오케스트라 구성 변화에 영향을 미쳤음을
추론할 수 있으므로, (A)가 정답이다.

CHAPTER 07 Insert Text

EXERCISE
pp.104-109

정답 | **01** (A) **02** (B) **03** (D) **04** (D)
05 1. 1(B) 2. 2(D) **06** 1. 1(D) 2. 2(C)
07 1. 1(C) 2. 2(D) **08** 1. 1(B) 2. 2(A)

01

영국의 지질학자 윌리엄 스미스는 19세기 초에 암석층을 연
구하다가 각 층이 주로 화석화된 유사종으로 구성되어 있는
것을 발견했다. ■(A) 그들 안에서 패턴을 발견한 스미스는 동
물군 천이의 법칙을 생각해 냈는데, 이는 화석화된 유기체는
예측 가능한 순서로 서로 연속된다는 말이다. ■(B) 예를 들어,
네안데르탈인의 뼈는 절대 공룡 뼈와 똑같은 층에서 발견되
지 않을 것이다. ■(C) 그 이유는 그들이 공존하지 않았기 때문
인데, 공룡들이 멸종하고 수백 만년 후에 네안데르탈인이 처
음 등장했다. ■(D) 이 원칙을 적용함으로써, 과학자들은 하나
의 층 내에서 발견된 화석들을 이용해 그 층을 식별해내고 연
대를 추정할 수 있다.

지문 어휘

stratum (암석 등의) 층, 단층 (*pl.* strata) fossilized 화석화된
detect 알아내다, 발견하다 come up with ~을 생각해 내다
the principle of faunal succession 동물군 천이의 법칙
organism 유기체 succeed 뒤를 잇다 predictable 예측할
수 있는 order 순서; (사회적) 질서 Neanderthal 네안데르탈인
coexist 공존하다 die out 멸종되다 date 연대를 추정하다

제시된 문장이 지문에 삽입될 수 있는 곳의 네모[■]를
선택하여라.

**하지만 층들의 안과 사이 모두에서 종들에게서 발견되는 미묘한
차이가 있었다.**

어휘 delicate 미묘한 distinction 차이

해설 제시된 문장의 however로 미루어 바로 앞 문장에 반대되는
의미가 나올 것을 예측할 수 있다. 층들 사이에 차이점도
존재한다는 것이 제시된 문장의 주요 내용이므로, 각 층이
유사한 종의 화석으로 이루어진다는 문장 다음에 반대되는
의미가 나오는 것이 자연스럽다. 따라서 정답은 (A)이다.

기원전 600년경 그리스 도시국가 아테네는 다른 수많은 그리스 도시국가들이 뒤이어 민주주의의 기반으로 삼은 초기 형태의 민주주의를 확립했다. 그럼에도 불구하고, 아테네의 민주주의만큼 안정되고 성공적인 것은 없었다. ■(A) 그것은 직접 민주주의이며, 국민을 대표하기 위한 입법기관이 선출되지 않았다는 뜻이다. ■(B) 솔론이 아테네에서 민주주의 체제를 처음 확립한 정치가였을 것으로 여겨지지만, 일부 반박이 있기는 하다. ■(C) 어느 쪽이든 간에, 아테네에서 가장 오래 통치했을 뿐만 아니라 가장 위대했던 민주주의 통치자는 분명 페리클레스였다. 그의 사망 이후, 이 제도는 과두 정치 혁명으로 두 차례 잠시 대체되면서 위태로워졌다가 에우클레이데스 통치 아래에서 부활하였다. ■(D)

지문 어휘

base upon ~에 기반을 두다 legislative body 입법 기관 elect 선출하다 statesman 정치가 dispute 반박하다 reign 통치하다 peril 위험 oligarchic 과두 정치의 restore (제도를) 부활시키다

제시된 문장이 지문에 삽입될 수 있는 곳의 네모[■]를 선택하여라.

대신, 시민들 각자가 정치적인 사안을 놓고 직접 투표를 했다.

해설 제시된 문장의 Instead로 미루어 바로 앞 문장에 반대되는 내용이 나올 것을 예측할 수 있다. 시민들 각자가 직접 투표를 했다는 것이 제시된 문장의 주요 내용이므로, 국민을 대표하는 입법 기관을 언급한 내용 바로 뒤에 오는 것이 자연스럽다. 따라서 정답은 (B)이다.

한 사회 내 개개인을 재산, 교육, 인종을 포함한 사회 경제적 요인에 근거해 분류하는 것을 사회 계층화라고 일컫는다. ■(A) 현대 서구 문화의 계층화 모델에서는 사람들을 3개 사회 계층으로 나누는데 상류층, 중류층 그리고 하류층이 그것이다. ■(B) 이러한 유형의 사회 계층 간의 구분은 봉건주의 형태의 사회에서 뚜렷하게 드러나는데, 이 사회에서는 상류 귀족 계층이 하류 소작농 계층과 극명한 대조를 이룬다. ■(C) 일반적으로, 사회는 복잡해질수록 더욱 계층화된다. 어떤 사회학자들은 사회 계층을 선진화된 사회에서 발생하는 긍정적인 힘으로 여긴다. ■(D) 하지만, 다른 사회학자들은 보다 부정적인 입장을 견지하면서, 계층화된 사회의 사회적 유동성 부족은 근본적인 불공평의 신호라고 주장한다.

지문 어휘

categorization 분류, 범주화 on the basis of ~에 근거해서 social stratification 사회 계층화 social strata 사회 계층 feudal 봉건 제도의 peasant 소작농 social mobility 사회적 유동성

제시된 문장이 지문에 삽입될 수 있는 곳의 네모[■]를 선택하여라.

그들은 그것의 근본적 목적을 지속적인 질서와 안정의 제공으로 본다.

어휘 provision 제공 stability 안정

해설 제시된 문장에서 질서와 안정의 유지는 사회 계층을 긍정적으로 보는 이유에 해당하므로, 사회 계층을 긍정적으로 보는 일부 사회학자들을 언급한 뒤에 오는 것이 자연스럽다. 제시된 문장의 they는 Some sociologists를, its는 social stratification을 가리킨다는 것을 파악하면 답을 빨리 찾을 수 있다. 따라서 정답은 (D)이다.

기후 변화는 어느 정도 자연 현상이지만, 온실가스 농도를 높여 지구의 하층 대기에 열이 모이게 만드는 인간 활동에 의해서도 발생할 수 있다. 오늘날 정확히 무엇이 기후 변화를 몰아가는지 밝히기 위해 과학자들은 우선 기후 시스템 내의 자연적 변동성을 제외해야 한다. 그 다음에 그들은 대규모 화산 폭발과 지구의 태양 공전 궤도 편차 같은 외적이지만 자연적인 동인들을 잘 생각해 봐야 한다. ■(A) 각 잠재 요인은 그것을 기후 변화의 동인이라고 식별해주는 고유한 지문을 가지고 있다. ■(B) 예를 들어, 일반적으로 지구에 도달하는 태양 에너지의 양을 증가시키는 태양 강제력은 배제되어 왔다. ■(C) 그 이유는 태양 강제력의 지문이 대기권 전체가 따뜻해지는 것으로 나타나는데도 현재 대기권 하층부만이 뜨거워지고 있기 때문이다. ■(D)

지문 어휘

trap 가두다, 모아두다 lower atmosphere 대기권 하층부 drive 추진시키다, 몰아가다 exclude 제외하다 natural variability 자연적 변동성 driver 추진 요인, 동인 volcanic eruption 화산 폭발 deviation 편차 orbit 궤도 potential 잠재적인 rule out ~을 배제하다 currently 현재

제시된 문장이 지문에 삽입될 수 있는 곳의 네모[■]를 선택하여라.

바로 이 사실이 온실가스의 증가가 현재의 기후 변화 뒤에 숨겨진 주요 요인이라는 것을 시사한다.

어휘 precisely 바로

해설 제시된 문장은 결국 온실가스 증가가 기후 변화의 원인일 수밖에 없다는 내용이다. 따라서, 태양 강제력을 예로 들며 자연적인 요인은 지구온난화에 큰 영향을 미치지 않는다고 설명한 다음에 온실가스 증가를 주요 요인으로 설명하는 것이 문맥상 자연스럽다. 그러므로 정답은 (D)이다.

미국에서 저널리즘의 중요성은 미국이 독립을 성취한 직후에 분명해졌다. ■[1(A)] 1791년에 헌법에 수정안 제1조가 추가되면서, 출판의 자유와 언론의 자유 모두가 보장되었다. ■[1(B)] 1690년에 벤자민 해리스는 정기적인 주간 신문의 창간호인 <공공 사건, 국내외 모두(*Publick Occurrences, Both Forreign and Domestick*)>를 발행했다. ■[1(C)] 불행하게도 그것은 또한 마지막 호이기도 했는데, 해리스가 당시만 해도 여전히 미국 식민지를 통치하고 있었던 영국 정부로부터 제대로 된 허가를 얻는 데 실패했기 때문이다. ■[1(D)] 18세기에 식민지가 번성하고 성장하자, 모든 주요 도시에서 신문이 등장하기 시작했다. ■[2(A)] 그 중 하나인 <뉴잉글랜드 신문(*The New-England Courant*)>은 벤자민 프랭클린의 형인 제임스 프랭클린에 의해 발행되었는데, 벤자민은 후에 미국 건국의 아버지들 중 하나가 될 사람이었다. ■[2(B)] 벤자민 프랭클린의 글은 그의 형의 신문에 게재되었는데, 그는 다수의 기사들이 비방의 성격을 띠고 있어서 당시 일반적 관행이었던 필명을 썼다. ■[2(C)] 미국 독립 전쟁 당시, 영국의 봉쇄가 잉크와 종이의 극심한 부족을 야기하여 정기적 발행이 방해받았다. ■[2(D)] 전쟁이 끝날 무렵, 새롭게 독립한 이 나라에는 합계 판매 부수가 주당 약 4만 호에 달하는 신문이 약 36종 존재하고 있었다.

지문 어휘

rule over ~을 지배하다 pseudonym 필명 common practice 관행 libelous 비방하는 acute 극심한 shortage 부족 hinder 방해하다 circulation 판매 부수 in existence 존재하는

1957년 10월 4일은 인간 우주 탐사의 시대가 공식적으로 시작된 날이었다. ■[1(A)] 그날, 소련은 최초의 인공 위성을 우주로 발사했다. ■[1(B)] *스푸트니크 1*호라고 알려진 이 인공위성은 지구 궤도를 돌며 배터리가 다 닳을 때까지 약 3주 동안 무선 신호를 전송했다. ■[1(C)] 1개월 후, 소련은 최초로 살아있는 생명체인 라이카라는 이름의 개를 태운 *스푸트니크 2*호를 우주로 발사했다. ■[1(D)] 그 이후, 우주 탐사는 계속 발전하고 변화했다. 아마 지금까지의 최대 성과는 1969년 인간의 달 착륙이라고 할 수 있을 것이다. ■[2(A)] 그보다 8년 전에는 소련의 우주 비행사 유리 가가린이 약 1시간 30분에 걸쳐 지구 궤도를 한 바퀴 도는 비행을 완수하며 우주에 간 최초의 인간이 되었다. ■[2(B)] 하지만 1969년 7월 20일에 *아폴로 11*호의 달착륙선 이글호가 성공적으로 달에 착륙했고, 닐 암스트롱은 최초로 달 표면을 걸은 인간이 되었다. ■[2(C)] 지금까지 총 12인의 우주 비행사가 달 표면을 걸었지만, 마지막으로 달 위를 걸은 것은 50년도 더 전인 1972년이었다. ■[2(D)] 이는 부분적으로는 우주 탐사의 초점이 우주 정거장의 건립으로 바뀌었기 때문인데, 우주 정거장은 비교적 큰 구조물로 지구를 몇 년 동안 선회하면서 그 안에 살고 있는 우주 비행사들의 실험실로서의 역할을 할 수 있다.

지문 어휘

exploration 탐사, 탐험 launch 발사하다 artificial satellite 인공위성 orbit 궤도를 돌다; 궤도 transmit 전송하다 run out (힘, 수명 등이) 다하다 to date 지금까지 lunar module 달착륙선 focus 초점 establishment 설립 reside 살다

---

1 제시된 문장이 지문에 삽입될 수 있는 곳의 네모[■]를 선택하여라.

하지만 미국 저널리즘의 역사는 그보다 훨씬 이전에 시작되었다.

해설 제시된 문장의 Yet으로 보아 의미상 반대되는 문장 다음에 와야 한다. 또한, 미국 저널리즘이 that보다 훨씬 이전에 시작되었다고 했으므로, 미국에서 출판과 언론의 자유가 모두 보장받게 된 시기를 언급한 문장 다음에 오는 것이 자연스럽다. 따라서 1(B)가 정답이다.

2 제시된 문장이 지문에 삽입될 수 있는 곳의 네모[■]를 선택하여라.

이것에도 불구하고, 식민지 미국의 신문 발행인들은 끈질기게 버텼다.

어휘 persist (끈질기게) 계속하다

해설 제시된 문장이 In spite of this로 시작하므로, 앞 문장에는 this가 가리키는 내용이 나올 것을 예상할 수 있다. 제시된 문장에서 끈질기게 버텼다고 했으므로, 신문 발행을 어렵게 만드는 요인이 언급된 다음에 제시된 문장이 오는 것이 자연스럽다. 따라서 정답은 2(D)이다.

1 제시된 문장이 지문에 삽입될 수 있는 곳의 네모[■]를 선택하여라.

그녀가 이 임무에서 살아남을 것이라는 기대는 전혀 하지 않았지만, 과학자들은 동물 비행을 인간 우주 비행 임무로 가는 필수 단계라고 여겼다.

해설 제시된 문장에서 과학자들이 동물 비행을 인간 비행 전 필수 단계로 여겼다고 했으므로, 임무(the mission)에 파견된 그녀(she)는 동물임을 짐작할 수 있다. 그러므로 이 동물에 대해 언급하는 문장 다음에 오는 것이 자연스럽다. 따라서 정답은 1(D)이다.

2 제시된 문장이 지문에 삽입될 수 있는 곳의 네모[■]를 선택하여라.

그와 그의 동료 우주 비행사들 중 한 명이 암석과 먼지를 수집한 후, 모두 무사히 지구로 돌아왔다.

해설 제시된 문장의 첫 단어 He가 누구인지 파악해야 한다. 달에 착륙하여 한 동료와 임무를 수행하고 나머지 동료들과 지구로 귀환했다고 했으므로, 바로 앞 문장에는 암스트롱이 달에 처음 착륙한 내용이 나오는 것이 자연스럽다. 따라서 정답은 2(C)이다.

고대 마야 문명의 고유 표기 체계는 상당한 정도로 해독이 된 유일한 메소아메리카 표기 체계이다. ■^{1(A)} 그것은 적어도 기원전 3세기 이래 계속 존재했으며 스페인의 정복으로 한때 거대했던 마야 제국이 종말을 고한 17세기까지 사용되었다. ■^{1(B)} 고대 마야 문자는 처음 이를 접한 초기 유럽 탐험가들에 의해 '상형 문자'라고 불렸는데, 고대 이집트 문자와 약간 비슷했기 때문이었다. ■^{1(C)} 그것은 도자기, 건물 벽, 나무 껍질로 만든 종이 위에 그려졌으며, 나무나 돌에 새겨지거나 치장용 벽토로 만들어지기도 했다. ■^{1(D)} 불행하게도, 그림으로 그려진 마야 문자는 거의 남아 있지 않아 고고학자나 언어학자가 이용할 수 있는 문자의 양이 제한되어 있다. ■^{2(A)} 그럼에도 불구하고, 현존하는 고대 마야 문자의 약 60퍼센트가 어느 정도는 해석이 가능한 것으로 추정되며, 이를 바탕으로 그 체계에 대한 기본적인 이해가 가능하다. ■^{2(B)} 그 문자는 일반적으로 블록(사각 덩어리)에 쓰이고 두 개의 블록 너비의 세로단으로 배열된다. ■^{2(C)} 각 블록은 명사구 또는 동사구를 나타내고, 블록들은 왼쪽에서 오른쪽으로, 위에서 아래로 읽는다. ■^{2(D)} 남아 있는 현대 마야 언어는 현재 로마자 알파벳으로 쓰인다. 하지만 고대 상형 문자 체계의 부활을 옹호하는 사람들도 있다.

지문 어휘

decipher 해독하다 substantial (양, 정도가) 상당한 date back to ~이래 계속 존재하다 conquest 정복 put an end to ~을 끝내다 hieroglyphics 상형 문자 resemblance 유사점 mold 만들다 stucco 치장용 벽토 extant 현존하는 column 세로단 revival 회복, 부활

1 제시된 문장이 지문에 삽입될 수 있는 곳의 네모[■]를 선택하여라.

그러나 그것은 실제로는 글자들이 전체 단어를 나타내고, 개별 음절을 나타내는 상형 문자들이 이를 보완하는 현대 일본어 표기 체계와 더 비슷하다.

어휘 glyph 상형 문자 complement 보완하다 syllable 음절

해설 제시된 문장이 however로 시작하므로 의미상 반대되는 문장 다음에 와야 한다. 실제로는 일본어와 비슷하다는 것이 제시된 문장의 요지이므로, 마야 문자가 이집트 상형문자와 비슷하다는 내용 다음으로 이어지는 것이 자연스럽다. 따라서 정답은 1(C)이다.

2 제시된 문장이 지문에 삽입될 수 있는 곳의 네모[■]를 선택하여라.

이 과정은 남은 세로단이 없을 때까지 계속되는 것이다.

해설 제시된 문장의 this process에 해당하는 내용이 바로 앞에 나올 것을 예측할 수 있다. 제시된 문장에서 '남은 것이 없을 때까지 계속한다'고 과정을 설명하고 있으므로, '위에서 아래로 읽는다'는 내용 바로 뒤에 와야 자연스럽다. 따라서 정답은 2(D)이다.

새의 이동은 유전적으로 조절되는 현상으로 그 시기 결정은 주로 낮의 길이 변화에 의해 촉발되는 것으로 보인다. ■^{1(A)} 이런 변화는 새들의 호르몬 수치에 영향을 미치는데, 이것은 이동을 시작하기 전 며칠 동안 가만히 있지 못하고 더욱 활동적으로 되는 것을 통해 관찰이 되고 있다. ■^{1(B)} 하지만 새들의 연례 이동의 시작을 유도하는 내부 메커니즘도 있는 것으로 보인다. ■^{1(C)} 낮 길이나 온도 변화가 없는 조건에서 새장에 갇힌 새들은 그들 종의 일반적인 이동 방향으로 날고 싶어하는 것을 포함하여, 이동 전의 야생 새들과 유사한 행동을 보인다. ■^{1(D)} 일단 이동이 시작되면, 새들은 자신들의 감각을 이용해 길을 찾는다. 일부는 태양을 나침반으로 이용하고, 또 다른 일부는 지구의 자기장을 탐지해서 따라가고, 또 어떤 새들은 시각적 주요 지형지물이나 후각적 단서에 의존하기도 한다. 대다수의 경우, 이런 방법들을 조합하여 사용함으로써 이동을 위한 길 찾기가 이루어진다. ■^{2(A)} '스프링 오버슈트'로 알려진 현상에서는 번식지로 돌아오는 새들이 목적지를 지나 결국 의도했던 곳보다 훨씬 북쪽에서 멈추게 된다. ■^{2(B)} 또 다른 경우에는, 비정상적으로 강한 바람이 새들을 경로에서 벗어나게 한다. ■^{2(C)} 이로 인해 새들은 정상 범위에서 수천 킬로미터 벗어난 지역에 내려 앉을 수도 있다. ■^{2(D)}

지문 어휘

genetically 유전적으로 timing 시기 선택 trigger 촉발하다 restless 가만히 있지 못하는 lead up to (결국) ~에 이르다 navigate 길을 찾다 magnetic field 자기장 visual 시각의 olfactory 후각의 cue 단서 breeding ground 번식지 alight (날아가) 앉다

1 제시된 문장이 지문에 삽입될 수 있는 곳의 네모[■]를 선택하여라.

체지방 축적량 증가를 포함한 생리학적 변화도 감지된다.

어휘 physiological 생리학적인

해설 제시된 문장에서 생리학적인 변화도 있다고 하였으므로, 낮 길이 변화가 호르몬 수치에 영향을 주었다는 말 다음에 생리학적 변화에 대해 추가적으로 언급하는 것이 자연스럽다. 따라서 정답은 1(B)이다.

2 제시된 문장이 지문에 삽입될 수 있는 곳의 네모[■]를 선택하여라.

이 길 찾기 기술이 아무리 복합적이라고 해도 잘못될 일이 절대로 없는 것은 아니다.

어휘 far from 절대 ~하지 않는 foolproof 잘못될 수가 없는

해설 제시된 문장은 길을 찾는 도중 일이 잘못될 수 있다는 것이므로, 뒤에 새들이 이동하면서 겪는 어려운 상황의 예시로 스프링 오버슈트나 강한 바람 등이 이어지는 것이 자연스럽다. 따라서 정답은 2(A)이다.

EXERCISE   pp.118-123

정답 | 01 (B), (C)   **02** (B), (D)   **03** (B), (D), (F)
      04 (A), (D), (F)

01

사방이 물로 둘러싸인 땅 덩어리라고 폭넓게 정의되지만, 섬은 어떻게 형성되었는지에 따라 몇 개의 하위 범주로 더 나뉘어질 수 있다. 하위 범주에는 대륙섬과 울타리섬이 포함되는데, 이들은 물리적인 유사성을 일부 공유함에도 불구하고 형성 방법에 있어서 굉장히 다르다.

크기가 매우 큰 편인 대륙섬은 한때 대륙에 붙어 있었고, 계속 대륙붕 위에 얹혀 있다. 그린란드와 마다가스카르 같은 몇몇 섬들은 지각의 움직임이 대륙 이동 현상을 야기시켰을 때 분리되었다. 반면에 또 다른 섬들은 지구 온도 상승으로 빙하가 녹아, 해수면이 상당히 상승했을 때 형성되었다. 예를 들어, 영국 제도는 한때 유럽 본토의 일부였지만, 저지대가 바닷물로 범람되었을 때 분리되었다.

이와 달리 울타리섬은 해안선과 나란히 뻗어 있는 길고 좁은 섬으로, 때로는 대륙섬과 마찬가지로 대륙붕에 받쳐져 있다. 그 이름은 대양과 본토 사이에 장벽을 형성해 석호나 해협을 보호해 준다는 사실에서 유래했다. 그것은 많은 울타리섬 형성의 원인인 해류에 의해 모래, 토사, 또는 자갈과 같은 퇴적물이 쌓인 것이지만, 녹아내리는 빙하가 천천히 지표를 가로질러 이동하면서 빙원 빙퇴석, 즉 주로 암석, 흙, 자갈로 이루어진 잔해가 쌓인 흔적을 남김으로써 형성된 울타리섬도 있다.

지문 어휘

1. subcategory 하위 범주 barrier island 울타리섬(보초도) strikingly 굉장히
2. continental island 대륙섬(육도) continental shelf 대륙붕 break away 분리되다 continental drift 대륙 이동 significant 상당한 the British Isles 영국 제도 low-lying 낮은, 저지대의 be subjected to ~을 겪다(당하다) flooding 범람
3. parallel to ~와 평행한 rest on ~에 받쳐지다 lagoon 석호 sound 해협 build-up 조성 gravel 자갈 ocean current 해류 landscape 지표 leave behind ~을 뒤에 남기다 glacial moraine 빙원 빙퇴석 trail 자국, 흔적 piled-up 쌓여 있는 debris 잔해 comprise ~으로 이루어지다

지문에서 가장 중요한 개념들을 나타내는 선택지 2개를 선택하여 요약을 완성하여라.

보다 폭넓은 정의 외에도 섬들은 형성 방식에 의해 더 작은 그룹으로 나뉠 수 있다.

(A) 울타리섬과 대륙섬은 둘 다 대륙붕에 위치한다는 기본적인 특성을 가지고 있다.
(B) 대륙섬은 일종의 분리가 발생하기 전에 한때 대륙의 일부였다는 특성을 공유한다.
(C) 길고 좁은 울타리섬은 침전물의 축적이나 빙하가 빙퇴석을 남김으로써 만들어진다.
(D) 대륙섬이 이곳저곳으로 천천히 표류하는 반면, 울타리섬은 본토에 가로막혀 있다.

어휘 accumulation 축적

해설 형성 방식에 따라 구분되는 두 종류의 섬에 대해 대륙에서 분리되어 형성된 대륙섬의 특징을 요약한 (B)와 침전물 또는 빙퇴석으로 형성된 울타리섬에 대해 요약한 (C)가 정답이다. (A)는 중심 내용이 아니고, (D)는 지문 내용과 다르다.

02

도시의 성장을 설명하는 데 쓰이던 최초의 이론적 모델 중 하나는 그 모델의 창시자이자 사회학자인 어니스트 버제스의 이름을 딴 버제스 모델이다. 1920년대에 제안된 그것은 도심에 위치한 중심 업무 지구(CBD)로부터 발달하여 각기 다른 구성과 목적을 가지고 동심원 형태로 확장되어 나가는 도시 토지 이용을 설명한다. 점이 지대는 CBD에 가장 가까이 자리하면서 주거적, 상업적 구조물의 혼합 지역이며, 그 다음 바깥 구역인 내부 교외는 노동자 계층 가정의 집이 있는 곳이다. 내부 교외 너머에는 도시의 중산층들이 거주하는 외부 교외가 있고, 마지막으로 CBD에서 일하는 부유한 사업가들이 거주하는 통근자 지대가 있다. 이 구역은 그 안에 위치하는 사업체들이 얻을 수 있는 수익뿐만 아니라, 그 안에 거주하기 위해 사람들이 지불할 용의가 있는 돈의 양에 따라 구분이 된다.

버제스 모델은 1940년대 다중 핵 모델이 발전하는 데 중대한 영향을 미친 것으로 언급되어 왔다. 이 모델은 도시가 CBD로부터 바깥으로 발전해 나간다는 것을 인정하면서도, 추가적인 더 작은 CBD들이 교외에서 형성될 수 있다고 본다. 이는 임대료가 높은 지역이 잠재적으로 더 짧은 통근 거리를 제공하므로 버제스가 제시한 것보다 더 복잡하고, 틀림없이 더 현실적인 모델을 만들어 낸다. 자동차가 전국적으로 선호되는 교통수단이 되어가는 시점에 만들어진 이 모델은 도시 거주자들이 필요로 하던 이동 편의성 향상에 바탕을 두고 있다.

지문에서 가장 중요한 개념들을 나타내는 선택지 2개를 선택하여
요약을 완성하여라.

**어니스트 버제스에 의해 만들어진 것과 같은 도시 성장 모델은
도시를 서로 다른 목적의 서로 다른 구역으로 나눈다.**

(A) 버제스 모델에서는 도시 주민들의 집과 업무용 구조물을 모두
점이 지대에서 찾아볼 수 있다.

(B) 다중 핵 모델은 버제스 모델이 보다 더 복잡해진 형태로 여러
CBD(중심 업무 지구)를 포함하고 있다.

(C) 버제스 모델과 마찬가지로 다중 핵 모델은 개인 차량에 대한
통근자의 수요가 높은 도시 지역을 구상한다.

(D) 버제스 모델에서 도시 구역들을 나누어 놓은 형태는 CBD
(중심 업무 지구)가 중심에 있는 일련의 동심원들이다.

어휘 present 제시하다, 나타내다 envision 상상하다, 구상하다
private vehicle 자가용 hub 중심, 중추

해설 도시 구조의 모델 중 다중 핵 모델의 핵심을 설명한 (B)와
동심원 형태의 버제스 모델을 설명한 (D)가 정답이다. (A)는
중심 내용이 아니며, (C)는 지문 내용과 다르다.

03

에게 문명은 에게 해에서 유래한 말로, 일반적으로 그 부근에
서 출현한 청동기 시대 사회를 가리킨다. 대략 1,800년에 걸
쳐 이어진 이 문명은 연대기상으로 각각의 특정 문화에 따라
세 시기로 구분되는데, 초기 청동기 시대의 키클라데스 문명,
중기 청동기 시대의 미노스 문명, 후기 청동기 시대의 미케네
문명이 그것이다.

키클라데스 문명은 기원전 3000년에 시작해 초기 이집트 및
메소포타미아 문명과 동시에 번영했던 것으로 보인다. 소아
시아에서 이주해 온 것으로 여겨지는 이 사람들은 청동 무기
와 도구 제작 기술을 가져왔다. 기원전 2200년 무렵에는 새
로이 도착한 사람들이 기존 문명과 충돌하면서 혼란이 발생
했다. 미노스 문명을 일으킨 이 새 이주자들은 말을 데려오고
크레타 섬의 정교한 성들을 건설하였으며, 시칠리아나 이집
트 같은 멀리 떨어진 문명들과 교역하기 위한 해상 네트워크
도 구축했다. 보편적으로 합의된 것은 아니지만 일부 고고학
자와 역사가들은 이것이 유럽 땅 최초의 선진 문명으로 여겨
질 수도 있다고 제안한다.

기원전 1450년 무렵 크레타 섬의 웅장한 성들은 화산 활동
으로 인한 것으로 보이는 파괴를 겪었고, 미케네인들의 등장
과 함께 호전적인 새 문명이 출현했다. 미케네 도시들은 견고
하게 요새화되었으며, 기하학적인 양식의 예술이 예전보다
더욱 지배적이게 되어 청동기 시대와 고대 그리스 예술의 가
교 역할을 했다. 미케네인들은 미노스 교역로에 대한 통제권
을 장악하고 부와 권력을 쌓았다. 그들은 기원전 1200년 무
렵에 발생한 것으로 보이는 전설적인 트로이 전쟁과 관련 있
는 문명이라고 여겨진다. 하지만, 그들의 제국이 망한 이유
에 대해서는 아직 학자들 사이에서 의견이 분분한데, 자연 재
해 때문이었거나, 북부 산악지대에서 이주해 온 그리스 종족
도리스인들의 침입 때문일 가능성이 높다. 여하튼, 그 붕괴는
에게 문명의 종말을 의미했다.

19세기까지도 현대 세계는 에게 문명의 존재를 알지 못했다.
고대 그리스 작가들은 이 시기를 '영웅의 시대'로 칭했지만,
그리스와 트로이의 전쟁을 묘사한 호머의 <일리아드>처럼
이 시기에 관한 이야기들은 신화와 거의 구별이 되지 않았다.
문학적인 단서 이외에 특정 고고학 발견물들이 그리스에 청
동기 시대 문명이 존재했음을 보여주었다.

지시문: 지문의 간략한 요약을 위한 도입 문장이 아래에 제시되어
있다. 지문에서 가장 중요한 개념들을 나타내는 선택지 3개를
선택하여 요약을 완성하여라. 어떤 문장들은 지문에 제시되지
않거나 주요 개념이 아니므로 요약에 포함되지 않는다. **이 문제는
2점에 해당한다.**

**고대 그리스의 문명인 에게 문명은 세 개의 다른 시기로 분류될 수
있다.**

(A) '에게 문명'이라는 말은 에게 문명이 발달한 지역 가까이 있던
에게 해에서 유래했다.

(B) 고고학 발견물로 그리스에 청동기 시대 문명이 존재했음이
확인될 때까지 에게 문명은 처음에 신화라고 여겨졌다.

(C) 소아시아에서 이주한 사람들은 도자기나 기타 유물에 종종
그려진 기하학적 예술을 미케네인들에게 전파했다.

(D) 초기 에게 문명은 키클라데스 문명으로 여겨졌으며, 이것이
미노스 문명으로 바뀌었다.

(E) 그리스에서 청동기 시대에는 배들이 시칠리아나 이집트 문명과 해상 네트워크로 교역하는 데 흔히 이용되었다.

(F) 미케네 문명은 어마어마한 방어용 기반 시설과 예술적 기량을 특징으로 하며 번성했지만, 불가사의한 몰락을 겪었다.

어휘 derive from ~에서 유래하다 perceive 감지하다, 인지하다 formidable 어마어마한 enigmatic 불가사의한

해설 에게 문명에 대해 고고학적 증거 발견 이전에는 신화와 다름없었음을 설명하는 (B), 키클라데스 문명에서 미노스 문명으로의 변화를 언급한 (D), 미케네 문명의 발전과 쇠퇴에 대해 요약하는 (F)가 정답이다. (A)와 (E)는 중심 내용이 아니며, (C)는 언급되지 않았다.

04

일부 육상 생물, 균류, 미생물과 마찬가지로 수많은 해양 척추동물과 무척추동물들도 빛을 만들어내고 발산하는 능력을 가지고 있는데, 이것이 생물 발광이라고 알려진 과정이다. 어떤 경우, 이 종들은 스스로 빛을 만들어 낼 수 있는 반면, 또 다른 어떤 종들은 특정 종류의 박테리아와의 공생 관계에 의존한다. 일반적으로 말해서, 생물 발광은 발광 분자와 효소가 관련된 화학 반응에 의해 발생한다. 루시페린으로 알려진 분자는 종별로 변이가 거의 없는 반면, 루시페라아제라고 알려진 효소는 종류가 매우 다양한데, 이는 생물 발광이 동물계에서 개별적으로 서로 다른 40여 개의 사례를 통해 진화해왔다는 증거이다.

생물 발광에 대한 관찰은 축축한 나무에서 때때로 희미한 빛이 발산된다는 걸 주목한 아리스토텔레스만큼 오래 전으로 거슬러 올라가지만, 이 현상은 19세기 말까지 제대로 연구되지 않았다. 어떤 종들은 위장을 목적으로 그것을 이용하고 또 어떤 종들은 먹이를 유인하거나 짝을 유혹하기 위해 그것을 이용하기에, 생물 발광은 단일한 진화적 목적에만 기여하지는 않는다. 위장의 경우, 생물 발광은 일부 오징어 종 같은 해양 생물들에 의해 반대 조명 목적으로 흔히 사용되는데, 이는 자신들의 아랫면이 물의 표면을 통과하는 빛의 밝기뿐만 아니라 파장에까지 맞도록 빛을 내는 일이다. 그 결과 그들의 실루엣은 눈에 덜 띄고 아래로 지나가는 포식자들이 그들을 알아챌 가능성이 줄어든다.

또 다른 해양 생물인 아귀 또한 생물 발광을 포식 원리에 활용하는 종의 좋은 예다. 극도로 어두운 환경에서 서식하는 심해어인 아귀는 두 눈 사이에 튀어나온 변형된 지느러미를 달랑거리는데, 그 안에서 공생 박테리아가 먹이를 아귀의 큰 입에 더욱 가깝게 유인하기 위해 빛을 발한다. 그리고 육지에서는 딱정벌레의 한 종으로 초여름에 숲이 우거진 지역을 밝게 비추는 것이 종종 보이는 반딧불이가 적합한 짝을 유인하기 위해 생물 발광 능력을 이용한다. 과학자들은 반딧불이의 생물 발광의 원래 목적이 유충들에게 있어 경고성 신호로 작용해 잠재적인 포식자에게 자기들이 맛없는 스테로이드를 가지고 있으며 (자기들을) 먹어서는 안 된다는 것을 알리는 것이었지만, 이후 이것은 성체들에 의해 짝짓기 전략의 한 부분으로 이용하게 되었다고 본다.

지문 어휘

1. terrestrial 육상의, 육지의 fungus 균류 (*pl.* fungi) micro-organism 미생물 emit (빛·소리 등을) 내다 bioluminescence 생물 발광 symbiotic relationship 공생 관계 chemical reaction 화학 반응 molecule 분자 enzyme 효소 luciferin 루시페린(생물 발광에 관여하는 물질) variation 변이, 변화 luciferase 루시페라아제(생물 발광 효소) instance 경우, 사례

2. investigate 조사하다 camouflage 위장 lure 꾀다 counterillumination 반대 조명 underside 아랫면 wavelength 파장 prominent 눈에 잘 띄는

3. predation 포식 dangle (들고) 달랑거리다 modified 변형된 protrude 튀어나오다 larva 유충, 애벌레 (*pl.* larvae) unpalatable 맛이 없는, tactic 전략

지시문: 지문의 간략한 요약을 위한 도입 문장이 아래에 제시되어 있다. 지문에서 가장 중요한 개념들을 나타내는 선택지 3개를 선택하여 요약을 완성하여라. 어떤 문장들은 지문에 제시되지 않거나 주요 개념이 아니므로 요약에 포함되지 않는다. **이 문제는 2점에 해당한다.**

생물 발광은 살아있는 생물들이 자체적으로 빛을 생산하고 발산하는 과정이다.

(A) 생물 발광은 포식자로부터 숨기, 먹이 사냥하기, 그리고 짝 유인하기 등을 포함한 다양한 용도를 가지고 있다.

(B) 아리스토텔레스는 최초로 생물 발광을 관찰한 사람 중 하나로, 축축해진 나무에서 그것을 발견했다.

(C) 두 종류의 주요한 생물 발광이 있는데, 하나는 루시페린이라고 알려져 있고 다른 하나는 루시페라아제라고 불린다.

(D) 일반적으로 생물 발광의 원천이 되는 것은 바로 분자와 효소 사이의 화학 반응이다.

(E) 성충 반딧불이는 유충들이 독성이 있는 먹이를 먹지 않도록 경고하는 한 방법으로 생물 발광을 사용한다.

(F) 어떤 생물들은 생물 발광을 자체적으로 만들어 내는 한편, 아귀와 같은 또 다른 생물들은 특별한 박테리아에 의존한다.

어휘 spot 발견하다 toxic 독성의 on one's own 혼자 힘으로

해설 생물들이 자체적으로 빛을 생산하고 발산하는 생물 발광에 대해 생물 발광의 용도, 원리, 방법의 중심 내용을 요약한 (A), (D), (F)가 정답이다. (B)는 중심 내용이 아니고, (C)와 (E)는 지문 내용과 다르다.

정답 | 1 (B)   2 (C)   3 (A)   4 (D)   5 (C)   6 (C)   7 (B)   8 (B), (C), (E)

문학적 장치

영어로 글쓰기를 시도하는 사람들은 독자들을 의도된 메시지에서 벗어나게 만들 수 있는 **특이하거나 지나치게 미화된 표현**을 사용하지 말라는 주의를 받으면서, 명료성과 간결함을 우선시하라는 조언을 자주 듣는다. 그럼에도 불구하고 작가들은 명료성을 포기하지 않고 미학적 매력을 강조하는 길을 찾으면서, 창의적인 방식으로 아이디어를 전달하고자 하는 경우가 있다. 다행히 영어는 이런 목적에 맞는 다양한 수단들을 제공하는데, 이것들은 흔히 '문학적 장치'라고 일컬어진다.

특정 문학적 장치들은 시적 허용을 이용하는데, 이것은 문학 작품과 시를 쓰는 작가들이 문법의 제약을 초월할 수 있게 해준다. 그런 장치의 하나는 접속사를 일부러 생략하는 접속사 생략이다. 이런 생략은 작가들이 '그리고'와 '또는'을 제거함으로써 그렇지 않았다면 번잡했을 표현을 간결하게 다듬을 수 있게 해주어, 문장의 리듬에 엄청난 영향을 미칠 수 있다. 접속사 생략의 효과는 흔히 번역되는 라틴어 어구 "*왔노라, 보았노라, 이겼노라*"를 "나는 왔고, 보았고, 이겼다."로 간결히 옮긴 것에서 분명히 드러난다. 문장을 압축하는 또 다른 수단은 **생략법**을 통한 것으로, 의미에 대한 이해는 희생시키지 않으면서 문법적으로 필수적인 단어들을 생략한다. 이 장치는 "나는 너를 도울 거고, 너도 나를."이라는 문장에서 두 번째 "도울 거야"의 경우를 없앤 것에서 볼 수 있듯이, 흔히 구어체 영어의 간결한 특성을 **반영한다.**

상반된 효과를 찾는 사람들에게는 단순한 마침표 하나면 충분할 곳에 불필요한 접속사들을 삽입하는, 연속해서 여러 접속사를 사용하는 것이 있다. 이 문학적 장치는 문장의 리듬을 늦춰 비중을 더하는 역할을 한다. 하나의 예를 <아기 돼지 삼형제> 우화에서 찾을 수 있는데, 고약한 늑대의 파괴적인 행동이 이렇게 묘사된다. "그는 숨을 내뿜었다, 그리고 그는 입김을 불었다, 그리고 그는 입김을 불어서 그 집을 넘어뜨렸다." 이런 방식은 한 현대 추리 소설에서도 볼 수 있다: "형사가 미스터리를 풀기 위해 범죄 현장을 면밀히 조사한 다음, 연구하고 분석했으며, 모든 증거를 세밀하게 조사했다." 이 의도적인 반복은 독자들에게 긴장감을 유발하는 리듬을 만들어 낸다.

■(A) 때로는 창의적인 작가들은 문법의 엄격한 경계를 밀어붙이는 대신, 문자 그대로의 해석을 초월하는 방식으로 아이디어를 전달하는 것을 목표로 삼는다. ■(B) 바라는 바를 마음껏 추구할 수 있는 능력을 의미하는 "세상에 못할 것이 없다"라는 관용구에서 보이듯, 은유법은 추상적이고 시적인 비유

이다. 반면에, '~처럼' 또는 '~ 같은'이라는 단어를 이용해 '얼음처럼 차가운' 같은 비유 표현을 만드는 직유법은 더 직접적이다. ■(C) 또 다른 비유적 문학적 장치는 과장법인데, 여기에서는 진지하게 받아들이기엔 너무 극단적인 과장된 말이 강조나 희극적 효과를 위해 사용된다. ■(D) 몸집이 큰 사람을 '덩치가 산만 한'이라고 묘사하는 것이 한 예가 될 수 있다. 관찰력이 좋은 독자는 이런 주장이 과장법을 이용할 뿐만 아니라 직유까지 포함한다는 점을 알아차릴 수도 있다.

반대로, 완서법도 있는데, 이것은 이중 부정을 활용한 절제된 표현을 통해 강조를 표현하는 장치이다. 완서법의 예가 문학에 아주 많기는 하지만, 그것은 크리스토퍼가 실제로 춤을 꽤 잘 춘다는 의미를 나타내는 "크리스토퍼가 춤을 못 추지는 않아." 같은 일상 표현에서 가장 흔히 찾아 볼 수 있다. 완서법의 남용이 오해나 명료성 부족, 또는 의사소통 오류로 이어질 수도 있지만, 언어에서 이것을 사용하는 것의 긍정적인 효과는 과시에 기대지 않고 요점이나 속성, 또는 성취를 강조할 수 있는 능력에 있다. 이는 더 완화되거나 절제된 어조를 원할 때, 중층적 의미를 지닌 문학적인 글의 풍성함을 향상시켜 주어 특히 효과적일 수 있다.

이것들은 영어로 글을 쓰는 작가들이 흔히 활용하는 소수의 문학적 장치들에 불과하다. 다른 많은 장치들이 존재하며, 분별력 있게 적절히 활용된다면 글에 활기 넘치는 신선함을 불어 넣어 사람과 장소, 그리고 사건들을 단순히 일상적으로 묘사하는 것 이상의 수준으로 끌어 올릴 수 있는 힘을 지니고 있다.

지문 어휘

1. prioritize 우선시하다 conciseness 간결함 embellished 미화된 aesthetic 심미적인 forgo 포기하다
2. transcend 초월하다 constraint 제약 cumbersome 번잡한 succinctly 간결하게 sacrifice 희생시키다
3. insertion 삽입 suffice 충분하다 scrutinize 면밀히 조사하다 unravel 풀다
4. literal 문자 그대로의 interpretation 해석 abstract 추상적인 exaggerated 과장된 observant 관찰력이 좋은
5. understatement 절제된 표현 abound 아주 많다, 풍부하다 attribute 속성 resort to ~에 기대다 subdued 완화된, 부드러운
6. judiciously 분별력 있게 in moderation 적절히 infuse 불어 넣다 vibrant 활기찬 depiction 묘사

어휘의 의미 파악 문제

1 지문의 단어 "unorthodox"와 의미가 가장 가까운 것은?
(A) 보통의
(B) 색다른
(C) 효과적인
(D) 불분명한

해설 unorthodox가 '특이한'이라는 뜻으로 사용되었으므로, 이와 유사한 뜻을 가진 (B) unconventional이 정답이다.

추론 문제

2 다음 중 첫 번째 단락이 문학적 장치에 대해 암시하는 것은?
(A) 작가들이 명확하고 간결한 표현을 위해 사용한다.
(B) 작가들이 그것을 통해 문자 그대로, 그리고 비유적으로 생각을 표현할 수 있다.
(C) 작가들이 독자들을 사로잡고 자신들의 글을 기억에 남게 만들기 위해 이용한다.
(D) 작가들이 전적으로 창의성 때문에 그것에 중점을 둔다.

어휘 figuratively 비유적으로 engage 사로잡다

해설 작가들이 창의적인 방식으로 생각을 전달하고 심미적인 매력을 강조할 수 있게 해주는 것이 문학적 장치라는 설명에서, 이것이 독자들을 사로잡고 기억에 남는 글을 쓰기 위한 방법임을 유추할 수 있다. 그러므로 정답은 (C)이다.

문장 재구성 문제

3 아래 문장 중 지문에서 음영 표시된 문장의 핵심 정보를 가장 잘 나타낸 것은? 오답 선택지들은 의미를 현저히 바꾸거나 핵심 정보를 생략한다.
(A) 생략법은 의미에 대한 이해는 유지하면서 문법적으로 필수적인 단어를 생략함으로써 문장을 줄이는 데 쓰이는 기법이다.
(B) 생략법은 의미에 대한 이해는 해치지 않으면서 추가 단어를 포함시켜 문장을 확장하는 데 쓰이는 기법이다.
(C) 의미에 대한 이해를 향상시키기 위해 과장된 단어가 추가되는 생략법을 통해 문장이 압축될 수 있다.
(D) 생략법 사용은 문장에 불필요한 단어를 포함시켜 확실히 내용을 완전히 이해할 수 있게 한다.

어휘 compromise 해치다, 손상시키다 redundant 불필요한, 여분의 thorough 완전한, 철저한

해설 생략법은 의미를 이해할 수 있게 하면서 문법적으로 요구되는 단어를 생략한다는 것이 핵심 내용이므로, 정답은 (A)이다.

어휘의 의미 파악 문제

4 지문의 단어 "mirrors"와 의미가 가장 가까운 것은?
(A) 완화하다
(B) ~와 일치하다
(C) 반복하다
(D) 반영하다

해설 mirrors는 '반영하다'라는 뜻으로 사용되었으므로, 동일한 뜻을 나타내는 (D) reflects가 정답이다.

수사적 의도 파악 문제

5 글쓴이는 왜 세 번째 단락에서 "<아기 돼지 삼형제>"를 언급하는가?
(A) 필요치 않은 세부 정보 추가의 예를 제공하기 위해
(B) 소설이 문학적 장치를 이용해 쓰일 수 있음을 암시하기 위해
(C) 연속해서 여러 접속사를 사용하는 것의 예를 보여 주기 위해
(D) 불필요한 접속사 생략의 중요성을 설명하기 위해

어휘 superfluous 필요치 않은 details 세부 정보

해설 연속해서 여러 접속사를 사용하는 것이 문장의 리듬을 늦춰 비중을 더하는 역할을 한다고 설명한 후, 그 예로 <아기 돼지 삼형제>에 쓰인 문장을 들고 있으므로, (C)가 정답이다.

지시 대상 찾기 문제

6 지문의 단어 "it"이 가리키는 것은?
(A) 강조
(B) 절제된 표현
(C) 완서법
(D) 문학

해설 it은 앞 문장에서 단수 명사를 가리키고, Although 절에서 완서법의 사례가 문학에 아주 많다고 한 다음, 일상적인 표현에서 완서법을 찾아볼 수 있는 경우를 it 뒤에 설명하고 있으므로, (C)가 정답이다.

문장 삽입 문제

7 제시된 문장이 지문에 삽입될 수 있는 곳을 가리키는 네 개의 네모[■]를 보아라.

이를 달성할 수 있는 흔한 방법은 은유법과 직유법, 즉 생생하면서 연상 작용을 일으키는 비유를 만드는 데 쓰일 수 있는 문학적 장치들을 활용하는 것이다.

이 문장이 들어갈 가장 적절한 위치는? 해당 네모[■]를 선택하여 이 문장을 지문에 삽입하여라.
(A)　　(B)　　(C)　　(D)

어휘 vivid 생생한 evocative 연상시키는

해설 주어진 문장의 this가 문자 그대로의 해석을 초월하는 방식으로 아이디어를 전달하는 것을 목표로 하는 것을 가리키며, 주어진 문장이 두 가지 문학적 장치인 은유법과 직유법을 소개하고 있으므로, 은유법과 직유법을 각기 설명하는 내용 앞인 (B)에 놓여야 문맥상 자연스럽다.

지문 요약 문제

8 **지시문**: 지문의 간략한 요약을 위한 도입 문장이 아래에 제시되어 있다. 지문에서 가장 중요한 개념들을 나타내는 선택지 3개를 선택하여 요약을 완성하여라. 어떤 문장들은 지문에 제시되지 않거나 주요 개념이 아니므로 요약에 포함되지 않는다. **이 문제는 2점에 해당한다.**

다수의 문학적 장치가 영어 글쓰기에 이용된다.

(A) 작가들은 어느 문학적 장치가 각 문장에 이용되는지를 우선시해야 한다.
(B) 문학적 장치의 이용으로 인해 작가들이 명료성을 희생시키지 않고 창의적으로 글을 쓸 수 있다.
(C) 일부 문학적 장치를 이용하려면, 작가들이 특정 단어들을 제외하거나 포함해야 한다.
(D) 접속사 생략은 많은 라틴어 어구에서 찾아 볼 수 있다.
(E) 문학적 장치의 이용은 관습적인 문법 규칙에 도전함으로써 글을 향상시킬 수 있다.
(F) 과거에는 아이들을 위한 우화가 주로 문학적 장치의 이용을 특징으로 했다.

어휘 predominantly 주로

해설 영어 글쓰기의 문학적 장치에 대해 글의 명료성을 지키면서 창의적 글쓰기를 돕는 점, 단어 생략이나 삽입이 문학적 장치의 예로 언급되는 점, 문법 규칙에 도전하여 글을 향상시킨다는 점을 설명한 (B), (C), (E)가 정답이다.

관련 지식 **아이러니(irony)**는 문학 작품에서 주로 사용되는 문학적 장치로, 반어(反語) 또는 비꼬는 말이라고도 하며, '위장'을 뜻하는 그리스어 에이로네이아(eironeia)에서 유래했다. 표현의 효과를 높이려고 말이나 문장의 의미와 실제 상황 사이에 모순이나 엇갈림을 발생시키는데,

'못났다'라고 생각하면서 '잘났다'라고 표현하는 것이 그 예이다. 실제 뜻하는 바와 반대로 표현하여 결국은 본래 뜻하고자 하는 내용을 성공적으로 나타내는 것이다.

PASSAGE 2

pp.132-135

정답 | **1** (D) **2** (A) **3** (C) **4** (A) **5** (C) **6** (B) **7** (B) **8** (B), (D), (E)

로마의 흥망성쇠

고대 로마 공화국은 기원전 6세기에 세워졌으며, 곧 이탈리아 반도의 대부분을 장악했다. 하지만 로마 공화국이 주변 영토로 진출해 정복함으로써 그 반도를 벗어나 국경을 확장하기 시작한 것은 기원전 3세기가 되어서였다. 어떤 면에서는 이미 하나의 제국으로서 기능하고 있었지만, 정치적으로 로마 공화국은 여전히 마을과 도시들로 구성된 공동체로서 군 사령관들의 통치와 중앙 원로원의 관리를 받고 있었다. 로마 시민들은 공화국의 일원으로서 자신들을 대표할 정치인들을 선출했는데, 이는 시민들이 직접적으로 나라의 정치적 의사 결정에 관여하는 민주주의와 다른 점이었다. 실제로 미국이 거의 2천 년이나 지나 부분적으로 모방하게 된 것은 고대 그리스의 민주주의가 아니라 바로 이 공화국 체제였다.

기원전 1세기 무렵 고대 로마 공화국은 영토를 넓히면서 거의 지중해 지역 전체를 포함하게 되었지만, 악영향을 끼치는 정치적 모의 및 음모들과 더불어 내전이 상당한 불안정을 초래했다. 나중에 카이사르 아우구스투스로 알려지게 되는 옥타비아누스가 기원전 31년에 마크 안토니와 클레오파트라를 상대로 거둔 승리가 이집트 프톨레마이오스 왕국의 점령으로 이어졌으며, 로마 제국 최초의 황제 자리를 향한 옥타비아누스의 등극을 알리는 시작점이 되었다. 옥타비아누스는 율리우스 카이사르의 양자였으며, 율리우스 카이사르는 3월의 중간 날(15일)에 브루투스라는 원로의 손에 당한 유명한 암살 사건이 있

을 때까지 사실상의 독재자로서 로마 공화국을 통치했다. 이 충격적인 사건 후에 옥타비아누스는 그 암살을 계획한 세력을 물리치고자 그의 아버지가 거느렸던 가장 충직한 사령관들 중 하나였던 마크 안토니와 손을 잡았지만, 두 사람은 나중에 숙적이 되었다.

■ (A) 마크 안토니를 물리치며 옥타비아누스의 놀라운 권력 강화는 기원전 27년에 공식화되었다. ■ (B) 두 세기 동안 새롭게 세워진 로마 제국은 전례 없던 평화와 번영, 그리고 사회적 안정을 누렸다. ■ (C) 이 기간은 팍스 로마나라고 알려지게 되었다. ■ (D) 때때로 외부의 여러 지방에서 반란이 일어나긴 했지만, 신속하고 무자비하게 처리되었다. 로마 제국은 곧 그 당시 전 세계에서 경제 문화적으로 가장 뛰어난 강대국들 중 하나가 되었다.

트라야누스의 통치 하에 로마 제국은 지배 영토의 측면에 있어 정점에 다다를 만큼 확장되었지만, 서기 180년에 권력이 코모두스의 손으로 넘어가면서 쇠락하기 시작했다. 이는 결국 로마 제국에 격동의 분열을 일으키며 두 개의 분리된 황실이 자리잡게 되었고, 서기 330년에는 제국의 수도가 로마에서 그리스인들이 세운 도시인 비잔티움으로 옮겨졌으며, 비잔티움은 그 후에 콘스탄티노플로 개명되었는데, 기독교로 개종한 최초의 로마 황제이자 동쪽으로의 이동(동로마 공격)을 배후에서 이끈 인물이었던 콘스탄티누스 1세의 이름을 딴 것이었다. 현재 이

도시는 오늘날의 이름인 이스탄불로 알려져 있으며, 튀르키예 공화국의 문화와 경제의 중심지이다.

로마 제국의 이 절반은 동로마 제국 또는 비잔티움 제국으로 알려지게 되었고 지중해 지역 대부분을 통치한 반면, 서로마 제국은 로마를 그리고 나중에는 근처 도시 라벤나를 수도로 유지했고 유럽의 넓은 지역을 지배했다. 하지만 결국 서로마 제국은 근처의 게르만족과 사나운 전사 아틸라가 유라시아 지역에 걸쳐 이끌었던 훈족 군대에 의한 대규모 침략 공세를 받아, 서기 476년에 붕괴했다. 한편, 동로마 제국은 이후 천 년 동안 다소 약화된 상태이긴 했어도 명맥을 유지하다가, 1453년에 콘스탄티노플이 오스만 제국 침략군에 넘어갔다.

지문 어휘

1. **peninsula** 반도 **advance into** ~으로 진출하다 **conquer** 정복하다 **oversee** 관리하다, 감독하다 **Senate** 원로원

2. **dominion** 영토 **intrigue** 모의, 음모 **conspiracy** 음모 **instability** 불안정 **conquest** 정복 **adopted** 입양된 **virtual** 사실상의 **dictator** 독재자 **assassination** 암살 **senator** 원로 **faction** 세력 **sworn enemy** 숙적

3. **prosperity** 번영, 번성 **Pax Romana** 팍스 로마나 (로마 제국의 황금기) **uprising** 반란 **swiftly** 신속히 **mercilessly** 무자비하게

4. **peak** 정점, 절정 **fall into decline** 쇠락하다 **cataclysmic** 격동의, 격변하는 **split** 분열 **convert to** ~으로 개종하다 **mastermind behind** ~을 배후에서 이끈 인물

5. **a large swath of** ~의 넓은 지역 **be besieged by** ~의 공세를 받다 **invasion** 침략 **fierce** 사나운

세부 정보 찾기 문제

1 첫 번째 단락에 따르면, 로마 공화국이 민주주의가 아니었던 이유는?
(A) 지방을 통치하는 중앙 정부가 없었다.
(B) 선거가 없었고 황제가 통치했다.
(C) 정치인들이 시민의 뜻을 대변하지 않았다.
(D) 시민들이 직접적으로 국가적 결정에 대해 투표하지 않았다.

어휘 election 투표, 선거

해설 시민들이 직접적으로 나라의 정치적 의사 결정에 관여하는 민주주의와 달랐다고 했으므로, (D)가 정답이다.

어휘의 의미 파악 문제

2 지문의 단어 "ascension"과 의미가 가장 가까운 것은?
(A) 상승   (B) 여행
(C) 도전   (D) 갈망

해설 ascension이 '(높은 지위에) 오름, 등극'을 의미하므로, '(지위의) 상승'을 뜻하는 (A) rise가 의미상 가장 가깝다.

지시 대상 찾기 문제

3 지문의 단어 "his"가 가리키는 것은?
(A) 율리우스 카이사르
(B) 브루투스
(C) 옥타비아누스
(D) 마크 안토니

해설 his father의 가장 충직한 사령관들 중 하나로 마크 안토니가 언급되고 있다. 따라서, his father는 황제인 율리우스 카이사르를, his는 양자인 옥타비아누스를 가리킴을 알 수 있다. 그러므로 (C)가 정답이다.

수사적 의도 파악 문제

4 지문에서 세 번째 단락의 목적은 무엇인가?
(A) 로마 제국이 누렸던 이상적인 시대를 설명하는 것
(B) 옥타비아누스와 마크 안토니의 전략을 대조하는 것
(C) 로마가 새 지도자를 선택했던 방식을 설명하는 것
(D) 로마 원로원의 극단적 변화를 설명하는 것

어휘 strategy 전략

해설 로마 제국이 전례 없던 평화와 번영, 그리고 사회적 안정을 누리면서 강대국으로 발전한 사실을 이야기하고 있으므로, (A)가 정답이다.

문장 재구성 문제

5 아래 문장 중 지문에서 음영 표시된 문장의 핵심 정보를 가장 잘 나타낸 것은? 오답 선택지들은 의미를 현저히 바꾸거나 핵심 정보를 생략한다.
(A) 콘스탄티노플은 서기 330년에 최초로 기독교로 개종한 로마 황제의 이름을 따서 명명되었다.
(B) 로마 황실의 분립으로 인해 그 제국의 기독교인 시민 다수가 동쪽으로 이주하기 시작했다.
(C) 로마 제국이 두 부분으로 분리되었으며, 제국의 수도는 로마에서 비잔티움으로 옮겨졌다가 나중에 콘스탄티노플로 개명되었다.
(D) 로마의 초대 황제인 콘스탄티누스 1세가 비잔티움을 장악함으로써 분열된 제국을 통일하기로 결정했다.

어휘 schism 분립 seize 장악하다

해설 로마 제국에 두 개의 분리된 황실이 생겼고 수도가 비잔티움으로 옮겨진 후 콘스탄티누스 1세의 이름을 따 콘스탄티노플로 개명되었다는 요지가 담긴 것은 (C)이다.

추론 문제

6 다음 중 네 번째 단락에서 로마 황제 트라야누스에 대해
추론할 수 있는 것은?
(A) 코모두스를 부러워했다.
(B) 현명하고 유능한 지도자였다.
(C) 탐욕으로 무너졌다.
(D) 겸손하고 종교적인 사람이었다.

어휘 envious of ~을 부러워하는 be undermined by ~으로
무너지다, ~에 의해 약화되다

해설 트라야누스의 통치 하에서 로마 제국의 영토 확장이 정점에
달했고 다음 황제 즉위 후 쇠락과 분열을 겪었으므로, 그가
뛰어난 지도자였음을 유추할 수 있다. 그러므로 (B)가
정답이다.

문장 삽입 문제

7 제시된 문장이 지문에 삽입될 수 있는 곳을 가리키는 네 개의
네모[■]를 보아라.

**로마 원로원은 그에게 새 군주국에 대한 황제의 권한을
부여했으며, 로마는 권력의 중심으로 지정되고 다양한
영토는 속주로 조직되었다.**

이 문장이 들어갈 가장 적절한 위치는? 해당 네모[■]를
선택하여 이 문장을 지문에 삽입하여라.
(A)   (B)   (C)   (D)

어휘 grant 주다, 부여하다 monarchy 군주국 designate
지정하다

해설 로마 원로원이 him에게 황제의 권한을 부여했다는 말이
있으므로, him이 가리킬 수 있는 사람인 옥타비아누스가 권력
강화를 시작한 사실이 언급된 문장 뒤인 (B)에 들어가는 것이
문맥상 자연스럽다.

지문 요약 문제

8 **지시문:** 지문의 간략한 요약을 위한 도입 문장이 아래에
제시되어 있다. 지문에서 가장 중요한 개념들을 나타내는
선택지 3개를 선택하여 요약을 완성하여라. 어떤 문장들은
지문에 제시되지 않거나 주요 개념이 아니므로 요약에
포함되지 않는다. **이 문제는 2점에 해당한다.**

**로마 공화국은 이탈리아 반도를 통치했지만, 곧 주변 영토를
장악하기 시작했다.**

(A) 미국의 정부 구조는 부분적으로 로마 공화국의 것을
바탕으로 하고 있다.
(B) 기원전 1세기에 율리우스 카이사르의 양자였던
옥타비아누스는 최초의 로마 제국 황제가 되었다.
(C) 마크 안토니와 옥타비아누스는 클레오파트라와
프톨레마이오스 왕국에 의해 패배할 때까지 함께 로마를
통치했다.

(D) 팍스 로마나는 로마 제국 초기에 평화롭고 번영했던
200년 동안의 시대이다.
(E) 로마가 쇠락하기 시작하면서 두 개의 각 제국으로
분리되었으며, 그 중 하나는 서기 476년에 붕괴되었다.
(F) 현재의 튀르키예에 위치한 주요 도시 이스탄불은
비잔티움과 콘스탄티노플이라는 두 개의 이름을 갖고
있었다.

어휘 modern-day 현재의

해설 로마 공화국이 영토 확장을 시작한 후 로마 제국이 세워지고
최초의 황제가 된 옥타비아누스, 로마 제국이 평화와 번영을
누리던 팍스 로마나에 대한 설명, 그리고 로마의 쇠락과 분리
과정이 지문에서 차례대로 나오므로 정답은 (B), (D), (E)이다.

관련 지식 **팍스 로마나(Pax Romana)**는 로마 제국에서 기원전
약 27년부터 서기 180년까지 지속된 상대적인 평화와
안정의 시기이다. 이 시기 동안 로마 제국은 경제적, 문화적,
사회적으로 발전하며 거대한 규모의 도로망과 통일된 통화

체계 등을 구축했다. 또한,
많은 영토를 통치하면서
다양한 문화와 인종을
수용했고, 상업 및 문화 교류가
증가하며 번영했다.

정답 | **1** (D)   **2** (C)   **3** (B)   **4** (D)   **5** (C)   **6** (A)   **7** (A)   **8** (A), (E), (F)

동굴 예술

동굴 및 석굴의 암벽에서 발견되는 그림과 조각된 문양은 후기 구석기 시대의 초기 인류에 의해 비롯되었는데, 이것은 대략 50,000년에서 12,000년 전에 나타났던 흔히 석기 시대라고 알려진 것의 세 번째이자 마지막 시기였다. 이 석기 시대 동굴 벽화들 중 현대에 처음으로 발견된 것은 스페인의 알타미라 동굴이라고 알려진 동굴 지대에서 발견됐고 그 후로 총 약 400개의 추가 장소가 계속 확인되었는데, 그 대부분은 프랑스와 스페인에 위치해 있다.

대부분의 동굴 벽화는 산화철로 만든 붉은색 안료나 숯으로 만든 검은색 안료 중 하나를 이용해 만들어졌는데, 그 반면 조각된 문양은 부드러운 암벽에는 사람의 손가락으로, 또는 더 단단한 표면의 경우에는 부싯돌 도구를 이용해 새겨진 듯 보인다. 이렇게 그려진 것들 중 일부가 전체적으로 또는 별개의 신체 부분으로 인간을 묘사하고 있지만, 모든 시대에 걸쳐 모든 지역의 동굴 벽화 대부분은 동물의 이미지에 집중되어 있다. 프랑스의 쇼베-퐁다르크 동굴에서 발견된 것과 같은 가장 초기 동굴 예술에는 사나운 동굴사자와 거대한 매머드를 포함해 그 후로 멸종된 어마어마한 동물들이 두드러지게 많다. 후기 동굴 벽화에는 말과 들소 같은 더 일상적인 동물들이 더 흔히 묘사되어 있는데, 흥미롭게도 새나 물고기 이미지는 거의 찾아볼 수 없다.

과학자들은 이 예술이 상징적이거나 종교적인 기능 둘 중의 하나, 또는 두 기능을 모두 제공했을 가능성이 꽤 큰 것으로 생각한다. 동굴 예술은 전 세계 많은 지역에서 동굴 입구 근처나 석굴의 노출된 벽면에 나타나 있지만, 외부의 빛이 거의 닿을 수 없는 동굴 내부 깊숙한 곳에 있는 예술 작품은 사실상 유럽에만 국한되어 있다. 석기 시대 주술사들이 의식의 일환으로 이 동굴들에 들어가 그곳에서 무아지경 상태에 빠진 후에 환영들을 경험한 다음, 그것들을 벽면에 그렸다는 이론이 제시되어 왔다. 동굴 예술의 목적과 관련된 또 다른 이론은 사냥꾼들이 직면할 수도 있는 다양한 상황을 예상하고 시각화함으로써 사냥이 성공하도록 도움을 주기 위해 만들어졌다는 것이다.

일부 연구가들은 심지어 특정 동굴 예술 이미지가 초기 형태의 원시 문자를 나타낸다고 제안하기까지 했다. ■(A) 하지만 동굴 벽면에 그려진 동물들이 흔히 편리한 사냥감으로 여겨질 수 있는 종이기는 했어도, 이 이미지들이 동굴 내부에서 발견된 동물 뼈와 항상 일치하지는 않는다는 점에 유의하는 것이 중요하다. ■(B) 예를 들어, 프랑스 라스코 동굴 지대의 석기 시대 주민들은 주로 순록 뼈를 남겨, 이것이 사냥으로 선호하는 종이었음을 나타냈다. ■(C) 하지만 그 동굴의 벽면에 그려진 이미지는 어느 것도 순록이 아니며, 대부분 말을 묘사하고 있다. ■(D)

또 다른 흔한 동굴 예술의 주제는 사람 손인데, 일반적으로 실제 손을 암벽에 갖다 대는 방법을 통해 만들어졌다. 그런 다음 그 주변 부분이 안료로 덮였으며, 중앙의 손 모양 공간은 점이나 대시 기호, 또는 매우 단순한 패턴으로 장식되었다. 이 손 예술의 평균 크기를 바탕으로 고고학자들은 그것이 주로 구석기 시대 공동체에 속한 여성들의 작품이었다고 생각한다. 그림과 조각된 문양보다 훨씬 덜 흔하기는 하지만, 이 시기에 만들어진 소수의 조각품도 동굴 내부에서 발견되었는데, 프랑스 피레네 산맥에 위치한 별개의 동굴들 내부에서 찾은 점토 들소 조각상과 실물 크기의 곰 모형이 여기에 포함된다. 머리가 없고 한때 실제 곰의 생가죽으로 덮여 있었던 것으로 여겨지는 이 곰 조각상은 아마도 창으로 그것을 반복적으로 찔렀을 공동체의 사냥꾼들이 이용했을 것이다.

지문 어휘

1. **engraving** (새긴) 문양, 조각 **be attributed to** ~에 의해 비롯되다 **Upper Paleolithic** 후기 구석기 시대의 **identify** 확인하다
2. **pigment** 안료 **iron oxide** 산화철 **charcoal** 숯 **etch** (뚜렷이) 새기다 **flint** 부싯돌 **predominate** 두드러지게 많다, 지배적이다 **mundane** 일상적인
3. **virtually** 사실상 **exclusive to** ~에 국한된 **shaman** 주술사 **ritual** 의식, 식 **vision** 환영 **trance** 무아지경 **anticipate** 예상하다 **visualize** 시각화하다
4. **go so far as to** 심지어 ~하기까지 하다 **proto-writing** 원시 문자 **expedient** 편리한, 편의주의의
5. **motif** 주제 **render** 만들다 **pelt** 생가죽 **impale** 찌르다

어휘의 의미 파악 문제

1 지문의 단어 "formidable"과 의미가 가장 가까운 것은?
(A) 멸종한
(B) 유독한
(C) 활기찬
(D) 인상적인

해설 formidable이 '어마어마한'을 의미하므로, (D) imposing이 의미상 가장 비슷한 단어이다.

수사적 의도 파악 문제

2 글쓴이는 왜 두 번째 단락에서 "새나 물고기"를 언급하는가?
(A) 동굴 예술이 어떻게 초기 인류에게 유익했는지 설명하기 위해
(B) 동굴 예술의 주된 종교적 기능을 소개하기 위해
(C) 동굴 예술에서 좀처럼 보이지 않는 동물의 예를 들기 위해
(D) 이 동물들이 흔히 사냥되었음을 암시하기 위해

어휘 benefit 유익하다 religious 종교적인

해설 후기 동굴 벽화에 말과 들소가 더 흔히 묘사되어 있고 새나 물고기 이미지는 거의 찾아 볼 수 없다고 설명하고 있으므로, (C)가 정답이다.

문장 재구성 문제

3 아래 문장 중 지문에서 음영 표시된 문장의 핵심 정보를 가장 잘 나타낸 것은? 오답 선택지들은 의미를 현저히 바꾸거나 핵심 정보를 생략한다.
(A) 동굴 예술은 전 세계의 다른 지역에서는 발견되지 않았기 때문에 유럽에만 국한되어 있는 듯하다.
(B) 동굴 예술이 전 세계 많은 지역에서 발견되지만, 동굴 내부 깊숙한 곳에 있는 예술 작품은 유럽에서만 볼 수 있다.
(C) 동굴 예술은 전 세계 많은 지역에서 동굴 입구 또는 노출된 석굴의 벽면으로만 제한되어 있다.
(D) 유럽은 동굴 예술이 동굴 입구 근처와 외부 벽면 모두에서 발견되는 유일한 지역이다.

어휘 be limited to ~으로 제한되다

해설 전 세계 많은 지역에서 동굴 예술을 찾아볼 수 있지만, 동굴 내부 깊숙한 곳에 예술 작품이 있는 것은 거의 유럽에만 국한되어 있다는 핵심 내용을 담고 있는 것은 (B)이다.

지시 대상 찾기 문제

4 지문의 단어 "them"이 가리키는 것은?
(A) 석기 시대 주술사들   (B) 이 동굴들
(C) 의식들   (D) 환영들

해설 석기 시대 주술사들이 visions를 경험한 후 벽면에 그렸을 것이라고 언급했으므로, 정답은 (D)이다.

세부 정보 찾기 문제

5 다섯 번째 단락에 따르면, 다음 중 손 이미지에 대해 사실이 아닌 것은?
(A) 손 주변에 안료를 도포해서 만들어졌다.
(B) 기호와 패턴으로 장식되었다.
(C) 주술사가 행한 의식의 일부였다.
(D) 대체로 여성 예술가들에 의해 만들어졌다.

해설 손을 암벽에 대고 그 주변을 안료로 덮었고, 중앙의 손 모양 공간을 기호나 단순한 패턴으로 장식했다고 했으며, 구석기 시대 공동체에 속한 여성들의 작품으로 여겨진다고 했다. 그러나 주술사가 행한 의식의 일부라는 것은 지문에 언급되지 않았다. 그러므로 (C)가 정답이다.

추론 문제

6 다음 중 다섯 번째 단락에서 곰 조각상에 대해 추론할 수 있는 것은?
(A) 사냥 기술을 연습하는 데 쓰였다.
(B) 여성 주술사들에 의해 만들어졌다.

(C) 흔히 동굴에서 동굴로 옮겨졌다.
(D) 벽면 그림만큼 오래되지는 않았다.

해설 곰 조각상을 창으로 반복적으로 찔렀던 사냥꾼이 이용했을 거라는 설명에서 그것이 사냥 기술을 연습하는 데 쓰였음을 유추할 수 있다. 그러므로 (A)가 정답이다.

문장 삽입 문제

7 제시된 문장이 지문에 삽입될 수 있는 곳을 가리키는 네 개의 네모[■]를 보아라.

그들은 그것이 달의 위상을 바탕으로 사냥감의 짝짓기 주기에 관련된 정보를 공유하는 데 쓰였을 수도 있다고 생각한다.

이 문장이 들어갈 가장 적절한 위치는? 해당 네모[■]를 선택하여 이 문장을 지문에 삽입하여라.
(A)   (B)   (C)   (D)

어휘 mating 짝짓기 phase (달의) 위상, 상

해설 주어진 문장은 복수 명사를 가리키는 They 및 단수 명사를 가리키는 it을 포함해 사냥감과 관련된 정보를 담고 있다. 따라서, researchers와 proto-writing이 언급된 첫 번째 문장과 사냥감으로 여겨졌던 종에 관한 내용을 담은 두 번째 문장 사이인 (A)에 놓이는 것이 자연스럽다.

지문 요약 문제

8 지시문: 지문의 간략한 요약을 위한 도입 문장이 아래에 제시되어 있다. 지문에서 가장 중요한 개념들을 나타내는 선택지 3개를 선택하여 요약을 완성하여라. 어떤 문장들은 지문에 제시되지 않거나 주요 개념이 아니므로 요약에 포함되지 않는다. **이 문제는 2점에 해당한다.**

후기 구석기 시대에 초기 인류에 의해 만들어진 예술 작품이 수백 개의 동굴 벽면에서 발견되었다.

(A) 대부분의 동굴 예술은 매머드나 들소, 또는 말 같은 동물을 묘사하며, 검은색이나 붉은색 안료를 이용해 만들어졌다.
(B) 곰 조각상은 프랑스와 스페인의 동굴에서 흔히 발견되었으며, 실제 곰 가죽으로 덮여 있었을 수도 있다.
(C) 순록은 초기 인류 사냥꾼들이 가장 좋아하던 사냥감이었기 때문에, 다른 동물보다 동굴 예술에 더 많이 나타나 있다.
(D) 동굴 예술이 있는 일부 동물의 벽면은 부드러운 암석으로 만들어져 있는 반면, 다른 곳들은 표면이 훨씬 더 단단하다.
(E) 초기 인류 공동체의 여성들이 암벽에 자신의 손을 그림으로써 동굴 예술에 기여했을 수도 있다.
(F) 동굴 예술은 종교 의식의 일부로서 또는 사냥 준비를 위해 만들어졌을 수 있다.

어휘 trace (윤곽 등을) 그리다, 긋다

해설 후기 구석기 시대의 동굴 예술이 많은 동굴 벽면에서
      발견되었다는 도입 문장 다음에 동굴 예술이 묘사하는 동물의
      종류와 안료, 여성들의 손을 이용한 예술 작품, 종교 의식과
      사냥 준비의 일환으로 기능했다는 설명으로 지문 내용을
      요약한 (A), (E), (F)가 정답이다.

관련 지식 **쇼베-퐁다라르크 동굴(Chauvet-Pont-d'Arc cave)**은
프랑스 남부 아르드쉬 지역에 있는 석회암 동굴로 이곳에는
다른 지역의 동굴 벽화에서는 볼 수 없는 매머드, 동굴사자,
동굴곰 등이 그려져 있다. 염료를 이용한 그림과 조각이
결합된 이 벽화들은 매우 역동적이며 선사시대 그림이라고
믿기 힘들 정도의 세련미를 보여 준다. 이 동굴은 약 2만

년 전에 암벽 붕괴로 폐쇄된 덕분에
1994년에 발견될 때까지 원시 상태
그대로 보존되어 있어서, 고대 예술과
문화 연구에 중요한 자료로 활용되고
있다.

PASSAGE 4   pp.140-143

정답 | 1 (D)   **2** (C)   **3** (B)   **4** (D)   **5** (A)   **6** (B)   **7** (C)   **8** (A), (C), (E)

고대 그리스 연극

기원전 7세기 초에 고대 그리스 연극이 번성하기 시작했는데,
도시 국가였던 아테네가 이 문화적 현상의 중심지 역할을 했
다. 궁극적으로 이런 발전으로 이어지게 된 이유는 바로 문자
언어보다 구어를 더 좋아한 그리스인들의 선호였다. 문학이 일
반적으로 성장이나 변화할 가능성이 없는 죽어 있고 고정적인
것으로 여겨졌던 반면, 이야기를 하는 것은 무한한 가능성을
지닌 살아 있는 것으로 여겨졌다. 기원전 508년 무렵에 연극
은 디오니소스제의 중심 요소로 제도화되었는데, 이 축제는 그
리스의 술의 신 디오니소스를 기려 개최되는 것으로 도시 디오
니소스제와 시골 디오니소스제의 분리된 두 개의 행사로 연중
다른 시기에 개최되었다. 세 가지나 되는 주요 연극 장르, 즉
비극과 희극, 사티로스극이 이 축제에서 나오게 되었고, 이 축
제는 나중에 여러 다른 그리스 도시로 전해졌다.

기원전 532년 무렵에 아테네에서 그리스 비극이 등장했는데,
당시는 테스피스의 시대로, 그는 현대 영어 단어로 '배우'를 뜻
하는 '테스피언'의 근간이 되는 이름을 가진 그리스 시인이었
다. 테스피스는 대본에 쓰인 한 등장 인물의 대사를 말로 했다
는 점에서 배우로서 무대에 선 최초의 인물이었다. 한 사람이
서로 다른 마스크 착용을 통해 여러 등장 인물을 구별하며 묘
사하는 형태의 공연을 그가 도입했을 때, 비극이 될 연극 장르
를 고안해 낸 사람이 바로 테스피스였다는 것은 거의 틀림 없
는 사실이다. 하지만 연극의 발전에 있어 그가 가지는 중요성
이 일부 역사학자들에게는 논쟁이 되고 있다는 점에 유의해야
하는데, 이들은 그를 때때로 알려진 바와 같이 '비극의 아버지'
라기 보다 소소한 공헌자로 여기고 있다. 기원전 323년에 시
작된 헬레니즘 시대에 이를 때까지 모든 그리스 비극은 디오니
소스를 기리기 위해 쓰여졌으며 단 한 번만 공연되었다.

나중에 고희극이라고 알려지게 되는 초기 아테네 희극은 비극
이 가장 인기 있는 연극 장르로 확고히 자리잡은 후 오랜 시간

이 흐른 기원전 487년에 도시 디오니소스제에서 처음 무대에
올려졌다. 아리스토텔레스에 따르면 희극은 기념 축제의 노래
에서 발전했지만, 진지한 연극 형태로 받아들인 사람이 거의
없었기 때문에 처음에는 그리스 연극 관람객들의 상상력을 사
로잡지 못했다. 그럼에도 불구하고 희극은 결국 합창 가무단이
중요한 서사적 역할을 하고, 정치적 풍자가 단순히 익살스러운
행동에 불과한 것으로 위장되는 대단히 짜임새 있는 장르로 발
전했다. 아테네의 고희극은 심각한 고통이나 불행을 초래하지
않는 방식으로 실수를 저지른 우스꽝스러운 사람들에 대해 이
야기했지만, 이 초기 희극 중 유일하게 현존하는 예는 아리스
토파네스가 쓴 11편의 연극뿐이다.

■(A) 디오니소스제에서 세상에 소개된 세 번째 장르는 사티로
스극이었는데, 그것은 일종의 짧은 공연으로 희극과 비극 모두
와 비슷했다. ■(B) 사티로스극은 줄거리와 언어가 비극과 비슷
해서 희극보다 비극에 더 밀접하게 연관되어 있는데, 도시 디
오니소스제에서는 전통적으로 사티로스극 한 편이 비극 3부
작과 함께 공연되었다. ■(C) 사티로스극과 다른 형태의 연극들
간의 차이는 사티로스극이 조악한 말장난과 함께 상반신은 사
람이고 하반신은 염소인 신화적 존재들로 된 합창 가무단을 포
함하고 있었다는 점이다. ■(D) 그럼에도 불구하고 사티로스극
은 각각의 도시 디오니소스제를 마무리하기에 적합한 유일한
공연으로 여겨졌다.

그리스 비극과 희극은 현대의 연극과 영화 모두에서 여전히 분
명하게 보이는 기본 구조 및 특징들로 세상이 연극을 바라보는
방식에 지속적으로 엄청난 영향을 미치기는 했지만, 희비극적
인 사티로스극은 점점 더 세련되어졌던 아테네 관객들에게 결
국 인기를 잃게 되어 기원전 4세기 이후에는 새로 쓰여진 사티
로스극이 소수에 불과했다.

세부 정보 찾기 문제

1 첫 번째 단락에 따르면, 다음 중 디오니소스제에 대해 사실인 것은?
(A) 시골 지역에서 아테네로 전해졌다.
(B) 원래 문학을 기념하는 축제였다.
(C) 현지의 포도주 제조자들로부터 재정적 지원을 받았다.
(D) 분리되어 개최된 두 부분으로 구성되었다.

어휘 financially 재정적으로

해설 디오니소스제가 두 가지 분리된 행사인 도시 디오니소스제와 시골 디오니소스제로 나뉘었다고 했으므로, (D)가 정답이다.

세부 정보 찾기 문제

2 두 번째 단락에 따르면, 다음 중 테스피스에 대해 사실이 아닌 것은?
(A) 배우로서 무대에서 공연한 최초의 인물이었다.
(B) 비극이 된 연극 장르를 만들어낸 사람으로 여겨진다.
(C) 연극 발전에 대한 그의 공헌이 모든 역사학자들의 인정을 받고 있다.
(D) 한 사람이 여러 등장 인물을 연기하는 공연 형태를 도입했다.

어휘 undisputed 모두에게 인정 받는

해설 연극의 발전에 있어 테스피스가 가지는 중요성에 대해 일부 역사학자들이 논쟁하고 있다고 했으므로, (C)가 정답이다.

어휘의 의미 파악 문제

3 지문의 단어 "blundered"와 의미가 가장 가까운 것은?
(A) 거짓말했다
(B) 실수했다
(C) 소리쳤다
(D) 웃었다

해설 '실수했다'를 뜻하는 blundered와 같은 뜻을 가진 것은 erred 이므로, 정답은 (B)이다.

추론 문제

4 다음 중 세 번째 단락에서 아리스토텔레스에 대해 추론할 수 있는 것은?
(A) 연극을 저급한 예술 형태로 여겼다.
(B) 고희극이 더 많은 인기를 얻도록 도왔다.
(C) 희극이 아이들의 상상력에 해가 될 수도 있다고 걱정했다.
(D) 연극의 역사에 관심이 있었다.

어휘 inferior 저급한 harm 해가 되다

해설 아리스토텔레스가 희극이 기념 축제의 노래에서 발전했다고 언급했다는 설명에서 그가 연극 역사에 관심이 있었던 것을 유추할 수 있다. 그러므로 (D)가 정답이다.

어휘의 의미 파악 문제

5 지문의 구 "fell out of favor"와 의미가 가장 가까운 것은?
(A) 인기를 잃었다
(B) 널리 확산되었다
(C) 금지되었다
(D) 익숙해졌다

해설 fell out of favor는 '인기를 잃었다'라는 뜻이므로, 동일한 뜻을 나타내는 (A) lost popularity가 정답이다.

수사적 의도 파악 문제

6 다섯 번째 단락은 네 번째 단락과 어떻게 연관되어 있는가?
(A) 다섯 번째 단락이 네 번째 단락에 제시된 일부 정보에 대해 의문을 제기한다.
(B) 다섯 번째 단락이 네 번째 단락의 주제에 대해 나중에 일어난 일을 설명한다.
(C) 다섯 번째 단락이 네 번째 단락에서 글쓴이가 제시한 의견을 요약한다.
(D) 다섯 번째 단락이 네 번째 단락에 제시된 사건의 문화적 영향을 강조한다.

해설 다섯 번째 단락은 네 번째 단락에서 설명한 사티로스극이 점점 더 세련되어졌던 아테네 관객들에게 결국 인기를 잃은 사실을 언급하여, 나중에 사티로스극에 일어난 일을 설명한다는 것을 알 수 있으므로, (B)가 정답이다.

문장 삽입 문제

7 제시된 문장이 지문에 삽입될 수 있는 곳을 가리키는 네 개의 네모[■]를 보아라.

> **하지만 그것의 많은 주제와 등장 인물들은 희극과 유사했으며, 두 장르 모두 관객에게 행복한 결말을 제공해 관객을 즐겁게 하는 특징을 공유하고 있었다.**

이 문장이 들어갈 가장 적절한 위치는? 해당 네모[■]를 선택하여 이 문장을 지문에 삽입하여라.

(A)　　　(B)　　　(C)　　　(D)

해설 대조를 나타내는 However와 함께 희극과의 유사성 및 앞서 제시된 두 가지 장르의 공통점을 언급하고 있다. 따라서 비극과의 밀접한 관련성을 설명하는 문장 뒤에 위치해 희극과의 유사성을 차례로 언급하는 흐름이 되어야 문맥상 자연스러우므로, (C)가 정답이다.

지문 요약 문제

8 **지시문:** 지문의 간략한 요약을 위한 도입 문장이 아래에 제시되어 있다. 지문에서 가장 중요한 개념들을 나타내는 선택지 3개를 선택하여 요약을 완성하여라. 어떤 문장들은 지문에 제시되지 않거나 주요 개념이 아니므로 요약에 포함되지 않는다. **이 문제는 2점에 해당한다.**

고대 그리스 연극은 기원전 7세기에 세 가지 주요 연극 장르가 출현하며 번성했다.

(A) 문자 언어보다 구어를 선호하는 것이 그리스 연극의 발전에 중요한 역할을 했다.
(B) 배우로서 최초로 무대에 등장했던 인물인 테스피스는 일반적으로 '비극의 아버지'로 인정 받고 있다.
(C) 초기 아테네 희극, 즉 고희극을 처음에는 그리스 연극 관람객들이 진정한 연극 형태로 받아들이지 않았다.
(D) 디오니소스제에서 소개됐던 세 번째 장르인 사티로스극은 비극보다 희극과 더 밀접하게 연관되어 있었다.
(E) 그리스 비극과 희극은 현대의 연극과 영화에 상당한 영향을 미쳤다.
(F) 희비극인 사티로스극은 그리스 연극 역사 전반에 걸쳐 인기 있는 장르로 남아 있었다.

어휘 be recognized as ~으로 인정 받다

해설 세 가지 장르를 중심으로 번성했던 고대 그리스 연극에 대한 지문에 제시된 요지들, 즉 그리스인들의 구어에 대한 선호로 연극이 발전했고, 처음에는 그리스 연극 관람객들이 고희극을 진정한 연극 형태로 여기지 않았으며, 그리스 비극과 희극이 현대의 연극과 영화에 상당한 영향을 미쳤다는 내용을 요약한 (A), (C), (E)가 정답이다.

관련 지식 **아리스토파네스(Aristophanes)** 는 아테네에서 활동한 그리스의 대표적인 희극 작가로, 대표작으로 〈아카르나이 사람〉, 〈기사〉, 〈구름〉, 〈소피스트와 소크라테스의 풍자〉, 〈벌〉, 〈개구리〉 등이 있다. 그의 작품들은 주로 그리스의 역사적 인물이나 상징적 인물들을 소재로 하며, 풍자와 비판을 통해 사회 문제를 다룬다.

그는 뛰어난 서정성과 천재적인 패러디 기법을 사용하여 44편의 희극을 썼지만 현존하는 것은 11편이다. 그는 자신의 희극을 통해 대중에게 웃음과 함께 깊은 사회 비판의 메시지를 전하고자 했다.

PASSAGE 5　　　　　　　　　　　　　　　　　　　　　　　　　　pp.144-147

정답 | **1** (C)　**2** (D)　**3** (D)　**4** (C)　**5** (B)　**6** (A)　**7** (C)　**8** (A), (B), (F)

최초의 아메리카 정착

크리스토퍼 콜럼버스가 신세계를 '발견했다'는 전통적인 개념에도 불구하고, 북아메리카와 남아메리카에 첫 번째 유럽인들이 도착하기 오래 전에 아시아에서 그곳으로 이주한 사람들이 살았다는 사실이 오래 전에 확인되었다. 하지만 정확히 언제, 그리고 어떻게 이 고대인들이 하나의 대륙에서 다른 대륙으로 건너갔는지에 관해서는 의견 차이가 여전히 있으며, 그들이 아메리카까지 멀리 이주하면서 거친 주된 경로와 관련된 논란도 상당히 많다.

최초의 이주자들은 한때 현재의 알래스카와 시베리아 동부를 연결했지만 지금은 물속에 잠겨 있는 육지인 베링기아에서 건너간 후 북아메리카에 도착한 것으로 여겨지고 있다. 미국 뉴멕시코 주의 작은 마을인 클로비스 근처에서 홍적세 시대의 동물상과 관련된 것으로 보이는 유물의 발견은 사람들이 빙하 시대가 끝나기 전에 아메리카에 도착했음을 시사하는 가설로 이어졌다. 이것은 고대인들이 베링기아가 완전히 빙하로 덮여 있을 때 어떻게 그곳을 가로지를 수 있었을까 하는 의문으로 이어졌는데, 그것은 통행이 불가능한 두께의 얼음으로 덮여 있었을 것임을 의미하기 때문이다. 이 의문에 대해 제안된 답변은 이 거대한 두 얼음 덩어리들 사이에 잠시 개방되었을 수도 있는 육로 회랑 지대와 관련이 있다. 대형 사냥감을 쫓던 고대 아시아의 사냥꾼들이 그때 이 회랑 지대를 횡단해, 아메리카에 정착한 최초의 사람이 되었고 두 대륙에 걸쳐 남쪽과 동쪽으로

서서히 퍼져 나갔을 것이다. 이 확산은 북아메리카 내륙을 관통하고 클로비스를 포함하는 경로를 통해 일어난 것으로 여겨지고 있다.

이것은 클로비스-최초 이론으로 알려져 있으며, 클로비스 근처 및 여러 다른 관련된 장소에서 발견된 유물의 연대를 측정하는 데 이용된 고도의 방사선 탄소 측정법을 바탕으로, 최초의 아메리카인들의 도착이 13,000년에서 12,600년 전 사이에 해당하는 것으로 보고 있다. 이 이론이 바탕을 두고 있는 근본적인 사실이 논리적으로 근거가 있다 해도, 그 후의 고고학적 발견은 사람들이 아시아로부터의 이주 물결을 타고 아메리카에 도착했음을 강력하게 시사하고 있으며, 그 중 일부는 분명히 클로비스 문화보다 수천 년 앞서 있었기 때문에, 클로비스-최초 이론의 '최초'라는 개념을 없애면서 중앙아메리카와 남아메리카로 이어지는 내륙 경로라는 개념에 의문을 제기한다.

■(A) 해안 이주 이론은 대체 경로를 제안하면서, 아메리카로 처음 이주한 고대인들이 신세계에 도달할 때까지 북동 아시아의 해안선을 따라 도보로 이동했고, 그곳에서 남쪽으로 해안을 따라 계속 이동했음을 시사한다. ■(B) 이에 대한 변형 이론은 실제로 이 이주자들이 가까스로 만든 원시적인 보트를 타고 이동했으며, 그로 인해 해빙 과정이 끝나기 전에 대륙들 사이를 건널 수 있었을 것이라고 주장한다. ■(C) 어느 쪽이든, 이 이론은 클로비스-최초 모델이 제안한 내륙 이동로와 현저히 다른 경로를 제시하는데, 순전히 해안을 통한 이동이 이주자들을 처음에는 중앙아메리카로, 그리고 나중에는 남아메리카로 데려갔다는 것이다. ■(D)

이 이론은 새롭게 도착한 이 사람들이 칠레 남부 지역과 베네수엘라 서부 지역에서 발견된 것 같이 알래스카에서 멀리 떨어진 해안 지역으로 어떻게 그렇게 빨리 퍼질 수 있었는지 설명하고 있다는 사실 덕분에, 과학계의 많은 구성원들의 지지를 이끌어 냈다. 하지만 이 이론은 명확하게 확정하기 어려운 것으로 판명되었는데, 주로 전 세계 해수면이 마지막 빙하기가 끝난 이후로 120미터 넘게 상승해 왔다는 사실 때문이며, 이는 그 고대인들이 따라갔을 해안선이 바다에 오래 잠겨 있어서, 그 사람들이 이동했던 정확한 경로를 추적하는 것이 오늘날 거의 불가능하게 되었음을 의미한다. 이주 경로와 방식이 여전히 의문으로 남아 있다는 사실에도 불구하고, 최초의 사람들이 대략 15,000년에서 20,000년 전에 아메리카의 해안에 도달했다는 데에는 전반적으로 의견이 일치되고 있다.

지문 어휘

1. be populated by ~이 살다 migrate 이주하다 controversy 논란
2. migrant 이주자 submerged 물속에 잠긴 Pleistocene-era 홍적세 시대(신생대 제4기의 첫 시기) glaciated 빙하로 덮인 impassable 통행 불가능한 corridor 회랑 지대(길게 뻗은 지형) in pursuit of ~을 쫓아 game 사냥감 traverse 횡단하다
3. radiocarbon technique 방사선 탄소 측정법 date 연대를 측정하다 valid 논리적으로 근거 있는, 타당한 predate (시간적으로) ~보다 앞서다 dispel 떨쳐 버리다, 없애다
4. alternative 대체의 variant 변형 assert 주장하다 manage 간신히 ~하다 deglaciation 해빙
5. glacial 빙하의

어휘의 의미 파악 문제

1 지문의 단어 "fauna"와 의미가 가장 가까운 것은?
(A) 장비
(B) 문화
(C) 야생 동물
(D) 토양

해설 fauna는 '동물상(한 지역에 있는 모든 동물의 종류)'을 의미하므로, 동의어는 (C) wildlife이다.

세부 정보 찾기 문제

2 두 번째 단락에 따르면, 빙하 시대에 베링기아를 건너는 것이 어려웠을 것 같은 이유는?
(A) 그 해안선이 수년 동안에 걸쳐 변화되었다.
(B) 빙하기 이전에 침수되었다.
(C) 북아메리카에서 멀리 떨어져 있었다.
(D) 거대한 얼음 판으로 덮여 있었다.

어휘 slab (넓적하고 두꺼운) 판

해설 베링기아가 완전히 빙하로 덮여 있었을 때 그곳을 가로지르는 것에 대한 의문이 제기되었다고 하면서 통행이 불가능한 두께의 얼음으로 덮여 있었을 것이라는 이유를 들고 있으므로, (D)가 정답이다.

추론 문제

3 다음 중 두 번째 단락에서 고대 아시아의 사냥꾼들에게 쫓겼던 종에 대해 추론할 수 있는 것은?
(A) 식량 공급원으로서가 아니라 놀이를 위해 사냥되었다.
(B) 대부분 빠르게 움직이지 않는 단독 생활 동물들이었다.
(C) 그 뼈와 가죽이 독특한 공예품을 만드는 데 이용되었다.
(D) 그 유해를 아시아와 북아메리카에서 발견할 수 있다.

어휘 sport 놀이, 재미 solitary animal 단독 생활 동물

해설 대형 사냥감을 쫓던 고대 아시아의 사냥꾼들이 아메리카에 처음 정착하는 과정에서 북아메리카 내륙을 관통해 지나갔다는 말에서 그들이 쫓던 사냥감의 유해가 아시아에서부터 북아메리카에 걸쳐 발견될 수 있음을 유추할 수 있다. 그러므로 정답은 (D)이다.

세부 정보 찾기 문제

4 세 번째 단락에 따르면, 다음 중 클로비스 유물에 대해
사실인 것은?
(A) 나중에 고고학자들에 의해 가짜인 것으로 공표되었다.
(B) 그 모습이 아시아의 유물과 크게 달랐다.
(C) 그 연대가 최첨단 기술을 이용해 측정되었다.
(D) 해양 활동과 관련된 도구들을 포함했다.

어휘 declare 공표하다 fake 가짜의 maritime 해양의

해설 클로비스 근처와 다른 관련된 장소에서 발견된 유물의 연대를
측정하는 데 고도의 방사성 탄소 측정법이 이용되었다고
했으므로, (C)가 정답이다.

어휘의 의미 파악 문제

5 지문의 단어 "endorsement"와 의미가 가장 가까운 것은?
(A) 경멸
(B) 지지
(C) 주의
(D) 자금

해설 endorsement는 '지지'를 의미하므로, 의미가 동일한 것은
(B) support이다.

수사적 의도 파악 문제

6 글쓴이는 왜 다섯 번째 단락에서 "전 세계 해수면"을
언급하는가?
(A) 한 이주 이론이 입증될 수 없는 이유를 대기 위해
(B) 베링기아가 절대 얼음 덩어리로 덮여 있지 않았다는
증거를 제공하기 위해
(C) 이주자들이 어느 경로를 택해 남아메리카로 향했을
가능성이 있는지 설명하기 위해
(D) 초기 아시아인들이 북아메리카로 이주하지 않았음을
시사하기 위해

어휘 verify 입증하다, 확인하다

해설 global sea levels 앞에 해안 이주 이론을 the theory로
지칭해 명확하게 확정하기 어려운 것으로 드러났다고 밝힌
뒤로 그 이유를 알리면서 전 세계 해수면을 언급하고 있으므로,
(A)가 정답이다.

문장 삽입 문제

7 제시된 문장이 지문에 삽입될 수 있는 곳을 가리키는 네 개의
네모[■]를 보아라.

**얼음 장벽과 맞닥뜨리자마자, 그들은 단순히 그 주위를 빙
둘러 항해함으로써 계속 앞으로 나아갈 수 있었을 것이다.**

이 문장이 들어갈 가장 적절한 위치는? 해당 네모[■]를
선택하여 이 문장을 지문에 삽입하여라.
(A)   (B)   (C)   (D)

어휘 encounter 맞닥뜨리다 barrier 장벽

해설 주어진 문장은 얼음 장벽을 맞닥뜨렸을 때 이주자들이
어떻게 계속 항해할 수 있었는지를 설명하고 있다. 원시적인
보트를 타고 해빙 과정이 끝나기 전에 이동한 사실이
제시된 문장 뒤에서 항해 중에 있었던 일을 설명해야 흐름이
자연스러우므로, (C)가 정답이다.

지문 요약 문제

8 **지시문**: 지문의 간략한 요약을 위한 도입 문장이 아래에
제시되어 있다. 지문에서 가장 중요한 개념들을 나타내는
선택지 3개를 선택하여 요약을 완성하여라. 어떤 문장들은
지문에 제시되지 않거나 주요 개념이 아니므로 요약에
포함되지 않는다. **이 문제는 2점에 해당한다.**

**최초로 아시아에서 아메리카로 향했던 인류의 이주를 둘러싼
몇 가지 이론과 논란들이 있다.**

(A) 클로비스-최초 이론은 최초의 이주자들이 베링기아를
건너 북아메리카에 도착했다고 말하지만, 고고학적
증거는 아시아로부터의 이주가 클로비스 문화보다 앞서
있었음을 시사한다.
(B) 해안 이주 이론은 최초의 북아메리카 이주자들이
해안선을 따라 이동했음을 시사하지만, 이 이론은
상승하는 전 세계 해수면으로 인해 확정하기 어렵다.
(C) 아메리카를 향한 인류 이주의 시초는 논쟁이 되고
있으며, 일부는 아시아인들이 최초의 유럽인들보다 앞서
도착했음을 시사한다.
(D) 뉴멕시코의 클로비스 근처에서 발견된 유물은 빙하기가
끝나기 전에 인류가 아메리카에 도착했음을 시사하면서,
고고학적 연대 측정법과 관련된 논란을 촉발시켰다.
(E) 알래스카와 시베리아를 연결하는 육지로서 현재는 물
속에 잠겨 있는 베링기아는 아메리카를 향한 인류의
이주에 중요한 역할을 하지는 않았으며, 당시에 존재했던
다른 육로 다리들에 가려 빛을 보지 못했다.
(F) 불확실성에도 불구하고, 인류가 약 15,000년에서
20,000년 전에 아메리카에 도착했다는 점에 대해서는
의견이 일치한다.

해설 아시아에서 아메리카로 향했던 인류의 이주에 대해 클로비스-
최초 이론과 그것을 반박하는 고고학적 증거, 해안 이주 이론과
그것을 확정하기 어렵게 만드는 원인, 여러 논란에도 불구하고
인류가 최초로 아메리카에 도착한 시점에 대한 의견 일치를
요약한 (A), (B), (F)가 정답이다.

관련 지식 **방사선 탄소 연대측정법(radiocarbon dating
technique)**은 탄소-14의 부식 속도를 이용하여 화석이나
유기 물질의 연대를 결정하는 과학적인 기술이다. 생물체가
살아있는 동안 그들은 대기 중의 탄소-14를 흡수하며,
이것은 생물체의 조직에 계속 누적된다. 생물체가
죽으면 그들의 탄소-14 흡수가 중단되고, 대신 탄소-

14가 점차적으로 부식되기
시작한다. 탄소-14의 부식 속도는
상대적으로 일정하기 때문에
이를 이용해 시간이 지난 기간을
정확하게 계산할 수 있다.

정답 | **1** (C)   **2** (A)   **3** (D)   **4** (B)   **5** (D)   **6** (A)   **7** (C)   **8** (B), (E), (F)

고대 이집트의 도자기

고대 이집트의 도자기는 특히 음식과 마실 것의 보관과 준비, 운반, 소비를 위한 그릇으로서 가정에서 실용적인 다수의 기능을 포함해 매우 다양한 역할을 했다. 그것은 의식에서도 사용되었고, 고인의 사후 여행을 같이 하도록 무덤에 넣어 둔 다양한 물품들 사이에서도 흔히 발견되었다. 도자기와 관련된 많은 것이 무덤 속 그림과 발굴된 도기 작업장 유적을 통해 파악되었는데, 여기에는 옛날 방식을 대체하는 것이 아니라 새로운 도자기 제조술이 왕국 도공들의 기존 레퍼토리에 단순히 추가되었다는 사실도 포함된다. 그러나 고고학자들은 그들이 (도자기를) 새긴 유형과 창조해 낸 모양 같은 기술을 면밀히 조사함으로써, 어느 정도의 확신을 갖고 각 개별 도자기를 특정 시대에 위치시킬 수 있다.

고대 이집트의 도자기 제작 과정은 적절한 재료의 선택으로 시작된다. 두 가지 가장 흔한 재료인 나일 찰흙과 이회토 찰흙을 구분하는 중요한 차이점이 있는데, 전자는 나일강을 따라 흘러가기 전에 에티오피아의 산맥에서 침식된 물질로 형성된 반면, 후자는 나일강의 강둑을 따라 이집트의 석회석 침전물 속에서 형성되었다. 도공들은 실용적인 가정 물품용으로 나일 찰흙을 이용하는 경향이 있었던 반면, 이회토 찰흙은 사람의 형상을 한 그릇 같은 장식용 물건들을 만드는 데 선호되었는데, 그런 물건들은 소유자의 사회적 지위와 위세를 상징하는 대략적인 사람의 모양을 한 아주 탐나는 물품들이었다.

일단 마르고 단단한 찰흙을 모으고 나면 물을 추가해 부드럽게 만들어야 했다. ■⁽ᴬ⁾ 그 후 적절한 점도가 되도록 반죽했는데, 이런 점도는 발로 밟거나 큰 찰흙 덩어리를 둘로 나눠 반으로 나눈 두 덩어리를 함께 두드려 얻을 수 있었다. ■⁽ᴮ⁾ 그 다음에 도공들은 수작업이나 그 과정을 용이하게 하도록 고안한 기구의 도움을 받아 찰흙의 모양을 빚었다. ■⁽ᶜ⁾ 마지막으로, 굽는 과정은 모닥불 위나 일종의 원시적인 오븐인 가마 안에서 진행되었다. ■⁽ᴰ⁾

이집트 도자기에 나타나 있는 여러 다른 종류의 장식은 제작 과정의 여러 다른 단계, 즉 굽기 전과 굽는 과정, 그리고 구운 후에 가미되었다. 굽기 전 단계에서 도공들은 흔히 금속이나

나무, 돌 같은 몇몇 다른 종류의 물체를 모조하도록 고안된 패턴을 새기기 위해 찰흙의 표면을 처리했다. 이 패턴들 중 일부는 아마도 원시적인 칼이나 단순한 잔가지였을 날카로운 도구로 새겨진 반면, 다른 것들은 도공의 손톱을 사용해 만들어졌다. 굽는 과정에서 사용된 인기 있던 장식 효과는 검정 테두리라고 부르던 것이었는데, 도자기 입구의 가장자리를 따라 탄화가 일어나는 불구덩이 속에서 도자기를 구워야 했다. 이런 효과를 일정하게 내려면 높은 수준의 기술적 지식이 필요했을 것으로 여겨지고 있다.

굽는 과정이 완료된 후에는 단단해진 도자기가 흔히 물감으로 장식되었으며, 특정 양식과 패턴이 일반적인 주제가 되었다. 여기에 포함되었던 것이 흰색 교차선 양식이었는데, 진홍색이나 적갈색 바탕에 흰색이나 크림색으로 기하학적 패턴이 그려진 반면, 흰색 바탕 양식에서는 형형색색의 장면이 흰색 바탕에 그려졌고, 푸른색으로 그려진 양식은 도자기 목 주변에 섬세하게 장식한 듯한 푸른색 안료로 그려진 연꽃과 꽃봉오리가 특징이었다.

지문 어휘

1. vessel 그릇 consumption 소비 tomb 무덤 the deceased 고인 remains 유적, 유해 repertoire 목록, 레퍼토리 potter 도공 incision 새기기
2. make a distinction 구별 짓다 marl 이회토(수중에서 퇴적되며 탄산 칼슘을 함유한 토사) eroded 침식된 limestone 석회석 utilitarian 실용적인 ware (특정 용도의) 물품, 용품 status 지위 prestige 위세, 명성
3. knead 반죽하다 consistency 점도 tread on ~을 발로 밟다 pound 두드리다 manually 수작업으로 implement 기구 kiln 가마
4. manipulate 처리하다, 다루다 imprint A with B A를 B로 각인시키다 imitate 모방하다 incise 새기다 rim 테두리 pit 구덩이 carbonization 탄화
5. adorn 장식하다 geometric 기하학적인 lotus flower 연꽃 bud 꽃봉오리 delicately 섬세하게 drape 장식하다

어휘의 의미 파악 문제

1 지문의 단어 "examining"과 의미가 가장 가까운 것은?
(A) 가르치기
(B) 보여 주기
(C) 조사하기
(D) 현대화하기

해설 '조사하기'를 뜻하는 examining과 의미가 동일한 것은 (C) studying이다.

추론 문제

2 다음 중 첫 번째 단락에서 고대 이집트 문화에 대해 추론할 수 있는 것은?
(A) 사후 세계에 대해 널리 퍼져 있는 믿음이 있었다.
(B) 장인들에 대한 존경심이 크지 않았다.
(C) 두 가지 다른 사회 계층이 있었다.
(D) 수많은 왕국이 있었다.

어휘 prevalent 널리 퍼져 있는 afterlife 사후 세계

해설 사후 여행을 함께 할 다양한 물품들을 무덤에 넣었다는 설명에서 사후 세계에 대한 일반적인 사회적 통념이 있었음을 유추할 수 있으므로, (A)가 정답이다.

수사적 의도 파악 문제

3 글쓴이는 왜 두 번째 단락에서 "에티오피아"를 언급하는가?
(A) 나일강의 지역적 중요성을 강조하기 위해
(B) 두 곳의 다른 지역에서 제작된 도자기를 비교하기 위해
(C) 이집트 도자기에 미친 외부적 영향을 설명하기 위해
(D) 도공들이 이용한 한 재료의 출처를 나타내기 위해

해설 나일 찰흙과 이회토 찰흙이라는 재료를 언급하면서 전자인 나일 찰흙이 에티오피아의 산맥에서 침식된 물질로 형성된 것이라고 했으므로, 정답은 (D)이다.

지시 대상 찾기 문제

4 지문의 구 "the latter"가 가리키는 것은?
(A) 고대 이집트   (B) 이회토 찰흙
(C) 침식된 물질   (D) 나일강

해설 the latter는 앞서 언급된 두 가지 중 두 번째 것을 가리킬 때 사용하므로, 두 가지 흔한 도자기 재료로 제시된 Nile clay and marl clay에서 두 번째 것인 (B)가 정답이다.

문장 재구성 문제

5 아래 문장 중 지문에서 음영 표시된 문장의 핵심 정보를 가장 잘 나타낸 것은? 오답 선택지들은 의미를 현저히 바꾸거나 핵심 정보를 생략한다.
(A) 첫 단계에서, 도공들은 금속이나 나무, 또는 돌 같은 다양한 물체를 이용해 찰흙의 모양을 빚었다.
(B) 찰흙을 처리하는 것의 주목적은 금속이나 나무, 또는 돌로 만들어진 것처럼 보이도록 하는 것이었다.
(C) 도공들은 강도를 향상시키기 위해 찰흙을 굽기 전에 흔히 금속이나 나무, 또는 돌 같은 물체를 찰흙에 추가했다.
(D) 도공들은 흔히 찰흙의 질감을 바꿔 다른 물체와 비슷한 패턴을 만들어 냈다.

어휘 enhance 향상시키다 texture 질감

해설 도공들이 다른 종류의 물체를 모조하도록 고안된 패턴으로 장식을 새기기 위해 흔히 찰흙의 표면을 처리했다는 핵심 정보를 제시하는 (D)가 정답이다.

세부 정보 찾기 문제

6 네 번째 단락에 따르면, 도공들이 왜 도자기를 불구덩이에 넣었는가?
(A) 도자기의 테두리를 따라 장식 효과를 내기 위해
(B) 찰흙 표면이 반드시 부드러운 상태로 유지되도록 하기 위해
(C) 도자기 가장자리가 검은색으로 변하는 것을 막기 위해
(D) 자신들이 가진 기술의 전반적인 수준을 향상시키기 위해

어휘 edge 가장자리 overall 전반적인

해설 검정 테두리라고 부르는 장식 효과를 내기 위해 불구덩이 속에서 도자기 제품을 굽는 방식이 필요했다고 했으므로, (A)가 정답이다.

문장 삽입 문제

7 제시된 문장이 지문에 삽입될 수 있는 곳을 가리키는 네 개의 네모[■]를 보아라.

이것은 흔히 도공의 물레라는 형태로 나타났는데, 찰흙을 중심축 위에서 회전시키면서 모양을 빚음으로써 도자기 제작을 훨씬 더 수월하게 만들어 주었던 상당한 기술적 진보였다.

이 문장이 들어갈 가장 적절한 위치는? 해당 네모[■]를 선택하여 이 문장을 지문에 삽입하여라.
(A)   (B)   (C)   (D)

어휘 rotate 회전시키다 central axis 중심축

해설 주어진 문장은 제시된 특정 방식이 도공의 물레를 이용한 것임을 언급하면서 도자기를 훨씬 더 쉽게 만들 수 있다는 장점을 나타내고 있다. 따라서 찰흙의 모양을 빚는 과정을 용이하게 해 주는 기구가 언급된 문장 뒤에 위치해 그 기구를 설명하는 흐름이 되어야 자연스러우므로, (C)가 정답이다.

지문 요약 문제

8 **지시문:** 지문의 간략한 요약을 위한 도입 문장이 아래에 제시되어 있다. 지문에서 가장 중요한 개념들을 나타내는 선택지 3개를 선택하여 요약을 완성하여라. 어떤 문장들은 지문에 제시되지 않거나 주요 개념이 아니므로 요약에 포함되지 않는다. **이 문제는 2점에 해당한다.**

고대 이집트에서 도자기를 만드는 데 이용된 과정들과 관련해 많은 것이 알려져 있다.

(A) 도자기는 보통 작업장에 있는 전문 공예가들에 의해 만들어졌으며, 새겨진 부분이 많이 있었다.
(B) 출처가 다른 두 가지 재료가 이집트 도자기에 이용되었으며, 각 재료는 특정 종류의 물품을 위해 선택되었다.
(C) 테두리를 따라 검게 탄화된 도자기는 질이 낮은 것으로 여겨졌기 때문에, 흔히 무덤 안에 놓였다.
(D) 도공들이 도자기를 장식하는 데 손톱을 이용하는 것을 선호했기 때문에, 기술적 발전이 거의 이루어지지 않았다.
(E) 도자기 제작 과정에는 찰흙 준비, 모양 빚기, 그리고 최종 제품을 만들어 내기 위한 굽기가 포함되었다.
(F) 도자기가 구워진 다음에는 흔히 그 위에 그려진 일반적인 패턴으로 장식되었다.

어휘 craftsman 공예가, 장인

해설 고대 이집트 도자기 제작 과정에 대해 도자기 재료와 서로
다른 용도, 도자기 제작 과정, 도자기를 구운 뒤의 장식 방법을
설명한 (B), (E), (F)가 정답이다.

관련 지식 **페이우므 도자기(Fayoum Pottery)**는 페이우므
지역에서 발견된 고대 이집트의 특별한 유물 중 하나로,
주로 고대 로마와 그리스의 영향을 받아 제작되었다.
실용적이면서 장식적인 형태가 특징인 이 도자기는 주로

일상적인 생활 공간에서 사용된 그릇과 용기로 구성되어
있으며, 보통 다양한 색과 장식적인 패턴으로 꾸며져 있다.

이 도자기는 고대 이집트 문화와
다른 나라들과의 교류 및 상업
활동에 대한 통찰을 제공해 주기
때문에 이집트 고고학 연구의
중요한 소재 중 하나이다.

CHAPTER 02 Social Science

정답 | 1 (D)   **2** (D)   **3** (C)   **4** (A)   **5** (A)   **6** (C)   **7** (B)   **8** (B), (D), (E)

향료 무역

향료 무역은 고대까지 거슬러 올라가며, 이때 아시아와 아프리카, 그리고 유럽의 고대 문명 사회에서 생강과 육두구, 계피를 포함해 아주 다양한 재배된 향료를 포함하는 무역에 처음 참여하기 시작했다. ■(A) 가장 초기의 해상 무역로들 중 일부는 인도네시아 선원들이 오갔는데, 이들은 일찍이 기원전 1500년에 동남아시아에서 재배한 향료들을 인도와 스리랑카 섬으로 운반했다. ■(B) 이윽고 이 교역로들은 규모와 범위가 모두 확대되어, 서기 1000년에 이르러서는 중동 지역과 아프리카 동부의 일부 지역들까지 포함할 정도로 늘어났다. ■(C) 향료 무역상들이 실제로 마다가스카르를 식민지화한 것이 바로 이때였는데, 현대의 인도네시아에서 현외 장치가 부착된 카누를 타고 인도양을 가로질러 그곳에 도착했고, 아프리카 앞바다에 위치한 이 거대한 육지에 사람이 살지 않는다는 것을 알게 되었다. ■(D)

이와 같은 시기 즈음에 현재의 에티오피아에 위치했던 악숨 왕국이 홍해를 정복해 내면서, 인도양과 지중해 사이에 놓인 그 지리적 위치를 이용해, 동양에서부터 당시 번영하던 로마 제국으로 향료를 실어 나르던 해상 무역로에 대해 상당히 큰 지배권을 장악했다. 이 경로는 홍해 가장자리에서 끝났으며, 그곳에서 향료를 내려 지중해 해안까지 육로로 옮겼다. 하지만, 7세기 즈음 아랍 세계에서 이슬람의 출현과 함께 악숨 왕국의 지배력이 점차적으로 약화되었고, 아랍 교역상들이 향료 무역의 주도권을 잡으면서, 동남아시아에서 지중해 동부 및 중부 지역의 상인들에게 향료를 옮겨다 주면, 이들이 그 후 그에 대한 수요가 늘어나고 있던 유럽 시장으로 전달했다.

이국적인 향료에 대한 유럽인들의 욕구를 자극했던 것은 원래 아시아를 가로지르는 육로였지만, 지도 제작 및 선박 제조 기

술이 지속적으로 발전하면서, 해양 경로가 곧 향료 무역에 절대적으로 필수적이게 되어 급속히 성장할 수 있게 해 주었다. 12세기 초에는 투르크족이 인도양에서 홍해를 거쳐 육로를 통해 지중해로 가는 무역로의 주인이 되었다. 하지만, 11세기 말에 기독교도와 이슬람교도 사이의 일련의 성전인 십자군 전쟁의 시작과 함께 모든 것이 바뀌었는데, 동양 문화에 대한 노출 증가가 서양에서 향료, 특히 후추에 대한 수요 상승으로 이어졌기 때문이었다.

이런 이유로 이탈리아의 해양 공화국인 베네치아와 제노바는 유럽과 아시아 사이의 교역에 대한 사실상의 독점을 확립할 때까지, 즉 엄청난 부와 권력을 가져다주고 15세기까지 지속되었던 그 상황에 이르기까지 향료의 수입과 유통에 점점 더 적극적이게 되었다. 하지만 1498년에 포르투갈의 탐험가이자 항해자였던 바스쿠 다가마가 유럽과 인도양을 잇는 새로운 무역로를 개척했다. 케이프 루트라고 알려진 이 경로는 아프리카 대륙의 최남단 끝자락에 위치한 희망봉 주변을 지나는 항해를 수반했다. 위험 요소투성이이긴 했지만, 이 경로로 인해 상인들이 홍해와 지중해를 통과하는 것을 피할 수 있었으며, 그로 인해 베네치아와 제노바의 숨통 조이기에서 벗어나, 포르투갈에게 향료 무역의 주요 역할을 떠맡기면서 결과적으로 유럽의 이 작은 나라가 거대한 식민 제국을 건설할 수 있게 되었다.

궁극적으로 향료 무역은 그에 관련된 모든 지역에 단순한 상거래를 훨씬 뛰어넘는 영향을 미쳤다. 이는 기술뿐만 아니라 종교와 문화까지 포함한 여러 주요 교류를 촉진시키면서, 문명 사회의 모습을 변화시켰으며, 아마 세계화를 향한 전 세계의 첫걸음에 해당했을 것이다.

1. antiquity 고대 nutmeg 육두구 ply 다니다 outrigger 현외 장치(배의 안정화를 위해 선체와 평행을 이루도록 부착한 나무 장치) uninhabited 사람이 살지 않는
2. geographical 지리적인 overland 육로로 wane 시들해지다 take the helm 주도권을 잡다
3. whet 자극하다, 돋우다 appetite 욕구 exotic 이국적인 cartography 지도 제작 vital 필수적인 commencement 시작 exposure 노출
4. importation 수입 virtual 사실상의 monopoly 독점 pioneer 개척하다 fraught with ~투성이인 stranglehold 숨통 조이기, 옥죄기 thrust 떠맡기다 colonial 식민지의
5. go far beyond ~을 훨씬 뛰어넘다 transaction 거래

추론 문제

1 다음 중 첫 번째 단락에서 고대 인도네시아 문명 사회에 대해 추론할 수 있는 것은?
(A) 농업을 강조하지 않았다.
(B) 주변국들로부터 교역에 대해 배웠다.
(C) 국제 무역에 관심이 없었다.
(D) 발달된 해양 기술을 가지고 있었다.

해설 첫 번째 단락에 현대의 인도네시아에서 현외 장치가 부착된 카누를 타고 인도양을 가로질러 갔다는 내용이 제시되어 있어 발달된 해양 기술을 가진 것으로 볼 수 있으므로 (D)가 정답이다.

어휘의 의미 파악 문제

2 지문의 단어 "culminated"와 의미가 가장 가까운 것은?
(A) 더 오래 지속되었다 (B) 연장되었다
(C) 시작했다 (D) 끝났다

해설 '끝이 났다'를 뜻하는 culminated는 (D) concluded로 대체할 수 있다.

문장 재구성 문제

3 아래 문장 중 지문에서 음영 표시된 문장의 핵심 정보를 가장 잘 나타낸 것은? 오답 선택지들은 의미를 현저히 바꾸거나 핵심 정보를 생략한다.
(A) 악숨 왕국은 유럽에서의 향료 수요 증가가 힘의 균형을 바꿀 때까지 아랍 세계에 대한 지배력을 유지했다.
(B) 이슬람이 더욱 강력해지면서 동남아시아의 향료 무역상들은 유럽과의 상업적 교류에 대한 흥미를 잃었다.
(C) 7세기에 아시아와 유럽 사이의 향료 무역에 대한 지배력이 악숨 왕국에서 아랍 세계로 옮겨졌다.
(D) 7세기는 유럽 국가들이 자체 향료를 재배하기 시작하면서 완전히 새로운 향료 무역의 시작을 알렸다.

어휘 transfer 옮기다, 이동시키다 mark the beginning of ~의 시작을 알리다

해설 7세기에 이슬람의 출현으로 인해 악숨 왕국의 지배력이 점차 약화되었고 아랍 교역상들이 향료 무역의 주도권을 잡았다는 내용은 향료 무역에 대한 지배력이 아랍 세계로 넘어갔다는 의미이므로 (C)가 정답이다.

어휘의 의미 파악 문제

4 지문의 구 "by leaps and bounds"와 의미가 가장 가까운 것은?
(A) 빠르게
(B) 변덕스럽게
(C) 자연적으로
(D) 점차적으로

어휘 erratically 변덕스럽게

해설 '급속히'를 뜻하는 by leaps and bounds와 의미가 가장 가까운 것은 (A) rapidly이다.

수사적 의도 파악 문제

5 글쓴이는 왜 세 번째 단락에서 "십자군 전쟁"을 언급하는가?
(A) 유럽에서 있었던 향료 수요의 상승 원인을 나타내기 위해
(B) 향료 무역이 동서양 사이의 균열을 초래했음을 시사하기 위해
(C) 11세기 동서양 사이의 교역에 대한 다른 접근법들을 대조하기 위해
(D) 동양의 상인들이 어떻게 유럽에 긍정적인 영향을 미쳤는지 보여 주기 위해

어휘 rift 균열

해설 세 번째 단락에 십자군 전쟁의 시작과 함께 동양 문화에 대한 노출 증가가 서양에서 향료에 대한 수요 상승으로 이어졌다는 내용이 제시되어 있으므로 (A)가 정답이다.

세부 정보 찾기 문제

6 네 번째 단락에 따르면, 포르투갈이 향료 무역에서 주요 참가국이 되도록 한 요인은?
(A) 중동 지역의 이슬람교도 군대에 대한 승리
(B) 유럽 선박 제조 기술의 변화
(C) 새로운 해상 무역로의 확립
(D) 홍해에서 시작되는 육로 건설

해설 네 번째 단락에 새로운 무역 경로의 개척으로 인해 결과적으로 포르투갈이 향료 무역에 있어 주요 역할을 하게 되었다고 쓰여 있으므로 (C)가 정답이다.

문장 삽입 문제

7 제시된 문장이 지문에 삽입될 수 있는 곳을 가리키는 네 개의 네모[■]를 보아라.

이 동일한 향료들이 그 후 육로를 통해 그리스와 로마 제국으로 흘러 들어갔다.

이 문장이 들어갈 가장 적절한 위치는? 해당 네모[■]를 선택하여 이 문장을 지문에 삽입하여라.

(A)　　　(B)　　　(C)　　　(D)

어휘　make one's way to ~으로 가다　via ~을 통해

해설　주어진 문장의 These same spices를 통해 앞서 향료가 구체적으로 언급되었음을 알 수 있고, 시간 순서를 나타내는 then과 함께 특정 향료의 이동 경로를 나타내고 있다. 따라서, 인도와 스리랑카 섬으로 운반된 향료들의 이후 이동 경로를 알리는 흐름이 되어야 자연스러우므로 (B)가 정답이다.

지문 요약 문제

8 **지시문**: 지문의 간략한 요약을 위한 도입 문장이 아래에 제시되어 있다. 지문에서 가장 중요한 개념들을 나타내는 선택지 3개를 선택하여 요약을 완성하여라. 어떤 문장들은 지문에 제시되지 않거나 주요 개념이 아니므로 요약에 포함되지 않는다. **이 문제는 2점에 해당한다.**

국제 향료 무역은 길고 흥미로운 역사를 지니고 있다.

(A) 향료 무역은 15세기 이후에 해양 경로에서 주로 육로로 바뀌었다.
(B) 인도양과 지중해 사이의 경로 지배권은 수세기에 걸쳐 반복적으로 소유자가 바뀌었다.

(C) 아프리카 남쪽 끝자락에 위치한 희망봉은 향료 상인들에게 많은 위험을 야기했다.
(D) 향료 무역에 대한 지배권의 주된 변화는 한 포르투갈 탐험가가 새로운 해상 무역로를 만들었을 때 일어났다.
(E) 향료 무역은 기원전 1500년경에 동남아시아의 선원들이 인도와 스리랑카로 향료를 전하면서 시작되었다.
(F) 베네치아와 제노바는 향료 무역을 지키기 위해 십자군 전쟁 중에 여러 이슬람 국가들과 함께 싸웠다.

어휘　predominantly 주로, 대부분　repeatedly 반복해서　change hands ~의 소유자가 바뀌다

해설　국제 향료 무역에 대하여 무역로 지배권의 변화, 포르투갈 탐험가의 신규 무역로 개척에 따른 변화, 향료 무역의 시작을 설명한 (B), (D), (E)가 정답이다.

관련 지식　**바스쿠 다가마(Vasco Da Gama)**는 유럽에서 출발하여 아프리카 남단 희망봉을 거쳐 아시아까지 이어지는 인도 항로인 케이프 루트(Cape Route)를 개척한 포르투갈의 항해자이다. 이 항로를 발견하기

위해 바스쿠 다가마는 약 2년에 걸쳐 42,000km의 험난한 원정을 견뎌내야 했다. 그의 발견은 포르투갈이 인도 무역을 독점하는 데 밑바탕이 되었다. 이후 그는 인도 무역의 확장에 힘썼으며, 국왕의 인도 정책 고문이 되기도 하였다.

PASSAGE 2

pp.160-163

정답 |　**1** (B)　　**2** (D)　　**3** (C)　　**4** (C)　　**5** (D)　　**6** (B)　　**7** (A)　　**8** (A), (D), (E)

지나친 벌목의 환경적 문제

벌목 행위는 나무를 베어 넘어뜨려 몸통 부분을 길이가 다양한 여러 부분으로 나눈 다음, 그 결과물인 통나무를 추가 가공 처리를 위해 제재소로 운반하는 작업을 수반한다. 과거에는 이 일이 오로지 사람 손으로만 이뤄졌고, 전 세계의 더 추운 특정 지역에서는 계속 수작업 방식으로 행해지고 있는데, 벌목꾼들이 겨울에 도끼로 각 나무를 베어 넘어뜨리면, 그 후에 말이나 황소 같은 짐수레 견인용 동물들이 이끄는 썰매로 그 통나무들을 얼어붙은 강의 강둑으로 운반한다. 봄철 해빙기가 다가오고 얼음이 녹으면, 그것들은 강을 따라 대기 중인 제재소로 떠내려가게 된다.

그러나 전 세계 대부분의 현대화된 국가에서 벌목은 고도로 기계화된 과정이 되었으며, 벌목이 전기톱을 이용해 이루어진다거나, 또는 나무를 집단적으로 거둬들이는 조림지에서는 심지어 단 한 번의 작동으로 다수의 나무를 잘라 쓰러뜨릴 수 있는 기계로 이뤄지고 있다. 이 통나무들은 트럭과 트랙터, 그리고 특히 일부 외딴 지역 같은 경우에는 헬리콥터를 포함한 동력 장치를 갖춘 운송 수단을 이용해 운반된다. 이 현대적인 기술의 이용은 전혀 놀라운 일도 아니며, 벌목 회사들에게 수없이 많은 혜택을 제공한다는 것도 의심할 여지가 없지만, 지나친 벌목에 따른 심각한 환경 문제의 원인이 되어 왔다.

지나친 벌목은 지속 불가능한 천연자원인 삼림에 대한 과잉 개발로 정의할 수 있으며, 회복할 수 없는 삼림 벌채 및 야생 동물 서식지의 영구적인 파괴 두 가지 모두로 이어질 수 있는 잠재성이 있다. 그러나 나무를 잘라 쓰러뜨리고 여러 조각으로 잘라 운반하는 과정에서 중장비와 현대적인 방식의 이용에 의해 생겨난 수월함이 일부 지역에서 지나친 벌목을 부추겨 오기는 했지만, 그것이 결코 이 문제의 유일한 원인은 아니다. 지나친 벌목은, 많은 다른 형태의 환경 악화와 마찬가지로 보조금으로 인해 흔히 나타나는 일부 결과인데, 이는 특정 상업적 활동을 장려하거나 저지하기 위해 정부에 의해 제공되는 금전적 보상책이다. 예를 들어, 미국에서는 국립 산림청이 납세자들의 세금을 이용해 국유림에 위치하는 벌목용 도로에 대한 토목 공사 및 건설 측면에 있어 벌목 회사들을 지원하고 있다. 그러한 보조금을 주는 것의 궁극적인 목적은 국가 경제력의 강화에 기여하는 것이지만, 이 경우와 다수의 다른 경우에 있어, 환경 보호 단체들은 그것을 정부 자금의 오용으로 여기고 있다.

지속 불가능한 특정 제품에 대한 소비자 수요는 지나친 벌목의 또 다른 중요한 요인이다. 예를 들어, 화장지와 종이 타월, 고급 화장지를 포함한 일회용 휴지는 많은 소비자들이 일상 생활에 필수적인 것으로 여기는 편리하고 가격이 적절한 제품일 수는 있지만, 그 제품들의 생산은 전 세계 각지의 삼림을 파괴하고 있는 지나친 벌목의 이면에 존재하는 원동력이 되었다. 비록 많은 소비자들이 지금은 100퍼센트 대나무 섬유로 만든 고급 화장지처럼, 제조 과정의 일환으로 목재 펄프를 필요로 하지 않는 제품으로 눈을 돌리고 있다고 해도, 그러한 대체 제품은 현재 전체 시장에서 오직 아주 작은 비율에만 해당한다. 그리고 전 세계 일부 지역에서는 지나친 벌목이 순전히 자본주의와 소비지상주의의 부산물만은 아니다. 예를 들어, 중국의 시골 지역에서는 과도한 벌목이 일어나도록 초래하고 있는 것이 바로 가정에서 연료로 쓰이는 나무에 대한 수요이다.

지나친 벌목이 전 세계 삼림에 미치는 영향은 극심하고 광범위한데, 한때 삼림이 울창했던 지역이 토종 야생 동물에게 쉼터를 거의 제공해 주지 못하고 침수에 취약한 관목림 지역으로 줄어들고 있기 때문이다. ■(A) 지나친 벌목에 따른 결과는 때때로 벌목 회사들에게 수입의 일부를 재식림 작업에 배정하도록 요구함으로써 완화될 수 있다. ■(B) 이는 벌목된 지역에 생물학적으로 다양하고 지역적으로 적절한 묘목의 식수 같은 활동들을 포함할 수 있다. ■(C) 지나친 벌목의 문제에 대한 해결책은 아니지만, 재식림은 지역 생물 다양성 및 지역 인구가 누리는 삶의 질 모두에 긍정적인 영향을 미칠 수 있다. ■(D)

지문 어휘

1. sawmill 제재소 exclusively 오로지 subsequently 그 후에 thaw 해빙기
2. felling 벌목 plantation (목재 생산용) 조림지 en masse 집단적으로 remote 외딴 undoubtedly 의심할 여지없이 contribute to ~의 원인이 되다, ~에 기여하다
3. unsustainable 지속 불가능한 irrecoverable 회복할 수 없는 by no means 결코 ~이 아니다 grant 주다, 부여하다 subsidy 보조금 financial 재정의 incentive 보상책 intent 목적, 의도 misuse 오용, 남용
4. disposable 일회용의 fiber 식물 섬유 consumerism 소비지상주의 rural 시골의 excessive 과도한
5. severe 극심한 brushland 관목림 지역 indigenous 토종의 susceptible to ~에 취약한 mitigate 완화시키다 earmark 배정하다 sapling 묘목 biodiversity 생물 다양성

지시 대상 찾기 문제

1 지문의 단어 "they"가 가리키는 것은?
(A) 벌목꾼들
(B) 통나무들
(C) 썰매들
(D) 강둑들

해설 they 뒤에 제재소까지 강물에 떠내려 가게 한다고 했으므로 앞선 문장에서 설명하는 통나무(logs) 운반 방식임을 알 수 있다. 정답은 (B)이다.

세부 정보 찾기 문제

2 세 번째 단락에 따르면, 미국 정부는 왜 벌목 회사들에게 도로를 건설하도록 돈을 주는가?
(A) 국립공원 내의 관광 산업을 촉진하기 위해
(B) 기술 발전을 가속화하기 위해
(C) 그들의 재식림 활동을 강화하기 위해
(D) 국가를 재정적으로 더 튼튼하게 만들기 위해

어휘 promote 촉진하다 bolster 강화하다

해설 세 번째 단락에 미국 정부가 벌목 회사들에게 제공하는 보조금의 궁극적인 목적이 국가 경제력의 강화에 기여하는 것이라고 쓰여 있으므로 (D)가 정답이다.

문장 재구성 문제

3 아래 문장 중 지문에서 음영 표시된 문장의 핵심 정보를 가장 잘 나타낸 것은? 오답 선택지들은 의미를 현저히 바꾸거나 핵심 정보를 생략한다.
(A) 지구의 삼림 파괴와 더불어 지나친 벌목은 가정용 제품에 대한 수요를 끌어 올린다.
(B) 그 편리함에도 불구하고, 일회용 휴지가 전 세계 삼림 벌채에 상당한 원인이 되고 있다.
(C) 사람들이 종이 제품의 편리함을 누리고 있기는 하지만, 그것을 구입하는 것이 지나친 벌목의 원인이 되고 있다.
(D) 일회용 휴지를 다른 종이 제품들 대신 사용함으로써, 소비자들이 지나친 벌목을 방지하는 데 도움을 줄 수 있다.

어휘 drive up 끌어 올리다

해설 일회용 휴지가 편리하고 가격이 적당하여 사람들이 그 제품들을 사용하고, 그로 인한 제품 생산이 지나친 벌목의 원동력이 되는 것이 핵심 정보이므로 (C)가 정답이다.

어휘의 의미 파악 문제

4 지문의 단어 "byproduct"와 의미가 가장 가까운 것은?
(A) 지표
(B) 반대
(C) 결과
(D) 경쟁자

해설 byproduct는 '부산물(주산물의 생산 과정에서 더불어 생기는 것)'을 뜻하며, 가장 의미가 가까운 (C) consequence가 정답이다.

추론 문제

5 다음 중 네 번째 단락에서 중국 시골 지역에 대해 추론할 수 있는 것은?
(A) 벌목 활동에 대한 현지의 반대가 많다.
(B) 생물 다양성이 재식림에 의해 향상되었다.
(C) 지나친 벌목이 현대화에 의해 악화되었다.
(D) 사람들이 집을 따뜻하게 유지하기 위해 땔감을 태운다.

해설 중국 시골 지역에서 과도한 벌목이 일어나는 원인이 가정용 연료로 쓰이는 나무에 대한 수요라고 쓰여 있어 집을 따뜻하게 유지하기 위해 나무를 태운다는 것을 알 수 있으므로 (D)가 정답이다.

세부 정보 찾기 문제

6 다음 중 다섯 번째 단락에서 재식림과 관련해 언급되지 않은 것은?
(A) 벌목 회사의 수익으로 자금을 제공받을 수 있다.
(B) 기계화에 의해 강화되었다.
(C) 야외에 어린 나무를 심는 작업을 수반한다.
(D) 현지 주민들의 삶을 향상시킨다.

해설 다섯 번째 단락에 벌목 회사들에게 수입의 일부를 재식림 작업에 배정하도록 요구하는 것과 적절한 묘목의 식수 같은 활동들을 포함하는 것, 그리고 현지 인구가 누리는 삶의 질에 미치는 긍정적인 영향이 쓰여 있으므로 (A)와 (C), 그리고 (D)를 확인할 수 있다. 하지만, 기계화에 의한 향상은 제시되어 있지 않으므로 (B)가 정답이다.

문장 삽입 문제

7 제시된 문장이 지문에 삽입될 수 있는 곳을 가리키는 네 개의 네모[■]를 보아라.

다행히 이것이 항상 되돌릴 수 없는 상황인 것은 아니다.

이 문장이 들어갈 가장 적절한 위치는? 해당 네모[■]를 선택하여 이 문장을 지문에 삽입하여라.
(A)   (B)   (C)   (D)

어휘 irreversible 되돌릴 수 없는

해설 주어진 문장은 특정 상황을 가리키는 this와 함께 항상 되돌릴 수 없는 것은 아니라는 의미를 나타낸다. 이는 해결 가능성을 제시하는 것으로서 문제점을 언급하는 문장과 해결책을 알리는 문장 사이에 위치해야 자연스러우므로 (A)가 정답이다.

지문 요약 문제

8 **지시문:** 지문의 간략한 요약을 위한 도입 문장이 아래에 제시되어 있다. 지문에서 가장 중요한 개념들을 나타내는 선택지 3개를 선택하여 요약을 완성하여라. 어떤 문장들은 지문에 제시되지 않거나 주요 개념이 아니므로 요약에 포함되지 않는다. **이 문제는 2점에 해당한다.**

벌목은 나무를 잘라 쓰러뜨린 다음, 제재소로 보내는 행위이다.

(A) 벌목 회사들에 대한 정부 보조금과 지속 불가능한 제품 사용은 지나친 벌목을 부추기는 두 가지 요인이다.
(B) 목재 펄프 대신 대나무로 만드는 고급 화장지는 환경 친화적인 대체품이다.
(C) 국립공원 내에 벌목용 도로를 짓는 것은 벌목 회사들의 중장비에 의해 초래되는 피해를 줄일 수 있다.
(D) 기계 장치의 이용을 포함한 벌목 기술의 현대화가 지나친 벌목에 기여했다.
(E) 지나친 벌목의 부정적인 영향이 나무 심기 같은 재식림 활동에 의해 부분적으로 상쇄될 수 있다.
(F) 지나친 벌목은 벌목꾼들이 주로 봄철 해빙기 후에 통나무를 운반하는 더 추운 지역에서 발생할 가능성이 더 크다.

어휘 offset 상쇄하다

해설 지나친 벌목의 주요 원인 두 가지를 설명하는 (A), 벌목과 관련된 기계와 기술을 언급한 (D), 지나친 벌목에 대해 제시된 해결책을 언급하는 (E)가 정답이다.

관련 지식 **식목일(Arbor Day)**은 나무 심기 행사를 하는 날이며, 많은 나라에서 기념하고 있다. 미국인 J. 스털링 모튼의 제안으로 네브래스카주에서 1872년 4월 10일에 최초로 식목행사가 개최되었다. 이때 심은 나무는 100만 그루가 넘었다고 한다. 이후 이날은 식목일로 제정되었고, 1885년에는 모튼의 생일인 4월 22일로 바뀌어 법정 주 공휴일이 되기도 하였다. 이후 미국의 많은 주에서도 각 주의 기후를 고려해 식목일을 제정하여 각자 행사를 진행하고 있다. 우리나라의 경우 1911년 4월 3일에 최초로 식목일이 제정되었으나, 1946년에 4월 5일로 변경되어 지금까지 유지되고 있다.

정답 | **1** (A)   **2** (C)   **3** (D)   **4** (C)   **5** (A)   **6** (B)   **7** (D)   **8** (B), (E), (F)

아동 발달에서 놀이의 역할

현대의 학부모와 교육자들은 이제 놀이를 아동 발달에 있어 필수적인 요소로 여기는데, 이는 (놀이가) 활동적이고 건강하게 지내는 방법을 그들에게 제공함과 동시에 사회적 능력을 터득하고 혼자 또는 또래들과 함께 보내는 시간을 즐길 수 있게 하기 때문이다. 하지만, 발달상의 혜택이라는 측면에 있어, 모든 놀이 형태가 균등하게 만들어지는 것은 아니다. 아이들 여가 시간의 상당 부분이 자유 선택 놀이에 할애되도록 보장하는 것이 중요하다.

자유 선택 놀이는 아이들이 놀이에 대해 스스로 결정하고 놀이가 진행되는 방향을 조절하도록 허용하는 특성을 공통으로 하는 아주 다양한 활동으로 구성된다. 이는 직접적이든 또는 간접적이든 부모나 다른 성인에 의해 이끌려가거나 고무되지 않고 그들 스스로의 본능과 관심, 그리고 상상력에 의존할 것을 요구한다. 어쩌면 자유 선택 놀이의 본질적인 의미를 규정하는 특징은 그에 참여하는 데 있어 옳고 그른 방법이 없다는 사실일 것이다. 아이들은 태어난 순간부터 십대 시절에 이르기까지 이런 체계화되지 않은 유형의 놀이를 필요로 하는데, 성공적인 성인으로 성장할 수 있는 충분한 삶의 기술을 습득하도록 보장할 뿐 아니라 신체적, 정신적 건강을 최적화하기 위해서이다.

놀이는 일반적으로 향후의 성공에 필요한 수단을 정신적, 신체적, 사회적인 세 가지 기본적인 방식으로 아이들에게 갖춰 준다. ■^(A) 정신적 발달 측면에 있어, 놀이는 아이들에게 자신감과 독립성, 호기심을 강화할 수 있는 기회를 제공한다. ■^(B) 어쩌면 가장 중요한 부분은, 여러 도전적인 상황에 대처하게 만들어 준다는 점일 것이다. ■^(C) 신체적으로는 특정 유형의 놀이가 지닌 이점은 명백한데, 달리기와 뛰어 오르기, 던지기, 또는 받기를 포함하는 즐거운 활동에 참여하면, 아이들은 민첩함과 체력, 조정력을 발달시키는 중요한 단계를 밟게 된다. ■^(D)

마지막으로, 다른 아이들과의 교류를 수반하는 놀이는 아이들이 나이가 들어가면서 건강하고 보람 있는 관계를 형성하게 해주는 유형의 사회적 능력을 발달시키는 데 도움을 준다. 단체 놀이가 예외 없이 갈등과 의견 불일치, 어쩌면 눈물까지도 수반하지만, 부모들은 이런 일이 발생할 때 아무리 불쾌해도 이를 순전히 부정적으로 치부하지 않는 법을 반드시 터득해야 한다. 이런 불화의 순간들은 놀이 중 공유 및 순서 지키기와 같은 조화의 순간들과 밀접하게 연관되어 있으며, 이는 아이들에게 자신들의 감정을 살피고 강한 감정들에 대처하면서 스스로를 효과적으로 표현하도록 가르쳐 준다.

놀이는 또한 부모들이 재미있고 편안한 방식으로 아이들과 교류하는 수단이 될 수 있는데, 이는 가족의 유대감을 강화하는 데 도움을 준다. 하지만 중요한 것은, 아이들의 놀이 활동에 참여하거나 단순히 도와줄 때, 일정 수준의 안전을 유지하는 데 필요한 것을 제외하고는, 부모들이 놀이가 흘러가는 방향을 통제하거나 규칙 또는 제한을 강요하지 않도록 신중히 주의를 기울여야 한다는 점이다. 그 이유는 놀이가 그 근본적인 핵심에 있어 자유와 선택에 관한 것이므로, 성인에게 모든 결정을 내리게 하는 것은 그 경험에서 순수한 기쁨을 상당 부분 없애버리고 아이를 성장 발달상의 혜택을 빼앗긴 상태로 만들 것이기 때문이다.

놀이의 일환으로 아이들이 스스로 도전 과제를 만들어 내고 의도적으로 불확실한 요소를 도입하는 것은 드문 일이 아니다. 특정 상황에서 그리고 일부 환경 속에서, 이는 부모들이 피하기를 바라는 수준의 위험을 만들어 낼 수도 있지만, 이 또한 놀이의 필수불가결한 일부이다. 이를 통해, 아이들은 스스로를 시험하고 자신의 한계가 무엇인지 정확하게 알아낼 수 있고, 위험한 상황에 대처하는 방법, 즉 필연적으로 이후의 삶에서 유용한 것으로 드러나게 될 능력을 배울 수 있을 것이다.

지문 어휘

1. **component** 요소 **peer** 또래, 동료 **when it comes to** ~의 측면에 있어, ~와 관련해서는 **be dedicated to** ~에 할애되다

2. **steer** 이끌다, 몰고 가다 **defining** 본질적인 의미를 규정하는 **unstructured** 체계화되지 않은 **optimize** 최적화하다 **sufficient** 충분한

3. **equip A with B** A에게 B를 갖춰 주다 **cope with** ~에 대처하다 **take part in** ~에 참여하다 **agility** 민첩성 **stamina** 체력 **coordination** 조정(력)

4. **interaction** 교류, 상호 작용 **rewarding** 보람 있는 **invariably** 변함없이 **discount** 치부하다 **discord** 불화 **go hand in hand** 관련되다, 함께 가다 **deal with** ~을 다루다 **effectively** 효과적으로

5. **familial** 가족의 **bond** 유대(감) **impose** 강요하다, 부과하다 **limitation** 한계, 제한 **core** 핵심 **make a decision** 결정을 내리다 **strip** 박탈하다 **innocent** 순수한

6. **intentionally** 의도적으로 **introduce** 도입하다 **uncertainty** 불확실성 **integral** 필수불가결한 **inevitably** 필연적으로 **prove** ~임이 드러나다

어휘의 의미 파악 문제

1 지문의 단어 "simultaneously"와 의미가 가장 가까운 것은?
(A) 동시에
(B) 이상한 방식으로
(C) 약간의 의구심을 갖고
(D) 그럴 만한 이유로

해설 simultaneously는 '동시에'라는 뜻으로 사용되었으므로 (A) at the same time이 정답이다.

세부 정보 찾기 문제

2 두 번째 단락에 따르면, 다음 중 자유 선택 놀이에 대해 사실이 아닌 것은?
(A) 아이들이 놀이의 그 전개 방식을 결정한다.
(B) 참여하는 데 있어 옳고 그른 방법이 없다.
(C) 부모가 아이들을 올바른 방향으로 안내해야 한다.
(D) 태어날 때부터 십대가 될 때까지 아이들이 즐겨야 한다.

어휘 unfold 전개되다

해설 아이들이 놀이의 진행 방향을 통제하는 것과 놀이 참여에 옳고 그른 방법이 없다는 점, 그리고 태어난 순간부터 십대 시절에 이르기까지 체계화되지 않은 유형의 놀이를 필요로 한다는 점이 제시되어 있다. 그러나 부모가 이끄는 것은 좋지 않은 것으로 언급되고 있으므로 (C)가 정답이다.

추론 문제

3 다음 중 체계화되지 않은 놀이를 경험하지 않는 아이들에 대해 추론할 수 있는 것은?
(A) 자신만의 체계화된 놀이를 만들어 낼 수 있다.
(B) 학교 공부에 더욱 집중하게 될 것이다.
(C) 부상당할 가능성이 더 적다.
(D) 성인이 되어서 힘겨워할 가능성이 더 크다.

어휘 struggle 힘겨워하다

해설 성공적인 성인으로서 성장할 수 있는 충분한 삶의 능력을 습득하는 데 체계화되지 않은 유형의 놀이가 필요하다는 내용이 제시되어 있으므로, 반대의 경우에 해당하는 어려움을 언급한 (D)가 정답이다.

수사적 의도 파악 문제

4 글쓴이가 네 번째 단락에서 놀이 중의 갈등에 대해 논의하는 이유는?
(A) 부모에게 체계화되지 않은 놀이의 있음직한 결과에 대해 경고하기 위해
(B) 놀이 방향을 자유롭게 선택하는 것이 위험할 수 있음을 시사하기 위해
(C) 놀이의 좋고 나쁜 순간이 모두 어떻게 이점이 있는지 설명하기 위해
(D) 아이들이 흔히 즐기는 두 가지 다른 유형의 놀이를 비교하기 위해

해설 놀이 중에 발생하는 불화의 순간들도 아이들에게 가르쳐 주는 것이 있음을 강조하는 내용이므로 (C)가 정답이다.

어휘의 의미 파악 문제

5 지문의 단어 "bereft"와 의미가 가장 가까운 것은?
(A) 빼앗긴
(B) 보장받은
(C) 대체된
(D) 강화된

해설 '빼앗긴'을 뜻하는 bereft와 의미가 가장 가까운 (A) deprived가 정답이다.

세부 정보 찾기 문제

6 여섯 번째 단락에 따르면, 다음 중 아이들이 놀이를 통해 배울 수 있는 것은?
(A) 불만스러운 환경 속에서 해야 하는 것
(B) 할 수 있는 것과 그렇지 않은 것
(C) 게임의 규칙을 따르는 방법
(D) 자신의 능력으로 또래들에게 깊은 인상을 남기는 방법

어휘 frustrating 불만스러운

해설 아이들이 스스로를 시험하고 자신의 한계가 무엇인지 정확하게 알아낼 수 있다고 했으므로 (B)가 정답이다.

문장 삽입 문제

7 제시된 문장이 지문에 삽입될 수 있는 곳을 가리키는 네 개의 네모[■]를 보아라.

이 모든 신체적 능력은 나중에 놀이터의 범위를 뛰어넘어 일상에서의 무수한 상황에 있어 필수적일 것이다.

이 문장이 들어갈 가장 적절한 위치는? 해당 네모[■]를 선택하여 이 문장을 지문에 삽입하여라.
(A)　　　(B)　　　(C)　　　(D)

어휘 a myriad of 무수한　above and beyond ~의 범위를 뛰어넘어

해설 주어진 문장의 All of these physical skills는 앞서 언급된 신체적 능력을 뜻하므로, 여러 신체적 능력과 관련해 설명하는 문장 뒤에 위치해 그 혜택을 알리는 흐름이 되어야 자연스럽다. 따라서 (D)가 정답이다.

지문 요약 문제

8 **지시문**: 지문의 간략한 요약을 위한 도입 문장이 아래에 제시되어 있다. 지문에서 가장 중요한 개념들을 나타내는 선택지 3개를 선택하여 요약을 완성하여라. 어떤 문장들은 지문에 제시되지 않거나 주요 개념이 아니므로 요약에 포함되지 않는다. **이 문제는 2점에 해당한다.**

오늘날 놀이는 아이의 성장 발달에 있어 필수적인 부분으로 여겨지고 있다.

(A) 체계화된 놀이와 체계화되지 않은 놀이의 엄격하게 규제된 균형이 아이들에게 최고의 장점들을 제공해 줄 것이다.

(B) 아이들이 참여하는 놀이의 일부는 삶에서 성공하는 데 필요한 능력을 터득하도록 보장하기 위해 자유롭게 선택되어야 한다.

(C) 자유 선택 놀이가 유용한 능력을 기르도록 아이들을 도울 수 있지만, 부모가 명확한 경계를 제시하는 경우에만 그렇다.

(D) 짧은 시간의 놀이는 아이들과 함께 참여하기로 선택하는 부모에게 즐거울 수 있다.

(E) 부모는 놀이 중에 아이들에게 스스로 결정을 내리도록 허용해야 하며, 때때로 일어나는 갈등에 대해 걱정하지 말아야 한다.

(F) 놀이는 아이들에게 본질적으로 정신적, 신체적, 또는 사회적일 수 있는 중요한 혜택을 제공한다.

어휘 regulated 규제된 occasional 때때로 일어나는 in nature 본질적으로

해설 놀이와 삶에서 성공하는 능력에 대해서 설명하는 (B), 놀이에 대한 자율성 및 부모의 태도를 설명하는 (E), 놀이가 아이들에게 주는 이점을 설명하는 (F)가 정답이다.

관련 지식 **마리아 몬테소리(Maria Montessori)**는 교육자이자 이탈리아 최초의 여의사로, 어린아이들의 정신병은 부모 관심의 부재가 원인이므로 치료가 아닌 도움이 필요하다고 생각했다. 그녀는 노동자 자녀들을 위한 유치원 '어린이의 집'을 개원하였고, 아이들의 능력과 의사를 존중하는 등 몬테소리 법(法)에 따른 교육을 했다. 어린이 개개인에게 알맞은 교육의 필요성을 주장했으며, 다양한 놀이 기구를 활용해 감각기관을 훈련시키고자 했다. 그녀의 사상을 기반으로 한 몬테소리 운동은 지금까지도 세계 각국의 유아 교육에 많은 영향을 주고 있다.

PASSAGE 4   pp.168-171

정답 | **1** (D)   **2** (D)   **3** (C)   **4** (A)   **5** (B)   **6** (A)   **7** (B)   **8** (C), (D), (F)

농업과 인구 증가

홀로세에 있었던 빠른 인구 증가는 수렵 채집 부족들의 유목 생활 방식에서 정착된 농업 공동체로의 전환에 의해 주로 촉진되었다. 이 공동체들이 쉽게 보존할 수 있는 식량의 생산 및 보관에 초점을 맞추면서, 인구 급증에 상당히 기여했다. 이 인구 증가에 동반되었던 것은 새로운 사회 경제 체제의 전 세계적인 출현으로서 농업 공동체에 두 가지 유익한 영향을 미쳤는데, 그 첫 번째는, 경작되던 각 토지 구획에서 더 높은 칼로리의 수확을 보장해 주었으며, 그리고 두 번째로는, 수많은 사람들에게 아주 많은 양의 식량을 분배할 수 있는 향상된 능력을 만들어 주었다.

하지만, 농업의 발전이 반드시 모든 문화에 즉각적이고 강력한 영향을 미친 것은 아니었으며, 그 가장 초기 단계에서 전 세계의 모든 지역에 균일하게 영향을 끼치지도 않았는데, 일부 공동체는 다른 곳들보다 훨씬 더 더디게 농업에 대한 의존을 지향했고, 어떤 곳은 심지어 식량을 얻는 주된 수단으로서 채집에 계속 초점을 맞추고 있었기 때문이다. 확인할 수 있는 고고학 증거를 바탕으로 볼 때, 많은 고대 공동체들의 공통된 특징이 채집과 농업 둘 모두의 특정 요소를 결합한 식량 획득 전략의 활용이었던 것처럼 보인다.

인구 증가와 더불어 아마 농업 사회로의 전환이 미친 가장 주목할 만한 영향은 초기 정착지들을 둘러싼 자연 환경에 미친 영향에서 볼 수 있을 텐데, 인간의 요구를 더 잘 충족하기 위해 상당한 변형을 거쳤기 때문이었다. ■(A) 그러한 경관 변형

활동의 출현이 약 12,000년 전에 시작된 것으로 전해지는 홀로세의 종말과 현세라고 제안되며 인류세로 알려진 것 사이의 경계를 표시하는 역할을 할 수 있다는 의견이 제기된 바 있다. ■(B) 많은 전문가들은 사실 인류세라는 바로 그 개념을 거부했으며, 대신 계속 홀로세를 현세로 여기고 있다. ■(C) 어느 쪽이든 물리적인 환경에 대한 인류의 이 부정적인 영향은 삼림 벌채와 토양 침식을 포함해 다양한 문제를 초래했으며, 이 두 가지는 모두 초기 농업 공동체를 애먹이면서 엄청난 폐해를 야기했다. ■(D)

그럼에도 불구하고, 농업 체제는 지속적으로 향상되고 시행되었으며, 그 직접적인 결과로 인구가 지속적으로 증가했다. 사회들은 점점 더 복잡해졌는데, 정치적으로 뚜렷이 다른 국가들이 형성되기 시작했고, 규모가 큰 도심 지역들이 전 세계 각지에서 우후죽순처럼 생겨났기 때문이었다. 하지만 농업 발전의 또 다른 부정적인 결과는 이 고대 문명들의 내부에 존재했던 사회적 불평등의 악화였으며, 그럼에도 불구하고 이 고대 문명들은 그들의 필수 작물의 생산을 크게 확대하면서 증가하는 인구에게 식량을 지속적으로 분배할 수 있었다.

이렇게 전반적인 식량 가용성이 증가했음에도, 인구 수의 빠른 증가에는 질병의 증가가 동반되었고, 결과적으로 평균 인류 수명의 감소를 초래했다. 이런 질병 및 조기 사망 모두에 의해 야기된 불행이 인류의 인구 증가를 멈추게 하지는 않았지만, 그것이 식량 부족 및 다른 기본 자원의 부족 문제 같이 갑자기 확장된 인구에 대한 대처와 관련된 다양한 수송상의 어려움이 그

랬던 것처럼 그것을 다소 둔화시키는 영향을 미쳤을 가능성이 있다. 하지만, 지속적인 인구 증가에 대한 이 모든 잠재적인 장애물들은 결국 기술 발전 및 문화 혁신을 통해 피하게 되었다.

오늘날, 기술 및 의학의 발전이 과거 그 어느 때보다 더 빠른 속도로 진행되면서, 농업이 미치는 덜 바람직한 영향의 많은 것들에 어느 정도 대응해 왔으며, 이로 인해 우리 지구의 인구가 계속 급속히 증가할 수 있었다. 2024년 초 기준 전 세계 인구는 80억 명이 넘는 수준에 이른 것으로 추정되었다.

지문 어휘

1. Holocene epoch 홀로세(현재까지의 마지막 지질 시대) nomadic 유목의 settled 정착된 focus on ~에 초점을 맞추다 preservable 보존 가능한 significantly 상당히 surge 급증 accompany 동반하다 emergence 출현 socioeconomic 사회 경제적인 return 수확(물)

2. necessarily 반드시 immediate 즉각적인 uniformly 균일하게 move toward ~을 지향하다 reliance 의존 foraging 채집 primary 주된, 주요한 employment 활용

3. transition 전환 undergo 거치다, 겪다 modification 변경 advent 도래, 출현 epoch (지질학의) 세, 시대 Anthropocene 인류세 deforestation 삼림 벌채 soil erosion 토양 침식 plague 괴롭히다

4. sprout up (많은 수로) 생기다 inequality 불평등 distribute 분배하다

5. in turn 결과적으로 lifespan 수명 misery 불행 bring about 야기하다 premature 너무 이른 halt 멈춤, 중단 logistical 수송의 circumvent 피하다, 면하다

6. desirable 바람직한 counteract 대응하다 as of ~ 현재 stand at ~의 수준에 이르다

문장 재구성 문제

1 아래 문장 중 지문에서 음영 표시된 문장의 핵심 정보를 가장 잘 나타낸 것은? 오답 선택지들은 의미를 현저히 바꾸거나 핵심 정보를 생략한다.
(A) 인구 증가가 식량 생산에서 식량 분배로 사회 경제 체제가 지닌 초점의 변화를 야기했다.
(B) 사람들이 농업 공동체에서 멀어지기 시작하면서, 두 가지 새로운 사회 경제 체제가 농업을 보호하는 데 필요했다.
(C) 경작된 작물의 칼로리 양이 증가했음에도 불구하고, 새로운 사회 경제 체제는 식량을 충분한 사람들에게 전달할 수 없었다.
(D) 새로운 사회 경제 체제는 농업을 통해 생산된 식량의 전반적인 칼로리 양을 증가시켰으며, 많은 인구에게 전달하는 데 도움을 주었다.

해설 새로운 사회 경제 체제가 더 높은 칼로리의 수확을 보장해 준 것과 수많은 사람들에게 아주 많은 양의 식량을 분배하는 능력이 개선되었음을 설명하고 있으므로 (D)가 정답이다.

세부 정보 찾기 문제

2 두 번째 단락에 따르면, 다음 중 채집에 대해 사실인 것은?
(A) 식량 획득의 수단으로서 농업을 대체했다.
(B) 고대 경제에 강력한 영향을 미쳤다.
(C) 전 세계에서 소수의 지역에서만 나타났다.
(D) 고대 사람들에 의해 농업과 함께 이용되었다.

어휘 a handful of 소수의

해설 많은 고대 공동체들이 채집과 농업 모두의 특정 요소를 결합한 식량 획득 전략을 활용했다고 언급되어 있으므로 (D)가 정답이다.

어휘의 의미 파악 문제

3 지문의 단어 "delineate"과 의미가 가장 가까운 것은?
(A) 약화시키다
(B) 논의하다
(C) 정의하다
(D) 가로지르다

해설 delineate은 '표시하다'라는 뜻으로, 해당 문장에서 경계를 '표시하여' 두 시기를 구분한다는 맥락으로 쓰였으므로, '정의하다'의 의미를 가진 (C) define이 정답이다.

추론 문제

4 다음 중 네 번째 단락에서 사회적 불평등에 대해 추론할 수 있는 것은?
(A) 농업에 의해 야기된 인구 증가 이전에 존재했다.
(B) 정치 단체의 도입에 의해 감소되었다.
(C) 많은 사람들이 채집에서 농업으로 전환하도록 만들었다.
(D) 일반 사람들이 충분한 영양분을 얻지 못하도록 막았다.

어휘 introduction 도입 political 정치적인 organization 단체, 기관 obtain 얻다 nutrition 영양(분)

해설 농업 발전에 따른 결과로서 인구 증가를 언급하면서 또 다른 부정적인 결과로 고대 문명 사회에 존재했던 사회적 불평등의 악화에 대한 내용을 제시하고 있다. 이는 농업 발전에 따른 인구 증가 이전에 이미 존재했던 불평등이 더 나빠진 것을 의미하므로 (A)가 정답이다.

5 글쓴이는 왜 다섯 번째 단락에서 "평균 인류 수명"을
언급하는가?
(A) 식량에 대한 접근성 증가가 어떻게 사람들에게
유익했는지 보여주기 위해
(B) 인구 증가의 부정적인 결과를 강조하기 위해
(C) 질병의 급격한 감소가 나타났음을 시사하기 위해
(D) 농업이 왜 식량 부족 문제를 막는 데 필요했는지
설명하기 위해

어휘 emphasize 강조하다 sharp 급격한

해설 인구 수의 빠른 증가에 질병의 증가가 동반되면서 결과적으로
평균 수명이 감소했다고 설명하고 있으므로 (B)가 정답이다.

지시 대상 찾기 문제

6 지문의 단어 "it"이 가리키는 것은?
(A) 불행
(B) 조기 사망
(C) 인구 증가
(D) 정지

해설 '불행이 인구 증가를 멈추게 하지는 않았지만'이라는 문장
뒤에서 it이 '그것(인구 증가)을 다소 둔화시켰다'라고 했으므로
(A)가 정답이다.

문장 삽입 문제

7 제시된 문장이 지문에 삽입될 수 있는 곳을 가리키는 네 개의
네모[■]를 보아라.

**하지만 이 생각이 널리 받아들여지지는 않았다는 점에
반드시 유의해야 한다.**

이 문장이 들어갈 가장 적절한 위치는? 해당 네모[■]를
선택하여 이 문장을 지문에 삽입하여라.
(A)　　　(B)　　　(C)　　　(D)

해설 this idea를 통해 앞에 이론 또는 의견이 제시되었음을 알 수
있다. 홀로세와 인류세의 경계에 관련된 의견을 제시한 문장
뒤와 많은 전문가들이 인류세라는 개념을 거부했음을 알리는
문장 사이에 위치해 그러한 의견이 받아들여지지 않았음을
지적하는 흐름이 자연스러우므로 (B)가 정답이다.

지문 요약 문제

8 **지시문**: 지문의 간략한 요약을 위한 도입 문장이 아래에
제시되어 있다. 지문에서 가장 중요한 개념들을 나타내는
선택지 3개를 선택하여 요약을 완성하여라. 어떤 문장들은
지문에 제시되지 않거나 주요 개념이 아니므로 요약에
포함되지 않는다. **이 문제는 2점에 해당한다.**

**농업 사회로의 전환은 인구 증가율을 확대하는 데 있어 큰
역할을 했다.**

(A) 인구의 갑작스러운 증가 후에 많은 고대 문명 사회들이
어쩔 수 없이 채집을 멈추고 농업을 시작했다.
(B) 일부 전문가들은 홀로세가 계속되고 있다고 생각하지만,
다른 이들은 그것이 끝나고 인류세가 시작되었다고
주장한다.
(C) 농업이 즉각적으로 모든 곳에 강한 영향을 미친 것은
아니었는데, 채집이 계속 일부 지역에서 큰 역할을 했기
때문이다.
(D) 농업을 받아들인 공동체들은 그들의 자연 환경을
변화시켰으며, 이는 부정적인 결과를 초래했다.
(E) 기술의 혁신과 발전은 농업 및 인구 증가의 부정적인
영향을 상쇄시키기에 충분하지 않았다.
(F) 증가한 인구가 더 많은 질병과 더 짧은 수명을
야기했으며, 인구 증가를 둔화시키기는 했지만 멈추게
하지는 않았다.

어휘 play a large role 큰 역할을 하다 ongoing 계속되는
assert 주장하다 embrace 받아들이다 natural
surroundings 자연 환경 neutralize 상쇄시키다,
중립화하다

해설 농업이 즉각적인 영향을 미치지 않은 점을 언급한 (C), 농업이
자연 환경을 변화시키고 부정적 영향을 미친 사실을 언급하는
(D), 질병의 증가와 수명의 감소로 인한 인구 증가의 둔화를
언급한 (F)가 정답이다.

관련 지식 **농업 혁명(Agricultural Revolution)**은 신석기
혁명이라고도 불리는데, 기원전 7000년경 농경과 목축이
시작되면서 수렵 채집 사회에서 농업 사회로 전환되는,
말 그대로 혁명적인 사건이었다. 이로써 인류는 자연을
이용하여 스스로 먹을 것을 생산할 수 있게 됨에 따라
식량을 안정적으로 공급할 수 있게 되었다. 정착 생활의

시작과 식량 공급의 안정화는
인구가 증가할 수 있는 여건을
마련해주었고, 이는 이후
도시와 사회 계급이 형성되는
토대가 되었다.

PASSAGE 1   pp.176-179

정답 | **1** (B)   **2** (B)   **3** (A)   **4** (A), (C)   **5** (B)   **6** (D)   **7** (C)   **8** (A), (C), (D)

토양 형성

지구의 표면은 공기, 물, 생물체들과 함께 암석이 풍화되면서 나온 유기물 및 광물 입자들로 대부분 구성된 비교적 얇은 토양층으로 덮여 있으며, 이들은 모두 느리지만 끊임없는 상호 작용을 하고 있다. 흔히 간과되기는 하지만 토양은 지구 생태계의 필수적인 구성 요소인데, 식물이 성장하고 번식하는 데 필요한 영양분을 얻는 곳이 바로 토양이며, 식물은 인간을 포함해 지구의 많은 동물에게 주요 식량원이다.

시간이 지남에 따라 토양이 형성되면서 두 가지 주요 유형, 즉 지표면과 가장 가까운 토양층인 표토와 바로 그것 아래에 위치한 심토가 나타난다. ■(A) 이들은 층위라고 알려진 더 작은 층들로 세분화될 수 있다. ■(B) 지구의 토양 대부분은 세 가지 층위를 포함한다. A층위는 표토 내에 있으며 부엽토와 영양분, 유기물이 풍부해서 바로 이 층에서 최고 수준의 생물학적 활동이 일어나는데, 이곳이 굴을 파는 곤충과 지렁이, 미생물과 함께 서서히 뻗어나가는 나무와 식물 뿌리의 서식 공간이기 때문이다. ■(C) A층위 아래에는 점토가 풍부한 심토층인 B층위가 자리잡고 있다. A층위만큼 비옥하지는 않으며 색이 더 옅고 생물학적 활동이 훨씬 더 적은 공간이지만 가장 많은 습기를 찾을 수 있는 곳이 바로 이곳이다. ■(D) C층위는 그 다음 아래층이며, 자연력에 의해 점차적으로 풍화되면서 A층위와 B층위에서 발견된 토양 대부분의 근원지 역할을 하는 암석층으로 주로 구성되어 있다.

이 풍화 작용 중 일부는 암석 덩어리들이 서로 충돌할 때 나타나는 마모처럼 본질적으로 물리적이다. 다른 물리적 풍화 작용의 형태에 포함되는 것으로 기온 변화와 서리의 형성이 있다. 암석이 토양으로 분해되는 것을 가속화하는 화학적 풍화 작용도 있는데, 이것은 암석 안에 있는 광물들이 물이나 공기, 또는 화학 물질과 반응할 때 일어난다. 마지막으로 생물학적 풍화 작용이 있는데, 이것은 생물체에 의한 암석 분해이다. 예를 들어, 굴을 파는 동물들의 활동으로 물이나 공기가 암석을 뚫고 들어가 점차적으로 부서지게 할 수 있으며, 식물 뿌리 또한 풍화 작용의 원인인데, 암석 표면의 균열을 파고들며 시간이 흐름에 따라 더 멀리 뻗어나가 암석 구조를 분리시킨다.

이 풍화된 암석의 광물들이 토양의 기반을 형성하기 때문에 분해된 암석 유형은 그것이 만들어 내는 토양의 특징에 강한 영향을 미친다. 예를 들어, 화강암에서 형성된 토양은 모래 같은 경향이 있고 특별히 비옥하지는 않은 반면, 풍화된 현무암에 의해 생성된 토양은 형성되는 환경이 충분히 습하다면 흔히 꽤 비옥하고 점토로 가득하다.

토양은 이런 광물들과 더불어 높은 수준의 부패한 유기물을 포함하고 있다. 식물이 죽으면 그 줄기와 잎, 뿌리는 자랐던 토양으로 되돌아가는데, 이 과정은 동물에 의해 식물이 섭취된 후 노폐물의 형태로 배설되는 경우에도 발생한다. 그리고 동일한 동물이 죽으면 그 사체도 분해되어 토양의 한 요소로 변환된다. 동물의 노폐물과 함께 이 동물 및 식물 유해가 토양 속에 살고 있는 박테리아와 지렁이, 균류에 의해 섭취되면, 결국 부엽토나 토탄, 목탄 같은 유기물로 변환되어, 토양의 구성 요소 및 특성을 상당히 변화시키게 된다.

지문 어휘

1. relatively 비교적 organic 유기의 mineral 광물 particle 입자 weathering 풍화 constant 끊임없는 overlook 간과하다 obtain 얻다 nutrient 영양분 reproduce 번식하다

2. topsoil 표토 subsoil 심토 horizon 층위 humus 부엽토 burrow 굴을 파다 earthworm 지렁이 micro-organism 미생물 weather 풍화시키다

3. abrasion 마모 chunk 덩어리 collide 충돌하다 frost 서리 accelerate 가속화하다 breakdown 분해 crumble 부스러지다 crack 균열

4. granite 화강암 basalt 현무암 provided (that) ~하다면 moist 습한, 촉촉한

5. decayed 부패한 excrete 배설하다 remains 유해 fungus 균류 (pl. fungi) peat 토탄(완전히 탄화하지 못한 석탄) charcoal 목탄(나무를 탄화시켜 만든 것) undergo 거치다

문장 재구성 문제

1 아래 문장 중 지문에서 음영 표시된 문장의 핵심 정보를 가장 잘 나타낸 것은? 오답 선택지들은 의미를 현저히 바꾸거나 핵심 정보를 생략한다.
(A) 토양은 번성하는 데 식물을 필요로 함에도 불구하고, 특정 동물의 사체 및 노폐물에 의해 생성될 수 있다.
(B) 식물은 토양 없이는 생존할 수 없고, 사람과 동물은 식물을 먹어야 하기 때문에 토양이 중요하다.
(C) 대부분의 식물 및 동물과는 달리, 인간은 필요한 식량을 공급 받기 위해 식물에 의존한다.
(D) 토양의 가장 덜 필수적인 요소는 그것이 포함하고 있는 영양분이지만, 이를 알고 있는 사람은 거의 없다.

어휘 thrive 번성하다 be aware of ~을 알고 있다

해설 토양이 식물에게 중요한 존재이며 그로 인해 인간과 동물까지 혜택을 얻고 있다는 것이 핵심 내용이므로, (B)가 정답이다.

지시 대상 찾기 문제

2 지문의 단어 "it"이 가리키는 것은?
(A) 시간
(B) 표토
(C) 표면
(D) 심토

해설 심토를 설명하면서 앞서 언급된 표토를 it으로 가리켜 둘 사이의 위치 관계를 나타내고 있으므로, 정답은 (B)이다.

추론 문제

3 다음 중 두 번째 단락이 표토에 대해 암시하는 것은?
(A) 심토보다 더 비옥하다.
(B) 심토보다 덜 흔하다.
(C) 심토보다 덜 빨리 형성된다.
(D) 심토보다 더 많은 점토를 포함하고 있다.

해설 심토층인 B층위가 표토 내에 위치한 A층위만큼 비옥하지 않다고 했으므로, (A)가 정답이다.

세부 정보 찾기 문제

4 두 번째 단락에서 다른 층위와 구별되는 A층위의 특징으로 언급된 것 **두 개를 고르시오. 두 개를 골라야 점수가 인정된다.**
(A) 풍부한 유기물
(B) 가장 많은 수분의 존재
(C) 최고 수준의 생물학적 활동
(D) 토양 대부분의 근원지

어휘 moisture 수분

해설 A층위에는 부엽토와 영양분, 유기물이 풍부해서 최고 수준의 생물학적 활동이 일어난다고 했으므로, (A)와 (C)가 정답이다.

어휘의 의미 파악 문제

5 지문의 단어 "penetrate"과 의미가 가장 가까운 것은?
(A) ~에서 달아나다
(B) ~으로 통과해 들어가다
(C) ~의 영향을 받다
(D) ~을 빙 둘러 가다

해설 penetrate이 '~을 뚫고 들어가다'를 의미하므로, 가장 비슷한 뜻을 가진 (B) pass into가 정답이다.

세부 정보 찾기 문제

6 네 번째 단락에 따르면, 현무암에서 만들어진 일부 토양이 비옥하고 점토로 가득한 이유는?
(A) 화강암층 근처에 있다.
(B) 유기물이 거의 들어 있지 않다.
(C) 지하 깊은 곳에서 찾을 수 있다.
(D) 습한 환경에서 형성된다.

해설 현무암에 의해 생성된 토양은 그 형성 환경이 충분히 습할 경우에 꽤 비옥하고 점토로 가득하다고 했으므로, (D)가 정답이다.

문장 삽입 문제

7 제시된 문장이 지문에 삽입될 수 있는 곳을 가리키는 네 개의 네모[■]를 보아라.

다량의 유기물을 포함하는 그 구성 요소 때문에, 그것은 나머지 층위들보다 색이 더 어둡다.

이 문장이 들어갈 가장 적절한 위치는? 해당 네모[■]를 선택하여 이 문장을 지문에 삽입하여라.
(A)　　　　(B)　　　　(C)　　　　(D)

해설 다량의 유기물을 포함하고 있어 색이 더 어둡다는 말은 풍부한 유기물이 언급된 문장 뒤에 추가되어, 인과관계를 알리는 흐름이 되어야 자연스러우므로, (C)가 정답이다.

지문 요약 문제

8 **지시문**: 지문의 간략한 요약을 위한 도입 문장이 아래에 제시되어 있다. 지문에서 가장 중요한 개념들을 나타내는 선택지 3개를 선택하여 요약을 완성하여라. 어떤 문장들은 지문에 제시되지 않거나 주요 개념이 아니므로 요약에 포함되지 않는다. **이 문제는 2점에 해당한다.**

토양층이 지구의 표면을 덮고 있다.

(A) 자연력에 의해 초래되는 암석의 풍화가 토양의 광물 요소를 형성한다.
(B) 표토는 아주 많은 암석들을 포함하고 있으며, 이들이 서로 충돌할 때 서서히 분해된다.
(C) 지구의 토양은 두 가지 주요 부분인 표토와 심토로 나뉠 수 있으며, 보통 세 가지 층위를 포함한다.

(D) 식물과 동물이 죽은 후, 그 사체는 부패해 토양의 일부를 구성하는 유기물이 된다.

(E) 굴을 파는 곤충과 지렁이, 그리고 미생물은 A층위에서 찾을 수 있다.

(F) 습한 지역에서 발견되는 토양은 표토와 심토 사이에 두꺼운 암석층을 가지고 있을 가능성이 더 크다.

해설 지구의 토양 형성에 관한 지문에서 암석의 풍화에서 비롯된 광물 입자들로 토양층이 구성되어 있다고 설명하는 (A), 표토와 심토, 그리고 층위에 관해 설명하는 (C), 동식물이 죽은 후 그 사체가 토양에 미치는 영향을 언급하는 (D)가 주요 요지이므로, 이들이 정답이다.

관련 지식 **화강암(granite)**은 지각의 광암석 중 하나로 주로 페가산암, 칼리암페가산암 등으로 구성되어 있다. 화강암은 매우 큰 암석 조각을 형성하는 데 사용되며, 자연적으로 발생하는 매우 단단하고 내구성이 높은 성질을 갖고 있는데, 대개 지각에서 심층까지 다양한 환경에서 용암이 냉각되고 결정화되는 과정에서 형성된다.

이러한 화강암은 건축물, 도로 포장재, 조각품 등 다양한 용도로 사용되며, 그 내구성과 아름다움으로 건축 및 조경 디자인에서 널리 인정받고 있다.

PASSAGE 2

pp.180-183

정답 | 1 (A) 2 (C) 3 (B) 4 (D) 5 (D) 6 (A) 7 (B) 8 (A), (C), (E)

종 사이의 상호 작용

생물학자들은 식물 및 동물 세계 모두에 걸쳐 물리적으로 아주 근접해 있는 한 쌍의 종이 매우 특정한 방식으로 상호 작용하도록 진화한 다수의 경우를 확인했다. 일반적으로 말해 이 이종간 관계는 상리 공생이나 기생, 편해 공생 중 하나로 분류될 수 있다.

간단히 말해 상리 공생은 두 종이 모두 상당한 혜택을 얻는 두 종 간의 관계를 일컫는다. 식물과 관련된 상리 공생은 지상 생태계가 건강하면서 제대로 기능하는 상태로 유지되도록 하는 데 있어 핵심적인 역할을 하는데, 그 주된 이유는 모든 육상 식물의 약 80퍼센트가 지표면 아래 뿌리계에 살고 있는 다양한 균류 종과의 상리 공생 관계에 의존하고 있다는 사실 때문이다. 이 특정한 상리 공생 관계는 무기물과 유기물의 교환을 수반한다. 더 구체적으로 말해 균류는 토양에서 뽑아낸 다양한 무기물을 식물에게 제공하는 반면, 식물은 **광합성** 과정을 통해 생성한 당분이나 지방질을 균류와 공유한다. 식물 종이 동물 종과 상리 공생 관계를 확립하는 것도 가능한데, 이것은 특정 동물이 먹는 열매를 맺는 식물의 경우에서 가장 쉽게 볼 수 있는 상황의 유형이다. 이 동물들은 자신들이 먹는 과일이 제공하는 영양분을 얻고, 결과적으로 씨앗을 퍼뜨릴 수 있는 효과적인 방법을 해당 식물에 제공하며, 그 씨앗은 그 동물의 노폐물로 배설된다.

반면에, 기생은 두 종 사이에서 두드러지게 더 일방적인 관계로서, 둘 중 한쪽이 나머지 한쪽을 희생시켜 이득을 얻는다. 기생 식물은 지구상에 존재하는 거의 모든 생물군계에서 발견되는데, 모든 꽃식물의 약 1퍼센트를 구성하는 4천 5백여 종이 해당된다. 이 기생 식물들은 모두 기생근이라고 부르는 특수 기관을 지니고 있다는 독특한 특징을 공유하고 있는데, 이것은 다른 식물의 부드러운 조직을 관통할 수 있어서 두 식물을 함께 고정시켜 기생 식물이 물과 질소, 탄소, 당분을 포함할 수 있는 다양한 자원을 숙주 식물로부터 추출할 수 있게 해 준

다. 기생 식물이 숙주 식물에 미칠 수 있는 부정적인 영향은 광범위하지만, 가장 흔한 결과는 극심하게 **저해된** 성장과 평소보다 더 높은 치사율이다. 일부 기생 식물은 심지어 숙주 식물의 새싹에 의해 공중으로 배출되거나 뿌리에 의해 토양으로 배출되는 특정 화학 물질을 감지함으로써 알맞은 숙주 식물의 위치를 찾을 수 있는 능력까지 발전시켰다.

기생과 거의 유사하게, 편해 공생은 한 쌍의 종 간의 **불균형적** 관계로서, 둘 중 하나가 결국 해를 입거나 죽게 된다. 그 두 관계 사이의 차이점은 편해 공생에서는 해를 입지 않는 종이 그 관계에서 직접적인 혜택을 얻지 못한다는 것이다. ■(A) 식물의 세계에는 두 가지 기본적인 편해 공생 유형이 존재하며, 첫 번째는 경쟁에 뿌리를 두고 있는데, 더 크거나 더 강력한 생물체가 자신의 크기나 힘을 이용해 더 작고 더 약한 경쟁자가 필수 자원을 얻지 못하게 하기 때문이다. ■(B) 어떤 경우에는 다 자란 나무의 뿌리계가 주변 토양의 모든 영양분과 수분을 흡수해 어린 나무에게 아무것도 남기지 않는 능력도 지니고 있을 수 있다. 다 자란 나무는 이 상호 작용의 영향을 받지 않는 반면, 어린 나무는 죽을 가능성이 있다. ■(C) 적대 관계로 알려진 나머지 편해 공생 유형에서는 한쪽 생물체가 적극적으로 특수 화학 물질을 활용해 나머지 한쪽을 죽이거나 손상시킨다. ■(D) 이는 검은호두나무라고 알려진 나무 종과 그 뿌리 영역 내에서 자라는 초본 식물들 사이의 상호 작용에서 볼 수 있는데, 그 뿌리 영역에서 검은호두나무는 초본 식물들에게 치명적인 물질을 토양 속에 분비한다.

지문 어휘

1. in close proximity 아주 근접하여 interspecies 이종간의 mutualistic 상리 공생의 parasitic 기생의 amensalistic 편해 공생의

2. inorganic 무기물의 lipid 지방질 generate 생성하다 furnish A with B A에게 B를 제공하다

3. at the expense of ~을 희생시켜 biome 생물군계
   organ (생물체의) 기관 haustorium 기생근 fasten
   고정시키다 host 숙주 inflict (영향 등을) 가하다 wide-
   ranging 광범위한 mortality rate 치사율, 사망률 shoot
   새싹

4. acquire 얻다 mature 다 자란 sapling 어린 나무
   antagonism 적대, 대립 deploy (효율적으로) 활용하다
   herbaceous plant 초본 식물(줄기 부분에 목재를 형성하지
   않는 식물) secrete 분비하다 fatal 치명적인

수사적 의도 파악 문제

1 글쓴이는 왜 두 번째 단락에서 "광합성"을 언급하는가?
   (A) 상리 공생 관계의 생물체들이 어떻게 혜택을 얻는지
       알려 주기 위해
   (B) 특정 식물이 열매를 맺게 해 줄 수 있는 과정을 설명하기
       위해
   (C) 식물 종이 동물들에 비해 이점이 있음을 시사하기 위해
   (D) 균류의 뿌리계가 하는 필수적인 역할을 설명하기 위해

어휘 have an advantage over ~에 비해 이점이 있다

해설 균류와 상리 공생 관계에 있는 식물은 광합성 과정을 통해
     생성한 당분이나 지방질을 균류와 공유한다고 했으므로, (A)가
     정답이다.

세부 정보 찾기 문제

2 두 번째 단락에 따르면, 다음 중 상리 공생에 대해 사실인
   것은?
   (A) 적은 비율의 식물들이 그것에 의존한다.
   (B) 흔히 식물이 무기질을 제공하고 당분을 가져가는 것과
       관련이 있다.
   (C) 식물은 동물과 상리 공생 관계를 가질 수 있다.
   (D) 오직 한쪽의 참가자만 그 상호 작용의 영향을 받는다.

어휘 proportion 비율 involve 관련되다, 포함하다 participant
     참가자 impact 영향을 미치다

해설 식물 종이 동물 종과 상리 공생 관계를 확립하는 것도
     가능하다고 하면서 특정 동물이 먹는 과일을 맺는 식물의
     경우를 예로 들고 있으므로, (C)가 정답이다.

어휘의 의미 파악 문제

3 지문의 단어 "stunted"와 의미가 가장 가까운 것은?
   (A) 노출된   (B) 저해당한
   (C) 가속화된   (D) 모방된

해설 stunted는 '저해당한'이라는 뜻으로 사용되었으므로, 동일한
     의미를 나타내는 (B) hindered가 정답이다.

세부 정보 찾기 문제

4 세 번째 단락에 따르면, 다음 중 기생 식물에 대해 사실인
   것은?
   (A) 해마다 비율이 적은 꽃식물을 대대적으로 죽인다.
   (B) 대부분의 비기생 식물만큼 빨리 자라지 않는다.
   (C) 숙주 식물을 끌어들이기 위해 많은 자원을 생산한다.
   (D) 거의 전 세계의 모든 생물군계에서 볼 수 있다.

어휘 attract 끌어들이다 virtually 거의

해설 기생 식물은 지구상에 존재하는 거의 모든 생물군계에서
     발견된다고 했으므로, 답은 (D)이다.

어휘의 의미 파악 문제

5 지문의 단어 "asymmetric"과 의미가 가장 가까운 것은?
   (A) 적대적인
   (B) 비정상적인
   (C) 오래 가는
   (D) 균형이 맞지 않는

해설 '불균형적인'의 뜻으로 쓰인 asymmetric과 가장 유사한 뜻을
     가진 (D) uneven이 정답이다.

추론 문제

6 다음 중 네 번째 단락에서 검은호두나무에 대해 추론할 수
   있는 것은?
   (A) 보통 그 기저 부분에서 자라는 식물이 거의 없다.
   (B) 흔히 근처의 다른 나무보다 키가 더 크고 폭이 더 넓다.
   (C) 같은 종의 어린 나무를 세심하게 보호한다.
   (D) 그 뿌리 근처에 많은 다른 종류의 초본 식물이 있을 수
       있다.

어휘 vegetation 식물, 초목 base 기저, 밑바탕

해설 검은호두나무가 자신의 뿌리 영역에서 다른 식물들에게
     치명적인 물질을 토양 속에 분비한다고 했으므로, 그 부분에서
     자라는 식물이 거의 없다는 것을 유추할 수 있다. 그러므로
     (A)가 정답이다.

문장 삽입 문제

7 제시된 문장이 지문에 삽입될 수 있는 곳을 가리키는 네 개의
   네모[■]를 보아라.

   **예를 들어, 어린 나무가 다 자란 다른 종의 나무 옆에서
   자라기 시작할 때, 성숙한 나무는 어린 나무에게서 생존에
   필요한 햇빛을 빼앗는 그림자를 드리울 수 있다.**

   이 문장이 들어갈 가장 적절한 위치는? 해당 네모[■]를
   선택하여 이 문장을 지문에 삽입하여라.
   (A)   (B)   (C)   (D)

어휘 deprive A of B A에게서 B를 빼앗다

해설 주어진 문장은 다 자란 나무가 어린 나무에게서 생존에
필요한 햇빛을 빼앗는 경우를 설명하고 있으므로, 더 크거나
더 강력한 생물체가 더 작고 더 약한 경쟁자에게서 필수
자원을 빼앗는다는 설명 뒤에 예로 제시되는 것이 자연스럽다.
그러므로 (B)가 정답이다.

지문 요약 문제

8 **지시문:** 지문의 간략한 요약을 위한 도입 문장이 아래에
제시되어 있다. 지문에서 가장 중요한 개념들을 나타내는
선택지 3개를 선택하여 요약을 완성하여라. 어떤 문장들은
지문에 제시되지 않거나 주요 개념이 아니므로 요약에
포함되지 않는다. **이 문제는 2점에 해당한다.**

**세 가지 기본적인 유형의 이종간 관계, 즉 상리 공생과 기생,
편해 공생이 있다.**

(A) 상리 공생에서는 두 가지 종 모두 혜택을 얻는 관계에
관여한다.
(B) 편해 공생 관계는 두 종이 모두 해를 입거나 죽게 되는
상호 작용이다.
(C) 기생 식물은 다른 종에게 해를 끼치는 방식으로 또 다른
유형의 식물에게서 이득을 얻는다.
(D) 상리 공생하는 종은 같은 자원을 두고 경쟁하지만, 결국
오직 한쪽만 성공한다.

(E) 편해 공생은 하나의 종이 나머지 종에게 직접적으로
이익을 주지 않으면서 피해를 입는 관계이다.
(F) 기생에서는 벌이 꽃을 수분하는 것처럼, 동물 종이 식물
종에게 혜택을 제공한다.

어휘 ultimately 결국 pollinate 수분하다

해설 두 종 사이에 일어나는 세 가지 공생인 상리 공생, 기생, 그리고
편해 공생과 관련해 두 종 모두 상당한 혜택을 얻는 상리 공생
관계에 대해 설명한 (A), 둘 중 한쪽이 나머지 한쪽을 희생시켜
이득을 얻는 기생에 대해 설명한 (C), 둘 중 하나가 피해를 입는
편해 공생 관계에 대해 설명한 (E)가 정답이다.

관련 지식 **광합성(photosynthesis)**은 식물, 미세조류, 박테리아
등이 햇빛과 이산화탄소, 물을 이용해 포도당과 산소를
생성하는 생물학적 과정이다. 이 과정은 광합성 1단계와
2단계로 구분된다. 광합성 1단계는 빛 에너지와 이산화탄소,
물을 이용하여 ATP 및 NADPH 등의 에너지 매개체를
생성하는 단계이며, 광합성 2단계는 생성된 에너지 매개체를
이용하여 이산화탄소를 포도당으로 변환하는 단계이다.

이는 지구 생태계에서 중요한 역할을
하며, 대기 중의 이산화탄소를
감소시키고 산소를 생성하여 환경을
안정화시킨다.

PASSAGE 3

pp.184-187

정답 | 1 (C) **2** (A) **3** (B) **4** (D) **5** (B) **6** (C) **7** (B) **8** (A), (D), (F)

텔로미어와 텔로머레이즈

인간의 몸은 수조 개의 특수 세포로 구성된 수많은 요소들로
구성되어 있으며, 각 세포는 세포핵이라는 중요한 세포 기관을
가지고 있다. 이 세포핵 안에는 염색체가 있는데, 한 세대에서
다음 세대로 전달되는 유전자 청사진을 보관하고 있는 실 같은
조직으로 된 정교한 집합체이다. 보통 우리의 '유전자'라고 지
칭되는 이 유전 암호는 핵염기 또는 단순히 '염기'라고 밝혀진
네 개의 뚜렷이 다른 생물학적 화합물을 포함하는데, 이들은
복잡하게 쌍을 이루고 연결되어 우리의 DNA를 구성하는 가
늘고 긴 나선형 사슬 같은 구조를 형성한다. 세포 복제 방법
인 체세포 분열 과정에서 이 유전 물질이 복제를 거치면서, 그
것의 반은 원래 세포 안에 남고 나머지 반은 새롭게 형성된 세
포로 옮겨진다. 이 중요한 과정의 정확성과 완전함을 보장하기
위해, 우리 염색체는 결함과 오류 방지에 도움을 주는 보호용
텔로미어(말단소립)를 갖추고 있다.

우리 염색체의 말단 끝에 자리잡고 있는 보호용 텔로미어는 최
대 15,000개까지 반복되는 염기쌍으로 이루어진 DNA 염기
서열을 구성하는 복잡한 구조물이다. 그것들은 의도하지 않은
염색체 DNA의 손실을 막고 염색체의 우연한 융합을 방지함

으로써, 체세포 분열을 세심하게 조정하는 데 중추적 역할을
한다. 그런 일들이 발생하는 것은 파멸적인 일로, 복제된 DNA
내에서 치명적인 결함이 생긴다. 그러므로 텔로미어는 없어서
는 안 되는 수호자로서 등장해, 세포 복제의 정확성을 보장해
준다. 하지만 텔로미어는 조정 과정에서 손상을 입기 쉽다. (텔
로미어가 붙어 있는) 숙주 세포가 각기 분열할 때, 텔로미어는
그 염기쌍의 200개까지 점진적으로 소모하게 된다. 시간이 흐
르면서 이런 누적 손실로 텔로미어의 길이가 계속해서 짧아져
'임계 길이,' 즉 복제가 중단되는 신호를 보내며 결국 세포가 사
멸하게 되는 한계점에 도달하게 된다. 그러나 이런 침식(길이
가 줄어드는 것)은 RNA(리보 핵산)와 단백질로 구성된 놀라운
효소인 텔로머레이즈(말단소립 복제효소)의 형태로 대응하는
힘과 맞닥뜨린다. 텔로미어에 염기쌍 서열을 붙여주는 특별한
능력을 가진 텔로머레이즈는 보호막의 역할을 하면서, 이 구조
물의 길이를 연장시키고, 그렇게 함으로써 임박한 세포사가 시
작되는 것을 지연해 준다.

광범위하게 존재하는 텔로미어에서 벗어난 텔로머레이즈의 활
동 영역은 인간의 몸의 특정 범위 내로 현저히 제한되어 있다.
그 움직임은 정자나 난자로 발달할 수 있는 특별한 잠재성을

지닌 생식 세포 안에서뿐만 아니라, 태아 조직과 암 종양 안에서도 주로 관찰된다. 이 특수한 영역들 외에는 그것이 몸의 다른 세포 내에서 나타나는 경우가 거의 없는데, 존재하는 경우에는 최소한의 활동만 한다. 이런 시나리오로 인해 텔로미어가 걷잡을 수 없이 줄어들어, 결과적으로 세포의 노화와 궁극적 사멸, 즉 노쇠라고 일컫는 현상을 촉진하게 된다. 이와는 아주 대조적으로, 더욱 활동적인 텔로머레이즈가 있는 세포는 추가와 유실이라는 반대되는 힘들 사이에 어느 정도 균형이 맞춰진다. 이 균형은 텔로미어의 가차 없는 소모를 효과적으로 중단시키며, 그로 인해 그 길이를 보존해 준다. 이론적으로 그런 세포는 무한히 성장과 분열을 영속화할 수 있는 능력이 있어서, '불멸 세포'라는 구어적 명칭을 얻는다. 이 대조적인 행동이 세포의 장수에 있어 텔로머레이즈의 중추적인 역할을 분명히 보여 주며, 그것이 없을 때 나타나는 거침 없는 노쇠의 진전과 그것의 존재 안에 압축되어 있는 잠재적인 영속성 사이의 아주 흥미로운 병렬을 제시해 준다.

이런 관점에서 불멸 세포라는 개념은 암이라는 치명적인 질병을 잠재적으로 없애기 위해 암 세포의 양태를 조사하는 과학자들뿐만 아니라, 인간 노화의 원인과 결과를 연구하는 과학자들의 마음도 사로잡고 있다. ■(A) 인간의 암 세포 안에 있는 텔로머레이즈는 정상 체세포 안에서 보이는 것보다 20배까지 더 높은 활동량을 보여 준다. ■(B) 텔로머레이즈의 움직임을 차단할 방법을 찾으면 암을 치료하고 어쩌면 고칠 수 있는 실현 가능성을 상당히 향상시킬 수 있을 것이다. ■(C) 더욱이 텔로머레이즈를 활성화시키거나 차단하는 스위치를 발견하게 되면, 먼 미래에 인간의 수명을 무한히 연장할 수도 있을 것이라는 낙관적인 기대감도 존재한다. ■(D) 이런 전망은 신화 속 젊음의 샘의 과학적 등가물에 비유되어, 그 분야의 획기적 발전에 대한 희망을 제공해 주고 있다.

지문 어휘

1. comprise 구성되다 organelle 세포 기관 nucleus 세포핵 (pl. nuclei) chromosome 염색체 assembly 집합(체) house 보관하다 genetic 유전의 gene 유전자 nucleobase 핵염기 base 염기 spiraled 나선형의 mitosis 체세포 분열 cellular 세포의 replication 복제 integrity 완전한 상태 be endowed with ~을 갖추고 있다 glitch 결함

2. intricate 복잡한 DNA sequence DNA 염기서열 pivotal 중심(축)이 되는 meticulous 세심한 inadvertent 의도하지 않은 avert 방지하다 fusion 융합 indispensable 없어서는 안 될 be prone to ~하기 쉽다 attrition 소모 cumulative 누적되는 threshold 한계점 cessation 중단 inevitably 필연적으로 enzyme 효소 append 부착하다 stave off 지연하다, 비키다 imminent 임박한 onset 시작

3. diverge from ~에서 벗어나다 niche 범위 fetal 태아의 cancerous tumor 암 종양 germ cell 생식 세포 sperm 정자 egg 난자 manifest 나타나다 unbridled 걷잡을 수 없는 transpire 발생하다 senescence 노쇠 halt 중단시키다 relentless 가차 없는 perpetuate 영속화하다 designation 명칭 immortal 불멸의 underscore 분명히 보여 주다 longevity 장수, 수명 juxtaposition 병렬 inexorable 거침 없는 encapsulate 압축하다

4. deactivate 정지시키다 feasibility 실현 가능성 cure 치유하다, 고치다 optimistic 낙관적인 prospect 전망 groundbreaking 획기적인

문장 재구성 문제

1 아래 문장 중 지문에서 음영 표시된 문장의 핵심 정보를 가장 잘 나타낸 것은? 오답 선택지들은 의미를 현저히 바꾸거나 핵심 정보를 생략한다.
(A) 유전자라고 부르는 우리의 유전 암호는 인간의 전체 DNA를 형성하는 핵염기를 포함하고 있다고 알려져 있다.
(B) 유전자는 핵염기라고 하는 생물학적 청사진의 네 가지 부분으로 나뉠 수 있고, 결국 DNA 구조를 구축한다.
(C) 우리의 유전자는 쌍을 이루고 연결되어 우리 DNA의 나선형 구조를 만드는 네 개의 뚜렷이 다른 핵염기로 구성되어 있다.
(D) 인간의 유전 암호는 긴 나선형 모양으로 변환되는 네 가지 요소로 구성된 것으로 보인다.

해설 네 가지 뚜렷이 다른 생물학적 화합물인 핵염기, 그것들이 쌍을 이루고 결합하는 양상, 그리고 나선형 DNA 구조 같은 핵심 내용이 모두 포함된 (C)가 정답이다.

세부 정보 찾기 문제

2 첫 번째 단락에 따르면, 체세포 분열 과정에서 텔로미어의 역할은 무엇인가?
(A) 결함과 오류를 막는다.
(B) 다수의 세포 형태를 만드는 데 도움을 준다.
(C) 유전자 내에 남아 있는 DNA를 보호한다.
(D) 염색체가 가능한 한 빠르게 자라게 해 준다.

해설 우리 염색체가 결함 및 오류를 방지하는 데 도움을 주는 보호용 텔로미어를 갖고 있다고 했으므로, (A)가 정답이다.

어휘의 의미 파악 문제

3 지문의 단어 "constitute"과 의미가 가장 가까운 것은?
(A) ~에 의존하다
(B) ~을 구성하다
(C) ~와 분리되다
(D) ~와 다르다

해설 constitute은 '~을 구성하다'라는 뜻이므로, 같은 의미를 나타내는 (B) make up이 정답이다.

추론 문제

4 다음 중 두 번째 단락이 세포사에 대해 암시하는 것은?
(A) 세포들은 죽은 후에 재생될 수 있다.
(B) 중요한 위치에 있는 숙주 세포에서는 절대 일어나지 않는다.
(C) 텔로머레이스가 세포의 사멸을 가속화한다.
(D) 점진적인 텔로미어의 감소에 의해 초래될 수 있다.

어휘 revive 재생하다

해설 텔로미어는 손상을 입기 쉬워서 점진적인 소모를 겪다가 세포사에 이르게 된다고 했으므로, (D)가 정답이다.

지시 대상 찾기 문제

5 지문의 단어 "it"이 가리키는 것은?
(A) 인간의 몸
(B) 텔로머레이스
(C) 태아 조직
(D) 정자

해설 앞선 문장의 주어로 쓰인 Its와 마찬가지로 첫 번째 문장에서 언급하는 텔로머레이스의 활동과 관련해 설명하는 문장이므로, (B)가 정답이다.

수사적 의도 파악 문제

6 글쓴이는 왜 세 번째 단락에서 "불멸 세포"를 언급하는가?
(A) 소모와 유실의 균형을 잡는 것이 얼마나 어려운지 설명하기 위해
(B) 세포 성장과 세포 사멸을 비교하기 위해
(C) 텔로머레이스의 기능을 설명하기 위해
(D) 사람들이 암에서 살아남을 수 있는 방법을 소개하기 위해

해설 텔로머레이스의 역할 한 가지를 설명하면서 불멸 세포를 언급한 다음, 이것이 텔로머레이스의 중추적인 역할을 분명히 보여 주는 것이라고 강조하고 있으므로, (C)가 정답이다.

문장 삽입 문제

7 제시된 문장이 지문에 삽입될 수 있는 곳을 가리키는 네 개의 네모[■]를 보아라.

이 고조된 텔로머레이스의 활동량이 암의 회복력에 상당히 기여하면서, 알려진 모든 의학적 치료 및 잠재적 치유법에 도전하고 있으며, 그 중 어느 것도 지금까지 신뢰할 수 있을 정도로 효과적인 것으로 판명되지 않았다.

이 문장이 들어갈 가장 적절한 위치는? 해당 네모[■]를 선택하여 이 문장을 지문에 삽입하여라.
(A)   (B)   (C)   (D)

어휘 heightened 고조된 resilience 회복력

해설 This heightened telomerase activity로 시작하는 문장이므로, 최대 20배 더 높은 활동량을 보여 준다고 언급하는 문장 뒤에 놓여 그런 활동량과 관련해 설명하는 흐름이 되어야 자연스럽다. 그러므로 (B)가 정답이다.

지문 요약 문제

8 **지시문**: 지문의 간략한 요약을 위한 도입 문장이 아래에 제시되어 있다. 지문에서 가장 중요한 개념들을 나타내는 선택지 3개를 선택하여 요약을 완성하여라. 어떤 문장들은 지문에 제시되지 않거나 주요 개념이 아니므로 요약에 포함되지 않는다. **이 문제는 2점에 해당한다.**

텔로미어와 텔로머레이스는 세포 복제에 있어 중요한 역할을 한다.

(A) 텔로미어는 우리의 염색체를 보호해 주지만 세포가 분열할 때마다 더 짧아지며, 이것은 결국 세포사로 이어진다.
(B) 어떤 활동적인 텔로머레이스도 없는 세포는 계속 무한히 성장하고 분열할 것이며, 이것은 어떤 면에서 그 세포를 '불멸의' 상태로 만든다.
(C) 세포는 체세포 분열이 너무 빠르게 일어나는 것을 막기 위해 텔로미어에 의존하는데, 이것은 암 종양의 형성으로 이어질 수 있다.
(D) 텔로미어가 너무 짧아지는 것을 막아 주는 효소인 텔로머레이스는 대부분 태아 조직과 암 종양, 그리고 생식 세포에서 발견된다.
(E) 텔로미어는 약 200개의 염기쌍으로 시작하지만, 텔로머레이스는 세포가 죽을 때까지 계속 염기쌍을 추가한다.
(F) 텔로머레이스는 일반 세포 안에서보다 암 세포 안에서 더 활동적이기 때문에, 그것을 차단하는 방법을 찾으면 암 치료에 도움이 될 수 있을 것이다.

해설 텔로미어와 텔로머레이스에 대해서 우리 몸 안 어디에서 어떤 역할을 하는지 설명한 (A)와 (D), 암 치료와 어떤 연관성을 가지고 있는지 설명한 (F)가 정답이다.

관련 지식 **인간의 염색체(chromosome)**는 세포핵 안에 있는 유전 물질을 담당하는 구조물이다. 인간 세포는 일반적으로 46개의 염색체를 가지고 있으며, 이는 23쌍으로 구성되어 있다. 이 중 한 쌍은 성에 상관없이 동일한 염색체를 포함하고 있다. 이 쌍 중 한 개는 아버지로부터, 다른 한 개는 어머니로부터 유전된다. 인간의 염색체는 성 전달과 질병 발생에도 중요한 영향을 미친다. 염색체 이상은 유전적 질환의 원인이 될 수 있으며, 염색체 구조의 변화는 다양한 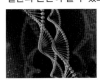 질병의 발생과 관련이 있을 수 있다. 유전학적 연구는 염색체의 구조와 기능을 이해하고, 질병의 예방 및 치료에 기여하는 중요한 분야이다.

정답 | **1** (B)   **2** (C)   **3** (D)   **4** (B)   **5** (A)   **6** (D)   **7** (D)   **8** (B), (C), (F)

우주의 나이

과거에는 과학자들이 우주의 나이를 구체적으로 파악하지 못했는데, 필요한 측정 작업을 할 수 있는 수단도, 정확한 이론을 만들어 낼 수 있는 지식도 없었기 때문이다. 실제로 20세기 초까지 내내, 전 세계에서 가장 높이 평가 받는 과학자들 대부분은 우주가 영원하며 그들이 '정상(定常) 상태'라고 일컬었던 것 안에 존재한다고 믿었는데, 이는 우주가 어떤 대규모의 변화도 겪지 않았고 겪지 않을 것이라는 의미였다. 따라서 우주에 나이를 부여하려는 어떤 시도도 그들의 눈에는 헛수고로 보였다.

우주의 나이가 실제로 수백만 또는 심지어 수십억 년이나 되었다는 생각을 수용한 것은 18세기에 처음 지배적으로 나타나기 시작했지만, 우주가 사실상 유한하다고 제안하는 최초의 공식적인 과학 이론들이 만들어진 것은 19세기 중반이 되어서였다. 이 이론들은 열역학 연구 및 엔트로피 개념을 바탕으로 했는데, 한 우주 안에서는 모든 것이 같은 온도이고, 그래서 항성이나 생명의 존재 가능성조차 배제한다는 것을 시사함으로써 무한한 우주라는 개념을 반박했다. 1915년에 앨버트 아인슈타인이 그의 획기적인 일반 상대성 이론을 출간했을 때, 우주는 무한하며 정상(定常) 상태로 존재한다는 지배적인 가설 하에 그렇게 했고, 나중에 그 이론을 이용해 우주에 대한 고정적 우주론 모델을 구축했다. 이 근본적인 오류 때문에, 그는 중력의 영향을 상쇄하고 정상 상태로 추정되는 우주를 설명할 자신의 방정식에 척력을 추가해야 한다는 것을 알게 되었다.

하지만 고정적 우주라는 이 관점에 대해 곧 미국의 천문학자였던 에드윈 허블이 이의를 제기했는데, 그는 우리 은하계의 먼지와 가스 구름이라고 생각되었던 것을 관측하는 과정에서, 자신이 실제로는 우리 은하계 밖에 있는 은하계들을 바라보고 있었다는 것을 깨달았다. ■(A) 이 은하계들은 크기가 어마어마하고 대단히 멀리 떨어져 있는 것으로 확인되었는데, 추가 분석을 통해 그것들이 우리 은하계에서 꾸준히 멀어지고 있으며, 이 은하계들이 더 멀리 떨어져 있을수록 더 빨리 움직이고 있는 것으로 추측됐고, 이 모두는 우주가 전혀 고정되어 있지 않으며 실제로 팽창하고 있다는 것을 보여 주는 강력한 증거였다. ■(B) 우주의 나이에 대해 최초로 이루어진 과학적 추정은 우주의 모든 물질이 언제 처음으로 단 하나의 점에서 바깥쪽으로 멀리 움직이기 시작했는지를 밝혀 내려 했던 계산에서 비롯되었다. ■(C) 하지만 허블이 관측했던 은하계들의 거리에 대한 그의 대략적인 계산이 지나치게 보수적이었다는 사실 때문에, 그가 우주의 나이로 제시한 수치는 너무 많이 낮았다. ■(D)

현재 오늘날의 천문학자들이 우주의 나이에 대한 측정치를 규명하려 할 때 이용하는 가장 정확한 방법은 초기 상태의 우주에 대한 직접적인 관측을 수반하며, 이는 138억 년이라는 대략적인 나이를 산출해 낸 방식이다. 그 일부가 마이크로파 배경 복사에 대한 관찰을 포함했던 수많은 연구에서 일치하는 점을 바탕으로, 이 측정치에 대한 불확실성의 범위가 앞뒤로 겨우 2천만 년으로 줄었는데, 이것은 그 수치가 인상적일 정도로 정확한 것으로 여겨질 수 있다는 뜻이다. 빅뱅 이후의 우주 냉각기가 추정될 수 있는 방법은 바로 우주에서 배경 복사를 측정하는 것인데, 이것이 우주가 팽창하는 속도에 대한 측정치와 합쳐지면 우주의 대략적인 나이를 제공할 수 있다. 이 추정된 나이의 좁은 범위는 (지구의 관점에서 본) 우주에서 관측 가능한 가장 오래된 항성에 대한 것과 일치하므로, 그것의 정확성에 대한 신뢰감을 한층 더 높여 준다.

지문 어휘

1. concrete 구체적인 make measurements 측정하다 eternal 영원한 steady state 정상(定常) 상태(우주가 팽창과 더불어 물질을 형성하여 밀도 등은 시간이 지나도 변함없는 상태) large-scale 대규모의 futility 헛됨, 무가치

2. finite 유한한 thermodynamics 열역학 entropy 엔트로피(물질의 열역학적 상태를 나타내는 물리량 중 하나) contradict 부정하다, 반박하다 preclude 배제하다 theory of general relativity 일반 상대성 이론 assumption 추정 cosmological 우주론의 repulsive force 척력(두 물체가 서로 밀어내는 힘) equation 방정식 counterbalance 상쇄하다 gravity 중력 account for ~을 설명하다 presume 추정하다

3. Milky Way 은하계, 은하(수) compelling 강력한, 설득력 있는 estimate 추정(치); 추정하다 conservative 보수적인 come up with ~을 제시하다

4. yield 산출하다 concordance 일치 microwave background radiation 마이크로파 배경 복사 uncertainty 불확실성 post-Big Bang 빅뱅 이후의 correspond with ~와 일치하다 perspective 관점 boost 높이다, 촉진하다 accuracy 정확성

세부 정보 찾기 문제

1 두 번째 단락에 따르면, 아인슈타인이 자신의 방정식에 척력을 추가해야 했던 이유는?

(A) 우리 은하계 밖에서 은하계들이 발견되었기 때문에

(B) 그것이 근본적으로 잘못된 생각에 근거한 것이었기 때문에

(C) 아인슈타인은 더 이상 우주가 무한하다고 믿지 않았기 때문에

(D) 중력의 개념이 아직 이해되지 않았기 때문에

어휘 misconception 잘못된 생각

해설 아인슈타인이 고정적인 우주론 모델을 구축했지만 그 근본적인 오류 때문에 방정식에 척력을 추가했다고 했으므로, (B)가 정답이다.

추론 문제

2 다음 중 세 번째 단락에서 에드윈 허블에 대해 추론할 수 있는 것은?

(A) 주로 우리 은하계를 연구하는 데 초점을 맞췄다.

(B) 우주가 고정적이고 불변하다는 것을 발견했다.

(C) 우리 은하계 외부의 은하계들에 대한 획기적인 관측을 해냈다.

(D) 앨버트 아인슈타인의 일반 상대성 이론이 틀렸음을 입증했다.

해설 허블이 우리 은하계 밖에 있는 은하계들을 관찰하면서 우주가 전혀 고정되어 있지 않으며 실제로 팽창하고 있다는 것을 보여주는 강력한 증거를 추정해 냈다는 설명에서 그가 우리 은하계 외부에 있는 은하계들을 획기적으로 관측해 냈다는 것을 유추할 수 있다. 그러므로 (C)가 정답이다.

어휘의 의미 파악 문제

3 지문의 단어 "monitoring"과 의미가 가장 가까운 것은?

(A) 거부

(B) 배열

(C) 정확

(D) 관측

해설 monitoring은 '관찰'의 의미로 사용되었으므로, 유사한 뜻을 가진 (D) tracking이 정답이다.

문장 재구성 문제

4 아래 문장 중 지문에서 음영 표시된 문장의 핵심 정보를 가장 잘 나타낸 것은? 오답 선택지들은 의미를 현저히 바꾸거나 핵심 정보를 생략한다.

(A) 과학자들이 빅뱅이 발생한 이후에 우주가 냉각되어 그렇게 빠르게 팽창하기 시작한 이유를 이해할 수 있는 방법은 오직 우주의 대략적인 나이를 알아내는 것이다.

(B) 우주의 나이는 우주에서 복사를 측정한 다음 빅뱅 이후에 우주가 냉각되는 데 얼마나 오래 걸렸는지와 얼마나 빨리 팽창하고 있는지 확인함으로써 추정할 수 있다.

(C) 우주가 처음 팽창하기 시작했을 때 빅뱅에 의해 발생된 복사를 측정했음에도 불구하고, 과학자들은 우주의 나이를 정확히 추정할 수 없었다.

(D) 빅뱅을 연구함으로써 우주가 결국 얼마나 뜨거워질지, 얼마나 빨리 팽창하고 있는지, 그리고 나이가 어떻게 되는지를 포함한 많은 것을 알 수 있다.

어휘 accurately 정확히

해설 우주에서 배경 복사를 측정해 빅뱅 이후의 냉각기를 추정할 수 있고, 우주 팽창 속도에 대한 측정치와 함께 우주의 대략적인 나이를 파악할 수 있다는 요지를 모두 포함하고 있는 (B)가 정답이다.

지시 대상 찾기 문제

5 지문의 단어 "its"가 가리키는 것은?

(A) 이 추정된 나이

(B) 관측 가능한 가장 오래된 항성

(C) 지구

(D) 우주

해설 its accuracy는 앞선 문장에서 언급한 측정 방식에 따른 우주 나이의 정확성을 의미하므로, (A)가 정답이다.

수사적 의도 파악 문제

6 네 번째 단락은 세 번째 단락과 어떻게 관련되어 있는가?

(A) 세 번째 단락에 제시된 부정확한 정보의 근원을 설명한다.

(B) 세 번째 단락에 제시된 이론의 과학적 불가능성을 보여준다.

(C) 세 번째 단락에 제시된 계산의 필수적 세부 사항들을 제공한다.

(D) 세 번째 단락에 제시된 발견의 현대적인 적용을 설명한다.

어휘 application 적용

해설 네 번째 단락은 세 번째 단락에 제시된 측정 방법을 현대의 과학자들이 이용한 사실을 설명하는 내용이므로, (D)가 정답이다.

문장 삽입 문제

7 제시된 문장이 지문에 삽입될 수 있는 곳을 가리키는 네 개의 네모[■]를 보아라.

그럼에도 불구하고, 오늘날의 더 정확한 추정치에 대한 토대는 현재 허블의 법칙이라고 알려져 있는 그의 관측에서 비롯된 공식에 의해 마련되었다.

이 문장이 들어갈 가장 적절한 위치는? 해당 네모[■]를 선택하여 이 문장을 지문에 삽입하여라.

(A)　　　(B)　　　(C)　　　(D)

해설 우주의 나이에 대한 허블의 계산이 아주 부정확했음을 알리는
문장 뒤에 추가되어, 그럼에도 불구하고 그가 오늘날 우주의
나이를 추정하는 데 있어 기여한 바를 언급하는 흐름이 되어야
자연스러우므로, (D)가 정답이다.

지문 요약 문제

8 **지시문**: 지문의 간략한 요약을 위한 도입 문장이 아래에
제시되어 있다. 지문에서 가장 중요한 개념들을 나타내는
선택지 3개를 선택하여 요약을 완성하여라. 어떤 문장들은
지문에 제시되지 않거나 주요 개념이 아니므로 요약에
포함되지 않는다. **이 문제는 2점에 해당한다.**

**과학자들이 우주의 나이를 추정할 수 있었던 것은 최근에
이르러서였다.**

(A) 앨버트 아인슈타인은 두 가지 위대한 발전을 이뤘는데,
그것은 상대성 이론과 우주에 대한 우주론 모델이다.
(B) 에드윈 허블의 관측은 우주가 역동적이며 팽창하고
있다는 사실에 대한 이해로 이어졌다.
(C) 과거에 과학자들은 우주가 무한하고 변화 없이 정상
상태로 존재한다고 믿었다.
(D) 우리 은하계 너머에 있는 먼 우주들에 대한 발견으로
과학자들이 빅뱅 이론에 의문을 제기하게 되었다.

(E) 연구에 따르면 우주에 있는 물체들이 서로 더 멀리
떨어져 있을수록, 더 빨리 반대 방향으로 움직이는
것으로 나타났다.
(F) 복사를 측정함으로써, 과학자들은 우주가 138억 년이 된
것으로 추정했다.

해설 우주의 나이 측정과 관련된 과학적 이론 및 발견에 대한
사실들, 즉 에드윈 허블의 관측으로 알게 된 사실을 설명한
(B), 과거 과학자들이 우주에 대해 가지고 있던 잘못된 통념을
설명한 (C), 현재의 측정 방식 및 그에 따라 얻은 결과를
설명하는 (F)가 정답이다.

관련 지식 **마이크로파 배경 복사(microwave background
radiation)**는 우주 전체를 덮고 있는 매우 낮은 온도의
전파이다. 이것은 우주의 초기 시점에서 생성되었으며,
빅뱅 이론에 따르면 우주가 생성된 직후의 열 역학적 평형
상태에서 나왔다. 마이크로파 배경 복사는 특히 빅뱅 이론의
예측을 확인하는 데 사용되고, 우주의 구조와 진화에 대한
중요한 정보를 제공한다. 또한,
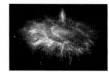
마이크로파 배경 복사의 미묘한
변화를 측정함으로써 우주의
구조와 확장에 대해 더 깊이
이해할 수 있다.

PASSAGE 5
pp.192-195

정답 | **1** (D)　**2** (D)　**3** (A)　**4** (C)　**5** (A)　**6** (B)　**7** (B)　**8** (C), (D), (F)

식물의 생식

식물과 동물이 자손을 만드는 것은 바로 생식 행위를 통해서
이며, 그로 인해 그들의 유전자를 새로운 세대에 전하고 각각
의 종의 연속성을 보장한다. 그러나 생식이라는 측면에 있어,
모든 동식물상 사이에 주목할 만한 차이점이 존재한다. 여우가
어울리는 짝을 찾아 숲을 자유롭게 배회하는 반면, 식물은 대
개 움직이지 못하는 상태로 번식하려면 더 큰 난관을 극복
해야 한다. 식물의 번식은 수많은 형태를 띠고 있을 수 있지만,
각 형태는 유성생식이나 무성생식 중 하나로 분류될 수 있다.

■ (A) 유성생식은 두 가지 다른 근원에서 나오는 생식 세포의
결합을 수반한다. ■ (B) 꽃을 피우는 식물의 경우, 바로 그 식물
안에 생식 기관이 들어 있다. ■ (C) 수술이라고 하는 줄기 꼭대
기의 작은 덮개인 꽃밥은 꽃가루 알갱이를 만들어 내는데, 각
기 한 세트의 남성 염색체를 가지고 있다. ■ (D) 생식을 시작하
기 위해서는 이 알갱이들이 반드시 암술의 끈적한 꼭대기 부
분인 암술머리에 부착되어야 하며, 이 부분이 바로 남성 및 여
성 생식 세포가 합쳐지는 곳이다. 이 과정은 수분이라고 알려
져 있다. 식물은 꽃밥과 암술머리가 같은 꽃 내부나 동일한 식

물의 다른 꽃들 내부에 위치해 있는 경우 발생하는 자가 수분
을 하거나, 한 식물의 꽃밥에 있는 꽃가루를 다른 식물의 암술
머리에 옮겨 타가 수분을 할 수 있다.

타가 수분은 여러 다른 방식으로 이뤄질 수 있다. 꽃을 피우는
일부 식물은 다른 생물체, 일반적으로 벌이나 나비 같은 곤충
에 의존해 타가 수분을 하며, 꽃의 색과 형태, 향기를 통해 대
기하고 있는 달콤한 꿀 저장고로 그 곤충들을 유혹한다. 곤충
들이 (꿀을) 먹는 동안 그 몸이 살포된 수술의 꽃가루를 덮어
쓰고, 그들이 방문하는 다음 꽃으로 그것을 실어 나르게 된다.
다른 꽃들은 바람에 의해 수분되는데, 이 식물들은 꽃잎이 없
는 꽃들과 그 꽃들이 만들어 내는 많은 양의 꽃가루로 흔히 확
인할 수 있고, 그 두 가지 모두 생식 과정을 더 신속하게 하는
역할을 한다. 그것이 어떻게 이뤄지든 성공적인 수분은 난세포
의 수정으로 끝이 나며, 이는 결국 새로운 세대의 식물로 성장
할 씨앗의 발생을 촉발한다.

반면에 무성생식은 외부의 힘으로부터 얻는 도움이 전혀 필요
없는 아주 다른 과정이다. 새로운 생명이 생식 세포의 결합 없

이 만들어지며, 이런 이유로 그 과정 중에 돌연변이가 나타나지 않는다고 가정하면, 단일 모체 식물의 유전적 복제물인 복제 자손이라는 결과를 낳는다. 무성생식은 두 가지 주요 형태로 구성되는데, 그 첫 번째는 영양생식이며, 두 번째는 무수정생식이다. 영양생식에서는 발아의 경우에서처럼 모체 식물의 일부분이 자손을 만들어 내며, 해당 식물체의 단 한 곳에 집중된 반복적인 세포 분열이 싹을 형성해 결국 분리되어 모체의 복제 식물로 성장한다. 무성영양생식의 또 다른 형태는 곰팡이류와 지의류에서 가장 흔히 나타나는 분절증식이다. 이는 성숙한 상태에 도달하자마자 모체 식물이 분열함으로써 유전적 복제물을 만들어 내는 과정을 수반한다.

식물 세계에서 나타나는 나머지 주요 무성생식 형태인 무수정생식은 켄터키 블루 그래스와 민들레 같은 흔한 종에서 볼 수 있다. 유성생식과 마찬가지로 씨앗의 성장 및 궁극적인 확산을 수반하지만, 그 씨앗이 수정된 배아에서 비롯되지 않으며, 다른 모든 무성생식 형태에서처럼 모체 식물의 복제물로 성장한다. 이러한 생식 유형은 일부 꽃 식물과 양치류에서는 흔하지만, 씨앗을 생산하는 다른 유형의 식물에서는 좀처럼 나타나지 않는다.

지문 어휘

1. offspring 자손 continuation 연속(성) respective 각각의 flora and fauna (모든) 동식물상 roam 배회하다 immobile 움직이지 못하는, 부동의 take on (특징 등을) 띠다 sexual reproduction 유성생식 asexual reproduction 무성생식

2. entail 수반하다 gamete 생식 세포 organ 기관 anther 꽃밥 stalk 줄기 stamen 수술 grain 알갱이 pollen 꽃가루 initiate 시작하다 pistil 암술 pollination 수분 self-pollinate 자가 수분하다 cross-pollinate 타가 수분하다

3. lure 유혹하다 nectar 꿀 dusting (가루) 살포 petalless 꽃잎이 없는 fertilization 수정 egg cell 난세포

4. clonal 복제의 duplicate 복제(물) mutation 돌연변이 comprise ~으로 구성되다 apomixis 무수정생식 budding 발아, 싹틈 mold 곰팡이류 lichen 지의류 fragmentation 분절증식 maturation 성숙

5. fertilized 수정된 embryo 배아 mature 성숙하다 clone 복제 (생물) fern 양치류

수사적 의도 파악 문제

1 글쓴이는 왜 첫 번째 단락에서 "여우"를 언급하는가?
(A) 식물이 직면한 심각한 위험의 예를 제시하기 위해
(B) 동물 무수정생식의 희귀성을 강조하기 위해
(C) 일부 식물이 왜 두 가지 유형의 생식을 필요로 하는지 설명하기 위해
(D) 식물의 생식과 동물의 생식을 대조하기 위해

어휘 rarity 희귀성

해설 여우를 예로 들어 동물의 생식과 식물의 생식 사이의 차이를 설명하고 있으므로, (D)가 정답이다.

어휘의 의미 파악 문제

2 지문의 단어 "proliferate"과 의미가 가장 가까운 것은?
(A) 지배하다
(B) 이주하다
(C) 경화시키다
(D) 증식하다

해설 '번식하다'를 뜻하는 proliferate과 의미가 가장 비슷한 (D) multiply가 정답이다.

추론 문제

3 다음 중 세 번째 단락에서 수술에 대해 추론할 수 있는 것은?
(A) 식물의 꿀 공급처 가까이에 있다.
(B) 꽃의 꽃잎과 동일한 색상이다.
(C) 타가 수분하는 식물에게는 필요하지 않다.
(D) 꽃밥이 있는 경우 꽃가루를 만들어 낼 수 없다.

해설 곤충들이 꿀을 먹는 동안 수술의 꽃가루를 덮어 쓴다는 말에서, 수술이 꿀 공급처 가까이에 있음을 유추할 수 있다. 그러므로 (A)가 정답이다.

어휘의 의미 파악 문제

4 지문의 단어 "expedite"과 의미가 가장 가까운 것은?
(A) 흩뿌리다
(B) 변형하다
(C) 가속화하다
(D) 조정하다

해설 '더 신속하게 하다'라는 의미를 가진 expedite과 가장 유사한 뜻을 나타내는 것은 (C) accelerate이다.

세부 정보 찾기 문제

5 네 번째 단락에 따르면, 다음 중 발아에 대해 사실인 것은?
(A) 아주 근접해 있는 많은 세포들이 둘로 나뉜다.
(B) 모체 식물이 다 자라면 두 부분으로 갈라진다.
(C) 특정 외부 요소들의 참여가 필수적이다.
(D) 단 하나의 씨앗이 소량의 꽃가루 알갱이에서 성장한다.

어휘 in close proximity 아주 근접하여

해설 발아와 관련해 해당 식물체의 단 한 곳에 집중된 반복적인 세포 분열이 일어난다고 했으므로, 이러한 방식에 해당하는 (A)가 정답이다.

세부 정보 찾기 문제

6 다섯 번째 단락에 따르면, 다음 중 무수정생식에 대해 사실이 아닌 것은?
(A) 씨앗 생산을 필요로 한다.
(B) 유성 또는 무성 중 하나일 수 있다.
(C) 복제 자손을 만들어 낸다.
(D) 흔히 양치류에 의해 활용된다.

해설 무수정생식은 식물 세계에서 나타나는 주요 무성생식 형태로 분류된다고 했으므로, (B)가 정답이다.

문장 삽입 문제

7 제시된 문장이 지문에 삽입될 수 있는 곳을 가리키는 네 개의 네모[■]를 보아라.

이는 반드시 자손이 부모 양측과 모두 유전적으로 달라지도록 해 준다.

이 문장이 들어갈 가장 적절한 위치는? 해당 네모[■]를 선택하여 이 문장을 지문에 삽입하여라.
(A)   (B)   (C)   (D)

해설 유성생식이 두 가지 다른 근원에서 나오는 생식 세포의 결합을 수반한다고 설명하는 문장 뒤에 위치해 그러한 방식에 따라 발생하는 결과를 나타내는 흐름이 되어야 자연스러우므로, (B)가 정답이다.

지문 요약 문제

8 **지시문**: 지문의 간략한 요약을 위한 도입 문장이 아래에 제시되어 있다. 지문에서 가장 중요한 개념들을 나타내는 선택지 3개를 선택하여 요약을 완성하여라. 어떤 문장들은 지문에 제시되지 않거나 주요 개념이 아니므로 요약에 포함되지 않는다. **이 문제는 2점에 해당한다.**

식물의 생식에는 유성과 무성이라는 두 가지 주요 형태가 있다.

(A) 무수정생식은 유성생식의 한 형태로, 유전적으로 다양한 자손으로 자라는 씨앗의 확산을 수반한다.
(B) 유성생식에서는 모체 식물의 일부가 분리되어 유전적으로 동일한 복제 생물로 성장한다.
(C) 무성생식에서는 생식 세포의 결합 없이 새로운 생명이 만들어지며, 복제 자손이라는 결과를 낳는다.
(D) 타가 수분은 두 가지 별개의 식물 사이에서 발생하는 반면, 자가 수분은 단일 식물과 관련되어 있다.
(E) 식물과 달리, 생식하기를 바라는 동물은 곳곳으로 이동하며 짝짓기할 어울리는 개체를 찾을 수 있다.
(F) 식물의 유성생식은 두 가지 다른 근원에서 나오는 생식 세포의 결합을 수반하며, 흔히 수분에 의해 촉진된다.

어휘 diverse 다양한 mate 짝짓기하다

해설 식물의 생식에 대한 이 지문에서 식물의 무성생식에 관련된 정보, 타가 수분과 자가 수분의 차이, 그리고 식물의 유성생식 과정을 요약한 (C), (D), (F)가 정답이다.

관련 지식 **인위적인 타가 수분(artificial cross-pollination)**은 사람이 직접 식물의 꽃가루를 수동으로 다른 꽃의 수술에 옮겨 놓음으로써 발생하는 교배 과정이다. 타가 수분은 일반적으로 여러 유전자를 서로 섞는 과정이기 때문에 식물이 가지고 있는 대립 유전자 간의 다양성이 증가하게 되며, 특히 순종끼리 처음 타가 수분을 해서 만드는 잡종  제1대는 무조건 우성 유전자가 발현하게 된다. 인위적인 타가 수분은 원하는 특성을 강조하거나 새로운 품종을 개발하는 등의 목적으로 사용된다.

PASSAGE 6

pp.196-199

정답 | 1 (D)   2 (A)   3 (B)   4 (C)   5 (C)   6 (B)   7 (B)   8 (A), (D), (E)

목성의 대기

태양계에서 가장 큰 행성이자 태양으로부터 다섯 번째로 멀리 떨어져 있는 목성은 질량이 너무 커서 태양계 내의 나머지 모든 행성의 질량의 총합을 2.5배 넘게 초과하는 가스상 거대 혹성이다. 고대 로마 신화에 나오는 신들의 왕 이름을 따서 명명된 이 행성은 암모니아 결정체로 된 영구적인 구름층으로 덮여 있으며, 그 구름층 밑에 아래쪽으로 약 3,000킬로미터 뻗어 있는 대기를 지니고 있다.

암모니아 구름층 자체는 두께가 약 50킬로미터이고, 더 두꺼운 구름들의 띠 꼭대기에 얹혀 있는 더 얇은 구름들의 띠로 구성되어 있는 것으로 여겨진다. ■(A) 목성의 대기에서 번쩍이는 번개를 탐지해 온 과학자들은 지구의 대기에서 나타나는 것과 다소 유사한 물 구름층도 암모니아 구름 바로 밑에 숨겨져 있을 거라고 생각한다. ■(B) 2011년에 NASA에서 발사한 뒤로 2016년부터 연구 임무를 띠고 목성 궤도를 계속 돌고 있는 주노 우주선도 이 행성의 대기 높은 곳에서 약한 번개를 탐지했다. ■(C) 아래쪽의 더 강력한 번개와 달리, 그것은 암모니아 구름에 의해 생성되는 것으로 보인다. ■(D)

아마 목성의 대기의 가장 잘 알려진 특징은 대적점일 텐데, 이 것은 일찍이 1665년에 지구의 천문학자들에 의해 관찰되었을 수 있는 폭풍으로, 그 크기와 수명, 맹렬함으로 과학자들을 계속 당황시키고 있다. 이 폭풍은 아래에 있는 구름 위 최대 약 8킬로미터의 고도로 이 행성의 적도 바로 남쪽에서 시계 바늘과 반대 방향으로 회전하는 어마어마한 소용돌이이다. 대적점은 한때 지구보다 더 큰 것으로 여겨졌고 이 행성의 영구적인 특징인 것으로 생각되었는데, 허블 우주 망원경과 목성 부근에서 우주 비행 임무를 수행했던 다양한 우주 탐사선에 의해 이뤄진 관측 결과를 바탕으로 볼 때, 지금은 점차적으로 크기가 감소하고 있는 것으로 여겨지고 있다. 그 뚜렷한 붉은색의 정확한 근원을 과학이 지속적으로 이해하지 못하고 있지만, 가장 가능성이 큰 설명은 그것이 암모니아와 아세틸렌 간에 계속되는 반응의 결과라는 점이다.

2017년에는 대기와 관련된 또 다른 특이한 특징이 목성에서 발견되었는데, 이것은 이 행성의 북극 근처에 위치해 있고 천문학자들에 의해 '대냉점'으로 불리고 있다. 대략적으로 길이 24,000킬로미터에 폭 12,000킬로미터의 인상적인 크기와 더불어, 가장 주목할 만한 특징은 주변보다 섭씨 200도 가량 더 낮은 것으로 추정되는 그것의 온도이다. 현재까지 그것에 대해 파악된 것은 거의 없지만, 대적점과 유사한 거대 소용돌이인 것으로 여겨지고 있고, 때때로 폭풍 전체가 사실상 사라지면서 그 형태와 강도가 어느 정도 규칙적으로 변화한다는 사실에도 불구하고, 처음 관찰된 이후 여전히 동일하게 일반적인 지역에 머물러 왔다.

대기 자체에 관해 말하자면, 대기의 약 90퍼센트를 차지하고 있는 분자 수소와 10퍼센트보다 약간 더 적게 차지하고 있는 헬륨으로 대부분 구성되어 있는 것으로 드러났는데, 이는 대략 태양과 일치하면서 전체적으로 이 행성의 구성 요소에 거의 변화가 없음을 보여 주는 비율이다. 질소와 황, 그리고 비활성 기체도 목성의 대기에서 찾아 볼 수 있지만, 이들은 태양에 있는 것을 3배 정도 초과하는 상대적 비율로 존재한다. 훨씬 더 적은 양으로 발견된 다른 화학적 혼합물에는 메탄과 암모니아, 그리고 물이 포함되며, 이 마지막 요소가 과학계의 큰 흥미를 끌고 있다. 주노가 이 행성의 적도 근처에서 저공 비행들 중 하나를 진행하면서 대기 샘플을 채취했으며, 그것에 대한 이후의 분석에 따르면 물 분자가 목성 대기의 0.25퍼센트를 차지하고 있는 것으로 드러났다.

지문 어휘

1. atmosphere 대기 solar system 태양계 gas giant 가스상 거대 혹성 mass 질량 exceed 초과하다 by a factor of ~배로 perpetual 영구적인, 끊임없이 이어지는
2. detect 탐지하다 launch 발사하다 orbit 궤도를 돌다
3. astronomer 천문학자 baffle 당황하게 만들다 ferocity 맹렬함, 흉포함 vortex 소용돌이 rotate 회전하다 counterclockwise 시계 바늘과 반대 방향의 equator 적도 altitude 고도 deem 여기다 probe 탐사선 mission 우주 비행 임무 elude ~에게 이해되지 않다 acetylene 아세틸렌
4. impressive 인상적인 noteworthy 주목할 만한 to date 현재까지
5. as for ~와 관련해서는 predominantly 주로, 대부분 molecular hydrogen 분자 수소 account for ~을 차지하다 proportion 비율 variation 변화 noble gas 비활성 기체 compound 혼합물 flyby 저공 비행

세부 정보 찾기 문제

1 두 번째 단락에 따르면, 다음 중 목성의 번개에 대해 사실인 것은?
(A) 주노의 우주 비행이 그것을 탐지하는 데 어려움을 좀 겪었다.
(B) 두 겹의 구름층 간의 반응에 의해 만들어진다.
(C) 그 안에 농도가 아주 높은 암모니아가 있다.
(D) 두 개의 다른 근원이 있는 두 가지 유형이 있는 것으로 보인다.

어휘 concentration 농도

해설 아래쪽에 더 강력한 번개가 있고, 그것과는 달리 암모니아 구름에 의해 생성되는 것으로 보이는 약한 번개가 있다고 했으므로, (D)가 정답이다.

수사적 의도 파악 문제

2 글쓴이가 세 번째 단락에서 "허블 우주 망원경"에 대해 논의하는 이유는?
(A) 일부 필수적인 정보의 출처를 제공하기 위해
(B) 대기의 한 가지 특징이 어떻게 발견되었는지 설명하기 위해

(C) 인간의 활동이 목성에 영향을 미치고 있음을 시사하기 위해
(D) 두 가지 다른 폭풍의 상대적 크기를 비교하기 위해

해설 대적점이 점차 크기가 감소하고 있는 것에 대한 근거로 허블 우주 망원경 및 다양한 우주 탐사선에 의해 이뤄진 관측 결과를 언급했으므로, (A)가 정답이다.

지시 대상 찾기 문제

3 지문의 단어 "it"이 가리키는 것은?
(A) 목성
(B) 그 뚜렷한 붉은색
(C) 과학
(D) 가장 가능성이 큰 설명

해설 it 뒤에 암모니아와 아세틸렌의 반응에 따른 결과라는 말이 쓰여 있어 주절에서 언급한 뚜렷한 붉은색의 생성 방식을 설명하는 내용임을 알 수 있으므로, (B)가 정답이다.

어휘의 의미 파악 문제

4 지문의 단어 "dubbed"와 의미가 가장 가까운 것은?
(A) 설치된
(B) 추정된
(C) ~이라고 명명된
(D) 발견된

해설 dubbed는 '~이라고 불리는'을 뜻하므로, 유사한 뜻을 가진 (C) named가 정답이다.

문장 재구성 문제

5 아래 문장 중 지문에서 음영 표시된 문장의 핵심 정보를 가장 잘 나타낸 것은? 오답 선택지들은 의미를 현저히 바꾸거나 핵심 정보를 생략한다.
(A) 분자 수소와 헬륨 사이의 극단적인 차이가 목성의 대기를 태양의 표면만큼 불안정하게 만드는 것이다.
(B) 목성 대기 안의 수소와 헬륨의 양은 매우 다른 반면, 태양에서는 그 둘의 양이 거의 동일하다.
(C) 목성의 대기는 대부분 수소와 헬륨으로 이루어져 있는데, 그 비율은 목성 전체와 태양 둘 다의 것과 유사하다.
(D) 목성의 대기는 많은 수소와 소량의 헬륨을 포함하고 있는데, 이로 인해 그 행성이 태양과 가장 밀접하게 닮아 있다.

해설 주어진 문장의 핵심 내용은 목성의 대기를 구성하는 요소와 그 비율이 태양 및 목성 전체의 구성 요소와 거의 유사하다는 것이므로, (C)가 정답이다.

추론 문제

6 다음 중 다섯 번째 단락에서 목성 대기의 물에 대해 추론할 수 있는 것은?
(A) 과거에 대기 중에서 발견되긴 했지만 더 이상 존재하지 않는다.
(B) 우주 탐사선에 의한 추가 조사의 대상이 될 것이다.
(C) 지구에서 발견되는 물과 다른 화학적 구성으로 되어 있다.
(D) 목성의 적도와 더 가까워질수록 양이 늘어난다.

어휘 investigation 조사 makeup 구성

해설 목성 대기의 물이 과학계의 큰 흥미를 끌고 있다는 말과 함께 탐사선 주노가 채취한 샘플 분석을 통해 물 분자가 목성 대기의 0.25퍼센트를 차지하고 있는 것으로 밝혀졌다고 했으므로, 이를 근거로 추가 조사 가능성이 있는 것을 유추할 수 있다. 그러므로 (B)가 정답이다.

문장 삽입 문제

7 제시된 문장이 지문에 삽입될 수 있는 곳을 가리키는 네 개의 네모[■]를 보아라.

이 번개에 의해 발생하는 전기 방전은 지구의 번개에 의해 만들어지는 것보다 훨씬 더 강력하다.

이 문장이 들어갈 가장 적절한 위치는? 해당 네모[■]를 선택하여 이 문장을 지문에 삽입하여라.
(A)　　　(B)　　　(C)　　　(D)

어휘 electrical discharge 전기 방전

해설 주어진 문장이 목성의 번개에 의한 전기 방전과 지구의 전기 방전을 비교하는 내용이므로, 목성의 번개를 언급하면서 지구의 대기와 비교하는 문장 다음에 와야 문맥의 흐름이 자연스럽다. 그러므로 정답은 (B)이다.

지문 요약 문제

8 **지시문**: 지문의 간략한 요약을 위한 도입 문장이 아래에 제시되어 있다. 지문에서 가장 중요한 개념들을 나타내는 선택지 3개를 선택하여 요약을 완성하여라. 어떤 문장들은 지문에 제시되지 않거나 주요 개념이 아니므로 요약에 포함되지 않는다. **이 문제는 2점에 해당한다.**

태양계에서 가장 큰 행성인 목성은 흥미로운 대기를 갖고 있다.

(A) 목성의 대기를 구성하는 주요 요소는 분자 수소이며, 그 다음은 훨씬 더 양이 적은 헬륨이다.
(B) 목성 대기의 온도는 예상보다 훨씬 더 낮으며, 최근 몇 년 사이에 계속 감소하고 있다.
(C) 주노는 NASA가 발사한 우주선이며, 현재 목성 궤도를 돌면서 그 행성의 대기를 조사하고 있다.
(D) 과학자들은 목성의 대기에서 점차적으로 크기가 변화한 대적점이라고 알려진 폭풍을 관측했다.
(E) 암모니아 결정체로 구성된 구름층이 그 행성 전체를 덮고 있으며 번개를 만들어 낸다.
(F) 태양에서 아주 먼 거리로 인해, 목성은 지구를 제외한 나머지 다른 행성들보다 대기에 물이 더 많다.

해설 목성의 흥미로운 대기와 관련하여 목성 대기의 구성 요소, 목성의 대적점과 관련된 정보, 암모니아로 구성된 구름 및 번개에 대해 요약한 (A), (D), (E)가 정답이다.

관련 지식 **허블 우주 망원경(Hubble Space Telescope)**은 NASA와 ESA가 협력하여 개발한 우주 망원경으로, 1990년에 4월 24일 우주왕복선 디스커버리 호에 실려 발사된 이래 계속해서 우주 관측 임무를 수행해 왔다. 지구 위 547킬로미터 고도에서 초속 8킬로미터로 약 95분에 한 번씩 지구를 돌고 있는 허블 우주 망원경은 지상 망원경과는 다르게 지구의 대기를 통과하지 않고 직접 우주 공간에서 관측을 수행하기 때문에 더 뛰어난 성능을 발휘한다. 이

망원경은 이를 통해 지구에서는 볼 수 없는 우주의 신비한 모습을 밝혀내고, 우주 탐사에 필요한 새로운 지식을 제공하고 있다.

ACTUAL
TEST ❶

정답 | **1** (A) **2** (A) **3** (C) **4** (C) **5** (B) **6** (C)
7 (D) **8** (D) **9** (C) **10** (B), (D), (E) **11** (D)
12 (A) **13** (C) **14** (D) **15** (B) **16** (A), (C)
17 (C) **18** (B) **19** (D) **20** (A), (D), (E)

Questions 1-10 pp. 202-213

이리 운하

허드슨 강에서부터 캐나다와의 국경에 위치한 5대호들 중 하나인 이리 호까지 이어지는 운하를 뉴욕주 북부에 건설하자는 제안이 처음 수면 위로 떠오르는 것은 1780년대였는데, 1808년에 정식 측량 작업이 마침내 이루어져, 1817년에 그 프로젝트를 시작하라는 정부의 승인이 내려졌다. 그 프로젝트의 주요 제안자는 뉴욕 주지사였던 드윗 클린턴이었으며, 그는 이 운하를 애팔래치아 산맥을 가로지르는 상품 운송 비용을 대폭 감소시키는 수단으로 여겼는데, 그 산맥이 뉴욕과 빠르게 발전하던 서부 지역 사이에서 지리적 장애물로 자리잡고 있었기 때문이었다.

클린턴의 정적들은 그것을 '클린턴의 도랑'이라고 비아냥거리듯 일컬으며 자신들이 쓸데없는 시도라고 주장하는 것에 대해 그렇게 많은 돈을 들인다고 그를 조롱했지만, 그는 1825년에 개통된 직후에 나타난 그 운하의 엄청난 성공에 힘입어 결국 자신의 정당성을 입증했다. 완공된 운하는 나중에 여러 차례 확장 공사를 거치게 되었지만, 오직 중국의 대운하 다음으로 당시에 두 번째로 긴 584킬로미터였으며, 폭은 12미터, 깊이는 1.2미터였다. 그 운하는 높은 공사 비용으로 인해 뉴욕주 경제에 부담이 되는 것이 아니라 압도적일 정도로 긍정적인 재정적 영향을 미쳤으며, 그곳을 통과해 운송되는 화물에 부과되던 통행료를 통해 얻은 수입이 10년도 채 되지 않아 공사 비용을 충당했지만, 이 통행료는 전국 각지에서 확산되면서 새로 건설되던 철도망과 경쟁하기 위해 이후 1882년에 폐지되었다.

이리 운하는 상업적 교통이라는 측면에 있어 1855년에 정점에 이르렀는데, 당시 총 약 33,000건의 운송 상품이 이 수로를 통해 제 갈 길을 찾아 갔다. ■(A) 이리 운하의 가장 큰 영향들 중 하나는 뉴욕과 국가의 농업이 존재했던 중서부 지역 사이를 오가는 운송비의 상당한 감소였다. 버팔로에서 뉴욕시로 제품을 수송하는 비용은 톤당 100달러에서 톤당 10달러 미만으로 감소해, 식품을 포함한 상품이 동부 해안 지역에 걸쳐 훨씬 더 저렴해졌다. ■(B) 예를 들어, 이제 밀가루 1배럴이 로체스터 시에서 뉴욕주의 주도 올버니까지 운하 건설 이전에 들었을 만한 비용의 단 일부만으로 운송될 수 있었다. ■(C) 이리 운하로 인한 또 다른 이점은, 이는 대체로 예기치 못했던 부분이었는데, 한때 행락객들이 기피했던 뉴욕 북부 지역들에서 나타난 관광 산업의 성장이었다. ■(D) 여객선들이 그 운하를 오가며 운항하기 위해 상업용 화물선들과 함께 줄지어 섰고, 관광객들이 운하를 따라 늘어선 야생 지역의 여유로운 경관을 즐기면서 뉴욕주의 재원에 훨씬 더 많은 수익을 안겨 주었다.

이리 운하의 시대는 국제적으로 그리고 국내에서 모두 다양하게 이뤄지던 대이주의 시기이기도 했는데, 지속적으로 이어지는 이민자들의 물결이 유럽에서 미국으로 유입되면서 짧은 역사를 지닌 미국의 대규모 서부 확장을 부채질했기 때문이다. 이 이민자들 중 일부, 특히 아일랜드에서 온 이민자들은 운하를 파는 데 필요했던 광범위한 인력에 합류했다가, 나중에 그 경로를 따라 이어지는 작은 마을들에 정착하면서 아일랜드계 미국인 공동체로 자리 잡았다. 이리 호의 몹시 추운 호반 지역인 뉴욕주의 북서부 구석에 위치한 정착지인 버팔로도 운하 건설에 따른 성장이라는 측면에서 큰 혜택을 입었고, 그 인구가 1820년에 주민 2,000명이었던 것이 불과 20년 후에는 18,000명이 넘는 사람들로 급증했다. 현재 버팔로는 인구 약 275,000명의 번성하는 도시이다.

이리 운하는 20세기 초에 일차적으로 철도와의 경쟁으로 인해, 그리고 20세기 후반에는 자동차가 국가적으로 선호하는 교통 수단이 되었기 때문에 트럭 운송업계에 의해 부정적으로 영향을 받으면서, 결국 이용되지 않게 되었다. 그 운하의 마지막 정기 운송 서비스는 1994년에 영구적으로 중단되었으며, 현재 이리 운하가 그 지역에서 얼마 되지 않는 호기심 어린 관광객들과 여가를 위해 보트를 즐기는 사람들을 계속 끌어들이고 있기는 하지만, 뉴욕주나 나라 전체에 더 이상 어떤 중요한 상업적 가치가 있지는 않다.

용어 설명
재원: 조직이나 정부가 사용할 수 있는 자금

지문 어휘

1. canal 운하 float 떠오르게 하다, (생각 등을) 제안하다 upstate 주(州) 북부 지역의 survey 측량 authorization 승인 grant 주다, 승인하다 proponent 제안자, 주창자 view A as B A를 B로 여기다 drastically 급격히 obstacle 장애물

2. sarcastically 비아냥거리듯 refer to A as B A를 B라고 일컫다 vindicate ~의 정당성을 입증하다 rousing 엄청난, 열렬한 expansion 확장 overwhelmingly 압도적으로 revenue 수입, 수익 toll 통행료 freight 화물 abolish 폐지하다

3. peak 전성기, 절정 in terms of ~의 측면에 있어 make one's way 가다, 나아가다 reside 존재하다 affordable 저렴한, 가격이 알맞은 fraction 일부, 부분 cruise 운항하다 line up 줄지어 서다

4. migration 이주 a steady stream of 지속적으로 이어지는 immigrant 이민자 fuel 부채질하다 extensive 광범위한 labor force 인력, 노동력 excavate 파다 settlement 정착지 frigid 몹시 추운 balloon 급증하다, 부풀어 오르다 thriving 번성하는

5. fall into disuse 이용되지 않게 되다 shut down 중단하다, 폐쇄하다 permanently 영구적으로 attract 끌어들이다 handfuls of 얼마 안 되는 value 가치

문장 재구성 문제

1 아래 문장 중 지문에서 음영 표시된 문장의 핵심 정보를 가장 잘 나타낸 것은? 오답 선택지들은 의미를 현저히 바꾸거나 핵심 정보를 생략한다.
(A) 그 산맥을 가로질러 상품을 운송하는 더 비용 효율이 높은 수단으로 운하를 구상한 것은 뉴욕주의 주지사였다.
(B) 드윗 클린턴이 뉴욕 주지사가 된 후, 운하를 건설하기 위해 많은 장애물을 극복해야 했다.
(C) 그 운하는 뉴욕과 미국 서부 지역을 분리하는 애팔래치아 산맥을 가로질러 건설되어야 했다.
(D) 드윗 클린턴이 당선된 주지사였기 때문에, 그 운하로 인해 서부 지역 사람들에게 제품을 운송하는 것이 더 수월해졌다.

어휘 cost-effective 비용 효율이 높은

해설 이리 운하 프로젝트의 제안자가 뉴욕 주지사였던 드윗 클린턴이었다는 사실과 그가 구상한 운하의 용도와 관련된 핵심 정보가 모두 포함된 (A)가 정답이다.

어휘의 의미 파악 문제

2 지문의 단어 "derided"와 의미가 가장 가까운 것은?
(A) 조롱했다   (B) 분석했다
(C) 포기했다   (D) 지지했다

해설 derided는 '조롱했다'라는 뜻으로 사용되므로, 동일한 의미를 가진 (A) ridiculed가 정답이다.

세부 정보 찾기 문제

3 두 번째 단락에 따르면, 뉴욕주는 왜 운하 운송에 대한 관세를 종료했는가?
(A) 연방 정부의 요구 조건을 충족하기 위해
(B) 운하의 통행량을 줄여 운송 속도를 높이기 위해
(C) 또 다른 운송 수단과의 경쟁력을 높이기 위해
(D) 운하 확장 자금을 예산에 포함하기 위해

어휘 tariff 관세 budget 예산

해설 운하 통행료가 당시에 새로 건설되던 철도망과 경쟁하기 위해 1882년에 폐지되었다고 했으므로, (C)가 정답이다.

어휘의 의미 파악 문제

4 지문의 단어 "shunned"와 의미가 가장 가까운 것은?
(A) 발전된   (B) 점검된
(C) 기피된   (D) 정의된

해설 '기피된'을 의미하는 shunned는 같은 뜻을 나타내는 avoided 로 대체할 수 있으므로, (C)가 정답이다.

수사적 의도 파악 문제

5 세 번째 단락의 목적은 무엇인가?
(A) 두 번째 단락에 제시된 두 가지 다른 원인을 대조하는 것
(B) 두 번째 단락에 소개된 아이디어에 대한 세부 정보를 제공하는 것
(C) 두 번째 단락에 있는 부정적 영향의 원인을 알려 주는 것
(D) 두 번째 단락에 있는 아이디어에 대한 글쓴이의 의견을 제공하는 것

해설 이리 운하가 뉴욕주 경제에 압도적일 정도로 긍정적인 재정적 영향을 미쳤다고 언급한 것과 관련된 예들이 세 번째 단락에 세부적으로 제시되므로, (B)가 정답이다.

세부 정보 찾기 문제

6 다음 중 네 번째 단락에서 언급되지 않은 것은?
(A) 유럽인들이 대규모로 미국으로 이민을 오고 있었다.
(B) 국가가 확장되면서 미국인들이 서쪽 방향으로 이주하고 있었다.
(C) 동부 해안 지역 도시들은 규모가 감소한 반면, 중서부 지역 도시들은 규모가 증가했다.
(D) 운하에서 일하려고 왔던 아일랜드 이민자들이 뉴욕에 정착했다.

해설 많은 유럽인들이 미국으로 이주했고, 미국이 확장되면서 사람들이 서부 지역으로 이주했으며, 운하 노동자로 온 아일랜드인들이 뉴욕에 정착했다고 했지만, 도시들의 규모 변화와 관련된 내용은 찾아볼 수 없으므로, (C)가 정답이다.

추론 문제

7 다음 중 네 번째 단락에서 버팔로에 대해 추론할 수 있는 것은?
(A) 처음에는 이리 운하를 건설하자는 제안에 반대했다.
(B) 전체 주민이 일시적으로만 증가했다.
(C) 뉴욕주에서 가장 다양한 인구 집단들 중 하나를 가지고 있다.
(D) 이리 운하가 이리 호와 만나는 곳 근처에 위치해 있다.

어휘 temporary 일시적인 diverse 다양한

해설 버팔로가 이리 호의 호반 지역에 위치해 있으면서 이리 운하 건설로 인해 크게 혜택을 봤다는 설명에서 이리 운하와 이리 호가 연결되는 곳에 위치한 도시임을 유추할 수 있다. 그러므로 정답은 (D)이다.

세부 정보 찾기 문제

8 다섯 번째 단락에 따르면, 다음 중 오늘날의 이리 운하에 대해 사실인 것은?
(A) 크기가 더 작고 상업적 교통이 한쪽으로만 이동한다.
(B) 길이 포장되어 현재 트럭 운전용 고속도로로 이용되고 있다.
(C) 국가와 주 경제 모두에 지속적으로 중요하다.
(D) 소수의 관광객들이 방문하고 있으며 운송용으로는 거의 쓰이지 않는다.

해설 현재 이리 운하에 얼마 되지 않는 관광객들과 보트를 즐기는 사람들이 방문하기는 하지만, 뉴욕이나 국가에 더 이상 중요한 상업적 가치는 없다고 했으므로, (D)가 정답이다.

문장 삽입 문제

9 제시된 문장이 지문에 삽입될 수 있는 곳을 가리키는 네 개의 네모[■]를 보아라.

기계 및 제품을 자사 공장에서 중서부 지역의 고객들에게 운송하던 동부 해안 지역의 업체들도 유사한 재정적 이익을 경험했다.

이 문장이 들어갈 가장 적절한 위치는? 해당 네모[■]를 선택하여 이 문장을 지문에 삽입하여라.
(A)   (B)   (C)   (D)

어휘 boon 이익, 혜택

해설 주어진 문장은 특정 업체들이 이리 운하 이용을 통해 얻었던 재정적 이익을 설명하고 있다. 따라서 이와 같은 경우를 첫 번째 예로 언급한 문장 뒤에 놓아 유사 정보를 추가하는 흐름이 되어야 자연스러우므로, (C)가 정답이다.

지문 요약 문제

10 **지시문:** 지문의 간략한 요약을 위한 도입 문장이 아래에 제시되어 있다. 지문에서 가장 중요한 개념들을 나타내는 선택지 3개를 선택하여 요약을 완성하여라. 어떤 문장들은 지문에 제시되지 않거나 주요 개념이 아니므로 요약에 포함되지 않는다. **이 문제는 2점에 해당한다.**

이리 운하는 19세기 초에 뉴욕주를 가로질러 지어졌다.

(A) 그 운하는 다른 유사 프로젝트들의 성공을 바탕으로 제안되었으며, 가장 주목할 만한 것은 중국의 대운하였다.
(B) 기차와 트럭을 포함한 다른 운송 형태가 더 인기를 얻으면서, 운송업자들이 그 운하의 이용을 중단했다.
(C) 버팔로는 그 운하의 건설로 인해 이리 호의 호반 지역에서 규모가 빠르게 커지던 작은 정착지였다.
(D) 그 운하의 통행료를 통해 거둬들인 돈은 10년도 채 되지 않아 건설 비용 전체를 지불하기에 충분했다.
(E) 그 운하가 뉴욕과 중서부 지역 사이의 운송비를 빠르게 내리면서, 물가가 하락했다.
(F) 미국인들이 서부로 이주하기 시작하면서, 뉴욕주는 그 운하에서 일할 충분한 인력을 찾기 힘들어했다.

해설 이리 운하에 대해 인기 있는 다른 교통 수단으로 인해 운하 이용이 중단되었다고 설명한 (B), 재정적으로 엄청나게 긍정적인 영향을 미친 점을 설명한 (D), 그 운하가 미친 큰 영향의 하나로 뉴욕과 중서부 지역 사이를 오가는 운송비의 상당한 감소를 언급한 (E)가 정답이다. (A)와 (F)는 지문 내용과 다르고, (C)는 중심 내용이 아니다.

Questions 11-20   pp. 214-225

화성의 물

하늘을 연구하기 위한 가장 기초적인 망원경의 첫 사용과 함께 시작해, 초기 천문학자들은 행성인 화성에서 물이 발견될 수 있을지에 대해 진지한 논의를 했다. 그들이 처음에 관측한 '수로'와 '바다'가 그 후로 오랫동안 관련 없는 자연적 특징으로 얼버무려져 왔지만, 현대적인 기술과 우주 탐사 덕분에 우리는 이제 두 가지 중요한 사실을 알고 있는데, 그 첫 번째는 비록 대기 중에 존재하는 소량의 물 수증기와 함께 거의 얼음의 형태로만 발견되기는 하지만 화성에 물이 있다는 점이며, 두 번째는 과거에 액체 형태의 물이 대량으로 존재했을 수도 있다는 점이다.

비록 얼음이 화성 북극의 만년설에서도 보이며 남극 만년설의 영구적인 이산화탄소 얼음 층 아래에도 숨겨져 있는 것으로 생각되고 있긴 하지만, 현재 화성에서 발견되는 얼음의 대부분은 지하에 있는 종류이다. 총 5백만 입방 킬로미터가 넘는 얼음이 화성의 표면이나 그 근처에 존재하는 것으로 알려져 있는데, 이것이 녹을 경우 35미터의 물로 그 행성 전체를 덮게 될 것

이다. 남아 있는 초미의 문제는 아주 먼 과거의 어느 때에 어느 정도의 물이 액체 상태로 존재했는지, 그리고 그 물이 행성 표면 전체에 걸쳐 자유롭게 그리고 엄청난 양으로 흘러 다녔는지 여부이다.

거의 40억 년 전에 화성의 대기는 밀도가 더 높고 표면의 기온은 더 높았던 것으로 생각되는데, 이는 방대한 양의 액체 상태인 물이 아마도 그 행성의 3분의 1을 덮었던 거대한 대양의 형태로 존재했을 수도 있다는 것을 의미한다. 또한 어쩌면 미생물에게 적합했을 만한 담수호들을 포함해 규모가 더 작은 액체 상태의 수역이 더 최근에 존재했을 가능성도 있다. 1971년에 NASA의 마리너 9호 우주선이 화성 궤도를 돌기 시작했을 때, 7,000장이 넘는 행성 표면 이미지들을 담아냈는데, 그 중 많은 이미지들이 액체 상태의 물이 한때 상당량 존재했음을 지형학적 특징을 띤 형태로 보여주는 최초의 구체적인 증거를 천문학자들에게 제공해 주었다.

그 이후로 화성에 있는 약 40,000개의 하곡이 연구가들에 의

해 지도로 제작되어 한때 흐르는 물이 이동했던 경로를 추적했는데, 그 중 일부는 수천 킬로미터에 이르렀으며, 그 길을 따라 표면 기반암을 침식시키면서 우리 행성의 일부 지역에서 발견되는 것과 거의 흡사한 깊은 계곡을 깎아냈다. 이 이미지들에 포함되었던 것으로 다수의 지류로 갈라졌던 개울들에 대한 증거도 있었는데, 이것은 그것들이 내리는 비에 의해 형성되었을 가능성이 가장 컸을 것임을 보여주는 지표이다.

이 개울 및 하곡들과 더불어 상당수의 호수 분지들도 화성에서 확인되었다. ■(A) 이들 중 일부는 지구에서 가장 큰 호수들과 대략 비슷한 규모이며, 한때 그 형성의 계곡들 사이로 흘렀던 강들이 그 수원이었던 것이 분명하다. ■(B) 개울들과 마찬가지로 이 호수들 중 일부는 강우에 의해 형성되었을 수도 있는 반면, 다른 것들은 솟아오르는 지하수에 의해 만들어졌던 것으로 보인다. ■(C) 이 호수들은 화성의 전반적인 환경이 비교적 따뜻하고 비가 잘 오던 먼 과거 이래로 계속 존재해 온 것으로 한때 추정되었다. ■(D) 아마도 화산 활동이나 운석 충돌, 행성 궤도의 변화 같이 대격변을 일으키는 모종의 사건으로 인해 화성의 대기가 지하의 얼음이 녹아 호수를 형성하기 시작하는 수준까지 따뜻해졌다는 가설이 제기된 바 있다.

한때 화성에서 물이 자유롭게 흘러 다녔음을 보여주는 또 다른 강력한 지표는 그 행성의 호수 바닥들 중 일부에서 발견된 삼각주들로, 강들에 의해 오래 전에 그 호수들 안에 침전된 퇴적물에 의해 형성된 부채꼴 모양이다. 이 삼각주들은 형성되려면 깊은 물과 오랜 시간이 모두 필요했을 것이라는 사실로 인해 중요하게 여겨지고 있다. 또한 이 물이 수위 측면에 있어 상당한 시간에 걸쳐 안정적으로 유지되지 못했다면, 그 퇴적물들은 쓸려 내려갔을 것이다. 이 모든 지형학적 증거는 화성이 풍부한 액체 상태의 물을 지니고 있었던 때가 있었음을 강력하게 시사하고 있으며, 이것이 생명을 지탱하는 데 필요한 근본적인 특징들 중 하나임을 고려할 때 특히 주목할 만한 정보이다.

지문 어휘

1. rudimentary 가장 기초적인 earnest 진심 어린 explain away ~을 얼버무리다 unrelated 관련 없는 exploration 탐사, 탐험 exclusively 오로지 vapor 수증기 atmosphere 대기 liquid 액체 quantity 양

2. subterranean 지하의 ice cap 만년설 permanent 영구적인 carbon dioxide 이산화탄소 melt 녹이다, 녹다 pressing 초미의, 긴급한

3. dense 밀도 높은 extensive 방대한, 광범위한 microbial life 미생물 orbit 궤도를 돌다; 궤도 geomorphic 지형학적인

4. map out ~을 지도로 제작하다, 세심히 계획하다 erode 침식시키다 bedrock 기반암 carve out ~을 깎아내 만들다 stream 개울, 시내 break off 갈라지다 branch 지류 indicator 지표

5. basin 분지, 유역 precipitation 강우 date back to ~이래 계속 존재하고 있다 hypothesize 가설을 세우다 cataclysmic 지각변동을 일으키는, 격변하는 meteorite 운석 impact 충돌, 충격

6. delta 삼각주 spot 발견하다 fan-shaped 부채꼴의 sediment 퇴적물, 침전물 deposit 침전시키다 stable 안정적인 abundant 풍부한 notable 주목할 만한

수사적 의도 파악 문제

11 글쓴이는 왜 첫 번째 단락에서 "초기 천문학자들"을 언급하는가?
(A) 망원경의 발명이 지니는 중요성을 강조하기 위해
(B) 화성에 있는 물의 기원에 관한 서로 다른 이론들을 비교하기 위해
(C) 화성의 아주 오래된 수로와 바다의 엄청난 규모를 설명하기 위해
(D) 화성의 물에 대한 과거의 오해를 소개하기 위해

어휘 misconception 오해

해설 초기 천문학자들이 과거에 관측했던 수로와 바다가 오랫동안 관련 없는 자연적 특징으로 여겨졌다고 했으므로, 화성의 물에 대한 과거의 오해를 소개하기 위해 그들을 언급했음을 알 수 있다. 그러므로 (D)가 정답이다.

어휘의 의미 파악 문제

12 지문의 단어 "copious"와 의미가 가장 가까운 것은?
(A) 풍부한   (B) 변동이 있는
(C) 감소하는   (D) 알 수 없는

해설 copious는 '엄청난, 방대한'이라는 의미를 나타내므로, 이와 가장 비슷한 뜻을 가진 (A) abundant가 정답이다.

어휘의 의미 파악 문제

13 지문의 단어 "hospitable"과 의미가 가장 가까운 것은?
(A) 치명적인
(B) 감지할 수 있는
(C) 알맞은
(D) 관련 없는

해설 hospitable은 '(환경 등이) 적합한'의 뜻으로 사용되었으므로, 유사한 뜻을 나타내는 (C) favorable이 정답이다.

세부 정보 찾기 문제

14 세 번째 단락에 따르면, 다음 중 마리너 9호에 대해 사실인 것은?
(A) 물을 찾기 위해 화성의 하곡에 착륙했다.
(B) 화성의 토양 샘플을 수집해 분석했다.
(C) 화성에 있는 거대한 바다의 사진을 처음 촬영했다.
(D) 한때 액체 상태의 물이 화성에 존재했음을 보여주는 증거를 제공했다.

해설 마리너 9호가 7,000장이 넘는 이미지들을 통해 화성에 액체 상태의 물이 한때 존재했음을 보여주는 구체적인 증거를 천문학자들에게 제공했다고 했으므로, 정답은 (D)이다.

문장 재구성 문제

15 아래 문장 중 지문에서 음영 표시된 문장의 핵심 정보를 가장 잘 나타낸 것은? 오답 선택지들은 의미를 현저히 바꾸거나 핵심 정보를 생략한다.
   (A) 화성의 표면은 기반암으로 만들어져 있으며, 그것을 가로질러 흐르는 물이 많은 깊은 계곡을 통과해 지나가게 한다.
   (B) 연구가들이 흐르는 물에 의해 화성의 표면에 침식된 강 수천 개의 경로를 확인하려고 하곡들을 이용했다.
   (C) 과학자들은 많은 연구 끝에 화성에서 발견된 약 40,000개의 계곡이 더 이상 어떤 흐르는 강도 가지고 있지 않다는 결론을 내렸다.
   (D) 화성에 있는 수천 개의 하곡들에 대한 연구에 따르면 그것들이 지구에서 발견되는 것들보다 훨씬 더 길고 깊은 것으로 나타났다.

해설 연구가들이 화성의 하곡들을 이용해 한때 물이 이동했던 경로를 추적한 점과 그 물로 인해 침식된 계곡 구조가 생겼음을 알아냈다는 것이 핵심 정보이므로, (B)가 정답이다.

세부 정보 찾기 문제

16 다섯 번째 단락에서 화성의 호수들이 형성되었을 수 있는 방식을 설명하는 **선택지 두 개를 고르시오. 두 개를 골라야 점수가 인정된다.**
   (A) 화성의 대기가 더 따뜻했을 때 비가 내렸다.
   (B) 큰 바다의 물이 줄기 시작하면서 호수들을 남겼다.
   (C) 그 행성의 화산 분출이 얼음을 액체 상태의 물로 바꿨다.
   (D) 우주에서 온 얼음 덩어리들이 그 행성과 충돌했다.

어휘 crash into ~와 충돌하다
해설 호수들이 화성의 환경이 따뜻하고 비가 잘 오던 먼 과거 이래로 계속 존재해온 것으로 추정되었다는 점과 화산 활동 등으로 인해 지하의 얼음이 녹아 호수를 형성하게 되었다는 가설이 제시되어 있으므로, (A)와 (C)가 정답이다.

세부 정보 찾기 문제

17 여섯 번째 단락에 따르면, 삼각주가 화성의 호수 바닥에 형성된 이유는?
   (A) 지하수가 뜨거워지기 시작해 그 행성 표면으로 솟아올랐기 때문에
   (B) 빠르고 강하게 흐르는 큰 강들이 기반암에 깊게 홈을 깎아 냈기 때문에
   (C) 오랜 시간에 걸쳐 암석과 토양이 강들에 의해 그 안으로 휩쓸려 들어갔기 때문에
   (D) 행성 궤도의 변화로 인해 그 표면이 불안정해지는 결과를 낳았기 때문에

어휘 groove 홈, 패인 곳   sweep 휩쓸다
해설 강에 의해 오래 전에 호수들 안으로 침전된 퇴적물에 의해 삼각주가 형성되었다고 했으므로, 정답은 (C)이다.

추론 문제

18 여섯 번째 단락에서, 글쓴이가 화성의 물에 대해 암시하는 것은?
   (A) 오래 전에 아주 짧은 시간 동안 존재했을 가능성이 가장 크다.
   (B) 그 행성에 한때 생명체가 있었음을 나타내는 것일 수 있다.
   (C) 지구에 있는 물의 근원이었을 수도 있다.
   (D) 수세기가 소요되는 주기로 생기고 없어질지도 모른다.

어휘 brief 짧은
해설 액체 상태의 물이 생명을 지탱하는 데 필요한 근본적인 특징들 중 하나임을 고려할 때 특히 주목할 만하다는 말에서 글쓴이가 과거의 생명체 존재 가능성을 시사하고 있음을 유추할 수 있다. 그러므로 (B)가 정답이다.

문장 삽입 문제

19 제시된 문장이 지문에 삽입될 수 있는 곳을 가리키는 네 개의 네모[■]를 보아라.

하지만 2010년에 실시된 연구를 통해 그 행성의 적도 근처에서 훨씬 더 최근에 존재하기 시작한 호수들에 대한 증거가 드러났다.

이 문장이 들어갈 가장 적절한 위치는? 해당 네모[■]를 선택하여 이 문장을 지문에 삽입하여라.
   (A)   (B)   (C)   (D)

해설 주어진 문장은 2010년의 연구를 통해 적도 부근에서 훨씬 더 최근의 시기에 시작된 호수들에 대한 증거를 찾았다고 말하고 있다. 따라서 더 이전의 과거에 형성된 호수들을 언급하는 문장 뒤에 위치해 형성 시점을 비교하는 흐름이 되어야 자연스러우므로, (D)가 정답이다.

지문 요약 문제

20 **지시문:** 지문의 간략한 요약을 위한 도입 문장이 아래에 제시되어 있다. 지문에서 가장 중요한 개념들을 나타내는 선택지 3개를 선택하여 요약을 완성하여라. 어떤 문장들은 지문에 제시되지 않거나 주요 개념이 아니므로 요약에 포함되지 않는다. **이 문제는 2점에 해당한다.**

천문학자들은 화성에 물이 존재하는지에 대해 오랫동안 관심을 가져왔다.

   (A) 화성에는 대부분 얼음의 형태로 물이 존재하며, 액체 상태의 물이 대량으로 존재했었을 수도 있다고 현재 알려져 있다.
   (B) 화성의 두 극을 덮고 있는 거대한 만년설이 있지만, 그것은 물이 아니라 오직 얼어붙은 이산화탄소만으로 구성되어 있다.

(C) 연구가들은 화성의 적도 근처에서 호수들을 발견했다고 생각했지만, 그것들은 그저 얼어붙은 지하수의 침전물이었다.

(D) 화성의 표면에 큰 호수 바닥들이 있으며, 그 중 일부는 그곳으로 흘러 드는 강들에 의해 생성된 삼각주들을 포함하고 있다.

(E) NASA의 한 우주선이 촬영한 이미지들은 수천 개의 하곡들을 포함해 흐르는 물에 대한 지형학적 증거를 밝혀냈다.

(F) 초기 천문학자들은 조잡한 망원경으로 화성을 보았으며, 자신들이 수로와 바다들을 보고 있다고 잘못 생각했다.

어휘 crude 조잡한, 대충의

해설 화성의 물을 소재로 한 지문에서 화성에 존재하는 물의 형태와 액체 형태의 물이 과거에 아주 많은 양으로 존재했었을 수 있다고 한 다음, 화성의 호수 바닥 및 삼각주 형성에 대해 설명하고, NASA의 우주선이 촬영한 이미지가 지니는 의미에 대해 설명하며 마무리가 되었으므로, 정답은 (A), (D), (E)이다. 나머지는 지문 내용과 다르다.

ACTUAL TEST ❷

정답 |

1 (C)	2 (D)	3 (B)	4 (A)	5 (B)	6 (C)
7 (A)	8 (D)	9 (C)	10 (B), (C), (F)		11 (B)
12 (B)	13 (C)	14 (A)	15 (D)	16 (D)	17 (A)
18 (B)	19 (A)	20 (A), (C), (E)			

Questions 1-10

pp. 226-237

초식동물이 식물 다양성에 미치는 영향

식물 다양성은 지구 생태계의 건강과 기능을 유지하는 데 필요한 아주 중요한 요소이다. 초식동물은 이 다양성이 사라지지 않도록 하는 데 필수적인 역할을 한다. 초식동물과 식물 다양성 사이의 관계에 대한 전통적인 관점은 상당히 단순한데, 초식동물의 식물 섭취가 어느 한 종이라도 경쟁 종에 대해 우위를 차지하지 못하게 함으로써 다양성을 보호한 것으로 여겨졌다. 이것이 중요한 이유는 일단 하나의 종이 우세해지면, 경쟁적 배제라고 알려진 과정을 통해 서식지를 공유하는 하위 종을 점차적으로 없애기 때문인데, 이 과정에서 더 약한 종은 생태계 자원에 대한 접근이 거부된다. 하지만, 이 사고방식의 근본 개념이 여전히 타당하게 여겨지고는 있지만, 과학자들은 이제 그 상황의 현실은 더욱 복잡하다는 것을 안다.

일반적으로 초식동물의 먹이 섭취 습성은 분명 식물 다양성의 증가로 이어진다. 환경이 식물에게 성장 및 번식하는 데 필요한 모든 자원을 제공해 주는 건강하고 생산적인 생태계에서는 적정 수준의 초식동물 섭식이 실제로 생태계의 생산성을 높여 주고, 전체 생물량의 증가로 이어질 수 있다. 초식동물이 우세 식물 종을 먹기 때문에, 그 개체 수를 줄여 하위 종에게 추가 자원을 풀어주며, 그로 인해 다양성을 유지한다. 하지만, 덜 생산적인 생태계에서는 반대의 상황이 발생할 수 있다. 자원이 풍부하지 않기 때문에, 초식동물의 섭식 행동이 오직 가장 강하고, 가장 잘 견디는 종만 생존할 수 있는 상황을 만들 수 있는 반면, 더 연약한 종은 멸종으로 사라지게 되어, 확실히 식물 다양성의 감소로 이어진다.

관련 초식동물의 크기는 생태계의 생물 다양성에 미치는 영향을 알아내는 데 도움이 되는 또 다른 요소이다. ■(A) 예를 들어, 식물 종이 필요로 하는 가장 중요한 자원 중 하나가 햇빛인데, 이를 두고 식물 종은 자신이 더 크게 자라면서 더 작은 경쟁자들에게 그림자를 드리우는 방식으로 경쟁한다. ■(B) 하지만, 대형 초식동물의 존재는 키가 더 큰 식물 종이 지닌 이점을 줄일 수 있는데, 섭취 대상이 될 가능성이 더 높기 때문이다. ■(C) 크기의 측면에 있어, 크기가 더 작은 초식동물일수록, 영향력이 덜할 가능성이 있는데, 크기가 작은 생물은 더 적은 영양분을 필요로 하고 물리적 환경에서 그저 미미한 지장만 있을 뿐이기 때문이다. ■(D) 하지만, 대형 초식동물은 훨씬 더 큰 영향을 미치는데, 많은 양의 우세 식물 종도 섭취하고 땅도 파내기 때문이며, 이는 사실 토양이 굳어지는 것을 방지해 주고 그 안에 추가로 산소가 들어가게 함으로써 토양의 질을 개선해 준다. 또한 많은 양의 배설물을 남기면서, 자신들이 섭취한 종의 씨앗을 퍼뜨리는 것뿐만 아니라, 토양의 영양분을 늘려 주는데, 이 모두는 그 생태계 식물들의 성장에 있어 전반적인 증진을 가능하게 해 준다.

초식동물이 생태계의 우세 식물 종을 섭취하는 경향이 있기는 하지만, 일부 경우에는 그저 기호성이 더 높기 때문에 하위 종을 목표로 삼는다. 이로 인해, 초식동물이 대규모로 먹이를 먹는 지역에서는 식물에 대한 기호성이 어느 종이 우세한 상태가 되는지에 영향을 미칠 수 있고, 기호성이 떨어지는 식물이 우위를 차지할 가능성이 더 높다. 식물은 흔히 '생장과 방어의 균형'이라고 부르는 것에 의지해 기호성에 따른 초식동물에 대한 취약성을 상쇄한다. 간단히 말해서, 배고픈 초식동물을 상대로 다양한 방어 기제들 중 어떤 것이든 활성화하기 위해, 식물은 반드시 내부 자원을 재분배해 결국 자신의 성장을 해치게 된다. 이러한 방어는 날카로운 가시나 외부 표면의 밀랍 층같이 물리적이거나, 또는 초식동물의 건강에 악영향을 끼치는 독소나 심지어 공중에 방출되어 초식동물의 천적을 끌어들이는 VOC라는 휘발성 유기 화합물의 경우처럼 화학적일 수 있다. 그 결과, 해당 식물이 개별 크기와 전반적인 규모가 감소하기는 하지만, 지속적인 생존을 지켜낸다.

[용어 설명]

휘발성 유기 화합물: 식물 유기체가 다른 유기체와 소통하고 외부의 위협으로부터 자신을 보호하기 위해 생성하는 기체성 화학 물질

지문 어휘

1. herbivore 초식동물 diversity 다양성 functionality 기능 ecosystem 생태계 vegetative 식물의 consumption 음식 섭취 attain 차지하다 eliminate 없애다 subordinate 하위의 competitive exclusion 경쟁적 배제 valid 타당한, 유효한

2. reproduce 번식하다 moderate 적정한 biomass 생물량(한 지역 내에 현존하는 생물의 총량) free up ~을 풀어주다 opposite 반대(되는 것) tolerant 잘 견디는 fragile 연약한 succumb to ~에 굴복하다, ~으로 죽다 extinction 멸종

3. biodiversity 생물 다양성 cast (그림자를) 드리우다 presence 존재 mass 크기, 양 nutrient 영양분 disturbance 지장, 방해 dig up ~을 파내다 compact 굳다, 다져지다 introduce 넣다, 삽입하다 fecal matter 배설물 disperse 퍼뜨리다 seed 씨앗

4. tend (~하는) 경향이 있다 palatability 기호성, 맛이 좋음 offset 상쇄하다 resort to ~에 의지하다 trade-off 균형 activate 활성화하다 defense mechanism 방어 기제 reallocate 재분배하다 to the detriment of 결국 ~을 해쳐서 thorn 가시 wax 밀랍 toxin 독소 adversely 부정적으로 release 방출하다 continued 지속적인

어휘의 의미 파악 문제

1 지문의 단어 "convoluted"와 의미가 가장 가까운 것은?
(A) 인공적인
(B) 유익한
(C) 복잡한
(D) 인정받지 못하는

해설 '복잡한'을 뜻하는 convoluted는 complicated로 대체할 수 있으므로 (C)가 정답이다.

문장 재구성 문제

2 아래 문장 중 지문에서 음영 표시된 문장의 핵심 정보를 가장 잘 나타낸 것은? 오답 선택지들은 의미를 현저히 바꾸거나 핵심 정보를 생략한다.
(A) 우세함의 중요성이 바로 일부 종들을 경쟁을 통해 경쟁자들을 죽이게 만드는 것이다.
(B) 더 우세한 종이 생존할 수 있게 하려면 하위 종을 없애는 것이 필수적이다.
(C) 이런 일이 일어나는 이유는 우세 종이 생태계의 자원을 두고 경쟁할 필요가 없기 때문이다.
(D) 이것이 중요한 이유는 우세 종이 더 약한 종이 필요로 하는 자원을 얻지 못하도록 차단함으로써 그들을 죽여 없애기 때문이다.

어휘 matter 중요하다 block 막다, 차단하다

해설 우세 종이 생태계 자원을 통제하여 하위 종을 제거하는 것이 핵심이므로, 이러한 경쟁적 우위를 차지하는 방식에 해당하는 (D)가 정답이다.

세부 정보 찾기 문제

3 두 번째 단락에 따르면, 다음 중 초식동물과 생태계 사이의 관계에 대해 사실인 것은?
(A) 생산성이 높은 생태계는 먹이를 먹는 초식동물로 인해 다양성에 가장 큰 위협에 직면한다.
(B) 초식동물은 더 약한 종이 죽도록 만들어서 덜 생산적인 생태계의 다양성을 감소시킨다.
(C) 생태계의 식물 다양성이 더 높을수록, 제공할 수 있는 자원이 더 적어진다.
(D) 하위 식물 종은 초식동물이 우세 종을 먹을 때 가장 크게 손해를 입는다.

어휘 threat 위협 suffer 손해를 입다

해설 덜 생산적인 생태계에서는 초식동물의 섭식 행동으로 인해 더 약한 종이 멸종하고 식물 다양성이 감소한다는 내용이므로 가장 부합하는 것은 (B)이다.

수사적 의도 파악 문제

4 글쓴이는 왜 세 번째 단락에서 "땅을 파내다"를 언급하는가?
(A) 초식동물이 어떻게 토양에 도움이 되는지 설명하기 위해
(B) 식물이 번식하는 방식을 소개하기 위해
(C) 강한 식물이 깊은 뿌리를 지니고 있음을 시사하기 위해
(D) 초식동물의 섭식 방식을 설명하기 위해

어휘 benefit 도움이 되다

해설 세 번째 단락에서 큰 초식동물이 땅을 파내 토양이 굳어지는 것을 방지하고 산소가 들어가게 해서 토양의 질을 개선한다고 설명하고 있으므로 (A)가 정답이다.

5 세 번째 단락에서 다음 중 글쓴이가 큰 초식동물과 관련해 언급하지 않은 것은?

(A) 키가 더 큰 식물을 먹음으로써 생태계의 식물 다양성을 보호해 줄 수 있다.

(B) 그들의 식단은 영양분을 거의 필요로 하지 않아서 확실히 거의 지장을 주지 않는다.

(C) 종종 토양을 휘저어 놓아서, 단단하지 않게 하고 산소 농도를 높여 준다.

(D) 그들의 배설물은 일부 식물의 씨앗이 퍼지도록 도움을 주고 토양에 영양분을 더해 준다.

어휘 disturb 휘저어 놓다

해설 식물 섭식을 통한 식물 다양성 보호를 뜻하는 (A)와 토양의 질 개선 및 산소 농도 증가를 의미하는 (C), 배설물을 통한 씨앗 확산 및 토양에 더해지는 영양분을 말하는 (D)는 언급되었지만, 큰 초식동물의 식단과 영양분에 대한 언급은 없으므로 (B)가 정답이다.

추론 문제

6 다음 중 세 번째 단락에서 키가 큰 식물에 대해 추론할 수 있는 것은?

(A) 그다지 생산적이지 않은 생태계에서만 존재한다.

(B) 키가 작은 식물보다 자신을 방어하는 수단이 더 적게 필요하다.

(C) 큰 초식동물이 먹기 더 편리한 위치에 있다.

(D) 우세 종보다 하위 종이 될 가능성이 더 크다.

어휘 means 수단 defend 방어하다

해설 키가 더 큰 식물 종이 섭취 대상이 될 가능성이 더 크다고 했으므로, 먹기 더 좋은 위치에 있다고 언급한 (C)가 정답이다.

어휘의 의미 파악 문제

7 지문의 단어 "susceptibility"와 의미가 가장 가까운 것은?

(A) 취약성　　　　　　(B) 불가시성

(C) 능력　　　　　　　(D) 적대감

해설 '취약성'을 뜻하는 susceptibility는 vulnerability와 같은 의미를 나타내므로 (A)가 정답이다.

세부 정보 찾기 문제

8 네 번째 단락에 따르면, 식물이 왜 자신의 성장을 희생시키는가?

(A) 초식동물의 눈에 띄지 않기를 원한다.

(B) 충분한 영양분을 이용할 수 없다.

(C) 하위 종과 자원을 공유한다.

(D) 자기 방어에 더 많은 에너지를 집중시킨다.

어휘 go unnoticed 눈에 띄지 않다 self-defense 자기 방어

해설 식물이 방어 기제의 활성화를 위해 내부 자원을 재분배하면서 결국 자신의 성장을 해치게 된다고 했으므로, (D)가 정답이다.

문장 삽입 문제

9 제시된 문장이 지문에 삽입될 수 있는 곳을 가리키는 네 개의 네모[■]를 보아라.

그들의 개체수가 감소하여 더 낮은 위치에서의 햇빛 이용 가능성이 높아지고, 그 때문에 식물 다양성이 더 커지게 된다.

이 문장이 들어갈 가장 적절한 위치는? 해당 네모[■]를 선택하여 이 문장을 지문에 삽입하여라.

(A)　　　　(B)　　　　(C)　　　　(D)

어휘 availability 이용 가능성

해설 주어진 문장은 their의 개체수가 감소하여 나타나는 결과이다. 키가 더 큰 식물 종이 더 작은 종에게 그림자를 드리워 경쟁한다는 내용 뒤에 오면, 그들의 개체수 감소로 낮은 곳에서의 햇빛 이용 가능성 증가와 식물 다양성의 확대라는 결과가 자연스럽게 이어지므로 (C)가 정답이다.

지문 요약 문제

10 **지시문**: 지문의 간략한 요약을 위한 도입 문장이 아래에 제시되어 있다. 지문에서 가장 중요한 개념들을 나타내는 선택지 3개를 선택하여 요약을 완성하여라. 어떤 문장들은 지문에 제시되지 않거나 주요 개념이 아니므로 요약에 포함되지 않는다. **이 문제는 2점에 해당한다.**

초식동물은 식물의 다양성을 유지하는 데 있어 중요한 역할을 한다.

(A) 대형 초식동물은 토양을 흐트러트리는 구멍을 파서 생태계에 심각한 물리적 손해를 초래할 수 있다.

(B) 초식동물의 먹이 섭취는 생산적인 생태계를 강화할 수 있지만, 덜 생산적인 생태계의 식물 다양성을 감소시킬 수도 있다.

(C) 식물 다양성은 초식동물의 크기에 영향을 받는데, 더 작은 초식동물은 미미한 지장을 주는 반면, 더 큰 초식동물은 생태계를 상당히 바꿔 놓는다.

(D) VOC(휘발성 유기 화합물)는 날카로운 가시와 위험한 독소처럼 식물이 초식동물을 상대로 사용하는 물리적 방어이다.

(E) 초식동물은 기호성이 더 높은 식물 종을 목표로 삼는 경향이 있으며, 그 식물 종은 초식동물이 대규모로 먹이를 먹는 지역에서 우위를 차지할 가능성이 더 높다.

(F) 초식동물로부터 자신을 보호할 방법을 발달시키기 위해 일부 종은 자신의 성장을 제한한다.

어휘 strengthen 강화하다 alter 바꾸다 restrict 제한하다

해설 초식동물과 식물의 다양성이라는 관계에 있어서 초식동물의 먹이 섭취가 생산적인 생태계와 덜 생산적인 생태계에 미치는 영향, 초식동물의 크기와 식물의 다양성 사이의 관련성, 식물 종이 초식동물로부터 자신을 보호하는 방식에 대해 요약한 (B), (C), (F)가 정답이다. (A), (D), (E)는 지문 내용과 다르다.

중국의 소금 생산과 거래

소금은 중국의 역사에서 엄청나게 큰 역할을 하면서, 중국의 사회적, 경제적 발전 전반에 걸쳐 강력한 영향력을 발휘해 왔다. 이에 대한 한 가지 이유는 중국의 요리에 필수적인 것으로 여겨지는 '다섯 가지 맛' 중 하나의 맛을 내는 배후 요소일 뿐만 아니라, 속담에도 나오는 '인생의 일곱 가지 필수품' 중 하나이기도 하다는 사실이다. 역사적으로 이 지역 전체에 걸쳐 다섯 가지 종류의 소금이 있었는데, 바다 소금이 가장 풍부하게 존재했다. 쓰촨성에서는 작업자들이 굴착 기술을 활용해 염정 소금을 얻었는데, 지표면 아래 깊은 곳에 있는 지하 소금 웅덩이를 퍼내는 방식이었다. 중국 서부 지역에서는 호수염과 토염이 각각 물과 땅에서 추출되었으며, 암염은 산시성과 간쑤성에 위치한 동굴에서 채취되었다. 역대 각 중국 정부의 유능함은 주로 소금의 생산과 유통을 얼마나 잘 관리했는지에 따라 평가됐으며, 관련 정책들이 민간의 부와 통치의 본질 자체에 대한 열정적인 사회적 논쟁을 촉발시켰다.

초기 정부들은 소금의 생산과 판매를 직접 통제하기를 자청했다. 서기 1368년에 명 왕조가 세워졌을 때, 새로운 정부는 전임 정부들처럼 소금의 생산과 판매를 계속해서 직접 통제했다. 하지만, 관료들이 나중에 그들에게 정부의 소금을 매입할 권리를 승인하는 증서를 상인들이 구입할 수 있게 하는 제도를 고안했으며, 이 소금은 그 후 오직 제한된 시장 내에서만 판매될 수 있었다. 이 국가 독점과 자유 시장의 이례적인 혼합은 결국 참담한 것으로 드러났는데, 상인들이 증서를 되팔기 시작했고, 소금은 비축되었으며, 투기 매매가 가격을 끌어 올렸기 때문이었다. 값비싼 정부 소금은 암시장 소금과 경쟁할 수 없었지만, 더 저렴하게 하는 대신, 관료들은 세수 할당액을 충족하기 위해 가격을 훨씬 더 높였다. 이로 인해 밀수된 소금이 훨씬 더 매력적이었으며, 얼마 지나지 않아 시장의 소금 3분의 2가 정부 독점 밖에서 나오면서 일련의 국가적 위기로 이어졌다.

명 왕조 시대에는 바다가 소금의 주요 원천이었으며, 소금을 추출하기 위해 바닷물을 바짝 졸이거나 증발이 일어날 때까지 햇빛에 놓아 두기도 했다. 시간이 많이 소요되는 이 과정을 수행하기 위해 때때로 죄수의 노동력이 활용되기도 했지만, 정부로부터 공식 소금 생산자로 지정된 가정의 구성원들에 의해 더 일반적으로 행해졌다. 명 왕조 시대 동안 이 소금 생산자들의 숫자는 급락했는데, 가족들이 정부로부터 산더미처럼 부과된 부담스러운 요구 조건을 피해 달아났기 때문이었다. 그 사이에 소금 정책에 대해 비판하는 사람들은 정부 관료들을 부유하게 만들면서 가난한 이들을 착취하기 위해 소금을 이용하는 것의 타당성과 도덕성에 반박하려고 지속적으로 시와 소설을 활용하였다.

17세기 중반에 청 왕조가 세워지면서 명 왕조를 대체하였고 마침내 무척이나 필요했던 소금 정책 개혁을 불러왔다. ■(A) 소금 업계는 이제 양저우가 중심이 되었는데, 소금을 북쪽 지역으로 운송하는 데 이용되었던 양쯔강 강변 지역에 위치해 있다는 사실 때문이었다. ■(B) 양저우 상인들이 그 지역의 소금 관련 권리를 통제하면서 대단히 부유하고 강력해졌지만, 황제가

이러한 권리를 철회하지 않도록 지속적으로 선물과 찬사를 바쳐야 했다. ■(C) 정부 소금 관리자들 역시 세수를 적게 신고하고 차액을 착복하거나 자신들에게 신세를 지고 있던 소금 상인들로부터 선물을 받는 방법으로 부를 쌓았다. ■(D) 또 다시 부패가 만연했고, 소금 수입은 감소했다.

1820년에 도광제가 즉위하였고, 골칫거리였던 아편 무역으로 인한 재정 위기에 직면하면서, 재정 개혁을 최우선 순위로 삼았다. 그는 타오주라는 이름의 한 관리에게 소금 산업을 개혁하는 책임을 맡겼다. 타오는 명 왕조의 잔재로 남아 있던 낡은 제도를 근절하고 어느 정도 자유 시장으로 대체함으로써 부응했다. 정부와 좋은 신용 관계를 유지하고 있던 상인들은 이제 원하는 만큼 소금을 구입해 원하는 곳 어디서든 판매할 수 있었다. 이러한 변화가 타오가 약속했던 이익을 즉각적으로 발생시키지 못하면서 타오는 강제로 은퇴하게 되었지만, 소금 무역의 전반적인 관리를 점차적으로 개선시킨 더 융통성 있는 제도를 만들어 냈다.

지문 어휘

1. outsize 대형의 assert 발휘하다 component (구성) 요소 proverbial 속담에도 나오는 drain 물을 빼내다 subterranean 지하의 extract 추출하다 respectively 각각 competency 유능함 successive 연속적인 distribution 유통 spark 촉발시키다 nature 본질, 특성 governance 통치

2. take it upon oneself 자청하다 predecessor 전임자 devise 고안하다 unconventional 이례적인 melding 혼합(하기) monopoly 독점 disastrous 참담한 hoard 비축하다 speculation 투기 매매 drive up ~을 끌어 올리다 black-market 암시장의 meet 충족하다 tax revenue 세수(정부가 세금을 징수하여 얻는 수입) quota 할당액

3. boil down 바짝 졸이다 evaporation 증발 carry out 수행하다 time-intensive 시간이 많이 소요되는 designate 지정하다 plummet 급락하다 flee from ~에서 달아나다 burdensome 부담스러운 heap A upon B A를 B에게 산더미처럼 주다 wisdom 타당성 morality 도덕성 exploit 착취하다 enrich 부유하게 만들다

4. exceedingly 대단히 ply A with B A를 B에게 공급하다 rescind 철회하다 superintendent 관리자 underreport 적게 신고하다 pocket 착복하다 beholden to ~에게 신세를 진 corruption 부패

5. ascend to the throne 즉위하다 troublesome 골칫거리인 opium 아편 fiscal 국가 재정의 eradicate 근절하다 more or less 어느 정도, 다소 in good standing with ~와 좋은 신용 관계에 있는 benefit 이점, 혜택 adaptable 융통성 있는 improve 개선하다

어휘의 의미 파악 문제

11 지문의 단어 "sparking"과 의미가 가장 가까운 것은?
(A) 분석하는
(B) 착수시키는
(C) 해결하는
(D) 금지하는

해설 '촉발시키다'를 뜻하는 spark와 유사한 의미를 지닌 동사는 '착수시키다'를 뜻하는 initiate이므로 (B)가 정답이다.

세부 정보 찾기 문제

12 첫 번째 단락에 따르면, 다음 중 소금에 대해 사실이 아닌 것은?
(A) 바닷물에서 추출한 소금이 가장 흔한 형태였다.
(B) 소금은 굴착 장치로 만든 깊은 우물에 보관되었다.
(C) 일부 지역에서는 동굴에서 암염이 채취되었다.
(D) 소금 관리가 정권을 평가하는 주요 기준이었다.

어휘 store 보관하다 criteria 기준 regime 정권

해설 염정 소금에 대해서는 소금을 얻은 장소로서만 언급되어 있고, 보관과 관련해서는 언급되지 않았으므로 (B)가 정답이다.

지시 대상 찾기 문제

13 지문의 단어 "them"이 가리키는 것은?
(A) 정부들
(B) 관료들
(C) 상인들
(D) 증서들

해설 them은 문장 내에서 정부 소금을 매입할 권리를 얻기 위해 증서를 구입하도록 허락된 사람들로 상인들을 가리키므로 (C)가 정답이다.

어휘의 의미 파악 문제

14 지문의 단어 "contraband"와 의미가 가장 가까운 것은?
(A) 인가받지 않은
(B) 중단된
(C) 비싸지 않은
(D) 복제된

해설 contraband는 '밀수의'라는 뜻이므로, 가장 의미가 가까운 것은 '인가받지 않은'을 뜻하는 (A) unauthorized이다.

세부 정보 찾기 문제

15 세 번째 단락에서 다음 중 글쓴이가 바다 소금을 추출하는 것과 관련해 언급하지 않은 것은?
(A) 자연 증발이 때때로 활용되었다.
(B) 그 과정은 완료하는 데 오랜 시간이 소요되었다.
(C) 종종 죄수들이 강제로 그 작업을 했다.
(D) 황실 사람들에 의해 관리되었다.

어휘 lengthy 오랜 royal household 황실

해설 자연 증발이 활용된 것과 오랜 시간이 소요된 사실, 죄수들이 동원된 내용은 제시되었지만, 황실에서 관리했다는 내용은 제시되어 있지 않으므로 (D)가 정답이다.

세부 정보 찾기 문제

16 네 번째 단락에 따르면, 소금 관리자들이 세금을 적게 신고한 이유는?
(A) 필요한 자산이 부족했기 때문에
(B) 황제가 그렇게 하라고 요구했기 때문에
(C) 지역 소금 상인들을 애처롭게 여겼기 때문에
(D) 자신들이 일부를 가지고 싶었기 때문에

어휘 take pity on ~을 애처롭게 여기다

해설 소금 관리자들이 세수를 적게 신고하고 차액을 착복하는 방법으로 부유해진 사실이 언급되어 있으므로 (D)가 정답이다.

수사적 의도 파악 문제

17 글쓴이는 왜 네 번째 단락에서 "양쯔강"을 언급하는가?
(A) 양저우가 엄청난 영향력을 가진 이유를 설명하기 위해
(B) 청 왕조에 의해 이뤄진 긍정적인 변화를 설명하기 위해
(C) 두 왕조의 소금 생산 방식을 대조하기 위해
(D) 소금 세수가 어떻게 소비되었는지에 대해 세부 사항을 전하기 위해

어휘 contrast 대조하다

해설 양저우가 소금 산업의 중심이 된 이유로 양쯔강 주변에 위치한 사실을 언급하고 있으므로 (A)가 정답이다.

추론 문제

18 다음 중 다섯 번째 단락에서 타오주에 대해 추론할 수 있는 것은?
(A) 소금보다 아편에 중점을 두었다.
(B) 자신의 새 제도로 인해 엄청난 비판에 직면했다.
(C) 명 왕조와 가족 관계였다.
(D) 장기적인 영향을 고려하지 못했다.

어휘 long-term 장기적인 implication 영향

해설 타오주의 개혁이 즉각적으로 이익을 발생시키지 못하여 강제로 은퇴하였으므로, 많은 비난을 받았음을 알 수 있다. 따라서 (B)가 정답이다.

문장 삽입 문제

19 제시된 문장이 지문에 삽입될 수 있는 곳을 가리키는 네 개의 네모[■]를 보아라.

하지만, 일이 잘 시작되지 않았다.

이 문장이 들어갈 가장 적절한 위치는? 해당 네모[■]를 선택하여 이 문장을 지문에 삽입하여라.

(A)   (B)   (C)   (D)

어휘 start out 시작하다

해설 제시된 문장은 어떤 일의 시작에 어려움이 있었음을 의미한다. 개혁의 시작을 언급한 문장 뒤에 위치하고, 부정적 상황에 대한 도입 문장의 역할을 하는 것이 자연스러우므로 (A)가 정답이다.

지문 요약 문제

20 지시문: 지문의 간략한 요약을 위한 도입 문장이 아래에 제시되어 있다. 지문에서 가장 중요한 개념들을 나타내는 선택지 3개를 선택하여 요약을 완성하여라. 어떤 문장들은 지문에 제시되지 않거나 주요 개념이 아니므로 요약에 포함되지 않는다. **이 문제는 2점에 해당한다.**

역사적으로 소금은 중국에서 중요한 경제적, 사회적 요소로 여겨졌다.

(A) 명 왕조와 청 왕조는 소금의 생산과 유통을 통제함에 있어서 서로 다른 정책을 채택했다.
(B) 청 왕조 시대에 황제가 임명한 관료가 소금 산업 개혁에 착수했지만 어쨌든 실패했다.
(C) 명 왕조 시대에 소금에 대한 국가 독점과 자유 시장 개념의 조합이 여러 위기를 초래했다.
(D) 소금 생산자들이 암시장에서 상품을 판매하면서, 정부 소금 가격의 무시무시한 하락을 야기했다.
(E) 부패한 소금 산업을 개혁하는 과정에서 청 왕조가 직면한 어려움에도 불구하고, 그들의 재정 개혁이 나중에 성공했다.
(F) 중국의 어떤 지역에서는 동굴에서 채취하는 방법을 통해 소금을 얻었다.

어휘 adopt 채택하다 undertake 착수하다 multiple 다수의 corrupt 부패한 pay off 성공하다

해설 중국 역사에서 중요한 사회적, 경제적 요소였던 소금과 관련하여 명 왕조와 청 왕조의 소금 산업 관리 정책, 국가의 소금 독점과 자유 시장 개념의 혼합으로 인한 명 왕조의 위기, 청 왕조의 소금 산업 개혁과 그 결과를 요약한 (A), (C), (E)가 정답이다. (B)와 (D)는 지문 내용과 다르고, (F)는 중심 내용이 아니다.

YBM TOEFL 80+
READING